God, Science, Sex, Gender

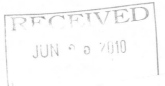

God, Science, Sex, Gender

An Interdisciplinary Approach to Christian Ethics

Edited by

PATRICIA BEATTIE JUNG

AND **AANA MARIE VIGEN**,

WITH **JOHN ANDERSON**

UNIVERSITY OF ILLINOIS PRESS

Urbana, Chicago, and Springfield

Publication was supported in part by a grant from
Loyola University Chicago.

Library of Congress Cataloging-in-Publication Data
God, science, sex, gender : an interdisciplinary approach to Christian
ethics / edited by Patricia Beattie Jung and Aana Marie Vigen, with
John Anderson.
p.   cm.
Includes bibliographical references and index.
ISBN 978-0-252-03537-1 (cloth : alk. paper)
ISBN 978-0-252-07724-1 (pbk. : alk. paper)
1. Sex—Religious aspects—Christianity—Congresses.
2. Christian ethics—Congresses. 3. Sexual ethics—Congresses.
4. Religion and science—Congresses. 5. Science—Moral and ethical
aspects—Congresses. I. Jung, Patricia Beattie. II. Vigen, Aana Marie.
III. Anderson, John.
BT708.G57   2010
241'.66090511—dc22   2009048713

Contents

Part 2. Reflecting on Human Sexual Diversity

Part 3. Sexual Diversity and Christian Moral Theology

Acknowledgments

This book would not exist were it not for the gracious and skilled contributions of many individuals. In fact, we received critical support and enthusiastic participation before there was even a draft manuscript. In particular, we are deeply grateful to three key partners at Loyola University Chicago: the Joan and Bill Hank Center for the Catholic Intellectual Heritage, the College of Arts and Sciences (hereafter CAS), and the Office of Research Services. Both the former and current Directors of the Hank Center, Adriaan Peperzak and Michael Schuck, offered substantial financial and logistical support so that we could convene and host three closed symposia at Loyola University Chicago in which scholars from various disciplines could openly share their work, ideas, and concerns with one another. The Hank Center also provided funding for a subsequent public conference on sexuality, gender, and ethics. Paul Voelker, currently a doctoral candidate in Theology and then a staff person at the Hank Center, was there at every turn to make sure the symposia and conference all went off without a hitch. Dr. Isaiah Crawford, Academic Dean of the CAS at the time, approved funding for both the symposia and public conference. A summer stipend awarded by the CAS in 2007 gave Dr. Vigen precious time to revise and edit the manuscript. Also at the manuscript stage, Loyola's Office of Research Services generously contributed funding to pay for various publication expenses.

We would like to thank the contributors and participants to the symposia and book. The conversations were thought-provoking and sincere. Several of these individuals wrote chapters for the book, but a few did not. Yet, they too made important contributors to our dialogue: we would like to honor Drs. James Garbarino, Paul Mueller, David Ozar, Jennifer Parks, and Diane Suter for the many ways they strengthened our conversations. Those who did write for the book made our job as editors much easier than it could have been. They composed compelling and well-crafted chapters and were responsive, timely, and constructive in replying to our few requests, suggestions, edits, and questions.

Finding the right publisher with whom to partner is an essential part of the process and we cannot thank Dr. Fred Kniss enough for introducing us to Kendra Boileau at the University of Illinois Press. As the editor overseeing the entire process, Ms. Boileau has been exceptionally helpful at every stage. Not only did she see the value in the work from the start, but she has stayed on top of all the details and kept the publication process moving steadily forward. Working with her has been a true pleasure. Similarly, Nancy Albright and Angela L. Burton were consistently efficient, accurate, and kind. They made the final editing go smoothly and painlessly. Also, we are grateful to Joy Simpson for creating two comprehensive and helpful indexes.

Finally, we would like to thank John Anderson, currently a doctoral candidate in Christian ethics at Loyola. He started out providing logistical support as a research assistant. But given both his interest and expertise in the subject matter, he took on more substantive tasks, including helping to edit initial drafts of the chapters, tracking down sources, fact-checking, and compiling the comprehensive bibliography. Doctoral student Grant Gholson later updated and expanded this bibliography.

For all these partners and people, we give our heartfelt thanks. Each took a risk in being part of this conversation. And their commitment and courage have made a much larger and ongoing conversation possible.

Introduction

PATRICIA BEATTIE JUNG

AND AANA MARIE VIGEN

What on Earth Is Going On?!

Iowa. Vermont. Maine. In April (Iowa and Vermont) and May (Maine), three states legalized same-sex marriage in 2009. They join Massachusetts and Connecticut. New York and New Hampshire may be next. The Matthew Shepard Act was passed by the U.S. Congress, and President Obama signed it into law in 2009. It extends federal hate crime protections to victims of crimes motivated by their actual or perceived gender identity and/or sexual orientation. In 2008, Thomas Beatie, a transgendered, legally male adult who is legally married to his wife Nancy in Oregon, made headlines (and appeared on *Oprah*) when the news broke that he was pregnant. He eventually gave birth to a healthy daughter.

In 2009, international officials insisted that Caster Semenya, an 18-year-old South African world champion runner who identifies as female, undergo testing due to elevated testosterone levels and complaints from her competitors. The testing and publicity were devastating for Semenya. The results showed that Semenya has internal testicles and lacks ovaries and a uterus. As of September 2009, it is not known whether Semenya will lose the world champion title and/or be ineligible to compete in future women's races.[1] Commenting on the situation, Arne Ljungqvist said, "the former medical commission chairman for track's world governing body . . . cautioned that a person's sex is not always easy to define. 'There is no simple, single lab test that can tell if you are a man or a woman . . . It is not black and white.'"[2] Semenya is, ironically, *both and neither* male or female. Rather, this person is best described as an intersexed individual—a person with both female and male biological attributes. Such a description defies traditional, dualistic "either or" male-female designations.

What is the world coming to? What are Christians to make of it all? Events such as these keep pushing the boundaries and call for reasoned and sustained public debate and attention—and Christians need to take part.

Christians *both* passionately celebrate *and* decry these events. To some, "the nature of things" is being turned upside down by a wayward culture; to others, there is hope that U.S. society and government laws will recognize individuals and couples who need and deserve protection, respect, and equality. Indeed, faithful, committed, sincere, (and vocal) Christians can be found on both sides of all the debates related to human sexuality and gender. And lamentably, Christians are often the most harsh and unforgiving when they speak of the Christians on "the other side."

Indeed, several Christian denominations vigorously debate questions of the inclusion of gay, lesbian, bisexual, transgendered (GLBT) Christians that cover a wide range of issues: Can they be members if they are open about their sexual or gender identity? Should congregations baptize their children? Can they be ordained if they remain celibate? Can they be ordained if they are not celibate? Should congregations and ministers (be allowed to) officiate at their weddings or bless their unions? Lutherans, Episcopalians, Presbyterians, Methodists, and Roman Catholics all continue to discuss, argue, denounce, defend, and reflect on matters related to sex and gender in various ways and to differing degrees. Sometimes there is provisional agreement; many times there is bristling conflict.

In short, sex and gender are "hot" topics in the church—this is both a new and ancient reality. It is ancient because there have been debates and discussion about both as far back as written history goes. And it is new because many in the United States palpably feel cultural sensibilities, views, practices, and structures actively (if still too slowly for some and entirely too quickly for others) changing in both society and faith communities in ways that are unprecedented.

The Impetus for the Book

Even as the public debates are heated, the formal scholarship by Christian ethicists is often more tepid. It often does not always reflect the full dimensions of "what on earth is going on" and fails to dig into all of the important sources of information. The problem is often that when Christian ethicists discuss or write about human sexuality and gender, they primarily consult biblical scholarship and their respective denominational teachings. Consequently, the scope of both the conversation and the invited dialogue partners is well mapped, even if outcomes of the ecclesial debates themselves are sometimes unpredictable.

In recent years, most discussions and arguments revolve around questions of welcoming, ordaining, and blessing gay, lesbian, bisexual, and transgendered Christians. Fissures often deepen as members and congregations threaten to split away depending on the policy adopted. Perhaps the most prominent example of this is the U.S. Episcopal Church. In protest at the 2003 ordination of an openly gay bishop, Gene Robinson, African Bishops of the world Anglican Church took the irregular and unsanctioned action of ordaining U.S. Episcopal priests as bishops of a splinter U.S. Anglican community in the summer of 2007. In an effort to avoid more dissent and division, U.S. Episcopal leaders promised to "'exercise restraint' in approving another gay bishop and to not authorize prayers to bless same-sex couples."[3] Yet, these concessions did not quell the protest. In 2008 a group of conservative Episcopal bishops, leaders, and congregations founded a rival denomination in the United States, the Anglican Church in North America.[4]

As most sides of any such debates will likely acknowledge, these discussions too often derail and devolve into the repetition of party lines and defensive postures without anyone really listening to anyone else, let alone learning anything new. Until 2009, U.S. Lutherans, for example, seemed to be stuck in a perpetual stalemate of not wanting to change policy *either to include more openly or to exclude* GLBT participation in the life of the Evangelical Lutheran Church in America (ELCA). The national assemblies, including the Churchwide Assembly of August 2007, opted to refer most of the matter to appointed task forces and vote only to affirm continued study and dialogue.[5]

However, in 2009 the stalemate was broken when the national ELCA convened again for a Churchwide Assembly and took rather bold action. Specifically, the assembly adopted a social statement on human sexuality and voted to approve two resolutions that will significantly affect the lives of GLBT members (both lay and ordained):

> *Resolution 1:* Adopted by a vote of 619–402: "Resolved, that the ELCA commit itself to finding ways to allow congregations that choose to do so to recognize, support and hold publicly accountable lifelong, monogamous, same-gender relationships."

> *Resolution 2:* Adopted by a vote of 559–451: "Resolved, that the ELCA commit itself to finding a way for people in such publicly accountable, lifelong, monogamous, same-gender relationships to serve as rostered leaders of this church."[6]

In a separate resolution, the ELCA also voted to "respect the bound consciences of those with whom they disagree" so that congregations not wishing to recognize same-sex relationships or call GLBT clergy are not obligated to do so. The full text of the resolution merits attention:

> *Resolution 4:* Adopted by a vote of 667–307 as amended: "This resolution called on members to respect the bound consciences of those with whom they disagree; declared the intent to allow structured flexibility in decision-making about candidacy and the call process; eliminated the prohibition of rostered (associates

in ministry, clergy, deaconesses and diaconal ministers) service by members in publicly accountable, lifelong, monogamous same-gender relationships; recognized and committed to respect the convictions of members who believe that the ELCA should not call or roster people in committed same-gender relationships; called for development of accountability guidelines; directed that appropriate amendments to ministry policy documents be drafted and approved by the Church Council; and urged that the church continue to trust congregations, bishops, synods and others responsible for determining who should be called into public ministry."[7]

The purpose of this last resolution is to allow for flexibility in how the prior resolutions are applied and to allow room for dissent. Specifically, bishops and congregations who do not wish to call or ordain GLBT persons or celebrate any same-sex ceremonies will not be forced to do so.

Yet, apart from whatever specific decisions are reached in any specific Christian denomination, it is unfortunate that too many of these heated, ecclesial exchanges are rather insular. Sometimes, participants refer to relevant information outside of religion, such as the natural sciences, but many times, they do not draw upon these sources in as direct or meaningful a way as they might. In the spring of 2006, we—a Catholic moral theologian and a Lutheran ethicist—wondered what might happen if we were to expand a Christian ethical dialogue on human sexuality and gender beyond their usual parameters to include in an integral way natural and social scientists and scholars from disciplines in the humanities. We then sought funding to host three symposia at Loyola University Chicago during the spring of 2007 and invited scholars from a variety of disciplines to participate: biology, sociology, anthropology, psychology, philosophy, theology, and English literature. We later hosted a public consultation in September 2007, featuring two keynote addresses: one by an evolutionary biologist, Joan Roughgarden, and the other by Catholic moral theologian, Stephen J. Pope. This conference also included two expert panels in that some of the symposia participants shared their respective reflections, insights, and questions.

In all, twenty-one scholars participated in some or all facets of this collaborative work and fifteen of the presentations have been revised for inclusion in this volume. It is important to note that each scholar graciously and courageously stepped outside of her or his comfort zone—working with unfamiliar texts, people, and disciplines—to do this interdisciplinary work. It has been an engaging and fruitful dialogue, that we are now pleased to share with our readers.

Before briefly signaling the content of the book's interdisciplinary chapters, a brief discussion of four wider contextualizing premises situates the analysis that follows. It is important to understand 1) the value of interdisciplinary scholarship on human sexuality and gender, 2) two theoretical underpinnings of this work, 3) the possibilities and limits for deriving any normative understandings about human sexuality from what is found in nature, and 4) a brief account of how we handle terminology, (e.g., "nature" and "natural") given that these terms often have very different meanings depending on the scholar and discipline employing them.

The Value of Interdisciplinary Scholarship for the Ethical Analysis of Human Sexuality and Gender

One of the symposia participants, philosopher David Ozar, used an especially illuminative metaphor to describe the need for interdisciplinary scholarship. He began with the familiar observation that "no person is an island" and added that what we perceive to be islands are, in actuality, just the tops of an undersea mountain range. Ozar then built on the metaphor to emphasize what he needs to do his work properly as a social philosopher:

> [T]o carefully describe what is below the surface when the islands are all that are easily visible, I need divers and undersea cartographers and many other experts. . . . For me to imagine those structures and to judge what is realistic, I need not only other disciplines' data, but the opportunity to dialogue with colleagues about what they imagine and what they judge to be realistically achievable . . . I cannot proceed . . . without the perspectives of other disciplines helping me see the mountains and valleys below the ocean's surface, helping me describe those deep structures accurately, and helping me to imagine them otherwise.[8]

Ozar is astute in observing that working with others from varying disciplines greatly expands one's field of vision and depth of perception. Sexuality and gender are complex and multifaceted realities that cannot be fully seen, much less understood, by using just one, or even two, disciplinary lenses. Indeed, in a sense, this entire book struggles with the contested and differing definitions of gender, sex, and sexuality. It is not surprising then that dialogues often "run aground" and get stuck on uncharted obstacles. Indeed, without the information and dynamic participation from multiple disciplines, any analysis of human sexuality or gender seems tragically undercut.

Yet, we do not assume that everyone agrees with us that such collaborative work is essential to an adequate descriptive, and/or normative, account of human sexuality or gender. So, we want to be explicit about what we see as the need for, and role of, interdisciplinary dialogue and scholarship, especially given how complicated and "messy" both can be when trying to talk about sex.

As Christian ethicists, we find interdisciplinary conversation integral, to our work in ethics in general and to the analysis of human sexuality and gender in particular.[9] The basic reason for this is the fact that essential knowledge about sex and gender exists quite outside of religious sources and within other disciplines (biology, history, philosophy, psychology, literature, sociology, etc.). Indeed, it is crucial that ethicists map the fleshy, physical, and social/cultural roots of humanity's sexual experiences with those attentive to these realities from varied disciplines.

Recalling a bit of history makes this point plain: There were tremendous developments in the Christian tradition—both Protestant and Catholic—about human sexuality in the twentieth century. Though many factors contributed to those developments, the increase in scientific knowledge about human sexuality proved to be very influential. Consider the eventual impact of the discovery of the ovum in 1828.

Though our understanding of the genetically active role of women in the reproductive process would not be more fully sketched until the mid-1900s, this scientific discovery eventually led to the transformation of church teachings because, for most of Christian history, a one-seed theory of reproduction—traceable back to antiquity and the Hellenistic world—dominated our understanding of natural human reproduction. According to this account, if the ground in which the semen was planted was not barren, then the heterosexual couple's fecundity was presumed to be potentially steady throughout the woman's menstrual cycle and essentially unlimited until menopause. This understanding of the biological design of human sexual reproduction, that we now recognize to be mistaken, was foundational to what all Christian churches taught to be natural in a normative sense. Even conjugal sexual activity was good if and only if intentionally procreative.[10]

However, as our understanding of human reproductive biology grew, such normative claims became increasingly untenable. Consequently, by 1930 Protestant denominations began to approve of contraception. In the 1950s in a dramatic development in Roman Catholic Church teaching, Pope Pius XII approved of what was then known as "the rhythm method." Couples—he argued—could engage in natural family planning, that is, they could intentionally restrict their sexual activity to infertile times in the woman's cycle in order to space their children, or if they had sufficiently serious cause, in order to avoid having children altogether. The church came to recognize that women are not potentially fecund every day of their lives until menopause. Sexual activity could then be considered moral even if heterosexual married couples made use of this fact of nature. Scientific discovery and knowledge informed and contributed to the ultimate revising of even Catholic teaching on sexual relations for married couples.

In addition, our increased understanding of the nature of the relationship between human reproductive and sexual activities has made it increasingly problematic to claim that procreative potential is the exclusive, primary, or even essential justification for all human sexual activity. Unlike animals that mate in rhythm with an estrus cycle, women experience sexual desire during periods of infertility and long after they are postmenopausal. In many quarters, this realization had implications for the ethical assessment not only of birth control, but also for activities like masturbation and oral sexual activities, that were traditionally condemned in large measure because they were not potentially procreative.

Moreover, numerous Christian scholars and authorities—across the conservative-liberal continuum—now all agree, and some even emphasize, that bonding, intimacy, and pleasure are all important, moral purposes of sexual activity. Conservative thinkers tend to specify that this activity must be limited to that of a heterosexual and married couple. More liberal thinkers may describe these purposes as valid for various others as well (e.g., widows and widowers; GLBT persons in committed and monogamous relationships; single, responsible, and consenting adults). The point is that, while they may disagree on who exactly can justify their enjoyment of these additional moral and good purposes of sexual acts, they nonetheless agree that there are other valid purposes for such sexual activity and relationships outside of procreation for at least some of the human population. And they have come to make this case, not only by appealing to sacred scriptures and theological arguments, but out of an evolving understanding of human sexuality that has been deeply informed by biological, psychological, historical, sociological, and anthropological findings.

Something analogous is occurring today. In the second half of the twentieth century insights into gender—coming from disciplines across the humanities as well as the social and physical sciences—have raised some challenging questions about the adequacy of the dimorphic[11] paradigm for human sexuality in general and consequently about the many church teachings that rest upon this paradigm. Consider just the genetic basis for human sexuality. While the vast majority of us are either male (XY) or female (XX), it is estimated that across the globe 5.5 million people do not fit genetically into this simple binary. This is just the tip of the proverbial iceberg of the mounting biochemical evidence against the adequacy of a dimorphic (rather than multidimensional) model for human sexuality.

During the three symposia gatherings in the spring of 2007, Dr. Diane Suter, a biologist, addressed the roles of several biochemical factors in the development of the anatomical parts and secondary sexual characteristics we commonly identify as male and female. While most of us do seem to divide in our outward appearance into one or the other of these two common anatomical types, it is also true that a significant number of us are intersexed.[12] Suter tracked just six of the biochemical factors that contribute to our physiological sexual identity.

She pointed out that every permutation in the combination of these six factors that exists mathematically *can and does* exist biologically in the human
population.[13]

The Pulitzer Prize–winning novel, *Middlesex*, by Jeffrey Eugenides imaginatively introduces the reader to one such person. Just one of the factors tracked
by Suter was missing in this protagonist, who was born with a clitoris and labia,
raised as a girl, and yet who grew into a boy during his adolescence. As our
knowledge of the many biochemical factors that contribute variably to our sexuality grows, we may find that the labels "male" and "female" mask more of the
complexity that is human sexuality and gender than they illumine.

In any case, the emergence of this multiplex concept of gender among biologists seems to be reinforced by the analyses of gender emerging from social
scientists and many scholars in the humanities. Together they challenge the
dimorphic account of gender complementarity that many official church teachings and Christian ethicists take to be axiomatic. They spark in us as Christian
ethicists several questions. What might insights from these many disciplines
mean for our interpretation of the notions of male and female as found in the
opening chapters of Genesis? What might it mean for the New Testament claim
that there is no male or female in Christ (Galatians 3:28)? For traditional teachings about sex and gender in heaven? For the role and inclusion of eunuchs in
the church community? And so on.

Admittedly these are pretty edgy questions. But that is precisely where most
interdisciplinary conversation takes us—to the growing edges of the tradition.
We believe Christians have no reason to fear going here. The Spirit has been
promised to guide us ever deeper into the truth. Whether such arguments, or
even these questions, reflect the work of the Spirit among us is not self-evident.
It is something we must test through rigorous debate and expansive, interdisciplinary exchange.

Theoretical Underpinnings

Yet, precisely because we are Christian ethicists, we do not think that such
debate/dialogue is "all there is" to reality. So, it is important to note two fundamental assumptions that underlie this work. The first is the assumption that
"truth" is still a worthwhile pursuit.

In the late twentieth and early twenty-first centuries, postmodern emphases
on the historical production of knowledge have challenged what seemed to be
"common-sense" assertions about human sexual diversity. Some cross-cultural
anthropological studies even suggest that our notions of what is masculine and
feminine may merely be cultural artifacts. The postmodern conviction that truth
and reality, at the least, are always socially constructed (through language, text,

customs, cultural taboos, laws, institutions, and other social structures) is an important corrective to those who too quickly assume what they "see" is the self-evident, "natural," objective, and eternal order of things. Caughie's chapter in this volume eloquently exemplifies such concerns.

Still, we maintain that social constructions are not all there is to "truth." Simply put, to say that social, political, religious, economic, cultural, historical, (and other) forces shape or construct the way particular human beings experience and interpret certain events and realities does not mean that there is no greater reality or truth to which their construction corresponds in a limited way. Not all of the contributors to this volume may agree with us on this point, but it is a grounding assumption that we, the two editors, believe critical to this dialogue.

We take this position because we are both Christian ethicists. Those of us called to engage in normative forms of cross-cultural and social criticism—that is, those who seek to judge some assertions about human sexual diversity as true and others as biased, some as fair and others as unjust—must uncover a "foundation" for such conversation. The fact is that we must find a way to talk—at least initially—about sexual and gender diversity as a shared human reality and not merely a product of individual choice or cultural construction. Some such "foundation" is prerequisite for all forms of normative analysis. It is the precondition for any and all forms of ethical analysis, theological or not, if it is to be based on something other than the sheer weight of popular opinion, ecclesial authority, or the power to control others.

The second grounding assumption is this: We the editors—as Christians and as ethicists—are convinced that current scientific knowledge and faith claims aren't mutually exclusive and won't ultimately contradict one another. That there can be no contradiction between faith and reason has long been, at least theoretically, central to the Catholic intellectual heritage. Unlike sectarian expressions of Christianity, the Catholic ethical tradition is radically confident that inductive reflection on human experience will yield intelligible moral norms, not only congruent with God's revelation, but also recognizable by all reasonable persons. On the basis of this axiom, we hope this book will foster explorations into what, if anything, reflection on information from evolutionary biology along with other disciplines might contribute to a faithful Christian account of human sexual diversity.

We presuppose that the basic goods constitutive of human happiness are objective, relatively stable across cultures, and knowable through inductive reasoning. Though we are different in tremendously important ways, we are also all human beings and share certain central defining experiences in common. One of the experiences we might recognize as shared in some sense is the experience of embodiment in general, and in particular bodily experiences like aging, mortality, hunger/thirst, and sexuality. Obviously, such experiences are constructed quite distinctively in various social contexts and historical epochs, but biology is attentive to the physiological dimensions of those experiences that we share in common and that enable us to talk across cultures about them.

To illustrate: Christian ethicist Lisa Sowle Cahill argues that the human body and sexuality as biological realities ground the relational (if not communal) character of human life minimally because they establish our generational connection to at least our biological parents.[14] For another Christian ethicist, Christine E. Gudorf, reflection on the bodily capacity of both men and women for sexual pleasure contributes to the recognition of (mutual) sexual pleasure as an ingredient of (morally) good sex.[15] Thus, in terms of the present work, one question we consider is: If evolutionary biology establishes that in general gender and sexual diversity serves in some way most species that reproduce sexually, how might sexual diversity serve human beings and communities in particular? What, if anything, might we learn about the purpose(s) of human sexual and gender diversity from the perspective of evolutionary biology? Certainly it is important not to overemphasize or absolutize the biological aspects of human persons and sexual activities.[16] However, there remain crucial and proper roles for biology as *one* of several illuminative perspectives on human sexuality.

What Can We Discern from "What Is" for "What Ought to Be"?

To affirm that nature, or that which exists in nature, possesses important insight for assessments of what ought to be in a moral or normative sense leaves much ambiguity. What relationship exactly is there between what exists and what we find as morally permissible/desirable? Vigen returns to this question in her concluding chapter to this volume.

What we want to note here is simply that deriving normative understandings about human sexuality from patterns, identities, and behaviors found among human beings is no obvious or simple matter. Moral philosophers David Hume and G. E. Moore (among others) cautioned respectively against hasty conflations of what exists with what ought to be (Naturalistic Fallacy) and against equating "The Good"—meaning the ultimate, eternal, perfect, ideal with any subjective, particular interpretation of something as good (Moore's Fallacy).[17] In other words, people should not confuse the absolute and eternal good with a specific, time- and context-bound reality or object that a particular person or community finds to be good. For example, it would be unwise to assume that democracy, socialism, or any other sociopolitical system are or will always be true and accurate reflections of the good in an ultimate sense. Just because something exists, or some person or community finds a particular object/reality/quality pleasing or desirable—"good"—does not mean that it is good in a moral sense.

Here is another—even more pertinent—example of the negative consequences of making rash or direct correlations or derivations with respect to reproduction. Christian ethicist Margaret Farley has pointed out that (mis)understandings of male and female reproductive roles have mistakenly been used to corroborate as reasonable interpretations of the "feminine as passive and the masculine as active, the woman as receptacle and the man as fulfiller, the woman as ground and the man as seed."[18] A historical case can be made that ancient and medieval conceptions of the human reproductive process actually contributed to the development and sanctification of these gender scripts. Many contend that such gender scripts are contradicted by human biology as we understand it today; at least reproductively, it is no longer reasonable to presume receptivity and activity to be gendered in the manner described above.

For us as ethicists, while we reject the notion that what is observable to us in nature automatically suggests a corresponding moral norm, many questions remain about how the life sciences can and ought to shape Christian sexual ethics. There are definite problems with making flat correlations for sure. And yet, it also seems equally unwise to deny that there may be some important relation between what is and what ought to be. For example, understanding ecological facts and the undeniably interdependent, and delicate, balance of relations among all living things tells us a lot (if we will attend to the realities) about how to enhance the flourishing of the planet and what we ought to do to live in an ecologically responsible and respectful manner.

So what might be the role of science in arriving at ethical conclusions? Is it possible to describe a positive function of science, rather than only warn against careless leaps from fact to moral values, prescriptions, and proscriptions? Given the plethora of scientific facts and discoveries available to us, it seems only responsible to discuss constructively the relationship between scientific fact and the formulation of ethics.

Stephen J. Pope, a contributor to this book, has described elsewhere the role, and limits, of science in ethical decision-making this way. "Science can provide assistance in determining the biological ends of human action, but religious and moral reflection bears the burden of discerning the morally proper ends of human action."[19] He contends that ethics can be informed by science, but not in such a way that it eliminates the need for moral reflection proper. In other words, ethics must not be solely based in, or conflated with, science, but rather maintain a relationship of mutual interdependence.

A pivotal figure in modern Christian ethics, James M. Gustafson, has argued similarly that empirical research ought not to replace ethical arguments. He notes that there has been a trend within the last few decades toward using scientific accounts of human development to explain certain actions. This trend sometimes has the effect of excusing persons from moral accountability. Gustafson does not deny the importance of empirical science in informing ethics. Rather, he warns against views of absolute determinism within this relationship. Empirical research can *inform* ethics in regard to the potential consequences of various courses of morally determined action, but not dictate *how* people ought to act. Using another example, Gustafson notes that ethical positions on economics must learn from and draw upon the formal economic sciences, but the economic sciences cannot determine moral norms of distributive justice and so forth.[20]

Yet, notably in his 2002 Warfield Lectures (published as *An Examined Faith* in 2004) Gustafson rightly argues that the future of theological ethics depends upon its ability to appropriate the findings of contemporary science into its analyses. This is so, Gustafson argues, for deeply theological reasons. Only such a wedding will enable theological ethics to reckon adequately with the divine ordering of the universe. Neither avoiding such dialogue nor naively inferring theological conclusions from scientific findings will do. In the model conversation that Gustafson has in mind, science could potentially both limit and license theological interpretations (without in either case specifying what ought to be said theologically).

The way by which reflection upon biological data can serve as a source of moral insight is surely a complex one. Biological facts, in and of themselves, are not normative in nature. Bodily needs, capacities, and tendencies do not incline us directly toward human moral goods, because these goods exist concretely only in socially constructed as well as biologically rooted complexes of needs and tendencies. The potential for conflict among these several goods has been underrecognized. The moral task is to harmonize and integrate our service of these multiple values and to humanize all that is constitutive of genuine happiness.

Nevertheless, what ought to be has some relationship to what is. Some of what the biological sciences tell us about our relatively invariant human bodies and experience of human sexual diversity will contribute to our normative understandings of human sexuality. Minimally, these normative understandings cannot contradict this data, when properly interpreted. In the long run, it is essential not only to reflect on the best, most adequate biology of our time as a descriptive source for moral theology but also to interpret such data by placing it in a mutually corrective dialogue with both revealed and other reason-based accounts of human sexuality.

Defining Terms: "Nature" and "Natural"

One of the things we quickly learned through the interdisciplinary symposia is that none of us can take the meaning of terms for granted! We spent a lot of time as a group defining and clarifying basic terms we all use—"nature," "natural," "authority," "normative," "sex," "gender," "sexuality"—once we discovered how their meanings vary across our disciplines. Indeed, the biologists had a somewhat different understanding of the terms "nature" and "natural" than did the philosophers and theologians, for example. Also the social and biological sciences had differing notions of authority—who possesses it, how it is arrived at, and so forth—than did those in the humanities, and again, the theologians had a particular notion of authority related to ecclesial sources. And it was surprising how differently various scholars defined and differentiated "sex" and "gender." Defining what constitutes a "male" or a "female" is not as obvious as it might seem. Rather than offer a glossary here, and since the authors use terms in particular ways in each of their chapters, look for each author's definitions of key terms within her or his chapter or endnotes.

Yet, to give a sense of how important it is to take time to define terms explicitly for one another in interdisciplinary conversation, we will highlight how different the meaning of nature/natural is depending on whether it is being used in a descriptive or normative way. When biological scientists use the terms "nature" or "natural," they are making a simple statement that something exists in nature. There is no qualitative or evaluative opinion about it. X simply exists in nature and/or has organic/inherent (natural) features/characteristics that are evident through objective observation and study. For example, in nature, and given *their* particular nature, lions walk on four legs whereas it is natural for human beings to walk on two. One way of getting around is not morally superior to the other—it is simply a statement of fact about the two distinct natures of two different species.

In contrast, ethicists mean something very different when they use the same terms. That which is considered normatively natural does include, inherently, morally evaluative content. When ethicists contend that it is natural for human beings to love and care for each other, they are making a normative claim that such behavior is essential to who we are as human beings and that it is what we are called to do for one another. James Gustafson uses the term "normatively human" to describe "what is to be valued and promoted in human existence, or what is fulfilling for humanity."[21] In other words, there is a moral claim on us to live into a particular nature, that is deemed integral to our being-ness, as described by a given ethicist or theologian.

In short, through the course of the interdisciplinary conversations, we deepened our understanding of how vital it is to not take the meaning of any term for granted or to assume that any definition would be shared by all. It is a simple lesson and yet an essential one. Dialogues about sexuality and gender screech to a halt when it starts to become clear that participants do not all mean the same thing by a given term. Then a time of backtracking, explanation, and translation is needed before conversation can return to the issue at hand. Simply sharing the differing definitions may not result in ever coming to a shared definition.

And that may not be necessary in all cases. It is more important to be aware of the different usages, to understand them on their own terms, and to be crystal clear about what one means in one's own usage of them.

Chapter Outline

This book is divided into three parts. The first part, "Establishing Basepoints for Dialogue," offers contextual background for understanding why debates about human sexuality in Christian contexts are so controversial and also suggests ways for moving beyond impasses. In chapter 1, theologian Jon Nilson outlines the modern and contemporary history of official Roman Catholic teaching on authority in the Church. He explains how and why the collaborative, consultative model that was demonstrated by the Second Vatican Council was never actualized. Consequently, the full scope of the data relevant to understanding sexuality and necessary to developing normative claims that might command wide assent are marginalized in the Church. Sociologist Anne Figert (chapter 2) complements Nilson's work on religious authority by exploring the meaning of scientific authority. Figert contends that in order to understand fully the debate and issues surrounding evolutionary biology, sexual differentiation, and Christianity, we need to understand how the boundary between science and religion has been made, negotiated, and contested. She examines the nature of scientific authority and how it forms and maintains its boundaries with other forms of authority, particularly religious or moral authority. In chapter 3, sociologist Fred Kniss then offers a kind of synthesis of chapters 1 and 2 as he examines the specific content of the historic and ongoing conflict between science and religion (particularly Roman Catholicism) over sexuality and sexual diversity.

With this multidimensional understanding of "authority" and "turf battles" in mind, philosopher and scholar of Aquinas, Francis J. Catania then steps back a bit in chapter 4 to consider ways in which Aquinas's method of scientific and moral inquiry may prove useful for contemporary questions and reflection related to human sexuality. The issue is not whether Albert (Aquinas's teacher) or Aquinas anticipated modern scientific findings (obviously neither did), but whether their thinking represents a cognitive attitude that is open to advances in scientific understanding of the world and specifically of human persons. Finally in this opening section, Patricia Beattie Jung identifies and critiques three traditional pillars of Christian sexual ethics—patriarchy, purity, and procreativity—and briefly reviews their historical development from the New Testament through the modern eras. Her chapter then explores the import of twentieth-century developments of these emphases, particularly within Roman Catholicism.

The chapters in Part 2, "Reflecting on Human Sexual Diversity," explore what the natural sciences reveal about the complexity and variety of sexuality and gender identities and relations in both human and other species. A prominent evolutionary biologist, Joan Roughgarden, opens the section with an especially provocative chapter that takes biologists to task. She argues that there are many species that do not fit into the mating paradigms put forth by Darwin's theory of sexual selection. As an alternative to it, Roughgarden then presents a theory of social selection that shows, she argues, how cooperation is a better paradigm than competition for understanding the sexual diversity that exists in the natural world. In response, biologist Terry Grande and colleagues argue in chapter 7 that sexual selection theory need not be abandoned but can be modified with respect to new data and that a melding of Roughgarden's social selection and traditional sexual selection theory is possible.

The section then moves to consider what scholars in the humanities might understand about human sexuality and gender and how both are, at least in part, socially constructed realities. In chapter 8 theologian John McCarthy discusses how contemporary Catholic statements issued by councils, Vatican congregations, and popes closely relate a theology of creation to a properly ordered understanding of gender and sexuality. McCarthy first imagines how the line of argument develops that defends an exclusive gender dimorphism/binarity, given the emphasis on created natural order within a theology of creation. He then suggests an alternative emphasis in a theology of creation and the effect its resultant hermeneutic of hospitality might have on our moral stance toward gender difference. English scholar Pamela L. Caughie, in chapter 9, then brings a literary perspective by analyzing gender and sexual identity in terms of cultural tropes. To conceptualize sex and gender as cultural tropes, Caughie contends, enables us to *read* sexual and gender identity as a historically specific narrative.

In significant contrast to both Roughgarden and Caughie's perspectives, anthropologist James Calcagno (chapter 10) emphasizes less subjective and social constructions of sex or gender and instead tends to trust what he sees as objective, observable facts discovered through scientific inquiry. The main purpose of his chapter, however, is to address what evolutionary biology, biological anthropology, and specifically primatology have to offer regarding our understanding of human sexual diversity, pair-bonding, and family structures. True to the anthropological tradition, this perspective is based on the premise that we can learn more about humanity through evolutionary comparisons with our closest relatives, the primates. Calcagno concludes that faith-based and evolutionary approaches can work in harmony toward a greater knowledge of ourselves, although they can also contradict one another in significant ways. The second section concludes by returning to the domain of theology and specifically to biblical interpretation. Biblical scholar Robert Di Vito explores how the subject of sexual diversity figures in recent Vatican documents and their interpretation of the Bible, with particular reference to Pope John Paul II's *Mulieris dignitatem.*

Part 3, "Sexual Diversity and Christian Moral Theology," focuses on sexual and gender diversity and implications for Christian theology and Christian ethics (also known as *moral theology*). The purpose here is to integrate the interdisciplinary knowledge gained in the previous sections with distinct contributions from Christian theology, poetry, and ethics. Renowned Catholic ethicist, Stephen J. Pope leads off the section with chapter 12, which analyzes the teachings of Pope John Paul II on human sexuality. It puts his "Theology of the Body" in conversation with the recent work on *Just Love* by Margaret Farley. It discusses how these papal teachings would benefit from more dialogue with biological insights, such as those brought to light by Joan Roughgarden.

After immersing themselves in substantive, analytical content, readers are invited to think about human sexuality and gender in a very different way: through the imaginative genre of poetry. In chapter 13 Frank Fennell elucidates and celebrates one of the most remarkable poetic celebrations of diversity—diversity in nature, diversity in human beings, diversity in created objects—all captured in Gerard Manley Hopkins's curtal sonnet "Pied Beauty." The chapter also briefly traces the intellectual and specifically religious origins of Hopkins's ideas about diversity. Theologian Susan A. Ross then imaginatively connects Christian feminist challenges of the significance of Christ's maleness for human salvation to consider ways that female images of the crucified Christ (e.g., Edwina Sandys's "Christa") can have profoundly positive effects on victims of sexual violence and how feminine dimensions of Christ have played roles in Christian spirituality. Her chapter (14) concludes by considering the significance of a more diverse Christology on Christian views of sexuality.

A Christian ethicist and an evolutionary biologist, Jung and Roughgarden, coauthor the next-to-last chapter, which some readers may find to be the edgiest of the entire volume. It challenges the Christian claim that variation from a heterosexual gender binary (male-female) is objectively disordered. The erosion of the biological basis for the dimorphic paradigm led the authors to retrieve other models of gender found within the Christian scriptures and early Christian eschatological traditions. Both the story of the Ethiopian Eunuch in Acts 8:26–40 and the gender fluidity endorsed by Gregory of Nyssa suggest that there might be some support for polymorphic models of human sexuality within the Christian tradition.

In her concluding chapter, Aana Marie Vigen takes a step back from sexuality and gender to reflect on matters of method in ethics. She makes the case that human experience ought be given more weight in moral reflection than it often is. And as she contemplates sources and the process of ethical deliberation, she also returns to the question of if/how Christian communities and ethics may derive normative claims about human sexual relationships and identities based on what scientists and others observe in nature. In reflecting on these issues, Vigen synthesizes key aspects of the preceding chapters.

The Beginning of a Dialogue

Before venturing into the chapters, two brief caveats are needed. First, we acknowledge that the theological insights are offered predominately by Catholic authors. This fact is due, in part, because the book grew out of a series of internal dialogues and symposia among scholars at Loyola University Chicago. The advantage of this process is that this book is not a disparate collection of unrelated essays, but reflects a thoughtful and ongoing conversation among the contributors. The authors have talked a lot together and have read one another's work and had this content in mind as they composed their individual pieces. However, and even more importantly, we want to underscore that the majority of the theological and ethical insights are not *uniquely* Catholic. Other Christian denominations endorse to varying degrees these same themes and share much of this same history.

Second, this book will not reach any unified conclusions about human sexuality and gender. It does not represent a group's consensus or a finalized set of ethical principles. Instead, together the essays serve as a *beginning* of a dialogue among these disciplines. It is a volume about the emerging data related to both human sexual and gender diversity and that wrestles with the implications of that data for multiple disciplines. Our goal is to foster dialogue and open, serious exchange across disciplines and perspectives.

In all, the central purpose of this book is to explore what theologians and ethicists might learn about human sexuality and gender from disciplines outside of theology and biblical scholarship. However, we are also interested in learning a bit about what evolutionary biologists might learn about human sexuality from this interdisciplinary conversation as well. Do philosophical, theological, sociological, and literary traditions suggest important new lines of inquiry and research for biologists? We look forward to hearing from scholars in the biological sciences about what they have learned from reading this book and engaging this conversation.

One thing we know already: Biological sciences must also be questioned for any biases or subjective assumptions that influence their research questions and conclusions. Just as theological concepts are sometimes rooted in scientific conclusions that have long been proven false by the scientific community, scientific hypotheses can also be influenced by cultural norms that remain veiled by a mystique of "scientific objectivity." Joan Roughgarden cautioned conference participants not to accept simply scientific data at face value. She raises the same concern in her work for this book. Roughgarden contends that both scientists and nonscientists have a responsibility to explore how scientific investigation is being done and who is doing it. Her concern is that sometimes scientists can comprise a fairly homogeneous group that is not as self-critical as needed. So, in this spirit, theological and moral reflection can unmask the harm done by sex and gender stereotypes implicit even in science and can push scientists to consider whether or to what extent these stereotypes affect how nature and scientific data are perceived and evaluated.

Undeniably, such interdisciplinary conversation on human sexuality and gender invites those interested (and bold enough) into what have proven historically to be tenuous partnerships. Nevertheless, as we originally invited the authors of this book, we now invite readers to engage one other in lively, gracious, and critical exchanges because we are convinced that those courageous enough to do so stand to learn a tremendous amount from one another.

Notes

1. Meghan Daum, "The Case of Caster Semenya."

2. The Associated Press, "Caster Semenya Withdraws from Competition."

3. Zoll, "Episcopal Leaders Promise Restraint on Electing Gay Bishops in Face of Anglican Demands."

4. Goodstein, "Episcopal Split as Conservatives Form New Group."

5. One notable exception to this description came in 2007 when the ELCA Assembly voted to ask ELCA bishops to avoid disciplining and removing gay clergy who are in committed same-sex relationships until a final decision about gay clergy and celibacy is reached at a future assembly. See Ramirez, "Lutherans Ask Bishops to Keep Gay Clergy in Ministry."

6. News Release, ELCA, "2009 ELCA Churchwide Assembly Addresses Variety of Topics."

7. Ibid.

8. David Ozar, Panel Remarks, September 27, 2007, Loyola University Chicago, unpublished address.

9. Patricia Beattie Jung wrestles primarily with sacred scriptures, traditional theological arguments, and church teachings about human sexuality in her scholarship. Aana Marie Vigen regularly draws upon sociological data, ethnographic case studies, and biomedical research in her work on medical ethics and bioethics.

10. It was permissible as a remedy for lust if nothing was done to prevent conception.

11. The terms "dimorphic" and "dimorphism" appear throughout this volume. By them, the authors refer to the predominant notion that human beings inherently exist in no more or less than two distinct forms—male and female.

12. The Intersex Society of North America (ISNA) broadly defines the word intersex as "a general term used for a variety of conditions in that a person is born with a repro-

ductive or sexual anatomy that doesn't seem to fit the typical definitions of female or male." The ISNA stresses that these definitions are constructed by human beings and have no inherent value. Thus, "nature doesn't decide where the category of 'male' ends and the category of 'intersex' begins, or where the category of 'intersex' ends and the category of 'female' begins. Humans decide." For more on the ISNA's discussion of the term, go to http://www.isna.org/faq/what_is_intersex.

13. Diane Suter, unpublished symposia paper, March 17, 2007, Loyola University Chicago.

14. Cahill, *Sex, Gender and Christian Ethics*, 60.

15. Gudorf, *Body, Sex and Pleasure*.

16. This would be to adopt a problematic form of physicalism as explained by Gula, *Reason Informed by Faith*, 226.

17. For an analysis of several versions of the Naturalistic Fallacy, see Curry, "Who's Afraid of the Naturalistic Fallacy?" 234–47.

18. Farley, "New Patterns of Relationship," 69.

19. Pope, "Descriptive and Normative Uses of Evolutionary Theory," 177.

20. Gustafson, "The Relationship of Empirical Science to Moral Thought," 429–30.

21. Cahill, *Between the Sexes*, 13. Cahill is referring to Gustafson, "Genetic Engineering and a Normative View of the Human," 46–58.

PART 1

Establishing Basepoints
for Dialogue

1

Red Hats

Catholic Sexual Ethics in the Face of Church Authority

JON NILSON

Ask any person on the street—or even the average Catholic in the pew—to describe the way moral teachings are developed in the Roman Catholic Church. Chances are good that his or her reply will be, "It's like a pyramid." At the apex of the pyramid stands the pope, surrounded by the curia, his advisors and assistants in Rome. On the next lower level stand the cardinals and one step below them stand the bishops of the Church. Then come the priests and finally, on the lowest level, are the lay people—the world's billion-plus Catholics. Official teachings are promulgated by the pope. All Catholics are expected to assent to them. The pope is also the chief governing officer of the Church. While others may exercise jurisdiction in the Church, they do so only as delegates of the pope. Many people assume (whether Catholic or not) that a common cliché represents the reality: the role of the billion-plus Catholics is simply to "pray, pay, and obey."

However, this description differs dramatically from the vision of a pilgrim church in constant need of reformation and development confirmed by the second Vatican Council (1962–65). After a rocky beginning,[1] the assembled bishops at Vatican II came to understand one dimension of their task to be that of completing the teaching of the first Vatican Council (1869–70). Vatican I, as we will see, had much to do with creating the pyramid. Vatican II, instead, envisions the Church as a set of concentric circles. It locates the pope as the successor of St. Peter within the College of Bishops. The bishops are successors to the twelve apostles, whom Jesus chose to continue his mission. Each bishop, assisted by his priests, stands at the center of a diocese, serving the people of God in that place as their chief teacher, priest, and overseer, as the Council's texts, *Lumen gentium* and *Christus Dominus,* make clear.

Each Catholic has a contribution to make to the life and mission of the Catholic community, so Vatican II exhorts the faithful to meet their ecclesial responsibilities. Among these is the duty to express their opinion on matters concerning the good of the Church, especially those matters in which they have expertise. The Council urges that forums be established in the Church to facilitate this process of discussion and collaboration (*Lumen gentium*, §37).

Nowhere does the Council suggest that the bishop is simply a middle manager between pope and people. Instead, Vatican II tells the bishop to act like a father toward his priests (*Christus Dominus*, §16) and to heed the voices of his people carefully (ibid., §13; *Lumen gentium*, §27). At times the bishop must bring the wisdom and insights of his people to gatherings of the universal Church. Vatican II recommends that the pope establish a "Synod of Bishops," a representative body elected from national or regional conferences of bishops throughout the world. The Synod would meet regularly in Rome to advise the pope on the central issues facing the Church (*Christus Dominus*, §6). Pope Paul VI implemented the Council's recommendation soon after its conclusion.

Vatican II makes it clear that the pope and the bishops are servants and guardians of the truths that God has revealed for the sake of our salvation. The Church develops its understanding of the meaning and implications of these truths by insight from the prayer, labor, and study of all the People of God (*Dei verbum*, §8; *Gaudium et spes*, §44). Even the pope is bound to inquire diligently into the "content" of divine revelation and learn how to express it more accurately and compellingly in each generation and situation (*Lumen gentium*, §25).

How, then, can we explain the perdurability of the pyramid model in the Church nearly half a century after the close of Vatican II? Why does the Church so often resemble and operate as a paternalistic dictatorship, especially when, over forty years ago, Vatican II clearly pointed the way toward a more dialogical, participatory exercise of authority? Why, consequently, will the best biology, sociology, psychology, philosophy, and theology do little or nothing to reshape official Church teaching on sexuality until and unless their results are accepted by the pope? Why in the Roman Catholic Church is wisdom always vulnerable to trumping by power?

Theology alone cannot answer such questions nor can any single discipline. A complete answer needs the collaboration of scholars like Anne Figert (especially her discussion of "boundary disputes") and Fred Kniss (especially his discussion of the inherent tensions between the Catholic intellectual heritage and science with respect to sexuality). Some history is needed, too. The purpose of this essay is to offer that history as an important complement to Figert's and Kniss's chapters (2 and 3) in this volume.

As Klaus Schatz points out, the gradual centralizing of power in Rome was not the result of a papal power grab.[2] The process was driven by the inability to resolve conflicts at the diocesan and regional levels. For instance, in the power vacuum created by the collapse of the Roman Empire, the office of the bishop became materially and politically, as well as spiritually, powerful. Episcopal elections could (and did) become contentious. Contested elections and other disputes that could not be resolved were appealed to the pope for adjudication.

A pivotal factor in establishing the pyramid model was the first Vatican Council, convoked by Pope Pius IX. Though he had been elected because he seemed open to new thought, he had been traumatized into a defensive conservatism by the murder of his appointed governor of the Papal States at the hands of an angry mob. In Pius's view, which was shared by many of the bishops who would play leading roles at Vatican I, civilization was in imminent danger of collapsing into bloody chaos. This danger was the consequence of the world's rejection of the Church's authority and age-old wisdom and its movement toward democracy. Thus, the Church's hierarchical structure needed to be strengthened in order to withstand the attacks of its enemies and to survive as the sole teacher and guardian of God's saving truth in the world.

For many Catholics—from Pius IX himself to the humblest layperson in the pews—one essential way to strengthen the Church (and, thus, preserve civilization) was to define clearly the supreme authority of the pope in teaching and governance. Ambiguous teaching led to severely diminished influence. Limiting papal jurisdiction left the Church vulnerable to a "divide and conquer" strategy, such as Roman Catholicism had suffered in France prior to and following the Revolution of 1789. Joseph deMaistre (d. 1821) spoke for many: "No European religion without Christianity, no Christianity without Catholicism, no Catholicism without the pope, no pope without the supremacy that belongs to him."[3]

But what exactly were those powers and prerogatives? A significant minority of bishops at Vatican I argued that these could be understood only in the context of a renewed understanding of the Church itself and of the role of the bishops within the Church. But, as the Council began this larger work of understanding, the majority got worried. The Council might end without a definition of papal authority. Political unrest in Europe was growing, and many bishops were longing to return home to their dioceses.

So the leaders of the majority urged Pius IX to intervene. Pius wanted the definition, too, so he accepted their proposal: first, to suspend work on the larger document on the Church; second, to extract the sections on the papacy from it in order to create a separate document; third, to prepare it for a vote; fourth, to pass and promulgate it—and only then would the bishops return to work on the larger document.

One English bishop foresaw that "infallibility" would turn out to be far less problematic than papal jurisdiction of the pope as framed in *Pastor aeternus*.[4] There Vatican I declares that papal power of governance over the Church is supreme, ordinary, immediate, and universal. Conciliar debates over the wording of the text show that these terms had specific denotations that differed somewhat from their connotations. "Supreme" meant that there is no higher authority in the Church than the pope. "Ordinary" meant that his jurisdictional authority comes with his office, not that it is exercised on some sort of daily basis. "Universal" meant that his jurisdiction extends over the whole Church, and "immediate" meant that he does not necessarily have to exercise his jurisdiction through intermediaries.

The minority bishops argued that these specifics should be part of the document to avoid misunderstandings. Moreover, the text ought to make clear that the power of the pope is to be exercised "for the building up" of the Church; that is, it is always to be a matter of service, not of any self-aggrandizement. Since the College of Bishops exists by the will of Christ himself, the text should also make clear that papal jurisdiction does not nullify the powers of teaching and governance that belong to bishops individually and corporately. Including these elements, they said, would make the document more complete and accurate.

But everybody in the Church knows what the terms "supreme, ordinary, immediate, and universal" mean, the majority responded. Why lengthen the text with elaborate explanations? Moreover, such explanations might lead to endless arguing about whether a particular exercise of papal jurisdiction was justified or not, when a crisis might call for rapid, decisive action on the pope's part.

The two sides could find no satisfactory compromise wording. When the final text was put up for a vote, only two bishops voted against it. The substantial minority had already left Rome by that time. They did not want to embarrass Pius IX with their "No" vote and they did not want the vote count to suggest that the Church was seriously divided.

Shortly afterward, the Franco-Prussian War broke out. The bishops never returned to Rome to complete the document on the Church and its bishops, which would have provided the broader context for understanding the role of the pope. A few voices continued to insist that only the records of the conciliar debates and discussions, as well as the *relatio* (i.e., the official explanation) of Bishop Gasser, could show the precise meaning of *Pastor aeternus*. By and large, however, Vatican I left the impression that the pope was a monarch and the bishops were simply his delegates. So, for example, Bismarck tried to use *Pastor aeternus* to weaken German Catholics' loyalty to the papacy. The German bishops' careful response to the Iron Chancellor (which was praised by Pius IX) that they had not made a monarch of the pope, did little to correct the new perception of the pope's jurisdiction as virtually unlimited and of his teaching authority as immune to criticism or correction. A fundamentalist interpretation of *Pastor aeternus* took hold in the Church.

When John XXIII, the pope who had convened Vatican II, died in 1963, the

Council was suspended, according to Church law. His successor, Cardinal Montini, had had misgivings about a Council, but had since become one of its leaders. His election to the papacy as Pope Paul VI showed that a majority of the cardinals now considered Vatican II crucial for the Church in the twentieth century.

It fell, then, to Paul VI, to help guide Vatican II to a successful conclusion, to begin the processes of its implementation, and to manage the gale-force winds of reform and reaction that the Council had inadvertently loosed upon the Church. His leadership strengthened regional and national conferences of bishops, as well as the new Synod of Bishops.[5] He sought to appoint bishops who were known and accepted as pastors to their people, the kind of men whom *Christus Dominus* had presented as a model. He refused to excommunicate those who disagreed with *Humanae vitae* (1968), in which he had reaffirmed the traditional prohibition against artificial contraception.

His journeys to India, the Philippines, the United States, and the Holy Land put an end to the image of the pope as "the prisoner of the Vatican" in a hostile world. For Paul, the journeys were evidence of a Church seeking mutual understanding and cooperation with other Christians, other religions, and "the world" that were envisioned by Vatican II. Nowhere were his initiatives more dramatic than in Jerusalem, when Paul VI embraced the Greek Orthodox leader Athanagoras and knelt to kiss his foot in respect and homage.

Paul VI died in 1978. His successor, John Paul I, had one of the shortest pontificates on record, thirty-three days. Then the cardinals broke the precedent of centuries by choosing a non-Italian, the Archbishop of Cracow, Karol Woytyla, to be Bishop of Rome as John Paul II. Because his pontificate was one of the longest on record, nearly thirty-years (1978–2005), his influence on the shape of authority in the Roman Catholic Church was—and is—vast.

Woytyla would never have become pope if he had been a known opponent of the Council. As John Paul II, he declared that implementing Vatican II was one of his chief responsibilities as pope—for example, "After its conclusion, the Council did not cease to inspire the Church's life. In 1985 I was able to assert, 'For me, then—who had the special grace of participating in it and actively collaborating in its development—Vatican II has always been, and especially during these years of my Pontificate, the constant reference point of my every pastoral action, in the conscious commitment to implement its directives concretely and faithfully at the level of each Church and the whole Church.'"[6]

It soon became obvious, however, that Woytyla's interpretation of the Council was quite his own, the product of his formative years as a young Polish Catholic under Nazism and as priest, bishop, and cardinal under Soviet domination. While he embraced enthusiastically certain conciliar teachings, he ignored others, particularly the teachings on authority that conflicted with his own views on the kind of authority that the Church now needed.

For instance, he repeated frequently the claim of the Pastoral Constitution on the Church in the Modern World (*Gaudium et spes,* §22) that the Incarnation meant that in Jesus Christ alone was to be found the deepest truth about humanity. Yet he (along with a number of the other Polish bishops at Vatican II) thought that the constitution's vision of a renewed Catholicism serving humanity by dialoguing with the world on the problems facing the human race was hopelessly naïve. Their experience of life under Nazism and Communism taught them that only a sizable, vigorous Church that presented a united front against its oppressors could withstand today's assaults on human dignity.

The Church, in their view, had little to learn from the world and much to teach it. Interdisciplinary symposia (like the one that inspired this book) might theoretically help the Church to learn from the natural and social sciences how to proclaim and defend human dignity more effectively. But such an outcome was hardly imaginable in a state whose educational and cultural institutions were controlled by dehumanizing ideologies. Thus, Church teaching had to be clear and it had to be delivered forcefully and dramatically.

Moreover, the public debate and even dissension among the bishops as they shaped Vatican II's teaching appalled Woytyla. In his view, such open conflicts could only weaken the Church and provide opportunities for its enemies, whether those enemies be totalitarian regimes or predatory capitalists. Woytyla loved his Church and humanity too much to let that happen. As John Paul II, he now had the power and prerogatives to apply the lessons of Poland to the life of the global Church. In so doing, John Paul II did not formally flout the teaching of Vatican II, since the Council had simply reaffirmed the teaching of Vatican I on the power and prerogatives of the pope, while couching its statements on participation, collaboration, and consultation in terms of desirability, not necessity. Thus, their implementation in the Church still depended on the pope.

John Paul II saw himself as the Church's chief missionary, using the symbolism of his office to extend the Church's influence throughout the world. Soon he became the most-traveled pontiff in history. Unlike Paul VI, he undertook his journeys not to enter into dialogue with the world, or even with his fellow Catholics but instead, to replicate the effect of the huge rallies staged by the Church in Poland under Communism. These massive events were designed to encourage the faithful and demonstrate the Church's moral power and influence.

While his journeys magnified the role and visibility of the papacy, they diminished the roles of the bishops in the Church, which Vatican II had sought to invigorate. John Paul II also weakened the authority of national or regional conferences of bishops, groups that the Council had sought to strengthen (*Lumen gentium,* § 23). He wanted bishops to exercise their authority vigorously to bring the local church's teachings and practice into line with Rome.

A number of these episcopal appointments turned out to be disasters. Most notable among these were Wolfgang Haas of Chur, Switzerland, where people lay down in front of the cathedral to force priests and bishops to step over them at his installation, and Hans Hermann Groer of Vienna, whose sexual abuse of young men under his supervision was verified by the other Austrian bishops. Nonetheless, John Paul continued to choose men he thought were cut from the same cloth as himself.

He also moved to limit the authority and influence of bishops' conferences, which, as noted earlier, Vatican II had tried to strengthen. In his view, these conferences could weaken Church authority and thus diminish the effectiveness of its mission. For example, Paul VI in *Humanae vitae* had rejected the advice of the majority of the commission he had appointed to study the issue. Instead, he had reaffirmed the immorality of artificial contraception. Soon thereafter, the German and U.S. Bishops' Conferences had reminded Catholics of the Catholic teaching that their conscience, not Paul's teaching, was the supreme moral norm.

In the 1980s, the U.S. Bishops' Conference issued two major documents, *The Challenge of Peace* (CP, 1983) and *Economic Justice for All* (EJFA, 1986). These texts had gone through multiple drafts. Each had been shaped by the bishops' wide consultation of experts and lay people alike. The bishops had even encouraged Catholic institutions of higher education to convene meetings and symposia on the issues of peace and the economy (i.e., conferences similar to the collaborative project that has produced this work on sexuality and gender).

For John Paul II and his advisors, however, the U.S. bishops' documents were problematic on account of the process that produced them. In their eyes, the extensive consultation leading to CP and EJFA highlighted the bishops as both learners and teachers—or, at least, as teachers whose credibility was only as good as the arguments they used to support their teaching. From John Paul II's perspective, such a process of consultation obscured the reason for viewing Church teaching as authoritative: the role of the Holy Spirit in the Church. One respected Church teaching not primarily on account of its arguments, but on account of one's convictions about the never-failing help of the Spirit in formulating and promulgating it. One difficulty with this view is that it seems to presume the Spirit is at work only among the ordained.

In late summer of 1998, John Paul II's *Apostolos suos* appeared. It limited the authority and influence of bishops' conferences. If he had issued it prior to 1983, CP and EJFA would have been stillborn, since *Apostolos suos* stipulates that all such teaching has to be approved unanimously. If a proposed teaching document could not win the bishops' unanimous agreement, it had to receive papal approval before it could be promulgated. Since this is a level of agreement that even a Council, such as Vatican I or Vatican II, does not have to reach and departs from long-standing Church practice, many observers reasoned that John Paul II wanted to centralize all official teaching in his office and his office alone.

Yet the teaching and practice of Vatican II highlighted the indispensable role of theologians in the Church and Bernard Lonergan explains it in his famous line, "A theology mediates between a cultural matrix and the significance and role of a religion in that matrix."[7] Theologians are responsible for facilitating a mutually corrective conversation between the Church and its particular matrices. But theologians cannot mediate if they are captive to the perspectives of their culture nor can they mediate if their role is restricted to explaining and defending the Church's current official teaching.

There is not enough space here to recount fully all the efforts to control Catholic theologians in the John Paul II era. Mention of a few cases will have to suffice.

Within months of John Paul II's election, the Congregation for the Doctrine of the Faith summoned Hans Küng to Rome on account of his work on papal infallibility, a book that had already been heavily criticized within the Catholic theological community. Revised directives for "pontifical faculties" of theology, that is, institutions that conferred degrees in theology under a license from Rome, were issued. These prescribed, among other things, that all candidates for tenure and promotion had to be approved by Rome. Charles E. Curran, who had taught on such a pontifical faculty at the Catholic University of America, was deprived of his position on account of his disagreement with Church teaching on contraception, homosexual activity, and so forth. He argued, to no avail, that he had always presented the Church's teaching in its best light and that he disagreed on matters not central to the Gospel. The revised Code of Canon Law (1983) required Catholic theologians in Catholic colleges and universities to seek a *mandatum* from their local bishop. A "Profession of Faith" and an "Oath of Fidelity," declaring the individual's assent to each and every element of Church teaching, were imposed on all those undertaking major new responsibilities in the Church.

Over the years, then, a disturbing trend became more and more clear. Since Vatican II's vision of the "shape of authority" had not been codified in the Church's procedures and legislation, wisdom from the natural and social sciences, philosophy, and other disciplines in the humanities that are demonstrably relevant to Church teaching on matters such as homosexuality, abortion, contraception, and the role of women—matters with serious implications for people's lives—can be ignored, dismissed, and repressed in the Church. An apparent uniformity of opinion in the Church can be imposed by exercises of jurisdiction, not by the authority of compelling argument and sufficient reason.

Therefore, until and unless the Roman Catholic Church elects a Bishop of Rome willing to implement the vision of Vatican II and to codify it in legislation, the shape of authority in the Church will always resemble a pyramid. Until such a time, most Catholic theologians will agree with Karl Rahner:

> On the one hand, there is the so-called permanence and clearly unchangeable character of human nature, as this is presumed by moral teaching on the laws of nature. On the other hand, we try to reconcile this with the fact that human beings with their constantly developing and changing genetic structure are to be situated within the whole history of evolution. It is not surprising then to be rather taken aback at times by the unambiguous and unchangeable tone of the Church's moral promulgation given that such certainties are not that obvious within human beings? [sic] Given this situation, theologians need to be careful and modest, but they must have the courage to proclaim their message and retain their own convictions.[8]

And theologians must have such courage for two reasons: first, to remind us all that the whole Church is not yet of one mind on issues of sexuality and, no less important, to give heart to those who have been marginalized in the Church for their sexuality and/or gender and who have suffered greatly on account of it.

Notes

1. Rynne, "The First Session," 3–134.
2. Schatz, *Papal Primacy.*
3. Quoted in Granfield, *The Limits of the Papacy,* 42.
4. Butler, *The Vatican Council 1869–1870,* 30.
5. Pope Paul VI, "Apostolica Sollicitudo," 720–24.
6. Pope John Paul II, "Fidei Depositum."
7. Lonergan, *Method in Theology,* xi.
8. Rahner, "Experiences of a Catholic Theologian," 13.

2

White Coats

Boundary Disputes between Scientific and Religious Authority

ANNE E. FIGERT

The popular history of Western science is often told as a series of conflicts with religion: Galileo versus the Catholic Church, Darwin versus Christian opponents of evolution, and recent charged debates over teaching intelligent design in public schools. In this heroic narrative, the inevitable truth of science and the scientific method is portrayed as eventually overcoming opposition from "superstitious" religious leaders and "dying but still powerful" institutions. It makes for exciting and interesting reading. It also overlooks the abundance of rich scholarship in the field of the history and social studies of science that has explored this relationship not only as a series of occasional conflicts, but also as cooperating and complementary ways of thinking.

It would be easy, but distorting and counterproductive, to approach a dialogue among scientists, theologians and other scholars about sexual and gender diversity assuming conflict is the only possible conversation mode. Instead, I want to offer an alternative approach to dialogue that will focus on two aims: 1) explore the complexity of the ideas and scholarship about the relationship between the sciences and religion; and 2) define "authority" and discuss why it is a central and useful concept in any interdisciplinary exchange about sex, science, and religion.

Scholars in the history and sociology of science have long debated and struggled to understand the relationship of science and religion.[1] This is not surprising given the importance of these two institutions in modern society. Indeed, many historians locate the central events and questions of Western civilization around the evolving nature of the science/religion relationship and raise questions such as: Are the roots of modern scientific thinking located within religious thought and traditions? Did modern science really replace religion as the authoritative voice about the natural world? Is there an inevitable conflict between scientific way of thinking and religious thinking? Brooke comments that "Since the seventeenth century every generation has taken a view on [these questions'] importance without, however, reaching any consensus as to how they should be answered."[2] How one answers these questions is just as complex as the questions themselves.

Science and Religion: A Complicated Relationship

In both scholarly and popular literatures of the twenty-first century, the relationship between science and religion in the West is usually explained with reference to one of three models: "conflict, complementarity, and complexity."[3] Throughout this volume, readers glimpse each of these models at work. For example, Calcagno's chapter defends clear distinctions between what science and religion can claim to "know" and notes the tensions between them. Catania and Pope also note the differences between the two, but take more of a complementary approach overall. Caughie, Jung, and Roughgarden certainly show the complexity—pertaining both to knowledge and to the relationships among distinct disciplines. Indeed, many of the contributors implicitly or explicitly draw upon one or more of these models in their attempts to make sense of the way that science and religion interact when discussing human sexuality or gender. After reading this discussion of the three models, the reader may wish to (re) read the other chapters with this typology in mind and see how they embody one or more of them. In what follows, I summarize each and provide examples in order to highlight the role of two major sociological concepts inherent in each model: institutional differentiation and authority.

CONFLICT MODEL

A conflict model is often seen as "the popular model" but it is also widely supported by social scientists and natural scientists.[4] It suggests that science and religion are separate institutions, separate ways of thinking and inherently incompatible ways of explaining the world. Notions of objectivity, facts, and "the truth about the world" have often led scientists to either distance themselves from the personal experience of religion or to attempt to study religion in a detached, "objective" manner. Max Weber, one of the founders of modern sociology, made a clear case for the separation of the two institutions and for scientific authority: "All scientific work presupposes that the rules of logic and method are valid; these are the general foundations of our orientation in the world; and, at least for our special question, these presuppositions are the least problematic aspect of science. Science further supposes that what is yielded by scientific work is important in the sense that it is 'worth being known.'"[5] Thus, science (as particularly opposed to religion) is the objective, logical and empirical study of the world.

As forms of knowledge and intellectual questioning, science and religion seek to ask different questions and arrive at different answers. When there is interaction, there is usually conflict over who has the authority or expertise to talk about and settle the factual matter at hand. When the debate is about factual matters about nature, science is usually perceived or presented as having the authority to settle the debate.[6] Indeed, recent work has found that social scientists are even less likely than other scientists to describe themselves as religious as well as an overall decline in religiosity among university-based scientists.[7] In short, in this model, science and religion are separate ways of thinking and separate institutions, that best operate separately in society.

A contemporary example of the conflict model in action is the popular work of the evolutionary biologist Richard Dawkins. Dawkins is not content with mere differentiation of science and religion. Instead, he argues for the superiority of the logic and thinking of science. Dawkins writes: "What expertise can theologians bring to deep cosmological questions that scientists cannot?" and "Why are scientists so cravenly respectful towards the ambitions of theologians, over questions that theologians are certainly no more qualified to answer than scientists themselves?"[8] In another publication he boldly professes: "Well, science is not religion and it doesn't just come down to faith. Although it has many of religion's virtues, it has none of its vices. Science is based upon verifiable evidence. Religious faith not only lacks evidence, its independence from evidence is its pride and joy, shouted from the rooftops."[9] Dawkins trusts the methods and facts of science implicitly.

In stark contrast, he views religion with great suspicion. For example, in terms of institutional differentiation, Dawkins warns that if allowed, religion would gladly intrude upon the rightful authority and work that belong to scientists alone: "Don't fall for the argument that religion and science operate on separate dimensions and are concerned with quite separate sorts of questions. Religions have historically always attempted to answer the questions that properly belong to science. Thus religions should not be allowed now to retreat away from the ground upon which they have traditionally attempted to fight. They do offer both a cosmology and a biology; however, in both cases it is false."[10] Thus, for Dawkins, the world would be better off if people relied solely upon science to search out the greatest mysteries of our existence. Religion cannot be trusted.

The conflict model suggests that science and religion are incompatible especially when one oversteps its institutional boundaries, and thus its authority and expertise, to comment on the domain of the other. The conflict model is usually a one-sided model on the part of science/scientists who are wary or hostile to religious interference in "matters of fact" about nature.[11] Some scientists ultimately believe that scientific expertise should win out—that the facts, truth, and the scientific method are more important than religion. Some scientists might concede that religious and ethical matters may be important, but quickly add that they are not factual.[12]

COMPLEMENTARITY MODEL

This model is related to the conflict model. It is based upon the notion of the institutional difference between science and religion, but it does not emphasize conflict. Rather, this model recognizes that there are the occasional conflicts between science and religion but emphasizes cooperation and respect for difference. Scientist and writer Stephen Jay Gould called this the "Principle of Noma or Non-Overlapping Magisteria": "Science tries to document the factual character of the natural world, and to develop theories that coordinate and explain these facts. Religion, on the other hand, operates in the equally important, but utterly different, realm of human purposes, meanings, and values—subjects that the factual domain of science might illuminate, but can never resolve."[13] For Gould, science and religion are not fighting on the "same battlefield" or "disputed territory" because they are talking about different things.[14]

Moreover, this model still suggests that science is the expert voice about the way that nature operates, and religion is the expert voice about matters of morals and cosmology. This is more of the "two worlds" view by scholars and scientists to show the compatibility of science and religion *as long as* one (religion) doesn't interfere with the other (science). Wilson notes, ". . . even those historians who were most significant in undermining the conflict thesis did not reject it entirely."[15] In other words, this model assumes a major caveat: both domains are valid and potentially helpful as long as religion stays out of science.

Key to the complementary model is the notion of "magisterium," which Gould defines as a "domain of authority in teaching."[16] Simply put, if you want to understand nature or why people act or think, you need to enter the realm of science and scientific authority. If you want to understand issues of ethics, morals, and the supernatural, enter the realm of religion and religious authority. Where Gould perhaps differs from more hard-line and conflict-model scientists such as Dawkins is his principle of "respectful noninterference—accompanied by intense dialogue between the two distinct subjects."[17]

Today this notion of "respectful noninterference" and dialogue between science and religion is getting increased attention thanks to The John Templeton Foundation. Founded by the late businessman and philanthropist John Templeton (1912–2008), the foundation has spent over seventy million dollars in awards, grants, and conferences promoting dialogue on "life's big questions."[18] The Templeton Foundation is one of the world's primary advocates of the complementary model. Johnson writes: "Templeton almost single-handedly sustains the modern movement to reconcile science and religion—or, as some see it, he is keeping it alive on its death bed with extraordinary means of support."[19]

The obituary for Sir John Templeton in the science journal *Nature* indicates how one of the institutional guards of science's borders assesses this influence. The obituary starts out affirming the primacy of science to investigate the world:

> This publication would turn away from religion in seeking explanations for how the world works, and believes that science is likely to go further in explaining human moral impulses than some religious people will welcome. Thus it shares a degree of suspicion with many in the scientific community at any attempt by religiously driven organizations to fund science.[20]

However, it ends with the following quasi-endorsement of the foundation's goals:

> A critical scrutiny of the foundation's scientific influence continues to be warranted, and no scientific organization should accept sums of money so large that its mission could be perceived as being swayed by religious or spiritual considerations. But critics' total opposition to the Templeton Foundation's unusual mix of science and spirituality is unwarranted.[21]

The "respectful wariness" expressed in the obituary shows that this "separate but respectful" model is alive and well in the world of science. The majority of the discussions on science, religion, and human sexuality in the symposia leading to this book reflected the complementarity model.

COMPLEXITY MODEL

Both science and religion are viewed as complex, historically situated institutions with different modes of inquiry in the complexity model.[22] This model is often associated with scholarship in the history of science. Its use reflects changes in the way we study history and particularly the way in which we think about and analyze science in a post-Kuhnian world where science is analyzed as a fully human activity and its knowledge is constructed and perspectival.[23] Bowler contends: "It now seems more reasonable to suppose that there are several different ways in which science and religion can be related to each other. They may interact in various ways, including conflict and cooperation, or they may come to an amicable agreement to stick each to its own territory. But there has never been a single attitude in play at a single time, and the balance between the various possibilities is always shifting."[24]

What distinguishes the complexity model from the previous models is precisely this analytic focus by which to understand both science and religion without privileging either of them. In the complexity model, neither science nor religion can be seen as static domains or purely objective. It also suggests symmetry to our understanding of both. For example, both science and religion have similar internal debates:

* What is the truth?
* Who gets to decide?
* Who has the authority/power to decide matters at particular points in time?
* Who possesses the expertise to settle matters of fact/truth?

In other words, both domains are historically situated and both have "baggage"!

Moreover, there is ". . . growing recognition among historians of science that the relationship of science and religion has been much more positive than is sometimes thought."[25] For example, the particular relationship between the Roman Catholic Church and science has often been portrayed as adversarial based upon the portrayal of the Galileo affair. More recent scholarship using the complexity model has shown how this historical debate and event were/are much more complicated than is often portrayed.[26] Harris explains:

> Almost every pope since Pius XI has taken pains to reaffirm the autonomy of science. This autonomy, they argue, is guaranteed on the one side by adherence to the methods of science and on the other by a theological view grounded in St. Augustine (354–430), who taught that scripture was not to be reread as a textbook on nature but as a guidebook to salvation. Moreover, they have repeatedly invoked the traditional Catholic doctrine of the "two truths" (i.e., natural or scientific knowledge can never contradict revealed or supernatural knowledge, since both issue from the same source) to maintain the separation between the domain of science and the domain of religion.[27]

In all, the history and relationship between science and religion is much more nuanced than some assume. Brooke maintains that "[t]here is no such thing as *the* relationship between science and religion. It is what different individuals and communities have made of it in a plethora of different contexts."[28] For some, this point means that we have to understand the historical and cultural specificity of both science and religion whenever the two interact. For others it means that each of the three models represents an equally valid way of making sense of the world.

In the symposia dialogues that preceded this book, the complexity model was often invoked by participants to understand the theological and scientific debate about human sexuality and gender. Stemming primarily from the complexity model, my own work involves pointing out the social and political implications of both the scientific and theological perspectives on human sexuality. Specifically, I focus on two major sociological concepts that are relevant and helpful in understanding the issues: institutional differentiation and authority.

Authority: What It Is and Why It Matters

In all three of the above models, science and religion have boundary disputes over the ownership or control of certain ideas, practices or events. And in each, two major sociological concepts are relevant: "institutional differentiation" and "authority." Institutional differentiation refers to the notion that institutions exist and develop in society to fill a societal need. Whereas science involves the extension of certified knowledge about the natural world, religion involves the things relative to what Durkheim called the sacred.[29]

Authority is derived in part from institutional differentiation. Merton's earliest work in the sociology of science highlights modern science's connection to organized religion dating back to the seventeenth century.[30] The authority of modern science is rooted in its institutional role and differentiation of modern professional expertise in modern society.[31] As already discussed, in each domain, there are different areas of expertise and thus different claims to authority. Historian Steve Shapin observes: "every culture must put in place *some* solution to the problem of whom to trust and on what basis."[32] The issue of authority usually revolves around questions of who has the power to legitimately "speak" about important matters. The authority and institutional rewards that accrue to science derive precisely from its distinctness from religion in explaining how the natural and biological world works. Religion likewise has a different kind of authority and reward system based upon the niche that it fills for society by answering questions about the unknowable and providing emotional and psychological comfort.[33] Thus the issue of authority and who gets to speak authoritatively on issues related to nature is rooted in the institutional differentiation of science as a modern social institution.

WEBER'S IDEAL TYPES OF AUTHORITY

I want to reflect upon Weber's widely used definition of authority, which derives from his discussion of power, in order to show why the notion of authority is a useful prism through which we can examine the relationship between science and religion in matters of human sexuality and gender. Weber defines power as the following: "In general, we understand by 'power' the chance of a man or of a number of men [sic] to realize their own will in a communal action, even against the resistance of others who are participating in the action."[34] Thus power is both interactive and, as we will see, built into the social statuses people occupy. What distinguishes illicit forms of coercive power from legitimate expressions of power is something called "authority."

Authority rests in the status or position that a person holds or occupies. The ability to exercise control by a person occupying a certain status is seen as right and sufficient, that is, it is legitimate power. Power is also limited to the exercise of that position. Weber defines three different and ideal types of authority. *Traditional authority* resides in long held and recognized status such as parental units, elders, or that of a hereditary monarchy. *Charismatic authority* rests upon an inspirational aura about a person that others then recognize and follow because of these almost supernatural or extraordinary features. *Rational-legal authority* rests in the formalized structure of a society or organization that dictates the rules—as seen in its laws, degrees, regulations, and so forth. At its heart, this third kind of authority is "based upon an *impersonal* bond to the generally defined and functional 'duty of office' . . . fixed by *rationally established* norms . . . in such a manner that the legitimacy of the authority becomes the legality of the general rule, which is purposely thought out, enacted and announced with formal correctness."[35]

SCIENTIFIC AND RELIGIOUS AUTHORITY

Under Weber's ideal types, "scientific authority" falls under the third category, rational-legal authority. The power or legitimated authority granted to science in modern society is rooted or based upon what scientists do and how they are supposed to act with the world or that impersonal relationship to duty of office. Religious authority in society is more complex because it can be traditional, charismatic, or in some cases rational-legal authority.

The authority granted to individual practitioners of each of the three ideal types is institutionalized and becomes accepted over time as part of the general culture. For religion, this cultural authority is recognized by the public when its expert practitioners speak truthfully about moral and spiritual matters; modern science has been given in our culture the authority to speak the "truth" about the social and natural world.

This functional separation of the institutions of religion, medicine, and science makes sense and generally works—except when it doesn't. And this of course is the interesting part: when boundaries get blurred, transgressed, or disputed. For example, in *Veritatus splendor* John Paul II was adamant about the Church's authority to speak on the connection between truth and morality. As indicated by the participation of scientists in this seminar, there is an interest and obligation for some scientists to speak about matters of faith and spirituality and not "leave it to the theologians."

For scientists, cultural authority turns into a cognitive authority, which is "the legitimate power (in designated contexts) to define, describe or explain bounded realms of reality."[36] The cultural or cognitive authority of science is portrayed as based on the technical competence of its practitioners and the truth of their factual conclusions. It is not based upon social, moral or other status attainments. The result in modern society is that "[s]cience is next to being *the* source of cognitive authority: anyone who would be widely believed and trusted as an interpreter of nature needs a license from the scientific community."[37] If this is the case, why does there continue to be controversy and debate about matters such as evolutionary biology? Why does the relationship between science and religion continue to matter, if science is "the source of cognitive authority" about nature? To explore these issues, I draw further upon the writings in the social studies of science.

OCCASIONAL BATTLES/SKIRMISHES AND SCIENTIFIC AUTHORITY

Shapin and Schaffer describe controversies over things such as evolution as a battle of cultural maps in which authoritative and authentic knowledge is debated and contested.[38] Gieryn points out that not all boundaries are contested and "[s]ometimes the cultural boundaries that separate realms of knowledge sit there peacefully, with little manifest attention from anybody, structuring everyday practices without noticeable contestation or doubt."[39] It depends where and when the cultural boundaries meet.

When the boundaries are contested, authority is not only rooted in institutional differentiation, but is also an *accomplishment of human actors*. Scientists (no less than other experts) engage in something called "boundary-work," which Gieryn defines as: "The attribution of selected characteristics to the institution of science (i.e., to its practitioners, methods, stock of knowledge, values and work organization) for purposes of constructing a social boundary that distinguishes some intellectual activity as non-science."[40]

When such challenges occur, we can see that both science and religion are much more driven by human politics, economics, and power struggles than their claims to the pure pursuit of the truth might suggest. For example, whether you call it creationism, creation science, or intelligent design, it doesn't matter. This is a boundary dispute between science and religion because religion is seen as encroaching upon science's space (and epistemic authority) to speak about the natural world. "Creation scientists" or "intelligent design" advocates for nonevolutionary theories of creation are not recognized by other scientists as scientific experts, even if they can produce scientific credentials. Rather, they are dismissed and treated as "frauds" and "religious zealots" because they are not publishing their scholarship in recognized scientific outlets.[41]

Take another example of disputed authority: Can embryonic stem cells cure diseases? Maybe, maybe not. To scientists this is a researchable question within the scientific community, and its pursuit ought not be prohibited from pulpits or the voting booth. There is public dispute about embryonic stem cell research because significant numbers of religious leaders and lay members believe harvesting these cells harms human (albeit embryonic) persons. So, they speak out against this particular form of scientific research and try to influence political decisions about what scientists can or can't do in this case. Scientists in turn see this position by religious leaders as "encroachment" upon their institutional turf and as a challenge to their authority and expertise as scientists.

Turning to the topic of sexuality, are people born sexually differentiated and thus by implication merely reflecting their genetic make-up? Or do they have free will and make choices about sexual behaviors? In other words, does a person have a "sexual preference" or a "sexual orientation"? Once again, to scientists this is a researchable question up for debate and discussion within the scientific community. However, for some within religious circles, *these questions are deeply moral questions that can and should be informed by scientific knowledge, but not necessarily decided only by scientists.* What is more, scientists constantly disagree among themselves about the "facts" and "theories" and "evidence" about sexual differentiation. This debate is usually held within the context of scientific conferences, journals, and other professionally recognized outlets and is rarely used in conversation with theologians or lay people who are struggling to address these issues in "good faith."

The way scientific controversies are settled and the consequences for the scientific community vary on whether the controversy is internal to the scientific community or external to it (with another profession or group such as religious leaders or politicians). Public controversies about what are seen as matters of science often get settled through a rhetorical exploitation of the authority of science, brought in to bolster arguments.[42] Assumptions about the rational nature of scientific discourse and methodology are important factors in how these scientific controversies get settled. As Nelkin points out: "The authority of scientific expertise rests on assumptions about scientific rationality. Interpretations and predictions made by scientists are judged to be rational because they are based on data gathered through rational procedures. Their interpretations therefore serve as a basis for planning and as a means for defending the legitimacy of policy decisions."[43]

When debates about scientific matters become public, they begin to take on an even more esoteric "technical" nature that tries to root the discussion and its settlement within the jurisdiction of science and not religion or politics. For example, Gilbert and Mulkay (1984) find an entirely different form of discourse that scientists use when talking in public, as opposed to when they talk among themselves informally in laboratories or at conferences. In employing these "empiricist repertoires" on public occasions, scientists present information in a way that preempts debate about its legitimacy. Gilbert and Mulkay state: "Each scientist's actions and beliefs, no matter how inconsistent they appear to be with those of other researchers, are presented as those of any competent scientist. The guiding principle of this repertoire appears to be that speakers depict their actions and beliefs as a neutral medium through which empirical phenomena make themselves evident."[44] The problem lies when social, religious and political values become difficult to distinguish from scientific facts during scientific controversies. As technical expertise becomes a resource, exploited by all parties to justify their moral and political claims, it becomes difficult to distinguish scientific facts from political values."[45]

More recent struggles, especially at the boundary of science and religion, indicate a potential problem for scientists and scientific authority. Since the 1980s, increasingly different tactics have been used and moral elements were introduced into the rhetoric of challengers as they challenged the morality of certain scientific practices or research. Nelkin writes: "By the end of the 1980s, protestors increasingly framed their attacks on science in the moral language of rights."[46] She goes on to warn that "controversies are increasingly expressing moral judgments as well as economic interests, and they are becoming crusades. The social movements organized to challenge science and technology are driven by a moral rhetoric of good and evil, of right and wrong."[47] Nelkin feared and accurately pinpointed that the authority of science is being challenged and undermined by this shift to political activity based upon a moral absolutism based upon religion.

Thus even as scientists assert their "right" to do their own institutionally mandated and internally driven work (authority and expertise) others can assert their own "right" to challenge the work on their moral principles, authority, and expertise. Controversies over the biological basis of human sexuality and stem cell research are examples of this challenge and how the disputes are centered upon authority issues. It also suggests why this type of dispute between science and religion will never be fully settled.

* * *

The complexity model of the science/religion relationship acknowledges both institutional differentiation perspectives about the authority of certain professions and the cultural/human agency perspective about authority. In the end, if an issue of knowledge, for example, the biological underpinnings of human sexuality, is not continually claimed and settled by scientists as fully scientifically settled, it will keep open the doors for moral challenges by religious leaders or in the minds of people of faith. But this also assumes that the questions to which scientists are making authoritative claims are answerable scientific questions. As one of the editors of this volume pointed out during the symposia dialogues, the scientific question about whether something is a human (as opposed to nonhuman) gamete is settled. But the question of when "personhood" begins is still wide open because it is not a scientifically answerable question.

Moral challenges to scientific knowledge may also be kept alive because of the general public's growing suspicion of experts. It gets at a very basic question: why do we believe what experts tell us is the truth about something? Is there something inherent in the ideas, theories, methods, or social actions of one group over another? Why accept the truth given to us by scientists about the natural world and not religious leaders? In his discussion about the current appeal about "scientific creationism" historian Brooke suggests that : "[i]n that gap between the lay person and the professional biologist lies a further reason for the growth of the movement—a growing suspicion of experts and frustration at having to take their word."[48] Moral challenges to scientific research that is built upon a rights language can significantly challenge the use of scientific authority to settle the debate over an issue because this issue is also claimed by moral or religious communities. The debate is not settled and thus may never be settled by scientists and their claims to expertise.

This reality may in part be due to the lack of comfort on the part of scientists to claim moral language and their tendencies to stick to the empiricist repertoires.[49] Scientists and social scientists are reluctant to argue and defend their conviction that "it is not immoral or unethical to do or be 'X' or to consider 'X.'" As indicated in the complementarity model, scientists offer a perception or claim that they do not have the training or expertise to speak about such issues. This may be changing according to a 2006 article in the *New York Times* discussion of recent books on science.[50] In an attempt to highlight attempts by scientists to promote the complementarity model, Dean argues that when boundary disputes between science and religion occur, "scientists have to be brave to talk about religion . . . Not denounce it, but embrace it." Just as theologians and ethicists have worked hard to understand scientific arguments, scientists could work harder to understand the theological and ethical debates rather than reject them out of hand. Recent books by Francis Collins (2006) and Joan Roughgarden (2006) are seen a positive step in this direction because they explore the compatibility of science and personal religious faith.[51]

Dialogues, conferences, and books about faith and science may indicate a greater willingness on the part of scientists to speak on matters of science and religion. As explored in this chapter, the bigger issue for the institution of science is *not* whether individual scientists have faith and religious practice. Some do. Others do not. What is not clear is whether the dialogue and willingness to discuss religious and moral issues helps or hurts the authority of science and individual scientists or whether the institutional differentiation between science and religion will continue to inhibit the conversation.

Notes

1. Westfall, *Science and Religion in Seventeenth-Century England;* Ferngren, *Science & Religion;* Brooke, *Science and Religion;* Merton, *Science, Technology and Society in Seventeenth-Century England;* Whitehead, *Science and the Modern World.*

2. Brooke, *Science and Religion,* 1.

3. Bowler calls these the "confrontation, cooperation and coexistence" models, but the elements of the models are similar. See Bowler, *Reconciling Science and Religion*.

4. Brooke, *Science and Religion;* Wilson, "The Historiography of Science and Religion."

5. Weber as quoted in Gerth and Mills, *From Max Weber: Essays in Sociology,* 143.

6. Kitcher, "The Many-Sided Conflict between Science and Religion"; Brooke, *Science and Religion;* Frickel and Moore, *The New Political Sociology of Science.*

7. Iannaccone et al., "Rationality and the 'Religious Mind'"; Ecklund, "Initial Findings from the Study of Religion among Academic Sciences"; Ecklund et al., "Secularization and Religious Change among Elite Scientists."

8. Dawkins, *The God Delusion,* 56.

9. Dawkins, "Is Science a Religion?"

10. Ibid.

11. Johnson, "A Free-for-All on Science and Religion."

12. Dawkins, *The God Delusion;* Kitcher, "The Many-Sided Conflict between Science and Religion." Ironically, Stenmark describes scientists like Dawkins as spokespersons for scientism, in which everything can and should be explained and understood in terms of science. These "science believers" are akin to religious believers for their faith and worldview. See Stenmark, "Science and the Limits of Knowledge."

13. Gould, *Rocks of Ages,* 4.

14. Ibid., 70.

15. Wilson, "The Historiography of Science and Religion," 21.

16. Gould, *Rocks of Ages,* 5.

17. Ibid.

18. http://www.templeton.org/about_us/

19. Johnson, "Agreeing Only to Disagree on God's Place in Science."

20. Obituary: John Templeton, 254.

21. Ibid.

22. Wilson, "The Historiography of Science and Religion."

23. Brooke, *Science and Religion;* Bowler, *Reconciling Science and Religion;* Olson, *Science and Religion, 1450–1900.*

24. Bowler, *Reconciling Science and Religion,* 6–7.

25. Ferngren, *Science & Religion,* ix.

26. Harris, "Roman Catholicism since Trent"; Olson, *Science and Religion, 1450–1900.*

27. Harris, "Roman Catholicism since Trent," 256–57.

28. Brooke, *Science and Religion,* 321.

29. Durkheim, *The Elementary Forms of Religious Life.*

30. Merton, *Science, Technology and Society in Seventeenth-Century England.*

31. Merton, *The Sociology of Science.*

32. Shapin, *A Social History of Truth,* 417.

33. According to Durkheim: "A religion is a unified system of beliefs and practices relative to sacred things, that is to say, things which are set apart and forbidden—beliefs

and practices which unite us into one single moral community . . ." (*The Elementary Forms of Religious Life,* 47).

34. Weber as quoted in Gerth and Mills, *From Max Weber: Essays in Sociology,* 180.

35. Ibid., 295–99.

36. Gieryn and Figert, "Scientists Protect Their Cognitive Authority," 67.

37. Barnes and Edge, *Science in Context,* 2.

38. Shapin and Schaffer, *Leviathan and the Air Pump.*

39. Gieryn, "Cultural Boundaries," 91.

40. Gieryn, "Boundary-Work and the Demarcation of Science from Non-Science," 782.

41. Gieryn et al., "Professionalization of American Scientists"; Nelkin, *The Creation Controversy;* Numbers, *The Creationists.*

42. See Gieryn and Figert, "Scientists Protect Their Cognitive Authority" and "Ingredients for a Theory of Science in Society"; Figert, *Women and the Ownership of PMS.*

43. Nelkin, *Controversy: Politics of Technical Decisions,* xviii–xix.

44. Gilbert and Mulkay, *Opening Pandora's Box,* 56.

45. Nelkin, *Controversy: Politics of Technical Decisions,* xix.

46. Nelkin, "Science Controversies," 445.

47. Ibid., 446.

48. Brooke, *Science and Religion,* 344.

49. Gilbert and Mulkay, *Opening Pandora's Box.*

50. Dean, "Faith, Reason, God and Other Imponderables."

51. At the Web site www.religionlink.org, there is a separate category for national scientific experts on the science and religion relationship and possible questions to ask them. Collins, *The Language of God,* and Roughgarden, *Evolution and Christian Faith,* are at the top of the list.

3

What's All the Fuss About?

The Conflict between Science and Religion over Sexual Diversity

FRED KNISS

When contemplating the intersection of evolutionary biology, human sexuality, gender, and the Christian tradition, it is "natural" (to employ a term contested by scientists and theologians) to expect some conflict. The history of dialogue between scientists and Christian authorities is replete with examples. Indeed, the chapters in this volume demonstrate various points of tension between the two perspectives. If we are to advance the dialogue between science and Christianity, it will be necessary to examine the conflict itself—asking what is at stake, what the outcomes of the conflict have been historically, and what directions the conflict may take in the future. Specifically, this chapter explores the relationship and conflict between science and the Catholic Church. My assumption here is that we should not be shy about acknowledging the conflict. In fact, conflict is implied by the very concept of dialogue. If there are no points of tension, there is no need for dialogue.

Conflict, even ideological or philosophical conflict, is inherently social. Its processes and outcomes are governed by social relationships of power, authority, and prestige. Several of the chapters in this volume (especially Nilson and Figert) make this point explicitly. And the interdisciplinary symposia that preceded this volume frequently generated questions and claims about the social relationships and structures that provide the context for discourse and debate about human sexuality. Frequently, our attention focused on procedural issues, highlighting the structures and processes that govern the relationship between science and religion. Nilson, for example, in his contribution to this volume, notes the historical contingencies involved in the rise of papal authority, while Figert points to the "boundary work" that goes on between science and religion.

In this chapter, I extend that discussion by focusing more on the *content,* rather than the form, of the conflict. What is the fuss really all *about?* What are the underlying issues at stake in debates over human sexuality, gender, and the various diversities in sexual orientation and practice? If we are to truly understand these tensions, we need to comprehend the substance of the issues for various contending groups. We must attend to how groups define and prioritize various factors in human sexuality, how such definitions might position them ideologically and philosophically vis-à-vis other groups, what ethical issues arise as a consequence of various positions, and what the social consequences of the conflict's outcome might be.

In previous work, I have found it helpful to consider two underlying dimensions in many of the political, cultural, and religious conflicts we observe in the public arena. The first dimension refers to the locus of moral authority, and the second explores how groups define their primary moral project.[1] Using these two dimensions, we can create a conceptual "map" that allows us to place different groups or points of view in an ideological space. The map (Figure 3.1) can help us understand the points of tension in various conflicts, as well as predict what the terms of debate are likely to be, where groups may find potential allies or opponents, how shifts in ideological or theological stances may affect relationships to other groups, and so forth.

As mentioned above, this map consists of two dimensions representing two central issues in any moral or political culture. One is the locus of moral authority and the other is what constitutes the moral project. The moral authority dimension is concerned with the primary basis for ethical, aesthetic, or epistemological (knowledge) standards. It answers this question: Who or what determines the predominant understanding of the good, of beauty, and of truth? In other words, who, or what body, has the power to arbitrate for a particular community or society what it understands as morally good or true? In contrast, the moral project dimension addresses the question of where moral action or influence should be targeted. What are a group's primary moral projects? In which concrete efforts (e.g., ending or preserving legal abortion, fostering or blocking prayer in public schools) should a religious community or society invest itself? Or, put another way, if specific notions of the good, beauty, and truth are to be pursued, how ought we attempt to attain them?[2]

The poles on both the moral authority and moral project dimensions represent the tension between the individual and the collective that most analysts of American political culture have noted. On the first dimension, moral authority may derive from the individual's reason or experience on one hand, or it may be located in the collective tradition on the other. On the second dimension, the primary moral project may be the maximization of individual utility or, at the other pole, it may be the maximization of the (collective) public good. Each of these dimensions represents a spectrum along which a wide variety of ideas and positions may occur. The two dimensions are crosscutting and interact in complex ways. Figure 3.1 depicts the ideological map resulting from crossing the two dimensions. It places various religious groups in relation to each other and the broader religio-political culture in the United States.[3]

At the individualist end of the moral authority dimension, the foundation for ultimate values is grounded in an individual's reason or experience—or, more often, reason as applied to and filtered through a person's experience and perceptions. This view shares much with modernist epistemologies (theories of knowledge or ways of knowing). Thus, the individualist conception of moral authority tends to downplay notions of traditional transcendent, absolute authority. Religious authority structures are subject to criticism and legitimation based on reason/experience. Further, moral authority is applied relativistically, because reason is located in particular individuals in particular times and places. Determining what is good, beautiful, and true requires the application of reason and experience to particular circumstances and will vary across contexts.

Within American religion, individualism, rooted as it is in modernism, has engendered much religious and social conflict, especially in the fundamentalist/modernist controversies in the twentieth century. The individualist view of moral authority legitimized the rational criticism of ecclesiastical and biblical

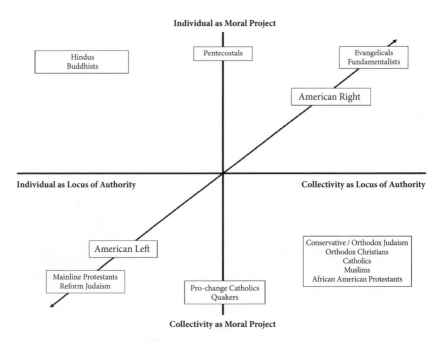

Fig. 3.1. Moral Order Map. Adapted from Kniss, 2003.

authority. As Hutchison pointed out, religious modernism held that religious ideas should be consciously adapted to modern culture.[4] Religious traditionalists, in the fundamentalist-modernist conflicts that were major drivers of American religious history in the past century, opposed the individualist/modernist view as an attack on fundamentals and a challenge to traditional authority.[5]

At the collectivist end of the moral authority dimension, groups hold that the authority to define ultimate values is grounded in the collective religious tradition. Where modernists view individual human agents as free actors, collectivists (or "traditionalists") see individuals as members of a collectivity, a social group defined by its relation to a higher authority—an authority that transcends the particularities of individual times and places, whether it is housed in a religious text or an ecclesiastical hierarchy. Collectivist views of moral authority, thanks to the elevation of collective tradition, have strong affinities with conservative religion, but it would be a mistake to equate the two. Dillon, for example, shows how progressive Catholics are able to pursue progressive agenda while still recognizing the authority of Catholic tradition.[6] Likewise, many progressive Muslims continue to emphasize and reinforce collective moral authority over individual self-interests.

The second dimension on the map in Figure 3.1 concerns the definition of the primary moral project, and again the extremes on the dimension are defined by the individualism-collectivism tension. At one end of the moral project continuum religious groups focus primarily on the individual. The primary moral project is the individual's salvation and moral improvement, and the problems of the world can be solved "one soul at a time." Congregations are networks of individuals in pursuit of religious goods, whether those are salvation, enlightenment, ecstatic experience, or personal well-being.

At the collectivist end of the moral project dimension, we find communalist projects. Here, the primary moral project is the collective good rather than individual utility. Communalism identifies the primary moral project as establishing a just and righteous social order rather than reforming individuals. Religious collectivists such as Christian liberation theologians are more likely to talk about social justice than about individual salvation.

It is tempting to think of the individualist end of the moral project continuum as identified with the religious right and collectivist positions as identified with the left. Certainly there are strong affinities or correlations in that direction, but there are also important anomalies. Collectivist notions, for example, are not exclusively the province of leftist theologians. As Hart shows, communalist ideas can be operative among mainstream Protestants and Catholics in the United States.[7] Most Muslims also view their primary moral project in collectivist terms.

While we might expect most groups to cluster around either individualism in the northwest corner of the map, or around collectivism in the southeast corner, in fact the dominant ideological configurations (at least within the United States) combine individualism and collectivism in either the northeast or southwest corners. Although they may have used different terms, various writers have noted the paradoxical combination of traditionalism and libertarianism in conservative or right-wing American ideology.[8] Although many scholars view this paradox as primarily a characteristic of post-1945 American conservatism, de Tocqueville, as far back as the 1830s, noted in *Democracy in America* that traditional religion in the United States had combined with unrestrained self-interest to promote the general welfare.[9] In contrast, the American left has combined modernism with communalism, supporting both the moral autonomy of the individual and the regulation of economic and political activity in defense of the public good.

Within this conception of the mainstream religious or political culture, Catholicism holds a somewhat anomalous position. Broadly speaking, Catholicism has held to collectivist ideas regarding both moral authority and the moral project. Certainly individual reason has played an important role in the development of Catholic theology and philosophy; but the exercise of reason is nearly always subject to the authority of the religious tradition and hierarchy. Kurtz (in 1986) and Burns (in 1990) documented this in their excellent studies of Catholic controversies over Modernist thought.[10]

For the purposes of this volume, there is likely no better nor more appropriate example of Catholic collectivism than the papal encyclical *Humanae Vitae*. This 1968 encyclical of Pope Paul VI "On the Regulation of Birth" is replete with explicitly collectivist argumentation regarding both moral authority and moral projects. He declares, for example:

> No member of the faithful can possibly deny that the Church is competent in her magisterium to interpret the natural moral law. It is in fact indisputable, as Our predecessors have many times declared, that Jesus Christ, when he communicated His divine power to Peter and the other Apostles and sent them to teach all nations His commandments, constituted them as the authentic guardians and interpreters of the whole moral law, not only, that is, of the law of the Gospel but also of the natural law. For the natural law, too, declares the will of God, and its faithful observance is necessary for men's [sic] eternal salvation.[11]

It is hard to imagine a clearer, more explicit statement of the authority of collective tradition and the need for individual reason to submit to it. In fact, its position in the document follows closely on the heels of a critical reference in Section 2 to "man's [sic] stupendous progress in the domination and rational organization of the forces of nature to the point that he is endeavoring to extend this control over every aspect of his own life."

Although the argumentation in *Humanae Vitae* is heavily weighted toward reinforcing traditional collective moral authority, the pope also considers childbirth and its regulation as a moral project for Catholics. Here, as well, the concern is for the collective. As Jung also explains in this volume, official Catholic teaching maintains that sexual intercourse is intended for "unitive" purposes in a marriage and for the reproduction of human life within the context of responsible parenthood. The purpose of sexual relations is articulated as a collective moral project: "Responsible parenthood, as we use the term here, has one further essential aspect of paramount importance. It concerns the objective moral order which was established by God, and of which a right conscience is the true interpreter. In a word, the exercise of responsible parenthood requires that husband and wife, keeping a right order of priorities, recognize their own duties toward God, themselves, their families and human society."[12] Thus, papal teachings not only instruct individual Catholics in their personal decisions, but also are meant to shape the collective social order of church, family, and society.

While papal documents make very clear the collective character of official Catholic moral thought, there is of course a range of positions within Catholicism "on the ground." The diversity within Catholicism, especially in the U.S. context and especially post–Vatican II, is such that any attempt to summarize Catholic thinking will hide much important and interesting variation. Dillon, for example, examines a diverse set of groups that she calls "pro-change Catholics."[13] These include gay and lesbian, pro-choice and pro-women Catholic groups that may seem to belong in the southwest quadrant of the earlier map, neighbors to liberal Protestants. But Dillon shows that while these groups apply individual reason and experience in their challenge to the authority of Catholic tradition, they also construct an identity that maintains continuity and solidarity with that tradition, thus recognizing its authority while promoting change within it. In another study recognizing Catholic internal diversity, Burns shows that, by separating political and economic issues from matters of faith and morals, Catholics are pulled in multiple directions.[14] In my terms, they are pulled toward the southwest where they find allies on issues such as economic justice (a collective moral project), and they are pulled toward the northeast where they find allies on personal moral issues (that highlight the collective moral authority).

How might this heuristic map help us understand conflict and change within Catholicism and between Catholics and others over issues of human sexuality and sexual diversity? Empirically, debates over most theological, moral, or political issues tend to orient themselves around one dimension or the other of the map. Often there is no inherent logic that would place a debate along one dimension or the other. Rather, the debate's mapping is a product of social factors, determined by how the most important contending parties frame the issues.

It is no coincidence, I believe, that most debates over things like sexual orientation, extramarital sexual practices, gender roles, abortion, contraception, and the like have been primarily located along the moral authority dimension. The family, especially the nuclear family as it has developed in western culture, is the most basic unit of collective authority. It has been the primary location for the legitimation of patriarchal and hierarchical authority, and for socialization into traditional collective authority structures. It is no surprise, then, that practices that are seen to threaten the patriarchal nuclear family (e.g., homosexuality, promiscuity, contraception, abortion) are opposed with a special tenacity by traditionalist groups. As Pope Paul VI noted in *Humanae Vitae*'s section appealing to public authorities, "The family is the primary unit in the state; do not tolerate any legislations which would introduce into the family those practices which are opposed to the natural law of God."[15]

We can observe this ideological conflict in the very terms of public discourse on matters of human sexuality. At the modernist pole, issues are framed in terms of individual rights and freedom of choice. At the traditionalist pole, issues are framed in terms of responsibility and obligation to others. In the rhetorical terms of the public debate, people can be "pro-choice" or they can be "pro-family" and never the twain shall meet (or so many assume).

Locating the discourse on human sexuality along the moral authority dimension also pits science against traditionalist religion. Scientific knowing is grounded in the authority of reason and empirical observation. It has an instinctive antipathy to authoritative appeals to tradition in discussions of natural processes like human sexuality. In fact, the scientific method is fundamentally about testing and disproving traditional understandings of reality.[16] This is as true of the social sciences as it is of natural science. Statistical methods cannot actually prove hypotheses about human behavior. Rather, they disprove null hypotheses. In their essential logic, they operate to disprove previous notions.

Thus, when the Catholic intellectual heritage attempts to incorporate scientific knowledge into the development of its thought about human sexuality or gender, it is engaged in very risky business. It is attempting to incorporate knowledge that is rooted in an epistemology that undermines the very basis of its own traditional authority. Small wonder then, that historically relations between the Roman Catholic Church and the scientific world have been so problematic.

When it engages science, the Catholic Church is faced with only a few options. One is to retreat into the shelter of tradition and ignore or deny the findings of science—and there are plenty of examples of this tactic. Just ask Galileo. Another more difficult option is to try to reach some accommodation between tradition and new scientific knowledge. This may involve an exercise in bricolage—picking and choosing which components of tradition and which components of science to incorporate. Many lay Catholics take just such a pragmatic strategy on issues such as contraception, for example. The pragmatic approach, however, is likely to be somewhat unsatisfying to any of the major parties involved—scientists, theologians, or church hierarchs—and it has the long-term effect of weakening the ties of authority and loyalty that hold the tradition together.

Another strategy might be to reinterpret the tradition itself, either abstracting it to its core general values while dropping particular dogmas, or by adopting scientific methods to critique and challenge traditional notions. Liberation theology did this, as do many of the "pro-change Catholics" that Dillon discusses.[17] This is likely to be a more satisfying strategy for theologians and scientists, but it makes church hierarchs nervous for obvious reasons; and the Vatican's crackdown on liberation theology is testament to such anxiety.

But there may be yet another possibility. As I noted above, there is no inherent reason why debates on issues should be located primarily on one ideological dimension rather than another. An interesting thought experiment is to consider how the discourse on human sexuality might be different if it were arranged along the moral project dimension rather than the moral authority axis. The issues would then concern the *consequences* of sexual behavior and policies/doctrines concerning it. Catholics, located at the collective end of the moral project dimension, would tend to consider sexuality as something that contributes to the collective character and well-being of human community. We see hints of that even in *Humanae Vitae* with its references to the "unitive" function of sexuality. Issues of sexual diversity or reproductive ethics take on a different hue in this light. Rather than being primarily concerned with preserving traditional authority structures (whether sexual or ecclesiastical in nature), the focus would be on how sexuality and sexual practices might contribute to building a healthy and just social order.

This sort of collectivist reasoning is not foreign to Catholics when they consider issues in moral project terms. The U.S. Catholic Bishops' 1986 pastoral letter on economics, *Economic Justice for All,* is a good example. The bishops note,

> As Catholics, we are heirs of a long tradition of thought and action on the moral dimensions of economic activity. The life and words of Jesus and the teaching of his Church call us to serve those in need and to work actively for social and economic justice. As a community of believers, we know that our faith is tested by the quality of justice among us, that we can best measure our life together by how the poor and the vulnerable are treated.[18]

The bishops claim that their comments on economics should be seen as moral teaching rooted in the fundamental notion of human dignity—but they define human dignity in collective terms.

Human dignity can be realized and protected only in community. In our teaching, the human person is not only sacred but social. How we organize our society—in economics and politics, in law and policy—directly affects human dignity and the capacity of individuals to grow in community. The obligation to "love our neighbor" has an individual dimension, but it also requires a broader social commitment to the common good. We have many partial ways to measure and debate the health of our economy: Gross National Product, per capita income, stock market prices, and so forth. The Christian vision of economic life looks beyond them all and asks, Does economic life enhance or threaten our life together as a community?[19]

It is not difficult to imagine shifting this basic moral logic to questions of how sexual minorities should be treated, or how marginalized groups should be incorporated into the moral economy of human sexuality. Some Catholic thinkers have already begun to take steps in this direction. Lisa Sowle Cahill is one who places issues of sex and ethics along what I would call the "moral project" dimension. She views human sexual behavior as pursuing three "projects" (my term)—reproduction, pleasure and intimacy. And, not surprisingly for a Catholic thinker, her arguments are more collectively oriented in that she views these projects as fundamentally social. She refers to sexuality as a "complex and *intrinsically relational* dimension of human being."[20] Moral arguments about particular expressions of sexuality are based in considerations of social justice, and they address how the particular matter in question enhances or hinders human flourishing (with "human" defined more collectively than individualistically).

Science would also have something to contribute to a conversation framed in this way, and the Catholic dialogue with science would not be so threatening because fundamental notions of authority would be less at stake. How might scientific perspectives be arrayed along the moral project dimension? On one hand, much of evolutionary biology's theoretical discourse seems to be located at the individualist pole. "Survival of the fittest" certainly has a libertarian air about it. The central role of mate selection and genetic mutation in the theory also lends itself to individually oriented notions of the consequences of sexual behavior.

But there are also more "communalist" aspects to evolutionary theory that might be of value to Catholic thinking about sexuality. Considerations of the evolution of a species or of various ecologies are more collective in their orientation and may provide insights for Catholic thinkers concerned with how sexuality can contribute to communal well-being. Joan Roughgarden's contribution to this volume, for example, argues for focusing on "social selection" rather than sexual selection. She points out a number of difficulties with the standard sexual selection theories of evolution and proposes an alternative evolutionary process driven by selection based on "offspring-rearing success," a much more collectively oriented project, and one that may do a better job of incorporating the sexual diversity found within and across species.

In addition to evolutionary biology, there may also be other scientific perspectives offering helpful insights in considering human sexuality as a collective moral project. Genetics and ecology leap immediately to mind as scientific fields with much to say about the value of diversity, for example. Sociological and anthropological research can provide insight into how various kinds of sexual bonding patterns affect social networks and communal well-being. The health sciences and epidemiology would also have much to contribute to questions of sexuality and community health.

I am suggesting in this essay that the traditional framing of human sexuality in the Roman Catholic Church (as a debate over the moral authority of the Church relative to individual needs and desires) has almost necessarily pitted itself against science. The attempt to engage science, as long as the terms of the debate remain the same, is going to be fraught with difficulties. On the other hand, reframing the questions about sexuality may permit a much more fruitful dialogue with science, as well as a helpful advance in Catholic thought about human sexuality. Such a radical reframing of a question where so much seems to be at stake is certainly no easy task, but it seems to me to be one worth undertaking.

Notes

This essay owes much to the many helpful comments from the editors and participants in our symposia, and to the research assistance of Laurie Cooper Stoll and Todd Fuist.

1. I developed this conceptual framework in previous work: first in a historical study of cultural conflict among U.S. Mennonites (Kniss, *Disquiet in the Land*), next in treating the contemporary "culture wars" (Kniss, "Mapping the Moral Order"), and most recently in analyzing the civic engagement of new immigrant religious groups (Kniss and Numrich, *Sacred Assemblies and Civic Engagement*).

2. I use the term "moral" here in a broad sense, encompassing considerations of "good, beauty, and truth." This use is more expansive than what may be the case for Christian ethicists, who often use the term more restrictively, denoting specific considerations of the individual or corporate "good" in particular behavioral situations. My broader use of the term is consonant with common usage by sociologists and anthropologists when they speak of, for example, the "moral order." It is similar, I believe, to McCarthy's use of "normativity," a term more familiar to theological ethicists (chapter 8 in this volume).

3. Adapted from Kniss, "Mapping the Moral Order."

4. Hutchison, *The Modernist Impulse in American Protestantism.*

5. Marsden, *Fundamentalism and American Culture;* Hunter, *Culture Wars.*

6. Dillon, *Catholic Identity.*

7. Hart, *What Does the Lord Require?*

8. Nash, *The Conservative Intellectual Movement in America;* Lipset and Raab, *The Politics of Unreason;* Himmelstein, "The New Right"; Platt and Williams, "Religion, Ideology and Electoral Politics."

9. de Tocqueville, *Democracy in America.*

10. Kurtz, *The Politics of Heresy;* Burns, "The Politics of Ideology."

11. *Humanae Vitae,* n. 4.

12. Ibid., n. 10.

13. Dillon, *Catholic Identity.*

14. Burns, *The Frontiers of Catholicism.*

15. *Humanae Vitae,* n. 23.

16. Social constructionist studies of science have, it must be noted, shown that scientific observation and analysis are often significantly shaped by the cultural traditions and social attachments that scientists bring to their task (e.g., Knorr-Cetina, *Epistemic Cultures;* Latour, *Science in Action;* Pickering, *Constructing Quarks*). But scientists themselves, even those who acknowledge the socially constructed character of the scientific enterprise, view such intrusions of tradition as essentially a failure of science to maintain its epistemological standards. For a good example of this, see Gould, *The Mismeasure of Man.*

17. Dillon, *Catholic Identity.*

18. *Economic Justice for All,* n. 8.

19. Ibid., n. 14.

20. Cahill, *Sex, Gender, and Christian Ethics* (italics in original).

4

Medieval Attitudes toward
Philosophia Naturalis in Relation
to *Scientia Moralis*

FRANCIS J. CATANIA

This chapter focuses on Thomas Aquinas and his teacher and mentor, Albertus Magnus, as a paradigm of what this book is all about. Albert was Aquinas's teacher; and while Aquinas himself did little by way of generating experimental knowledge of the world, Albert has extensive recordings of his observations of flora and fauna and was undoubtedly a great influence on Aquinas's attitude toward experience of the world.[1] In particular, attention to their methods for exploring the world help us appreciate that for a very, very long time, Christian theological and ethical teachings have drawn upon the sciences in a significant way. Furthermore, their methods are important because both thinkers occupy primary, even if by no means exclusive, places among Christian thinkers noted for interdisciplinary dialogue.

Referring to Thomas and Albert, however, raises some formidable questions about the choice of these two as sources of insight: 1) Obviously, evolutionary biology was not part of the curriculum in thirteenth-century University of Paris, so the question is a fundamental one: while evolutionary biology seems to fit nicely within the concept of "modern science" how does it fit within whatever turns out to be the meaning of "medieval science"? 2) Did medieval theologians regard "science"[2] as compatible with their religious faith? 3) Did knowledge of the world generated by "scientific" investigation affect moral judgments? Thus, the issue is not whether Albert and Aquinas anticipated modern scientific findings (obviously they did not), but whether their thinking represents a cognitive attitude that is open to advances in scientific understanding of the world and specifically of human persons. This claim goes beyond saying that theology and science have their own methods so that the one doesn't bear on the other; it goes to affirming a strong sense of complementarity between them.

An Illuminative Digression: "Intelligent Design"

Posing these three questions suggests still another issue: the recent and recurring attempts to engage evolutionary science with "intelligent design" as a scientific alternative. First, note that for Albert and Aquinas the phrase "intelligent design" is redundant: All design, of its nature, is intelligent. Second, both believed that our world is created by God; yet, "being created" is not at all incompatible with the world developing in a particular manner or even existing eternally. An eternally existing and evolving world is a reasonable position (even on analyses of matter and motion within Aristotelian physics) and its reasonableness is actually one of the assumptions of Aquinas's ways to demonstrate the existence of God. Third, neither Albert nor Aquinas had any disagreement with the position of fourth-century St. Augustine who, in his commentary on the creation story in the *Book of Genesis* where all of creation occurs "in six days," offers as an explanation of the disparity between "everything being created together" and the observable fact of "new things coming into existence." Augustine resolves what some might see as a mutually exclusive contradiction between two truth claims by articulating the doctrine of "seminal reasons." This doctrine holds that the "seeds" of everything were created "together," although individuals and kinds would appear only over time.

Said differently, the issue is not "scientific" but attitudinal. "Seminal reasons" is not a scientific anticipation of "evolution," but it does express a cognitive stance that is open to what experience and reason tell us about the world. In chapter 10 in this volume, James Calcagno notes that "theological perspectives should [not] alter how science is done." Albert and Aquinas would agree. In fact, a good case can be made that "the primary patron of scientific learning throughout the Middle Ages remained the Church," as David Lindberg notes.[3] What Albert and Aquinas saw as purposeful activity (i.e., teleological) in nature—translated into functional terms as, for example, William Harvey's discovery that the function (purpose) of the heart's beating is to circulate the blood—might more fruitfully be understood as Darwinian evolution wherein "the purposive appearance of biological phenomena is the result of a large amount of blind unpurposeful heritable variation."[4]

Contemporary science has dispensed with teleology for at least two reasons. First, because teleology suggests that things happen because of God, so the purposes are God's purposes and not those of the natural agents. Second, because nonteleological mechanism is much better at predicting natural phenomena and so is verifiable. But even Albert noted that "we would not presume to investigate the causes of the divine will, but we are free to investigate—in detail and specifically—the natural causes that are the instruments of the divine will."[5] The distinction is an important one to keep in mind, especially when exploring and discussing matters related to human sexuality, gender, Christian theological and ethical teachings, and data revealed from the natural sciences.

Theology and Science

But what can we look to in Aquinas for insight into the relationship between theology and science? For the most part, not to individual texts. For example, Aquinas quotes Aristotle in his depiction of female as "failed male,"[6] and refers to the intellectual limits of women and the attendant subordination of the roles of women to those of men.[7] Such claims on the basis of what we now know to be faulty biological assumptions are not of much use to us in present discussions of human gender or sexuality.

At the same time, however, it is also important to note places where Aquinas makes rather radical claims about marriage given his historical context. Specifically, Aquinas describes marriage as the "greatest friendship" between husband and wife;[8] especially surprising because friendship requires equality between friends as a necessary condition to sustain their long-term commitment to each other. Thus, Aquinas's efforts to bring together different traditions generate tensions in the texts as he strives to emphasize a "both/and" rather than "either/or" approach to the relationship between faith and reason.

What is crucial to understand is that Albert and Thomas are as much products of their own times as we are of ours. Thus we find in them—as in the Medievals generally—a focus on the male (as far as gender issues) and on marriage (as far as sexual issues). Beyond individual texts, we need to explore Aquinas's basic methodology and explanatory principles. It is here that Aquinas can be of real use to the issues treated in this book.

Basic Approach to Disputed Theological Questions: Interdisciplinarity

As to his style, Aquinas's writings do not contain much of what should be regarded as settled positions. Rather, they comprise themes to which he returned again and again—a work in progress of a master in the art of leaving questions open[9]—which he himself at the end of his life described as "so much straw."[10] The style of his writings owes much to the Disputed Question format that structured most thirteenth-century university teaching: This format encouraged taking seriously the wide range of perspectives on a given topic. Beyond this format, however, being ready to listen to a wide variety of voices suited Aquinas's idea of intellectual investigation: the inquiry that was necessary before any attempt to come to judgment.

A key element of that inquiry is a theory of explanation rooted in telos (end, goal, or purpose). Aquinas believed that God creates and sustains the universe through the formal structures of things, that is, their "natures," which give, at the same time, the directionality of their activities. This "natural teleology" in turn characterizes human attitudes in exploring nature. The significance of science for Aquinas lies in the encounter with nature itself (including the human nature), an encounter that is a discovery (*via inventionis* "the path of discovery") and that needs to be assessed in order to become part of a "scientific" understanding (*via judicii* "the path of judgment").[11] We learn from nature-as-experienced-and-assessed and so remain open to newness. Albert and Aquinas's conception of knowledge of the natural world is that it develops on its own methods, formally distinct from, but quite compatible with theology.

Further, Aquinas maintains the analogous unity of all knowledge, that several formally different disciplines contribute to the oneness of the whole. This is why "complementarity" rather than simple "compatibility" better expresses the relationship among the disciplines. In other words, each discipline contributes to a fuller understanding of a very complex, multifaceted whole. Yet, not each and every finding from distinct sources will neatly line up in a seamless fashion, because the whole is so complicated that we cannot easily see how all the pieces fit together. Too many loose, unsorted jigsaw puzzle pieces escape our placement. Complete knowledge and vision of the entire picture comes only in the next life after this.

A Revisionist Approach to Homosexuality

A full discussion of nature/natural [*natura/naturalis*] in Aquinas would take us far beyond the limits of this chapter; a brief note, however, on nature—together with a reference to Stephen Pope's discussion of homosexuality as "unnatural"—may be helpful. We begin by noting that "nature" has a range of meanings, which Aquinas learned from Boethius.[12] The fundamental meaning of "nature" is "source of activities"; this meaning is the foundation of the methodological principle, *agere sequitur esse*: as a thing is, so it acts; and, conversely, we come to know a thing through discovering (*via inventionis*) and assessing (*via judicii*) its actions. The range of meanings includes the following: the most universal natural order; all the created world (i.e., everything other than God); a particular type of being (e.g., a human person, a nonrational animal); the individual within a type (e.g., the historical Socrates, my pet dog); whatever is other than reason in the human person (generically animal powers).

Catholic ethicist and contributor to this volume, Stephen Pope, discusses the challenge that scientific information and theories poses to natural law ethicists' argument that homosexuality is immoral because "unnatural."[13] A discussion of homosexuality is a sort of test case, just because the traditional interpretation of natural law in characterizing homosexuality as "unnatural" forces confrontation with what is "natural." Pope's discussion is two-pronged: 1) he discusses particulars of experimental psychology, genetics, and physiology that bear upon regarding homosexuality as "natural," and 2) he appeals to the distinction between the descriptively human and the normatively human, pointing out that one cannot merely assume—without further argument—that the former includes the latter. The reason is that human experience of human persons draws from fallen human nature and needs to be adjusted teleologically to provide a moral norm. Here Pope—the theologian—considers whether revealed natural law can provide the normative basis that descriptions of human activity of themselves cannot.

Pope's own solution is to propose a "middle way" (a "revisionist natural law") between the position that because science depicts homosexuality as natural, moral reflection is thereby complete and the position that revealed natural law separates what science can say about homosexual orientation from scriptural condemnations of homosexual activity. That middle way is to suggest that science can make a significant, limited contribution to natural law ethics by focusing on what actually "constitutes genuine human flourishing in lived human experience."[14] Pope goes on to explain:

> The revisionist [finds] the warrant for the moral legitimacy of homosexual activity . . . in its potential for playing a constructive part in human flourishing.[15]
>
> The central moral issue, then, is not genetic or statistical naturalness but rather whether homosexuals can respond (at least, that is, as well as heterosexuals) to the universal human challenge to train and habituate their sexual passions—naturally oriented to various goods but existentially disordered by concupiscence—in a way that contributes to their flourishing.[16]

Revisionist Roots in Aquinas

There are two points in Pope's position that bear further discussion, one implicit, the other explicit, both supported to some extent in Aquinas. First, the implicit point, which is featured in Aquinas's texts, is that the human person is both continuous with and discontinuous from the rest of nature and, especially, nonrational animals. Aquinas contrasts human nature as characterized by reason with the nonrational aspects of human nature that human persons share with nonrational animals and other natural agents.[17] When homosexuality is labeled as *contra naturam, naturam,* may refer to that part of God's creation that is other than reason and that reason "does not establish but only beholds."[18] That is, "nature," in this sense, has a built-in teleology to which reason is to submit because it expresses God's intention. The question would remain, however, as to how human persons come to know that teleology.

Aquinas's ontology provides that all evil is a defect in what is otherwise good. Human activity is morally wrong if that activity is defective and the defect of the activity is due to a deficiency in its source. "The human person [*homo*] like any other being [*res*] naturally has an appetite for the good; and so if this appetite incline away to evil, this is due to corruption or disorder in some one of the principles of the human person [*principiorum hominis*]: for it is thus that sin occurs in the actions of natural things."[19] The *principia hominis* are intellect, sense appetite, and will.[20] When a person experiences desire [sense appetite], that experience of desire—good in itself—needs to be submitted to "rational ordering" [intellect] to judge that its good is appropriate to that person in order to act [will] on it. To act on the experience of desire assessed as rationally disordered is to sin. In effect, the pleasure of the anticipated sexual activity is chosen as if it were an end in itself rather than as part, say, of developing a committed friendship.[21] Thus, promiscuous same-sex sexual activity under this description would be wrong—as would adultery and the promiscuous use of persons of the opposite sex.

This point leads us to a deeper issue. If we regard same-sex behavior as "disordered" (as Aquinas does, based on a notion of what he regarded as "normal" sexual activity), same-sex behavior as implementation of the experience of desire when recognized as disordered is not the same as same-sex activity that is an expression of a disordered nature. The two are categorially different: 1) activity that is founded on a disordered will (same-sex sexual activity); and 2) activity that is founded on a disordered nature (homosexual orientation). Aquinas is quite clear that the disorder that grounds moral evil is in the will. As a consequence, activity founded on a disordered nature is of a different moral species than activity founded on a disordered will.

Aquinas describes this difference by referring to the difference between the specific nature and the individual nature. Because of some "corruption of nature," what is not natural to the human person considered as a natural kind or species of being becomes "connatural" to some individual.[22] This corruption of nature may be due to some bodily defect or from custom; in the words of one commentator: "hereditary causes or diseases or . . . habit induced either by conditioning beyond one's choice or by activity freely chosen."[23] Neither Aristotle nor Aquinas asks the further question of whether such a "connatural" orientation is in itself "disordered" or is disordered only by reference to the understanding of human nature that is taken to be normative.

Why did Aquinas characterize homosexuality as *contra naturam?* For at least three reasons: 1) This was the characterization of the taxonomy of sins bequeathed to thirteenth-century theologians. 2) It is so characterized in Aristotle and in traditional interpretations of the epistle to the Romans. 3) It clearly lay outside the "normal range" of human activity. If Aquinas had available to him the data about human sexual diversity discussed in this anthology, he would have had to address the issue differently. In developing a "science of ethics" both Aristotle and Aquinas proceed under the rubric that "natural rectitude in human acts depends, not on what is accidentally in one individual but on that which is proper to the whole species."[24]

The requirements of moral science as a science, namely, that it refer to what is proper to the whole species, leaves underdeveloped the experience of those who fall outside what is understood as "the whole species."[25] At the same time, the attitude that is open to learning about nature, including human nature, supports development of the meaning of "the whole species."

Contributions of Science to Ethical Analysis

This brings us to the second point in Pope's discussion: what we learn from experience of human nature needs to be adjusted teleologically. I think this is correct. *Scientia* (in this case *scientia moralis*) is constructed not by reading off empirical findings from nature (although that is a first step) but by assessing what is discovered in terms of causes that are the explanatory principles. In the case of human actions, the fundamental explanatory principle is the final cause, the end, the purpose from which the action gets its moral significance. For Aquinas, as for Aristotle before him, the beginning of ethics is a reflection on the "end" or "purpose" of the human being. All agents act on account of an end, either by the agent moving itself or by being moved by another; the former movement is through reason since such agents have authority [*dominium*] over their free judgment [*liberum arbitrium*], which is their power of will and of reason; the latter movement is through a natural inclination, that is, by being moved by another since such agents lack reason and do not know the meaning of "end."

Because human persons are both natural agents (as part of the created world) and also intentional agents (as "source [*principium*] of [their] works, as having free judgment and power over their works"),[26] teleology in human events is bifurcated: There is the natural, "built-in" teleology by reason of coming under the creative causality of God; there is the conscious intentionality originating in the mind of the human person. It is an ontological claim that God created human persons, intending union with Him. It is a question of ethics to ask about the relationship of that intention to the actual intentions of human persons.

To affirm essences or natures, accordingly, is really a claim about the fundamental intelligibility of the world, not a claim that at any particular point we have learned all that there is to learn about any natural kind—including the human person. In this sense, far from having settled the question of "who or what is the human person?" Aquinas today would be open to what science—including natural and social science—can say about persons. Even Aquinas's quoting Aristotle that "female is a failed male" rests on an error in biology—a more accurate account of the causal factors involved in the reproductive process may well have led to a different position. So, Aquinas discusses "a human nature" as an abstraction based on observed communalities and functioning as a basis for general scientific statements. At the same time, he also discusses "individual natures" as the ground of concrete ethical decisions, the domain of practical wisdom exercised by this individual with this individual's understanding and loves, in this time and in this place.

This point is significant if we read Aquinas's ethics as one of several "incommensurable readings"[27] of a "natural law ethics," since Aquinas describes human nature as "the participation of the human person in God's providence" and, as such, is the proximate foundation of natural law. But the point is significant also if we read Aquinas's ethics as "virtue ethics," since, as Alasdair MacIntyre has pointed out, giving an account of the goods, rules, and virtues that define our moral life will be inadequate unless it explains how that form of life is possible for beings who are biologically constituted as we are. Such a position needs to give an account of our development toward and into that form of life.[28]

Aquinas and Albert developed not one but two accounts of the human condition: In one, the ultimate purpose of human existence is communion with the Divine, a telos beyond human achievement without divine assistance (revealed through the Scriptures); in the other, this purpose (elaborated to some extent in Aristotle's *Ethics*) is a life of practical wisdom, justice, courage, and the reasonable direction of the passions, enhanced in friendships. These two accounts are related inasmuch as the first is the perfection of the second without destroying it.

Although quite aware of the debility of the human will (which Aristotle called "akrasia" and which Aquinas referred to the doctrine of "original sin"), Albert's and Thomas's accounts argue that we can order and control our passions—not only that we can, but that at times it was a good thing to do. This is one of the meanings of *virtus;* it is translated as "virtue," but its root meaning is "power"—power over ourselves, within greater or lesser limits—to become what in God's eyes we are. This is part of moral development: that we moderate our desires and infuse them with knowledge and wisdom so that our feelings are not blind but informed.[29] Further, we learn to desire such moderation and to find excess and even addiction undesirable. But—further still—reason itself demands that the use of reason be interrupted at times.[30]

The teleology of the human species is connected with the teleology of the individual through the conception of the good human person as including an essentially societal dimension. Excellence in practice is not fixed and determined for all time but is linked to the nature of one's society, which limits and/or enhances the activity of its members. That is, the human person is, in Aristotle's term, a sociopolitical animal; we are not alone but interdependent economically, psychologically, and morally. We need friends—all these other persons who require optimum environments to flourish along with their willingness (or not) to accept responsibility for the general good. Thus, it is possible, in Aquinas's view, to think meaningfully about the general good because that's what thinking and willing are for a social being. At the same time, Aquinas recognizes that the teleology of the individual may not coincide with the teleology of the human species. He argues that the teleology of sexual activity, from the point of view of the human species, is the common good, namely—the preservation of the species.[31]

So Aquinas's openness to scientific knowledge of the world needs to be complemented with his understanding of how teleology supplies a context for an account of human activities.

Aquinas and the Theory of Social Selection

Aquinas's position resonates with Joan Roughgarden's proposal to meet the problems of Darwin's theory of sexual selection with her own theory of social selection. Roughgarden argues that a careful account of the variety of sexual practices among nonhuman animals casts doubt on the theory that the only function of sexuality is to ensure that eggs are fertilized with sperm. Rather, a careful account suggests that the "natural" function of sexuality is to sustain the bond between animals that comprises the social system within which offspring are raised. She concludes that genital contact may simply be the form of intimate communication that happens to be sexual. For Aquinas, while he has nothing good to say about the promiscuous use of persons (of either sex), he clearly fosters nonprocreative sexual activity between husband and wife to promote their cooperative fellowship in the education of their children even when further procreation is not at issue.[32] This is the context in which Aquinas describes marriage as the "greatest friendship" between husband and wife.

Of particular interest for our attempts at interdisciplinary conversation, is Aquinas's theory of love and its highest expression in friendship. Interestingly, Aquinas's fundamental understanding of love is expressed in the way he contrasts how the tyrant loves the polis with the way the morally good ruler loves it. The political good is not found when someone loves the state in order to possess it, that is, to dominate it; this is to love oneself more than to love the state, desiring this good for oneself, not for the state. But to love the good of the state so that it might be preserved and defended is to love the state itself, and this constitutes the political good.

All that Aquinas has to say about love, sex, and friendship may be understood from the perspective of this distinction between the love that dominates and possesses and the love that preserves and fosters. Even if we disagree with a particular position of his, we can understand that position from that perspective. Not every love has the character of friendship, but only that love that is benevolent, mutual, and founded on communication.[33] Scripture provides Aquinas with a specific term to characterize this communication: *conversatio*. Among the basic meanings of *conversatio* is "abiding with" or "intercourse"—not necessarily or exclusively sexual. What is affirmed in this characterization is intimacy. Aquinas identifies the intimacy provided by both human friendship and divine charity as the life of mind and heart to mind and heart. Perhaps bodily intimacy may be seen as a symbol of the more fundamental spiritual intimacy whereby the human mind and heart are united to another human mind and heart as well as to the divine.

Pope's suggestion that "the warrant for the moral legitimacy of homosexual activity [lies] in its potential for playing a constructive part in human flourishing"[34] suggests a sort of "moral consequentialism." That is, that the moral assessment of any proposed activity is determined by its expected results: In order to achieve a state of flourishing or *eudaimonia* (Aristotle's term) or *beatitudo* (Aquinas's term) we ought to do such and such.

But that suggestion is mistaken; Aquinas's position is not consequentialist. The virtues are themselves worthwhile because their practice represents the sort of person we wish to become. We achieve the good life in that happiness accompanies the practice of the virtues. In the case of sexual activity, in addition to temperance (in Pope's terms "to train and habituate their sexual passions") the fundamental virtue—supernaturally—is *caritas;* naturally, it is friendship. The meaning of *caritas* is drawn from the experience of friendship. This is problematic both for Aristotle as well as for Aquinas. The reason is that "equality" is a necessary condition for friendship, and there can be no equality between the human and the divine. For Aquinas, God raises the human person to God's own life: Thus, this virtue is supernatural; but human friendship provides the essential content of what *caritas* means, even if human friendship is insufficient to bring about *caritas*.

At least within the Catholic intellectual traditions, Albert and Thomas give us reason to expect that moral theology can be enhanced by what sciences can teach us about, in MacIntyre's words, "our resemblances to and communality with other intelligent animal species" as well as about our specific differences.[35] Christian convictions can influence science not by attempting to substitute religious faith for science but by emphasizing two points: First, the human attempt to engage our world is a complex of many strands. They include science and technology, but also spiritual, esthetic, philosophical, and moral perspectives as well. Science is important, but not absolute and needs the other perspectives as context. The model that comes to mind to express Albert's and Thomas's approach is that of a conversation around a table with representatives of several disciplines—rather than a solitary meditation (à la Descartes) or a journal article, polemically attacking and/or defending a specific point. Second, as a human activity, science itself has a moral dimension. To be human and to be morally significant are one and the same thing. The moral dimensions of science show up both in how science is conducted and how it is applied: how conducted, insofar as it exhibits respect for nature and what constitutes nature; and how applied as it fosters fulfillment and flourishing rather than death and destruction.

Notes

1. See Catania, "Science," 864–65.

2. The English word *science* translates the Latin *scientia,* which in turn translates the Greek *episteme.* In Plato, *episteme* represented the summit, the ideal of cognitive accomplishment: the end or purpose of a ladder of cognitive attitudes. In Aristotle, we find the same exalted connotation, but systematized and expressed (in *Posterior Analytics*) as "cognition through causes." Such *episteme* is characterized as "universal, certain, and necessary." This is usually read by commentators as an ideal and not actually reached—perhaps not reachable—in the practice or generation of cognition. John Jenkins argues that this ideal is exactly what Aquinas had in mind with respect to *scientia;* and, Jenkins argues, this is exactly what Aquinas tries to accomplish in his *Summa Theologiae* and what characterizes his use of the term "scientia divina" and its synonym "theologia." Where, then, is "science" in our contemporary usage? Its medieval counterpart is "philosophia naturalis." "Philosophia naturalis" is the safer, less ambiguous term for our purposes; besides, it is enshrined in a major scientific (in our sense of the term) work, *Philosophiae naturalis principia mathematica* of Isaac Newton. I refer only to the continuity of the term, "philosophia naturalis," since Newton's natural philosophy was based on controlled experiments, and not simply descriptive experience.

3. Lindberg, "Medieval Science and Its Religious Context," 60–79. Not all scholars agree with Lindberg's assessment. In addition to those who maintained that the Church repressed scientific investigation, Roger French and Andrew Cunningham (*Before Science, the Invention of the Friars' Natural Philosophy*) argue that natural philosophy was not science in the modern sense at all. David Lindberg, building on the pioneering work of Pierre Duhem, Anneliese Maier, Alistair Crombie, and Lynn Thorndike employs "medieval science" and its synonym "medieval natural philosophy" to refer to the process by which Western scholars received, assimilated, criticized, modified, and extended the fruits of Greek and Muslim thought about nature; and to the products of this process, expressed in lectures and texts.

4. See Rosenberg, *Philosophy of Social Science,* 62–63; 146–49.

5. Lindberg quotes St. Augustine: "Even a non-Christian knows something about the earth, the heavens, and the other elements of this world, about the motion and orbit of the stars and even their size and relative positions, about the predictable eclipses of

the sun and moon, the cycles of the years and the seasons, about the kinds of animals, shrubs, stones, and so forth, and this knowledge he holds to as being certain from reason and experience. Now it is a disgraceful and dangerous thing for an infidel to hear a Christian, presumably giving the meaning of Holy Scripture, talking nonsense on these topics [from *The Literal Meaning of Genesis*]." Quoted by Lindberg, "Medieval Science and Its Religious Context," 72.

6. Aquinas, *Summa Theologiae* [hereafter *S.Th.*], I, q.92, a.1, obj.1 and ad 1.

7. *S.Th.*, I, q.92, a.1, ad 2.

8. Aquinas, *Summa Contra Gentiles* [hereafter *SCG*], III, 123.

9. See Kerr, *After Aquinas*, 14–15. Kerr quotes von Balthazar, "On the Tasks of Catholic Philosophy in Our Time," 147–87.

10. See Torrell, *Saint Thomas Aquinas*, 293, for a brief discussion of the meaning of "straw" as indicating the limits of words used to refer to divine things.

11. *S.Th.*, I, q.79, a.8 and 9.

12. Boethius, "A Treatise against Eutyches and Nestorius," 76–81.

13. Pope, "Scientific and Natural Law Analyses of Homosexuality," 89–126.

14. Ibid., 111.

15. Ibid., 114.

16. Ibid., 114–15.

17. *S.Th.* I-II, 31, 7.

18. Aquinas, *Commentary on the Nicomachaean Ethics*, Book 1, lect. 1.

19. *S.Th.*, I-II, 78, 1.

20. Ibid.

21. Ibid.

22. Ibid., q.51, a.1.

23. Daly, "Aquinas on Disordered Pleasures and Conditions," 608.

24. See *SCG*, III, 122.

25. This attitude is quite compatible with our contemporary view of scientific method which recognizes but does not find significant "outliers" in statistical tables until their number reaches a point where they can no longer be ignored.

26. S.Th. I-II, Prologus.

27. Kerr, *After Aquinas*. 97–113.

28. MacIntyre, *Dependent Rational Animals*, x.

29. For the phrase "informed feelings" see Code, *What Can She Know?* 102.

30. See *S.Th.*, I-II, 34, 1.

31. *S.Th.*, II-II, 153, 3.

32. *SCG*, III, 122.

33. *S.Th.*, II-II, 23, 1.

34. Pope, "Scientific and Natural Law Analyses of Homosexuality," 114.

35. MacIntyre, *Dependent Rational Animals*, 8.

5

Patriarchy, Purity, and Procreativity

Developments in Catholic Teachings on Human Sexuality and Gender

PATRICIA BEATTIE JUNG

My goal in this chapter is quite modest. I simply want to introduce recent developments in contemporary Roman Catholic teachings on human sexuality, so that readers of this volume might engage in a fruitful conversation about this particular tradition and its growing edges from a full range of disciplinary perspectives. In order to get a vivid sense of the import of recent developments within Church teachings about human sexuality, it is necessary to know something about their earlier formulations and preceding status. Otherwise, it is easy to miss the significance of these recent, subtle shifts. It should be noted as well that while this chapter focuses on Roman Catholic teachings, other Christian denominations endorse to varying degrees these same themes and share much of this same history.

The bulk of this essay focuses on the historical development of three traditional pillars of Catholic sexual ethics, namely, Church teachings about patriarchy, purity, and procreativity. This overview is divided into four parts, touching upon key developments in Church teachings during the New Testament period, among the early Church Fathers, during the Middle Ages, and then finally during the twentieth century.

New Testament Origins

Given its comparative priority in the Christian writings of later antiquity, the New Testament has remarkably little to say about sexuality per se. Yet, no survey of Christian sexual ethics makes sense apart from a consideration of the way the gospels portray Jesus in this regard, along with Pauline and later testimonies preserved in Christian scriptures. Here I will touch on the New Testament witness in regard to the body in general, patriarchy, and purity.

HUMAN EMBODIMENT

Christians give great value and status to the human body. Because of their convictions about the goodness of Creation, the Incarnation of God in Jesus of Nazareth, the Resurrection of Christ, and the promised resurrection of the body in the life of the world to come, Christians honor the body, considering it a "temple of the Holy Spirit." St. Paul's conception of human embodiment is worth noting in some detail.

For St. Paul, human beings did not just simply have a body; they *were embodied*. Thus, what one did with one's body really mattered. The body was not a disposable outer shell, but integral to the person and hence of great import. Paul did not hold the body in disdain, as did many in antiquity. When coupled with the call to whole-hearted loving devotion both to God and neighbor, as well as self, this assumption about human embodiment required that disciples of Christ integrate body (Gk. *soma*) and soul in their witness. Sometimes this entailed the discipline of the flesh (Gk. *sarx*), that is, of all those desires that keep us from God, but it did not mandate a rejection of the body per se. The body is considered by Christians to be part and parcel of the glorious life to come. In contrast to views of embodiment that prevailed in much of the rest of the ancient, first-century Mediterranean world, the anthropological conception of persons as an integral unity of body and soul is rightly considered distinctively Christian.

PATRIARCHY

Jesus's stance toward women was also strikingly countercultural. The way Jesus is portrayed in the Christian scriptures is remarkably egalitarian. The ancient Mediterranean world was thoroughly patriarchal. In contrast, Jesus affirmed the full agency of women who studied with and followed him. These women were the first to be sent as apostles to bear witness to the Risen Christ. Paul too appears to be notable in this regard, citing women as evangelical colleagues and quoting favorably the early Christian baptismal formula, which declared that "there is no longer Jew or Greek, there is no longer slave or free, there is no longer male or female; for all of you are one in Christ" (Galatians 3:28).

From our vantage point in the twenty-first century, it is easy to miss the full implications of this shift. Patriarchal systems endorse the domination of men over women, as well as the restriction (if not seclusion) of women to certain domestic arenas and servile roles. We know the Jesus movement challenged many such restrictions. But in addition, patriarchy establishes sexual and gender roles as well, restricting "good" women to sexually passive roles "headed" by men. In antiquity, coitus was generally thought to always embody this order, because women were presumed to be naturally unequal to men. Of course, male dominion could also be signaled by anal intercourse, with both same- and other-sex partners.

In the ancient world, generally speaking in order for male-to-male genital activity to be acceptable, a "passive" male partner needed to be obviously "unequal," that is, a captive, a vanquished soldier, a slave, a young boy, and so forth. Male same-sex activity between social peers was generally not accepted, at least in part, because it "feminized" the "passive" male partner and thereby challenged the patriarchal order in general. In general, same-sex activity among females evoked less of a negative response because it did not iconically castrate any male.[1] Nevertheless, it too challenged key premises of the patriarchal order (such as the presumed need of women for male headship.) We do not know whether Jesus intended to extend his challenge to patriarchy to these sexual stereotypes; many believe St. Paul clearly did not. Indeed, some biblical scholars today interpret St. Paul's negative reference in Romans to same-sex desires as expressive of precisely this patriarchal viewpoint on same-sex genital activity.[2]

It is important to understand that the challenge to patriarchy associated with the Jesus Movement was very dangerous.[3] The practice of baptizing women and slaves without their fathers'/husbands' and masters' permission tore at the very core of patriarchy. In this sense, it was not unreasonable to consider such activity treasonous. Households were the basic political and economic unit in society; even slight changes in the way they were ordered threatened to transform every aspect of their way of life. As early martyrs such as Sts. Perpetua and Fecilitas came to know only too well, such Christian practices that challenged patriarchy evoked violent responses from family and state alike.[4]

Today some biblical scholars theorize that in order to reduce the appearance of posing such a grave threat to the social fabric, some New Testament communities adopted more traditional household codes and organizational patterns. Some communities coupled their radically transformative baptismal and Eucharistic practices with calls for female and slave submission in order to reduce the threat of persecution. Patriarchal household codes typical of their era were adopted by some early Christian communities not only to make Christianity appear less threatening but perhaps also to increase the appeal of Christianity to those who had more power within the patriarchal system (that is, to increase the conversion rate of patriarchs and their households). Most scholars agree that the early Christian versions of these codes (such as those found in the letter to the Colossians in the New Testament) somewhat "soften" and transform patriarchal structures by prescribing in some cases mutual loving submission rather than unilateral obedience. Many note that these fateful cultural accommodations continue to compromise the full Christian witness to the life of the world to come.[5]

Perhaps the historically most significant accommodation to patriarchy was merely an imaginative failure, rather than a conscious accommodation. We can't know for sure. But certainly the connotations of Paul's gendered metaphor found in his letter to the Ephesians for the relationship between Christ and the Church, in which Christ is identified as a loving Groom who benevolently cares for his (obviously inferior!) Bride, the Church, still reverberate through the ages, sanctifying the submission of women to men, as well as denoting the love of God for the faithful.

PURITY

As portrayed in the gospels, Jesus was primarily concerned with establishing the primacy of the love command and calling disciples to whole-hearted devotion to God. Nowhere in sacred scripture is Jesus linked explicitly with virginity or celibacy, but Christian tradition has long held that he died a virgin. He spoke of celibacy as given only to some.

Despite his own probable status as celibate, Jesus welcomed children and began his public ministry by celebrating at a wedding feast in Cana. And yet, Jesus's public ministry entailed the abandonment of his parents' household. This decision—coupled with his apparent decision not to marry and have children—would have been considered a serious (though not unheard of, for example, among the Essenes) breach of filial duty. His pattern of denouncing the "family first" mentality most typical of antiquity was foreshadowed in his childhood when, for example, as a young teen, Jesus failed to stay home with his family and instead went "about his Father's business" in the temple.[6] Repeatedly in the gospels Jesus is portrayed as challenging the primacy of family ties, structures, and duties (even one as "sacred" as burying the dead) and as distancing himself from "blood ties."[7] He announced and established a new kind of "family" rooted in discipleship and baptism.[8] Some texts even say Jesus came to set family member against family member and that Christian discipleship requires "hating" one's family.[9] Jesus challenged as misplaced the priority that was often given to such family ties but did not denounce such intimate relationships.

We don't know whether St. Paul was widowed or divorced, but we do know that at least after his conversion, he was celibate. Through his celibacy, St. Paul aimed to free himself from the anxieties he associated with having a spouse and children. In comparison to some of the Christians in Corinth who believed that the "singleness of heart" required by discipleship could be achieved only by dissolving their households, St. Paul's views of marriage and celibacy seem moderate. He affirmed marriage, while expressing some ambivalence about it. St. Paul clearly thought marriage divided the heart and thus would prove to distract the faithful from God. But, because he believed the end-time was near,

St. Paul suggested that those who were married remain so. To those who were single, he commended celibacy over marriage. He preferred celibacy because it would leave the faithful disciple free from the worrisome distractions that accompany family life.[10] Nevertheless, St. Paul saw marriage as a licit remedy for sexual desire. He commended marriage to all those who might be overwhelmed by lust.[11]

Development by Early Church Fathers

Once it became clear that St. Paul was mistaken about the imminent arrival of the end-time, Christians set about trying to discern what it would mean to witness to the Risen Christ over the course of a lifetime. As noted earlier, discipleship would have to entail as normative the task of integrating one's body and soul and orienting this integral whole toward God over an entire lifetime. Only such an integral witness could characterize unyielding and wholehearted devotion to God.

TOWARD A CULTURE OF CELIBACY

In the earliest centuries, facing the threat of martyrdom offered Christians a clear, if terrifying, way to imitate Christ. But after the Emperor Constantine's conversion ended persecution in the fourth century of the Common Era, celibacy offered another dramatic form of witness. This "bloodless" form of martyrdom built upon an impulse toward sexual asceticism established earlier. In the early church, most people thought celibacy was the best way to imitate Christ.

Celibacy refers to a state of life in which a person has made a permanent commitment to abstain from marriage and sexual intimacy. Traditionally, Christians believed that while marriage was good, celibacy was better. Early church fathers interpreted the remark attributed to Jesus in the gospel of Matthew—that in heaven people will neither marry nor be given in marriage—to mean that celibacy would best embody the life of the world to come. It would best enable the believer to witness here and now to the purity and singleness of heart enjoyed in heaven. Because they were seen as "entangling" us with others, many perceived sexual desires as obstacles to such undivided devotion to God.

In view of the expectation that everything—including the body—would be gloriously transformed in the life of the world to come, many Christian theologians of this era argued that in this new creation the body would be "spiritualized" or gutted of all its impure visceral emotions. So it was that late in the second century, St. Clement of Alexandria declared that even in marriage coitus should take place only for reproductive purposes. Sex pursued for venereal pleasure, even for the gracious affection created by the sharing of pleasure, was not good. Clearly this judgment rested on a conflation of all sexual passion with lust. As a result of this premise, for much of its history, the Church would misidentify sexual desire per se as impure/pathological and hold sexual pleasure (even in marriage) to be morally suspect.[12]

Even the comparatively moderate views of the late fourth-century church father, St. Augustine of Hippo, arguably the single most influential Christian theologian in regard to sexuality, basically reflect this viewpoint. He presumed that marriage—along with sexual differentiation and reproduction (though devoid of desire)—was part of God's original blessing in Paradise. Nevertheless, as St. Augustine understood them for the vast majority of his life, marriage and reproduction, along with the passion and pleasure he associated with "the Fall," would have no place in the new heaven and earth.[13]

The story of how the distinction between lustful and graceful experiences of sexual desire became blurred in Christianity is quite complex but undoubtedly, the Christian adoption of the Stoic procreative and passion-free ideals proved central. Within the various dualistic worldviews that pervaded the ancient Mediterranean world, the material world—including the body and its sexual passions and reproductive functions—was thought to be a threat to reason and freedom. Since such visceral emotions were thought to be especially evident in women, femininity was particularly associated with what was irrational, involuntary, intensely emotional, and hence morally dangerous. In contrast virtue and virility were closely linked; the more masculine the person's personality/character, the better from an ethical point of view. Because sexuality was not identified with the person's core identity, everyone—*including women*—could potentially become more masculine, and hence, more virtuous.[14]

The reality of marriage in the ancient world—which frequently involved old men marrying very young women for economic, political, or procreative purposes—also contributed to the Church's sanctification of celibacy. For the richer male citizens of the ancient Mediterranean society in which Christianity arose, sexuality was not routinely confined to marriage, and marriage was not associated particularly with sexual pleasure. Sexual slavery and sex trade were fairly commonplace. In addition, maternal and infant mortality rates were high. As a result, Christians frequently adopted Stoic prescriptions that frowned upon not only the involuntary "intemperance" of most sexual passions but also upon even the tender affections sometimes shared by lovers. Along with indifference and control, emotional detachment and autonomy were admired and commended as morally ideal within Stoicism.

Wealth, power, and pleasure, even a sense of immortality, were often tied to and transferred through marriage and kinship systems in the ancient world.[15] In such a context, sexual continence vividly signaled the renunciation of such worldly pursuits. The endorsement, and eventual idealization, of virginity, celibacy, and widowhood signaled the refusal to prioritize such concerns. Through celibacy, these early Christians thought they might transform their bodies, imitate Christ, and bear witness to the resurrected, pure life to come.

It is important to note that a world in which sexual abuse, sexual slavery, and rape are accepted as ordinary features of life was not unique to antiquity. Lest in hindsight we judge too harshly the tendency of early Christians to conflate all sexual desire and lust, remember that though many condemn such practices as decadent today, various forms of sexual exploitation still flourish underground in the West and remain accepted as commonplace in other parts of the world.

Some liberally minded Christian ethicists may take issue with this next point, yet I think it is a vital one to acknowledge if we are committed to an honest appraisal of human sexuality that takes social and interpersonal justice seriously. Though in the end I think they are incompatible with Christian convictions about human embodiment, dualistic modes of thought that elevate the mind/spirit and denigrate the body make sense of much of human experience of sexuality. The fact is that all sexual contact is boundary blurring, but when such contact is disordered, it is boundary violating.

We know that sexual appetites can be addictive and compulsive. Passion can seduce, instead of serve, people, forging relationships that are abusive and destructive of human dignity. Sexual desire can fuel relationships wherein people take, rather than share, pleasure. It can draw and bind people into relationships that are marked by possessiveness and domination. Our bodily availability to one another and our longing for such intimate engagement leaves us extremely vulnerable to sexual forms of aggression and humiliation. So yes, Stoicism distorted early Christian views of sexuality and it is hard to underestimate its influence. Yet, sexual desires were held in suspicion and sexual activity was thought to require justification, also in part because the distinction between the desire for sexual pleasure and lust does, as a matter of fact, blur easily. There is, as Susan Ross has underscored in this volume and elsewhere, a profound ambiguity about human embodiment.[16]

The absence of sexuality in the visions of the new heaven and new earth that prevailed in the early church's eschatological imagination contributed to the idealization of celibacy as well. In the "culture of celibacy" that emerged, sexual lifestyles were ranked according to their purity in a descending order of acceptability. According to most church fathers, virginity was best, and then perpetual celibacy; these were followed by widowhood, temporary continence within marriage, and finally procreativity within marriage.[17] In sum, the Church taught that the best sex—even in marriage—was no sex at all.

PROCREATIVITY

For the most part from the third to the sixteenth centuries, the notion that celibacy was a superior path of discipleship went virtually unchallenged.[18] Still, celibacy was not a viable option for all. A good, even if inferior, way had to be found to incorporate sexual desires into the life of discipleship. The expression of sexual desire in marriage had to be more than merely the remedy for lust suggested by Paul; it had to serve a positive, rational purpose. So it was that Christians came to adopt as morally normative the Stoic emphasis on procreation. Needless to say, the sanctification of this rule also influenced the course for Christian sexual ethics for the subsequent two millennia.[19]

For most of its history, the Church taught that sexual activity—even in a just and loving marriage—could be chaste if, and only if, it was intended to be reproductive. Though St. Augustine believed celibacy to be superior to marriage, he rejected the notion that marriage was evil. In fact, he argued marriage could be a sacramental sign of God's fidelity to all that is. Procreation was another good associated with marriage.

St. Augustine taught that only when spouses engaged in sexual activity exclusively for procreative purposes could such activity be completely without sin. To "indulge" in sexual activity that was not intentionally procreative—even if done not to satisfy one's own desires, but simply to "remedy" the lustful desires of one's spouse—was gravely sinful. If spouses intended their sexual activity to be procreative as well as pleasurable, they still sinned, but only a little (venially).[20] If they did anything to avoid procreation, they sinned grievously.

St. Augustine argued that patriarchy was God's original design for male-female relationships, and as far as he could tell, women were created exclusively for procreative purposes. Still, he upheld the primacy of love for Christians. But St. Augustine did not think spousal love had any connection with human sexual activity. He speculated that in the Garden of Eden human genitalia might (or might not) have been used for reproductive purposes, but if they had been so employed, such activity would have been without physical pleasure. In its original design, human reproduction would have been rational and deliberate, not ecstatic.[21]

Historically, this emphasis on procreativity has had tremendous effects on Christian sexual norms. On the positive side, the procreative norm is essentially social. It firmly underlines the connection of morally good sex with service to values relevant not just to the individual or couple, but to the wider commonweal. For example, all coital activity outside the stability of marriage was usually forbidden, since procreative activity entailed the responsibility to rear children properly, which required stable parental relationships.

Negatively, this emphasis on procreativity blurs the distinction between reproductive and sexual activity. Consequently, most Christian denominations condemned contraceptive activity until the twentieth century, and the Catholic Church continues to do so today. Furthermore, all noncoital forms of sexual activity—digital, oral, and anal sexual activity, whether practiced by same-sex or other-sex couples, along with masturbation and the sexual activity of post-menopausal women—were for most of Christian history condemned. They were judged perverted at least in part because they were nonprocreative. All (except the sexual activity of postmenopausal women) are still condemned by the Catholic Church today, if they lead to orgasms apart from coitus.

Formulations during the Medieval Era and Beyond

ST. THOMAS AQUINAS ON CHASTITY, CELIBACY, AND THE MORAL GOOD OF SEXUAL ACTIVITY

Within a Thomistic schema, passions in general are viewed as ontologically good because they are presumed to incline us naturally, if not existentially, toward what is good-for-us. Of course, they are not yet necessarily morally good. Because of human freedom, people can focus their desires on objects that for a variety of reasons do not contribute to human flourishing, or they may pursue them in situations that would pervert their authentic purpose. In this sense, St. Thomas Aquinas understood that all desires must be humanized.

Virtues channel human desires toward what is fitting; they humanize our passions. Temperance is one of the cardinal virtues under which St. Thomas considered sensual desires for food, drink and sex. Reason dictates that the temperate person will channel and moderate consumption of the objects of these desires. For example, the virtuous person avoids in general both habitual over- and undereating. Ideally anyway, temperance should habituate its practitioner to the proper, rational enjoyment, as well as disciplined control, of the impulse to eat so that it promotes human health and flourishing.

As Cristina Traina has suggested, given the general framework developed by St. Thomas, it would have been reasonable to expect him to have described chastity as a learned way of channeling sexual passions so that they formed the faithful disciple's experience of erotic desires, integrating them within the person and ordering them to their proper purpose(s) so that the respect due every body and the dignity inherent in all persons is reverenced in every sexual relationship.[22] Despite the connotations of chastity to the contrary, given this overarching schema, sexual virtue should not be exclusively, or even primarily, about the suppression or denial of sexual passion. Of course, sometimes living chastely would require such continence. But within the understanding of the roles of virtues in the moral life as elaborated upon by Aquinas, chastity should have been about the proper cultivation, as much as the containment, of sexual desire. It should have been about the integration of sexuality into all personal relationships, though of course not necessarily about sharing the delights of intimate companionship and genital pleasure with everyone, or even anyone.

In fact, however, Aquinas was not able to break out of the "culture of celibacy" into which he was immersed, despite the presence of philosophical distinctions and tools that could have enabled it. Francis Catania discusses this issue at greater length in chapter 4 in this volume. Here, it is sufficient to note that as Traina has indicated, Aquinas does not begin with the consideration of excessive or inadequate expressions of touch and then treat coitus as a special case. Instead, for him, chastity concerns only coitus, whose proper purpose is to serve humanity through procreation. St. Thomas Aquinas does not recognize touch as essential to human health and flourishing. Consequently, virginity is not the frustration of sexual passions, but simply a choice not to use this faculty. A refusal to pay the "marital debt" (to have sexual intercourse) is simply an intemperate moral deficiency or an effort to avoid procreation.

Disappointing as St. Thomas Aquinas's treatment of chastity may be, an important breakthrough occurs in his thought. Aquinas does take note that coitus appears to contribute to the proper rearing of children (which is part of the procreative good properly conceived) by contributing to the couple's bond of friendship. This may be the first explicit and affirmative connection (however tenuous) of sexual activity to lovemaking in the history of Christian thought since their disconnection during the patristic era. Thus, Aquinas makes a crucial, even if only initially sketched, contribution to a nuanced sexual ethic, because his thought attends not only to what people do, but to the quality of the social and relational bond between them.[23]

"SINS AGAINST NATURE"

Around this same era, the twelfth and thirteenth centuries, the notion of "sins against nature" emerged. When blended with earlier sexual teachings, this eventually produced a two-tiered classification system for sexual sins. Sins against nature (which included all contraceptive activity, solitary and mutual forms of masturbation, oral intercourse, anal intercourse, and bestiality) were judged more grievous than sins committed in accord with nature (which could include some types of fornication, adultery, incest, rape, and sexual abduction).[24]

By the fourteenth century, sins against nature were labeled intrinsically evil. This in effect precluded (with only rare exceptions) the further consideration of the legitimacy of these activities.[25] By the eighteenth century, all sexual desires and subsequent sexual activities that were not conjugal and open to procreation were considered mortally sinful. The overall impact was that the evaluation of sexual desires and activities was isolated from consideration of their wider personal, interpersonal, and social contexts. To my knowledge, moral theology treated no other area of human life this way. For example, while homicide is always judged an ontic evil, it may not be immoral, that is, murderous. That judgment depends upon a consideration of the agent's intention and relevant circumstances.[26]

Twentieth-Century Developments

During the second half of the twentieth century, these traditional Catholic emphases on patriarchy, purity, and procreativity were significantly modified. Assessing these changes and suggesting direction for their further development may be useful for envisioning how Christian ethics and thinking on sexuality, and by extension gender, could evolve in both faithful and constructive ways in the future.

RECENT CHALLENGES TO THE EMPHASIS ON PROCREATIVITY

It may come as a surprise, even to many Catholics, that the Roman Catholic Church currently teaches that people should transmit life only in responsible ways and that such responsibility may entail the regulation of birth. The Church teaches that natural forms of family planning (hereafter NFP) might in some cases not only be permissible, but even obligatory. Nevertheless, the Church still teaches that every sexual act must remain open to the possibility of procreation. That possibility (however remote) is judged natural to each and every authentically human sexual act. Therefore, there should be no "artificial" interruption of, or interference with, this generative potential identified with sexual desire. Procreativity is no longer seen as the exclusive, or even the primary, purpose of sexuality, but it is still seen as essential to it. Let's review how it was that the contemporary Church came to this conclusion.

In response to the growing acceptance of contraception worldwide, especially the acceptance of it by the Anglican Communion at its Lambeth Conference in 1930, Pope Pius XI issued an encyclical, *Casti connubii,* that same year. In it, he declared contraception to be an "unspeakable crime." The conjugal act, he taught, is of its very nature designed for procreation. It is sinful to deprive this act through human interference of its natural power to procreate life; openness to life, Pope Pius XI argued, can be expressed only by noninterference with this potential. It was effrontery to call children a troublesome burden.

And yet, Pope Pius XI conceded that sexual continence could be permissible in marriage with the consent of both spouses. For him procreation remained the primary goal of marriage, yet not its only end. This pope emphasized the importance of the formation of intimate partnership in marriage.

In what many mark as a decisive "turning point" in Catholic teaching on sexuality, his successor, Pope Pius XII, declared in his 1951 "Address to Italian Midwives" that rhythm or "natural family planning" could be morally acceptable in certain circumstances for grave reasons. Sexual activity need not be intentionally procreative; under certain circumstances, spouses could licitly engage in sexual activity, in a manner consciously designed to avoid conception.

In his 1968 encyclical *Humanae vitae* Pope Paul VI described contraception as "unlawful," again by virtue of the nature of the sexual act. However, Pope Paul VI also argued that grave negative consequences would accompany contraception. He predicted that the practice of "artificial" forms of birth control would lower moral standards (by which he presumably meant increase fornication), increase marital infidelity, result in wives being used merely as sexual "instruments" for their husbands' pleasure, and provide people with no bulwark to use against claims on the part of the state to have a right to control the couple's reproductive activities.

At the same time, Pope Paul VI reiterated Pope Pius XII's declaration that recourse to natural infertile periods for the sake of spacing births (NFP) was lawful, but he required only that there be reasonable grounds for such family planning. These grounds included according to Pope Paul VI: preserving harmony and peace in the marriage, assisting the nurture and education of children already born, and proving to be therapeutic for the mother (if not directly contraceptive or sterilizing).

In 1981 Pope John Paul II also rejected contraception as wrong "based on the nature of the human person and his and her acts." Noting that the Church was aware of the problems associated with transmitting life in responsible ways, he mentioned some of the problems that may accompany unregulated population growth. Still, he concluded that "the panic" about overpopulation was exaggerated. Such undue fear stemmed, he thought, from an antilife, "contraceptive mentality" that had become widespread.

In an unprecedented (and hence remarkable) move, Pope John Paul II declared there to be an inseparable connection between the unitive and procreative meanings associated with sexuality. He taught that in order for a couple's sexual activity to be truly lovemaking, it must be open to the possibility of baby making. Otherwise, they fail to give fully of themselves to each other. He interpreted the "withholding" of a person's reproductive potential in a sexual encounter as a withholding of an integral part of her/his embodied self.

The full elements of this vision of the heterosexual "spousal significance" of the human person were summarized in 2004 by the Congregation for the Doctrine of the Faith in its "Letter on the Collaboration of Men and Women in the Church and in the World" (hereafter CMW). Here, heterosexual differentiation is linked not only with reproduction, but also additionally, with the human capacity to love truly and thereby image God (CMW, 5 and 9).

RECENT CHALLENGES TO THE "CULTURE OF CELIBACY"

As seen in the example of creating a positive space for NFP, during the twentieth century the excessive suspicion of sexuality expressed in the Catholic Church's "culture of celibacy" was partially overcome. Several theological developments contributed to the growing appreciation of the grace of the body in general and of human sexuality in particular. Theologians generally see human erotic love as imaging the divine self-giving love essential to God's Triune Reality.[27] Creation is seen as expressive of God's joyous abundant and fecund desire for relationship, while the story of Redemption is the story of God's persistent pursuit of reconciliation and communion with all that is. The Providence of God is understood to supply us all good things—including sexual pleasure—richly for our enjoyment (1 Timothy 6:17).

Moreover, it is widely recognized now as mistaken to have thought of human loves as "distracting" us from God, as if God were simply another possible object for our affections alongside and competing with human lovers, particular friends, and children for our loyalty and affections. God is the Ground of all that is and can be loved precisely through such relationships.[28]

For these reasons, in 1965 at the Second Vatican Council the bishops of the Catholic Church proclaimed the call to perfection to be universal. All Christians—*lay and religious, single, married, and celibate alike*—can bear such witness to God in and through their specific sexual vocations. In terms of this call to perfection, there is nothing second class about marriage. They declared love to be of the very essence of marriage. Marriage was defined as an exclusive, permanent, intimate partnership of both life and love.

Sexual activity within marriage was recognized as a positive source for mutual sanctification (as well as a concession to lust).[29] At the Council at least some recognized that sharing sexual pleasure could be lovemaking, in proportion to what we extend as gift. This is why most theologians recognize sexual intercourse as the primary symbol of sacramental marriages.[30]

However, in his 1981 Pope John Paul II reasserted that celibacy was morally superior to marriage.[31] In his theology of the body Pope John Paul II generally affirmed the unity of body and spirit in the person, but his acceptance of a strong version of the distinction between body and spirit found expression in his ambiguity about human corporeality. For him, the original psychosomatic unity of the person was ruptured by sin, so that there is an untrustworthy center of resistance to spirit within the body. While he saw the body as the expression of, and identified with, the person, he nevertheless identified the human's likeness to God (the *imago Dei*) with the person's ability to transcend and dominate her/his body. For Pope John Paul II, sexual passion appeared mainly as an obstacle to love. Consequently, sexual desires mainly required self-control.

CHALLENGES TO PATRIARCHY

Church teachings about gender and the equality of the sexes changed most dramatically over the course of the second half of the twentieth century. Many find the end result still to be ambiguous. While the Church gradually came to argue for the equality of women both at home and in society, at the same time, it began to teach a relatively new and rigid form of gender essentialism, concluding that women have a "special nature," different from, yet complementary to, that of men. Though the theory of gender complementarity has been asserted in several recent Vatican documents, there is an apparent reluctance to identify specific traits or roles as masculine or feminine—with one notable exception. As parents, women are seen (because of their maternal personality) as having a "special genius" for nurture, while men are seen as best able to represent God to other family members! Let me sketch the history of these developments.

As late as 1930 in his encyclical *Casti connubii* Pope Pius XI defended the primacy of husbands over wives and commended the ready submission and willing obedience of wives. Opposed to women's suffrage, this pope condemned as unnatural not only the domestic and ecclesial, but also the economic and political, equality of men and women. His successor, Pope Pius XII, noted in the 1950s that both sexes were equal in the eyes of God, but because they were essentially different, women belonged at home where they would flourish under the benevolent male headship of their fathers and/or husbands.

In the 1960s Pope John XXIII would teach that women should for the most part be treated as equal to men in the public sphere, but because of their "different nature," women should remain subject to men at home. Similarly, Pope Paul VI affirmed the equality of the sexes in society but defended their differential treatment in the Church. (He did not address the issue of women's comparative status, authority, and power at home.) Yet, in a truly remarkable reversal of nearly 1,900 years of constant Church teaching, Pope John Paul II taught in his encyclical *Mulieris dignatatum* (On the Dignity of Women) that women should be considered equal to men both in the wider society and at home. (Like his predecessor, Pope Paul VI, Pope John Paul II would argue that women's iconic inability to represent Christ required that they be treated differentially in the Church.)[32]

One point seems crucial to underscore in conclusion. It is important to see that Church teachings in the area of sexual ethics have changed over the centuries and, indeed, developed dramatically in the twentieth century. Even after Rome has spoken, Church teachings change. The factors behind such developments are complex, but as Frank Catania's chapter makes clear, the methodology of St. Thomas Aquinas would suggest that we have nothing to fear from the changes that interdisciplinary conversation might suggest.

Notes

1. Some interpret Jesus's absolute prohibition of divorce, even of wives caught in adultery, as posing a similar challenge to patriarchy. This is why the disciples grumbled: It is not expedient to marry! Otherwise, they would risk being dishonored/"castrated"

by having to live with adulterous wives. They would have to become eunuchs for the kingdom (Matthew 19:1–11).

2. For a discussion of this important text and a thorough review of the contemporary literature on this topic, see Martin, "Heterosexism and the Interpretation of Romans 1:18–32," *Sex and the Single Savior*, 51–64.

3. The challenge to patriarchal family structures can be traced directly back to the activities and teachings of Jesus. For example, see Mark 3:31–35 and Luke 11:27–28. The picture is of course complex because at other times Jesus appears to be very supportive of and sympathetic toward family. Most scholars conclude, however, that at the very least Jesus appears to relativize first-century family values.

4. See Brown, *The Body and Society*, 140–59.

5. See Fiorenza, *In Memory of Her*, 243–333.

6. Luke 2:41–51.

7. Luke 9:59–62.

8. Mark 3:31–35.

9. Matthew 10:21–22, 34–36; Luke 12:51–53.

10. 1 Corinthians 7:1, 32–35.

11. It is important to note that while from their earliest origins, Christians were noted for their hospitality toward and care for children, there is no special emphasis on, or even a discussion of, procreation in the New Testament. Paul certainly assumed sexual activity would be procreative but he found it acceptable within marriage primarily as a remedy for lust. 1 Corinthians 7:2, 9.

12. See Brown's discussion of Clement of Alexandria, 122–139.

13. There is some newly discovered evidence that at the end of his life (around 421 CE) St. Augustine began to distinguish between lawful experiences of sexual desire in marriage and "concupiscence of the flesh," what we would call lust today. In *Epistle 6* Augustine concedes that there might have been a sinless experience of sexual desire in Paradise, if there had been no Fall. See *St. Augustine on Marriage and Sexuality*, Clark, ed., 10, 99–105.

14. Reuther, *Religion and Sexism*, 160–61.

15. It has never been part of Christian belief that personal continuity is established through reproduction or ensured by ancestor worship. Hence, procreation was never seen as essential to the life of the world to come; indeed, for most of Christian history, celibacy was idealized as iconic of the life to come.

16. For an extended discussion of the theological and moral significance of ambiguity, see Ross, *Extravagant Affections*, 64–93.

17. Jovinian in the late fourth century and Julian of Eclanum in the early fifth went against this tide and argued powerfully for the equality of marriage with celibacy. Both were condemned as heretics. For a more detailed discussion of what little we know about their perspective, see Brown, 359–61, 377, 408–15.

18. Then, in the context of the Protestant Reformation, Martin Luther argued that while the gift of celibacy might be given "for the sake of the kingdom" to a few, such a special calling was quite rare. Most who attempted to travel this path were self-deceived. They were most likely in denial of God's remedy for human lust graciously provided in

the holy estate of marriage. As Luther saw it, efforts to live a celibate life usually ended in promiscuity. John Calvin, too, saw celibacy as a "special gift," but this state of life has no greater spiritual or moral value than marriage. The marriage, which was for him a higher estate, was mostly, if not entirely, free of sexual lust. At first John Wesley upheld the celibate life as "perfect," but he later revised his thinking, citing only the special advantages of being single. For a more detailed discussion, see Jordan, *The Ethics of Sex,* 57–62.

19. Key elements of current Church teachings regarding sexuality still rest heavily on assumptions about human sexuality that we now recognize to be androcentric, that is, they rest on aspects of male sexual and reproductive physiology. For example, the conclusion that "each and every" sexual act must be open to the possibility of procreation rests on the distinctive way sexual and reproductive physiology are intertwined for men, for whom alone this is a natural, biological possibility. In contrast, "each and every" sexual activity of a woman is not biologically potentially reproductive.

Furthermore, when persons are reduced to their biology, such "physicalism" can be dangerous to human welfare. Still, while Vatican officials and Catholic moral theologians alike recognize that sexual scripts are socially constructed, they argue that these gender roles and public policies about the family and wider social structures must engage and build upon "the facts" of human sexuality, if those personal norms and social policies are to prove humanizing. The problem is that many Church teachings appear to hinge on inaccurate and outdated biological information about human sexuality. The Catholic intellectual heritage has long contended that bodies school and discipline persons in humbling ways; both an ethics and a theology of sexuality must attend to and learn from, as well as dialogue about, these "facts" with conversation partners from the humanities and social and physical sciences.

20. See Clark's selections from Augustine's "The Goods of Marriage," 42–51.

21. Other Church fathers—e.g., Gregory of Nyssa, Ambrose, and Jerome—held sexual desire in even greater disrepute. See Brown, 376–77, 399.

22. Traina, "Under Pressure," 78–80.

23. Aquinas, *Summa Contra Gentiles,* XIV.18. Apart from contemporary writings, the endearing and tender, "love-making" qualities of sexual activities receive their most explicit endorsement in the writings of the seventeenth-century Anglican bishop, Jeremy Taylor, especially in *Holy Living.*

24. Aquinas, *Summa Contra Gentiles,* XIV.5–9.

25. It was generally taken to be axiomatic that in regard to sexual sins there was no parvity of matter.

26. For a detailed discussion of this methodological problem in Catholic moral theology see Jung, "Constructing a Consistent Ethic of Life," 61–80.

27. Rogers, *Sexuality and the Christian Body,* 193–275.

28. Ferder, *Tender Fires.*

29. Second Vatican Council, *Gaudium et spes,* no. 48.

30. It is interesting to note that the Church has always taught that it is the ability to engage in sexual intercourse, and not the ability to reproduce, that is the essential requirement for marriage.

31. Pope John Paul II, *Familiaris consortio*, no. 16.

32. It matters whether one emphasizes points of commonality or difference in one's theology of the body. In his theology of the body, Pope John Paul II sometimes recognized that people—at the most fundamental level—were somatically homogeneous. What we share in common runs deeper than what differentiates us. The other is "bone of my bone, flesh of my flesh" (For example, see *Mulieris dignatatum*, 6). At other times, however, he treated sexual differentiation as constitutive of and essential to human personhood, so that one could not be a human person without being either male or female, (for example, see *Mulieris dignatatum*, 18). For the most part, Pope John Paul II reduced human embodiment to sexual differences. Being male or female he treated as two different ways of being a body, a person. He then specified that for women their sex/gender dictated their vocation, their "special genius" for being virgins and mothers. (He made no analogous specification for men.)

PART 2

Reflecting on Human Sexual Diversity

6

Evolutionary Biology
and Sexual Diversity

JOAN ROUGHGARDEN

The perplexing discord concerning sex, gender, and sexuality that greets us everyday in the political and religious dimensions of our lives is encountered in science as well. The discovery of unanticipated expressions of sex, gender, and sexuality throughout the animal kingdom is finding biologists unprepared to catalog and account for the findings. Furthermore, the explanations offered for even the most familiar expressions of gender and sexuality are increasingly suspect as internal logical conflicts are encountered and contradictory information is amassed. Overall then, science is challenged when asked to supply an accurate picture of sex, gender expression, and sexuality in nature, and this limitation impedes a scientifically informed moral and theological discussion of these issues.

Within my discipline of evolutionary biology, the scientific narrative of sex roles has changed little since Darwin enunciated what is known as the theory of sexual selection. Darwin introduced this theory because of traits like the peacock's tail, which are termed ornaments and that are not readily understood as adaptations for survival. Instead, Darwin hypothesized that such traits find their evolutionary value in how they promote mating. The process that causes traits to evolve because of how they contribute to mating is called "sexual selection," which Darwin contrasted with "natural selection," the process causing traits to evolve that promote survival.[1]

Darwin claimed that females prefer to mate with males who possess elaborate ornaments. As a result, males evolve such ornaments because males lacking them leave few descendants. The rationale for females to mate with ornamented males is that their own sons will be likewise endowed, and thus given an advantage when their time comes to mate. This proposition seems plausible, and at first glance perhaps innocent—its truth is presumably determined by seeing whether peahens do in fact prefer to mate with peacocks that have splendid tails. If it should turn out that females do not preferentially mate with males possessing a splendid tail, one might expect that sexual selection would be rejected as the explanation for the peacock's tail, settling the matter once and for all, at least for peacocks. And similarly, for other species in which males possess ornaments. If females in such species don't prefer the males with ornaments, then one might anticipate that Darwin's account of sexual selection would simply be discarded.

There's more. Darwin also observed that males in some species possess not *beautiful* ornaments but *majestic* armaments, such as the antlers on deer. Darwin suggested that males in such species fight with one another for access to females. This would lead to the evolution of well-armed males because those without effective armament would leave few descendants. Meanwhile, as the story goes, females obligingly prefer to mate with the males most successful at male-male combat because in doing so they tend to ensure that their own male offspring are well armed and effective at acquiring mates. Darwin's picture of sexual selection for antlers is also plausible and also presumably subject to empirical test. Are stags that breed the victors in male-male combat that have vanquished the nonbreeding males, and do females prefer to mate with victorious stags? If not, then one again might anticipate that Darwin's theory of sexual selection would be discarded. The distinction between selection of male traits by females, and the selection of male traits resulting from male-male combat, is today referred to as intersexual selection and intrasexual selection, respectively. Darwin envisioned that intersexual selection by females reinforced intrasexual selection among males.

When Darwin proposed his theory of sexual selection, he took the peacock and peahen, and the stag and doe, as emblematic of males and females generally. He asserted generalizations like "Males of almost all animals have stronger passions than females," and "the female . . . with the rarest of exceptions is less eager than the male . . . she is coy."[2] Notice the phrase, "almost all" and "rarest of exceptions," and he amassed examples that seemed to support these claims of universality. Sexual selection thus enunciates a *norm* of natural sexual conduct. Species that depart from the sexual-selection templates of passionate male and coy female are then seen as "exceptions" meriting special discussion to account for their deviant behavior.

The plot thickens. The stories of inter- and intrasexual selection are supposed to explain why males have ornaments and armaments, traits referred to collectively as "secondary sexual characters," in contradistinction to the "primary sexual characters" consisting of testes, ovaries, and associated plumbing. What then are we to make of species in which males do not possess secondary sexual characters, so that males and females are virtually indistinguishable, as with the guinea pigs many people raise as pets, or birds like penguins, where sexes can be distinguished only by careful inspection of the genitals?

Conversely, what are we to make of species in which males are distinguishably different from females, but are not passionate, and in which females consistently pursue the males, but are not coy? Female alpine accentors from the central Pyrénées of France, for example, solicit males for mating every 8.5 minutes during the breeding season. Ninety-three percent of all solicitations are initiated by the female approaching the male, the other 7 percent by him approaching her.[3] This frequent sexual contact greatly exceeds that needed specifically to fertilize the relatively few eggs that are reared.

Or what are we supposed to make of the sea horses and pipefish in which the male is drab and the female ornamented, and in which the male raise the young in a pouch into which the female deposits eggs? Such species exhibit what biologists call "sex role reversal." The females are said to compete for access to males, with the males choosing females for their ornaments resulting in showy females and drab males, the reverse of the peacock. Why would this happen? Surely therefore, sex roles cannot be said to follow directly from gamete size— (meaning the assumption that the cheapness of sperm invites passionate male promiscuity and the expensiveness of eggs necessitates female coyness during their careful choice of good-gene–bearing males). After all, male sea horses make tiny sperm just as male peacocks do, and female sea horses make large eggs just as peahens do, but nonetheless male sea horses care for the young and female sea horses entrust their eggs to a male's pouch. Could these cases mean nature has no universal roles for male and females?

And on and on, the counterexamples accumulate. In many species, multiple types of males and females, each with distinct identifying characteristics, carry out special roles at the nest both before and after the mating takes place. In the sandpiperlike European ruff, black-collared males build nests in small defended territories called "courts" within a communal display area called a "lek." Meanwhile, white-collared males accompany females while the females feed. The white-collared males then leave the company of the females and fly to the lek where they are solicited by the black-collared males to join them in their courts. When the females eventually arrive at the lek to lay eggs, they are romanced by pairs of males—one black-collared male paired with one white-collared male in some courts—as well as by single black-collared males in courts by themselves.

Evidently, females prefer to lay eggs in nests hosted by a pair of black-collared and white-collared males at which both males serve as parents, rather than in nests hosted solely by one black-collared male, perhaps because the white-collared male has formed a bond with the females while he was accompanying them during their feeding. Perhaps white-collared males serve as "brokers" that introduce females to the black-collared males that have not previously had the opportunity to meet females while they were busy setting up and defending courts in the leking area. What are we to make of animal family organizations consisting of trios such as the ruffs, or of many other species with reproductive social groups that consist of more than one male and one female tending offspring together after mating takes place, or even participating jointly in courtship before mating takes place? Could this mean nature privileges no particular family structure as a norm?

In some species with multiple types of males, one of the types more-or-less resembles the females, as in bluegill sunfish in lakes of North America, and the ruffs just mentioned also possess a third type of male that has neither a black or white collar—no collared ornament at all, just like the females. Moreover, male sunangel hummingbirds of the Andes from Venezuela through Columbia, Ecuador, Peru, to Bolivia, have feathers called a gorget, a broad band of distinctive color on the throat and upper chest. Museum specimens reveal that some sunangel hummingbird species include "masculine females" with gorgets just like the male. Also, some males have female coloration. All in all, of 42 studied species, seven have both masculine females and feminine males, nine have masculine females and no feminine males, two have feminine males and no masculine females, and 24 have neither masculine females nor feminine males.[4]

Does not such natural variation in gender expression contradict the Darwinian prescription of one template, or norm, per sex—the passionate armed and ornamented males on one side and coy, drab females on the other? Does such natural variation in gender expression point to multiple norms for each sex, a multiplicity of possible roles evolutionarily negotiated within each species depending on local circumstance? In *Evolution's Rainbow*, I have gone so far as to suggest that each of the discrete norms for a sexed body might be considered as a "zoological gender."[5] This allows me to speak of a bird species as having, say, three genders of males—one with black collar, one with white collar, and one with no collar—and perhaps one or two genders of females; or of a fish with three genders—one gender of lifelong females, one gender of lifelong males, and one gender that begins life as female and changes to male in midlife.

And what are we to make of the same-sex sexuality so evident (and yet underreported) in many species? In over 300 species of vertebrates, same-sex sexuality has been documented in the primary peer-reviewed scientific literature as a natural component of the social system.[6] Examples include species of reptiles like lizards; birds like the pukeko of New Zealand and European oystercatcher; mammals like giraffes, elephants, dolphins, whales, sheep, monkeys; and one of our closest relatives, the bonobo.

A museum in Oslo recently initiated exhibits that introduce the public to the extent of homosexuality in nature. The museum earned international coverage and acclaim for its courage to present what Discovery Channel and other nature-show media avoid in their laundered accounts of animal social life. Does not homosexuality in animal societies cast doubt on the idea that the only function of sexuality in nature is to ensure that eggs are fertilized with sperm? Doesn't both homosexuality in the species just mentioned, as well as the extremely frequent sexuality in alpine accentors, suggest that the natural function of sexuality is to sustain the bonds between animals that comprise the social system within which offspring are reared, and only occasionally to directly effect the fertilization of an egg with a sperm?

What then is the present-day descendant of Darwin's sexual-selection theory to do about this cornucopia of diversity in gender expression and sexuality? The last fifty years have witnessed a great expansion of Darwin's sexual-selection narrative that was originally focused rather narrowly on secondary sexual characters like peacock tails and deer antlers. I have written at length criticizing these elaborations that attempt to reconcile the extraordinary diversity of reproductive social behavior that is now known with Darwin's original narrative, and this is not the place to rehearse my criticisms in detail.[7] It suffices here to observe that these extensions invariably paint a picture of animals that "lie, cheat, and steal" from one another.

To experience hell, one need not descend to the bowels of the earth. It is sufficient to be reincarnated as a nonhuman animal here on earth. According to Darwin's original narrative, the plight of a male in any arbitrary species is to fight with other males to control access to females, or if unable to win at combat, to make the "best of a bad situation," as biologists say, by coercing a female to have sex with him against her wish and out of sight of the male that possesses her, or to masquerade as a female and surreptitiously mate with his harem, or to submit to homosexual mountings to tire the controlling male and then mate with his harem once he is exhausted. And the female . . . well, she may entrap him to remain monogamous with threats to mate elsewhere, and she may succumb to sexual violence and coercion directed against her because she "wins by losing," as one biologist put it. And so on.

The diversity of special stories manufactured to account for real-life diversity in gender expression, sexuality, and family structure among animals reads like an orgy of dime-store novels. And they have about as much basis in fact. These stories of animals lying, cheating, and stealing from one another are never independently tested, merely asserted *ex post facto* to cover up yet another species whose actual behavior departs in one major way or another from the original Darwinian templates. And these stories employ a dime-store novel's vocabulary to trivialize and pathologize any departures from the sexual-selection norm. In the primary peer-reviewed literature, males are described as being "cuckolded," females as "faithful" or "promiscuous," offspring as "legitimate" or "illegitimate," non-territory-holding males as "sexual parasites," feminine males as "female mimics" or even as "transvestite serpents," and so forth.

But if we step back from the vocabulary that poisons any claim of scientific objectivity for today's sexual-selection theory and undermines its explanatory capability, we can discern even more fundamental difficulties. Sexual-selection apologists deride my critique of how sexual-selection theory deals with diversity by claiming that such diverse species are "exceptions," and that my critique of sexual selection ignores the supposedly many cases in which the sexual-selection narrative is correct, thereby throwing the baby out with the bathwater. Well, is this rejoinder true? Is there any baby in the bathwater, or just dirty water?

I contend that sexual-selection theory does not work even with the species for which it was designed, as is becoming increasingly clear from data based on huge long-term studies. The collared flycatcher is a small migratory woodland bird of central and eastern Europe studied by Swedish investigators for over twenty-four years on the Swedish island of Gotland yielding a cumulative sample of over 8,500 individually marked individuals.[8] This species would appear to be a perfect exemplar of classic sexual-selection theory. The males have a conspicuous white spot on their foreheads, called a "badge." The background to a landmark report in 2006 perfectly sets the stage for a definitive demonstration of the sexual-selection narrative, once and for all. The investigators write: "Previous research has documented the importance of the male flycatcher's ornament (a conspicuous white forehead patch) in sexual selection through male-male competition, sperm competition, and mate choice. Sons inherit their fathers' forehead patch size. Females prefer to mate with males with a large forehead patch, especially late in the season, and receive fitness benefits from doing so." But what did these investigators actually find? First, they confirm that male badge size does have a statistically significant heritability of moderate, though not negligible magnitude ($h2[\male\text{-badge-size}] = 0.38 \pm 0.03$).

Fine so far, but now the showstopper. The major problem is a near absence of heritability in male fitness[9] ($h2[\male\text{-fitness}] = 0.03 \pm 0.01$). That is, although males may vary among themselves in how many offspring they sire, very little of this variation is genetically determined, rendering it pointless for a female to attempt to ascertain which males have the best genes, because whatever variation there is in male reproductive success has almost nothing to do with their genes. Not surprisingly then, there is almost no heritability for female choice of male badge size. That is, if a female does happen to prefer males with large badges, this preference is itself not inherited among her daughters ($h2[\female\text{-choice-of-badge-size}] = 0.03 \pm 0.01$). Therefore, these negligible heritabilities result in a zero genetic correlation between female choice and male badge size ($r[\female\text{-choice-to-}\male\text{-badge}] = -0.02 \pm 0.17$), the sine qua non of sexual selection.

Hence, the investigators conclude that "genes coding for mate choice for an ornament probably evolve by their own pathways instead of 'hitchhiking' with genes coding for the ornament." In other words, preference by females for the badge on male collared flycatchers has nothing to do with trying to endow their sons with genes for the badge in expectation that their sons will be desired as mates by future females. Instead, some immediate ecological benefit to her own reproductive success must underlie a female's choice of mate, rather than some indirect genetic benefit realized in the fitness of her sons. If a study of this intensity, rigor, and perseverance can't demonstrate sexual selection, does it even exist? Anywhere? Instead of thousands of cases that supposedly show sexual selection in nature with only a few exceptions, do we not have instead thousands of cases that depart from sexual selection's expectations, and only a few, perhaps even none, that actually confirm it?

Similarly, another class of studies has focused on what are called extra-pair matings. A "pair" in this context refers to a male and female that jointly tend eggs in a nest—the set of eggs in the nest is called a "clutch." A clutch usually contains a few eggs, one of whose parents differs from the birds tending the nest but is instead a male or female from a nearby nest. This extra-pair parentage (EPP) results from extra-pair copulation (EPC). The literature on extra-pair parentage is filled with pejorative and value-loaded language, but we pass over that matter here. This issue before us is why EPP takes place. Sexual-selection theorists postulate that EPCs represent "cheating" by a female that is paired with a genetically inferior male and that seeks a genetic upgrade by mating with an adjacent male that she ascertains to have better genes than her pair-male. A neighbor might have genes for a bigger badge in the case of the collared fly-catchers just mentioned. Indeed, the authors of the collared-flycatcher study report the following, by way of background: "Forehead patch size has also been directly implicated in a good-genes process because extra-pair offspring that are sired by highly ornamented males fledge in relatively better condition and therefore have higher survival chances than within-pair offspring."

We have already seen that data showing that female choice of the pair-male in collared flycatchers cannot be explained as a quest for his badge-size genes with which to endow her own sons. But could the "good-genes" rationale nonetheless still apply to the choice of extra-pair males? Biologists hope so. Research on EPP might reveal the importance of indirect genetic benefits without the "complication" of any direct ecological benefits that the pair-male may provide, because all the extra-pair male is presumably providing a female is his genes. However, the possibility that extra-pair males do in fact provide some form of benefit such as protection or risk sharing is never checked. By stipulation, the extra-pair male provides only his genes.

Erol Akçay has compiled a survey of over 100 studies of extra-pair paternity in birds, spanning over 50 species.[10] His manuscript reports that only 40 percent of the studies report some kind of indirect genetic benefit accruing to females that pursue extra-pair matings, and 60 percent actually found that genetic benefits were absent. These statistics might suggest that the quest for EPPs by females is the pursuit of genetic benefits, at least in a minority of cases, but not a general explanation for the phenomenon.

Yet even that summary is probably too generous. What is the null hypothesis here? It is that genes are irrelevant to female choice of mates, either within-pair or extra-pair. Therefore, by coincidence, 50 percent of the time whatever females are choosing for in their males happens to coincide with a genetically determined marker like a badge, and 50 percent of the time it doesn't coincide with a genetically determined marker. So, the statistics on EPP studies, far from showing that genetic benefits matter at least some of the time and must be counted as part of any overall explanation for the phenomenon, actually suggest that genetic benefits are completely irrelevant to female choice.

Is it surprising that detailed studies of mate choice in birds fail to confirm sexual-selection theory? I don't think so. In my opinion, it is an obvious a priori that sexual-selection theory is false because it is logically self-contradictory. The problem is simply that if females continually select males with the best genes, bad genes are quickly eliminated, so after several generations when all males have become genetically equivalent, females no longer need bother selecting males on the basis of their genes.

This difficulty is attracting increasing attention in the biological literature where it has become known as the "paradox of the lek." A recent article describes it thus: "over time directional selection should erode the genetic variation for secondary-sexual traits, so that females will no longer profit from discriminating among males based on these traits and such female preferences should eventually disappear. Yet, females continually display strong preferences for males with relatively elaborate traits. This situation has been called the 'lek paradox.'"[11] This paper places itself among seven theoretical studies since 1995 focused specifically on "resolving" the paradox. Some authors propose elaborate genetic models postulating that secondary sexual characters are polygenic and incur very high mutation rates, thereby accumulating a steady supply of bad genes to discriminate against. Such propositions have not been tested, much less validated.

The study just cited offers the most ingenious proposal to date. The authors postulate that beautiful ornaments in a male do not indicate anything about the male himself but indicate instead that the male has a good mother, because the health of the offspring depends on maternal ability. A male presumably carries genes for his mother's maternal capability, and therefore a female should choose a beautiful male as a mate to endow her daughters with good maternal capability. While this narrative gladdens my feminist heart, it doesn't solve the paradox of the lek. It replaces that paradox with another one that might be termed the "paradox of the creche." If females are selecting beautiful males because beauty indicates genetically determined maternal capability, after several generations all the females should be equally good mothers, again erasing any grounds for females choosing their mates on the basis of his genes. The growing literature of the last dozen years aimed at "resolving" the paradox of the lek is itself testimony that the paradox has not been resolved. Perhaps it cannot be resolved. Perhaps the paradox of the lek is a fundamental, fatal flaw to sexual-selection theory.

Indeed, the data on collared flycatchers is precisely what one would expect if the paradox of the lek is actually valid. The existence of a moderate heritability for male badge indicates that it is not being subject to significant directional selection, because if it were, its heritability would have dropped to near zero. However, the heritability of fitness *is* near zero among flycatcher males indicating that male flycatchers have already been selected to be well adapted genetically to their environment.[12] Therefore, the male badge must be meaningless as an indicator of good genes because all the genes are equally good by now, and so no inherited female preference for the badge evolves. The collared flycatcher data set is exactly what one would expect if sexual selection does not occur at all, in accordance with what has been anticipated in the paradox of the lek. Although biologists have been devoting increasing attention to resolving the paradox of the lek, few seem prepared to appreciate its gravity.

In summary, considering the many diverse expressions of gender and sexuality that depart from the Darwinian sexual-selection "norms," the many data that do not confirm the sexual-selection expectations, even in cases that seemed to accord with the sexual-selection norms, and the presence of irreconcilable logical self-contradictions within sexual-selection theory, I have concluded that the entire theoretical system of sexual selection is incorrect and should be abandoned. So, where does this leave us? With a rare opportunity to carry out possibly long-lasting basic research on foundational issues in evolution—to rethink the science of sex, gender, and sexuality. Since *Evolution's Rainbow* appeared, my laboratory has been primarily engaged in developing a possible alternative to the theoretical system of sexual selection that we term, "social selection."

We suggest that Darwin started off in the wrong direction to begin with when focusing on mating, which is at most only one component of reproduction. Obviously, offspring are impossible unless some mating takes place, but quantity of matings per se is only distantly related to number of offspring reared. Nonetheless, sexual selection always refers to a reproductive social behavior as comprising a "mating system." Within a mating system, evolutionary change arises from differences in "mating success," and particular behaviors are understood by how they contribute to attaining this end. Male/female social dynamics revolve around females as a "limiting resource" for males. Males compete for access to, and control of, mating opportunities with females. Sexual selection elevates a component of reproduction, namely mating, into an end in itself.

In contrast, social selection views reproductive social behavior as comprising an "offspring-rearing system." Within an offspring-rearing system, evolutionary change arises from differences in "offspring-rearing success," and particular behaviors are understood by how they contribute to building, or maintaining, the social infrastructure within which offspring are reared. Male/female social dynamics determine bargains and exchange side payments that establish control over offspring and manage the offspring-rearing social infrastructure. Beyond this primary difference in focus—mating success vs. offspring-rearing success—social selection also differs from sexual selection in offering alternative hypotheses on a variety of specific subsidiary issues that I have detailed elsewhere.[13] Here, briefly, are some of these issues.

Social selection views the advantage of sexual reproduction to be that in every generation all the matings throughout the population rebalance the portfolio of genetic diversity residing in a species' gene pool. This continual rebalancing of a species' portfolio of genetic diversity is lacking in an asexual species, which eventually suffers from overspecialization when environmental conditions fluctuate back and forth over time.[14] In contrast, sexual selection has two views of the function of sexual reproduction. On one hand, some sexual-selection theorists consider sexual reproduction to be a mechanism that eliminates deleterious mutations, assuming that genetic variation is generally harmful.[15] Alternatively, other sexual-selection theorists envision that species are in a never-ending arms race and must continually evolve to stay even. This idea is called the "Red Queen hypothesis"[16] and assumes that a sexual species can evolve a favorable genetic combination faster than an asexual population, which must await multiple favorable mutation events. Although the genetic recombination in sex does bring favorable mutations together, it also splits them apart. Calculations have shown that the time to fix a double favorable mutant in a sexual population is only marginally better, if at all, than in an asexual population, thereby rendering the Red Queen hypothesis as theoretically invalid.[17]

Social selection views the evolution of a sperm/egg size difference, which is the evolutionary origin of the male female binary, as an adaptation to physically increase the sperm/egg contact rate.[18] The contact rate between individual gametes realized when two "clouds" of gametes, both the same size, collide is lower than when two clouds collide, one cloud with relatively few large gametes (eggs) and the other with huge number of tiny gametes (sperm). Sexual selection views the evolutionary origin of the sperm/egg size difference as a conflict between gamete types, one of which becomes tiny (cheats) to minimize its commitment of resources to the zygote while the other becomes larger to compensate—a battle of the sexes writ small, and played out between the proto-egg and proto-sperm.[19]

A further issue is how sperm and egg producing ability is packaged into whole bodies, which is to say, whether a male/female binary evident at the gametic level translates into a male/female binary at the whole-organism level. Social selection views the "one-sex-in-one-body" condition as derived from the "both-sexes-in-every-body" condition seen in plants, most marine invertebrates, and many fish. Sexual selection regards the occurrence of a simultaneous or sequential ability to produce both egg and sperm within the same body as derived from an initial condition of separate sexes in distinct bodies. The sexual-selection position is not consistent with the family tree of evolutionary descendancy among major phylogenetic groups.

Social selection views the covenant between male and female as initially one of cooperation because both parties have agreed to place their genes together in a joint evolutionary bank account. Sexual conflict then may result secondarily from a failure to successfully negotiate a division of labor at offspring rearing. Sexual selection, in contrast, views sexual conflict as present initially in every male-female interaction, even seeing the very origin of the male/female binary as a battle of the gametes. According to sexual selection, any male/female co-operation that transpires is a fleeting secondary development.[20]

Another major issue is how social behavior is to be modeled. Social selection models social behavior with a two-tier formulation. The behavioral tier consists of equations from cooperative game theory that describe how animals interactively develop their time budgets into various social activities. The evolutionary tier consists of equations for how the payoff matrix in the social game evolves. The behavioral tier refers to a "within-generation time scale" and the evolutionary tier to a "between-generation time scale."[21] In a two-tier approach, a social system emerges developmentally in behavioral time from a payoff matrix that itself has evolved during evolutionary time. Behavioral activities are therefore not genetically determined in and of themselves, but they emerge indirectly from the genetic substrate that determines the evolutionary payoffs to various actions.

In contrast, sexual selection takes a single-tier approach in which behavioral activity is directly regarded as an evolutionary strategy.[22] This approach forces narratives of genetic determination for behavior, as in the "gene for" shyness or aggressiveness, bellicosity or pacifism, and so forth. For vertebrates, behaviors are well known to have very little genetic component, and even invertebrates like insects may have more learned behavior than commonly thought. Single-tier sexual-selection theory requires that social behavior be described solely through the lens of competitive game theory, whereas two-tier social-selection theory allows the behavioral tier to include cooperative game theory even though the evolutionary tier is approached as a noncooperative game. The two-tier approach to modeling allows a cooperative game of social behavior to be nested within a noncooperative evolutionary game.

The cooperative games of social-selection theory provide first-class standing for friendships. Chess and monopoly illustrate the difference between competitive and cooperative games. In chess, the players cannot communicate and are aware of only each other's moves. In Monopoly, players can talk, form partnerships, and make side payments. Similarly, in social-selection theory, organisms can make agreements and work in teams. Teamwork involves both coordinated action and the perception of a common goal. In social-selection theory, the evolutionary function of physical intimacy, including mutual grooming, preening, and yes, even homosexuality, is to keep animals literally "in touch" with each other so that they may make coordinated moves and perceive each other's welfare as contributing to their own pleasure. Being able to account evolutionarily for friendship in the sense of acting jointly and taking pleasure in one another's welfare is a central asset of social-selection theory, whereas sexual-selection theory regards friendships as manipulation in disguise.

Social selection also features different narratives for particular traits that have figured prominently in sexual-selection studies. Extra-pair parentage, as discussed previously, is viewed by sexual selection as "cheating" by a female to acquire better genes from an extra-pair male than her pair-male provides. In social-selection theory, pairing in birds is regarded as an economic arrangement, not necessarily a genetic arrangement—an agreement to work as a team of one male and one female to rear young. The paternity may be distributed across an array of nearby nests to spread the risk of mortality from weather like storms or from predators like hawks, foxes, and snakes. Furthermore, extra-pair parentage may be a side payment between adjacent pairs to stabilize a pairing arrangement when the nest qualities in the habitat are very asymmetric.[23]

Even secondary sexual traits like the peacock's tail find an alternative narrative in social-selection theory. Observation in the field often show that displays of secondary sex characters like the cock-a-doodle-doo, comb, and brilliant feathers of a rooster are not directed toward hens, but toward other males. Social selection views these traits as expensive "admission tickets" to monopolistic cliques. A male lacking these traits would be denied entry into the clique and then be unable to reproduce. Similarly, female spotted hyenas possess penises that are full replicas of the male penises. These curious traits, originally noted by Aristotle, are used by females to facilitate interaction within female power cliques. Social selection views secondary sexual characters as "social inclusionary traits" without which an animal cannot participate in the offspring-rearing social system.[24] The lack of such traits is reproductively lethal and is the source of strong selection for their elaboration and maintenance.

The flip side of social inclusion is social exclusion, "zoological prejudice." According to social-selection theory, the threat of social exclusion through zoological prejudice causes the evolution of secondary sex characters. On the other hand, species without secondary sexual characters, like guinea pigs, penguins, and so forth, presumably have social systems in which the optimal coalition is the coalition of the whole so that monopolistic cliques do not develop. Many more ideas spring forth once the chains of sexual-selection theory are cast off. The topics just mentioned offer a glimpse of exciting new directions that await evolutionary biology as it considers the extraordinary diversity of sex, gender, and sexuality now known to exist.

I turn now to mention some theological implications of the information now available about sex, gender, and sexuality in nature. The issue before most Christian denominations is whether to endorse full membership of gay, lesbian, and transgender people into communities of faith. In March 2007, the Episcopal house of bishops released a resolution adopted in response to the worldwide Anglican communion's demand that the U.S. Episcopal church cease and desist from blessing same-sex unions and ordaining noncelibate gay and lesbian bishops.[25] The resolution includes this passage:

> We proclaim the Gospel that in Christ there is no Jew or Greek, no male or female, no slave or free.
> We proclaim the Gospel that in Christ all God's children, including women, are full and equal participants in the life of Christ's Church. We proclaim the Gospel that in Christ all God's children, including gay and lesbian persons, are full and equal participants in the life of Christ's Church. We proclaim the Gospel that stands against any violence, including violence done to women and children as well as those who are persecuted because of their differences, often in the name of God.

This unusual, powerful, and moving declaration of inclusion and social justice brings tears to lesbian, gay, and transgender persons who daily suffer from the stigma that demeans their sense of self-worth, and it alleviates at least temporarily the fear the they will be forced to abandon their house of worship to pray to God on the streets along with the other dispossessed.

Yet, the bishops' resolution does not address the grounds presently used to underwrite the persecution of lesbian, gay, and transgender persons, and it is difficult to imagine how full inclusion can be realized without placing these grounds on the table for examination. Both science and religious doctrine are complicit in the persecution of gay, lesbian, and transgender people. These people are condemned as both unnatural and sinful. Indeed, to some, being unnatural is sinful in itself. Is the diversity in gender and sexuality that lesbian, gay, and transgender people embody either unnatural, sinful, or both? If the answer is yes, abiding by the bishops' resolution invites hypocrisy or some damning work-around like "love the sinner, hate the sin." If the answer is no, we should commit ourselves to cease and desist in the continued persecution of lesbian, gay, and transgender people.

Scientists are remarkably unaware of how their enterprise serves as a weapon of oppression and are happily content to think of themselves as "objective." Yet not long ago, science and medicine were actively underwriting the Nazi effort to exterminate Jews, Gypsies, gays, and the handicapped in Nazi Germany.[26] The "scientific consensus" was that these peoples contained deleterious genes that needed to be removed from the wider gene pool to protect the general good. Scientists today dismiss the role of science in Nazi Germany as an aberration that certainly isn't taking place today and, indeed, never could take place again.

Yet it is clear that evolutionary biologists have not reported on how widespread homosexuality is in nature, and have consistently downplayed its significance and often contributed to its being considered pathological. It took a young, out, gay scholar with a PhD in linguistics, Bruce Bagemihl, to summarize the citations in the primary literature to gay and gender variant social behavior.[27] No evolutionary biologist would summarize this material, and review articles on homosexuality were nonexistent. When Bagemihl's book appeared, biological reviewers trashed it—it was the work of someone untrained and somewhat naive in matters of evolutionary biology, and thus someone vulnerable, even though its contribution to revealing the extent of homosexuality in the primary scientific literature was unprecedented and revolutionary.[28]

The situation has not improved. I've documented the homophobic and transphobic reviews that greeted *Evolution's Rainbow* upon its publication a few years ago.[29] Even today, the homophobia of evolutionary biologists continues to be manifest. A recent paper[30] purporting to be the first attempt to account for the evolution of homosexuality in nature ignores the many hypotheses that view homosexuality as an adaptive trait, including the hypothesis I've advanced in prominent scientific journals that homosexuality, like other forms of physical intimacy between animals, is a mechanism to enable team work—coordinated action that furthers a common goal. Instead, the authors mention only scenarios in which homosexuality is assumed to be a deleterious trait whose presence is explained by some scheme, such as sex-antagonistic pleiotropy.[31]

This example of poor science selectively quotes pejorative hypotheses from among all those available about homosexuality in an attempt to encode homophobic narratives into the hypothesis structure of evolutionary biology. The authors are among those advocating for "sexual-conflict" as the basic male-female dynamic in animal families, and therefore must extend this philosophical stance about the ubiquity of conflict in nature to same-sex sexuality lest anyone dare think that cooperation and friendship are possible among animals. The journal, *Nature,* went on to publicize this study in a news-and-views section,[32] thereby continuing the homophobic policies of *Nature*'s editorial staff that I've previously observed. Just as Jews, Gypsies, gays, and their allies had a responsibility to challenge the science of eugenics in Nazi Germany, today, gays, lesbians, transgender people, and their allies must challenge the credibility of homophobic scientists and demand that the highest standards of science be met—that all hypotheses be put on the table, not just some subset that postulates homosexuality as a defect and that differ only in details of the genetic mechanism concocted to explain how a deleterious gene might be retained in the gene pool.

Overall, it is clear that homosexuality is not some peculiar anomaly found only in human beings. It is a natural component of the social systems of many animal species. The natural history of these species suggests that homosexuality, together with other forms of physical intimacy, sustains the social infrastructure within which offspring are raised. Homosexuality is not against nature, it is an adaptive part of nature. The pejorative stance of medicine toward such people is scientifically uninformed. To the extent that information about nature can inform theological discourse on human and biological diversity, the message for full and proper inclusion of gay, lesbian, and transgender persons is clear and unequivocal.

Notes

1. Many have since noted that sexual selection might more properly be considered as a special case of natural selection in some broad sense. Natural selection specifically on behalf of traits that promote survival might be considered natural selection in a narrow sense, and natural selection for traits that promote mating is sexual selection.

2. Darwin, *The Descent of Man, and Selection in Relation to Sex.*

3. Davies et al., "Female Control of Copulations to Maximize Male Help," 27–47.

4. Bleiweiss, "Widespread Polychromatism in Female Sunangel Hummingbirds," 291–314; Bleiweiss, "Asymmetrical Expression of Transsexual Phenotypes in Hummingbirds," 639–46.

5. Roughgarden, *Evolution's Rainbow.*

6. Bagemihl, *Biological Exuberance.*

7. Roughgarden, "The Myth of Sexual Selection," 18–23; Roughgarden et al., "Reproductive Social Behavior," 965–69; Roughgarden, "Challenging Darwin's Theory of Sexual Selection," 1–14; Roughgarden, "Social Selection vs. Sexual Selection," 421–63. Several paragraphs here closely follow my exposition in Chapter 2 of *The Genial Gene,* 23–60.

8. Qvarnström et al., "Testing the Genetics Underlying the Co-Evolution of Mate Choice and Ornament in the Wild," 84–86.

9. The heritability of fitness among females is also near zero, and is the same as that in males.

10. Akçay and Roughgarden, "Extra-Pair Reproductive Activity in Birds," 855–68.

11. Miller and Moore, "A Potential Resolution to the Lek Paradox through Indirect Genetic Effects," 1279–86.

12. These two statements draw on what is known as the "fundamental theorem of natural selection" stated by the population geneticist Ronald Fisher in his 1930 book, *The Genetical Theory of Natural Selection.* Fisher's theorem is that the rate of change of fitness during evolution by natural selection equals the additive genetic variance of fitness. "Fitness" means the ability to breed, which is measured as the product of survival probability and fecundity. The heritability is defined as the additive genetic variance

divided by the total phenotypic variance. Therefore, the heritability is zero when the additive genetic variance is zero. The way the evolutionary process works is that the speed of evolutionary change (i.e., the rate of change of fitness) starts out fast when there's lots of genetic variation in the ability of the organisms to breed. As evolution progresses, its speed slows down as the genetic variance disappears, because most of the types remaining in the population are those that breed well. The evolutionary change then grinds to a halt when all the individuals are equivalent in their ability to breed, and this state is marked by a zero heritability of fitness. This state is observed in the collared flycatchers. The existence of a moderate heritability in the badge size means that it has little contribution to male fitness because if males with large badges were being selected by females, the genetic variance in badge size would then disappear.

13. Roughgarden, "Challenging Darwin's Theory of Sexual Selection," 1–14, and "Social Selection vs. Sexual Selection," 421–63.

14. Roughgarden, "The Evolution of Sex," 934–53.

15. Haigh, "The Accumulation of Deleterious Genes in a Population—Muller's Ratchet," 251–267; Chao, "Fitness of RNA Virus Decreased by Muller's Ratchet," 454–55.

16. Van Valen, "A New Evolutionary Law," 1–30.

17. Karlin, "Sex and Infinity," 155–94; Christiansen et al., "Waiting with and without Recombination,"199–215.

18. Iyer and Roughgarden, "Origin of Male and Female."

19. Parker etal., "The Origin and Evolution of Gamete Dimorphism and the Male-Female Phenomenon," 529–53.

20. Parker, "Sexual Conflict over Mating and Fertilization," 235–59; Parker, "Behavioural Ecology," 23–56.

21. Roughgarden et al., "Reproductive Social Behavior," 965–69.

22. Smith, *Evolution and the Theory of Games.*

23. Akçay and Roughgarden, "Extra-Pair Reproductive Activity in Birds."

24. Roughgarden, *Evolution's Rainbow.*

25. http://www.episcopalchurch.org/3577_84148_ENG_HTM.htm

26. Proctor, "The Destruction of 'Lives Not Worth Living,'" 170–96.

27. Bagemihl, *Biological Exuberance.*

28. Adkins-Regan, "The Love That Dare Not Bark Its Name," 926–27; Harvey, "A Bestiary of Chaos and Biodiversity," 402–03.

29. Roughgarden, "Challenging Darwin's Theory of Sexual Selection," 1–14.

30. Gavrilets and Rice, "Genetic Models of Homosexuality," 3031–38.

31. Sex-antagonistic pleiotropy refers to a gene that is deleterious in one sex and beneficial in the other sex. In this case, a gene for homosexuality is postulated to be deleterious in males and beneficial in females.

32. Savolainen et al., "Genetics and Bisexuality," 158–59.

7

The Evolution of Sex

TERRY GRANDE AND JOEL BROWN

with Robin Colburn

Human beings within and across cultures, and within and across historical periods, have displayed, and continue to display, just about every form of sexuality and mate-bonding found across the fifty-five hundred or so species of described mammals. Harems, polyandry (one woman with multiple mates), serial polygamy, promiscuity, transgender, homosexuality, eunuchs, and non-breeding castes can all be found throughout the animal world. And, all of these are found in human beings as well—displayed by individuals, genders, cultures, and whole societies.[1] By way of example, Trevithick estimated that among the world's "marriageable males," 1 percent were in polyandrous unions, 4 percent in polygamous unions, and 4 percent in homosexual unions.[2] Furthermore, Borgerhoff Mulder in a study of the Pimbwe people of Tanzania concludes that females benefit more than males from serial monogamy.[3] Studies of human mating strategies are legion and varied.[4] Is it foolhardy or Sisyphean to suggest or even speculate on the Darwinian function of these manifold types of behavior, physiologies, and morphologies associated with gender and sexuality in human beings?

There is a large, wonderful, and often bizarre assortment of literature on human sexuality and its Darwinian context and roots. To provide a successful Darwinian perspective on human sexuality, we feel it is necessary to unbundle the sophisticated package of traits and adaptations. We aim to delve deep into the "History of Life" and focus on the appearance and likely Darwinian function of each plausible step from the exchange of genetic material in eukaryotes (bacteria and the like), through meiosis and gamete formation in single-celled protists such as *Chlamydamonas,* up to the present, where the term "sex" connotes much more than just the fusion of parental gametes into a potential offspring. This perspective aims to provide clarity, simplicity, and some thought-provoking hypotheses—some new and untested, some well developed by many others.

We aim to concatenate a series of hypotheses for the evolution of sex, genders, sexual selection, and human sexuality as it currently exists and functions. This will allow us to see sequences of adaptations as a series of unintended consequences emerging from each simple evolutionary transition. This sequence leads us to modern-day human beings, who are probably the species that is most acclimated to the environment for which they did *not* evolve. Many human behavioral traits, sexual or otherwise, are likely "evolutionary illusions," meaning that present stimuli elicit behaviors in them that may have been adaptive in the past but are not necessarily relevant in the "modern" world of human beings. The sequence of hypotheses may not be correct, and most are not mutually exclusive. Failure of one does not impugn the validity of another, but, rather, it illustrates the alternation of adaptation and unintended consequences that may have set the stage for evolution. We shall also argue that the actions and behavior of modern human beings can be understood only in the context of unintended consequences whereby behavioral adaptations are *now operating in environments and social circumstances for which they neither evolved nor are adapted in a Darwinian sense.*

In what follows, we develop three topics: First, we review the evolution of sex and the field of sexual selection where courtship, gender, gender roles, and mating are seen as adaptations. We then relate these ideas to human beings with the goal of understanding the original environmental context and Darwinian function of human sexuality. Finally, we suggest that modern human sexuality is no longer evolutionarily stable in the sense that modern humans appear to function for "utility" maximization rather than maximizing the Darwinian fitness of births and deaths. A sense of positive "utility" may have been a proximal motivator for prompting adaptive behaviors under some past circumstances. The sense of utility remains even as the adaptive behaviors for the new circumstances may have shifted. This opens the possibility that the sexuality of modern humans may be under selection to change—we may be evolving even as this is being written. Based on that premise, we can extrapolate how human beings may continue to evolve as a consequence of this marvelous disconnect between the environment for which they evolved and that which they have largely engineered for themselves.

Evolution by Natural Selection

Our discussion will be couched within three key evolutionary concepts: heritable variation, fitness, and selection. An understanding of these basic principles of evolution by natural selection (i.e., the engine of evolution that produces adaptations and new species) is foundational for this discussion. To begin, individuals within populations are variable. This variation among individuals is heritable. From parent to offspring like begets like, but with mutations producing and contributing to heritable variation.

What, then, is *fitness?* There have been many definitions proposed from comparing growth rates to comparing long-term survival rates. The textbook definition of fitness commonly used by population geneticists is: the relative reproductive success, as governed by selection in a particular environment, or the extent to which an individual contributes genes to future generations. Fitness is often referred to as "lifetime reproductive fitness," or the number of individuals/offspring an organism produces that survive to reproduce in the next generation. In this sense, sex is tightly linked to reproduction. For our purposes, however, we define fitness as the per capita growth rate of a heritable phenotype or evolutionary strategy.[5] In this way, fitness is an ecological property that relates to the "struggle for existence," where all populations have the capacity to grow exponentially under ideal conditions, but there are limits to growth. No population can grow exponentially forever.

Natural selection happens because the heritable variation influences the struggle for existence. Given the ecological and environmental conditions, particular phenotypes have higher fitness than others. Individuals with better-adapted phenotypes are more successful at surviving and reproducing. Hence, the reproduction of surviving individuals within a population is not random with respect to phenotypes. Favorable traits, those conferring higher fitness, are tied to variation. Again, individuals with more favorable traits for a given environment will better survive and reproduce. These favorable traits are said to be *selected for.* So, simply stated, natural selection preserves and selects for adaptations that allow individuals to survive and reproduce better given the circumstances.

Evolution of Sex

Our discussion of variation and diversity begins with the evolution of sex (i.e., recombination) and sex-determining systems. Before proceeding, it is important to clarify a few fundamental matters. First, there is a big difference between the scientific definition of a "theory," and the way nonscientists use the term. In a nonscientific vernacular, a theory may simply be conjecture based on intuition. In science, a theory is an explanation that is broad in scope, generates new hypotheses, and *is supported by a large body of evidence.* This distinction is crucial because although evolution exists per se, when examining past evolutionary events (as opposed to population genetics experiments involving changes in gene frequencies occurring in real time), we can only hypothesize about what might have happened. Evolutionary hypotheses (like theories) are, however, more than scenarios or mere storytelling; they are grounded in testable experiments and an understanding of the biology of extant taxa.

For example, to investigate the factors that triggered the initial invasion of the earliest tetrapods from water to land, it is reasonable to study living animals that engage in similar transitions. By doing this, we can hypothesize that the shift from aquatic to terrestrial life was triggered by factors such as a decrease in resources, decreasing reproductive opportunities, and an increase in intraspecific and interspecific competition. Living air-breathing fishes, such as the bichir (*Polypterus* sp.), the walking catfish (*Claris* sp.) and the climbing perch (*Anabas* sp.), regularly engage in terrestrial excursions in response to naturally occurring or experimentally induced dwindling resources or increased population densities.[6] Rhipidistian fishes (precursors to early tetrapods) may have also engaged in similar terrestrial sojourns. In a similar vein, the mammalian middle ear ossicles (i.e., malleus, incus, and stapes) are hypothesized to be homologous (similarity due to common ancestry) to the jaw suspension bones of fishes.[7] Data for this hypothesis come from the fossil record, and, more recently, from developmental fate map experiments (i.e., experiments designed to trace the history of cells, tissues or organ rudiments during the course of vertebrate body development).

A second preliminary matter: terminology. Before going further with the analysis, two definitions are in order. First, the terms "natural" and "nature" in this chapter simply refer to the biotic environment and the interactions of organisms within their environment. This is in contrast to an artificial or laboratory setting, where conditions can be manipulated by the experimenter. Second, "natural selection" refers to the process leading to differential reproduction or the survival of replicating organisms caused by factors that are not directed by human beings, whereas with artificial selection, there is direct human intervention (e.g., domestication of dogs, hybridization of plants or animals).

With these definitions in mind, the first question to be asked is: "What is the function of sex?" Let's consider two basic modes of reproduction: nonrecombinational (or asexual reproduction) and recombinational (i.e., sexual reproduction, defined as the exchange of genetic material between organisms). Examples of asexual reproduction include fission (e.g., anemones), cloning (e.g., hydras and amoebas) and fragmentation (e.g., strawberries). These particular organisms evolved from ancestors that have never had sex.

Some asexual organisms however, like the whiptail lizard (*Cnemidophorus* sp.), are recent evolutionary offshoots from sexual species with distinct males and females. In the case of *Cnemidophorus,* asexual reproduction doubles the population's potential for producing offspring over their sexual congeners. In some asexual organisms (e.g., fish genus *Poeciliopsis*), copulation is needed to start and stimulate reproduction, even though fertilization through the combining of gametes does not occur. Generally, in asexual species (regardless of how recent the reproductive strategy evolved), the maternal genotype is preserved because offspring are formed from a parental cell via mitosis (simple cellular division), and the potential for producing a substantial number of offspring is high. Essentially, they repeatedly make copies of themselves. In these species, genetic variation is derived only by mutation.

So, if asexual reproduction occurs in nature and sex is unnecessary to reproduce, why is recombination the dominant and common form of reproduction among vertebrates? It could be argued that the commonality of recombination demonstrates that it has some benefit. However, there are great costs to sexual reproduction, and just because a feature is conserved, or is widespread, does not necessarily mean that it is beneficial or good for the organism. Sex may simply be difficult to eliminate.

From a biological perspective, the costs and difficulties associated with sexual reproduction are numerous: Sex is energy inefficient. Sex requires two individuals (even hermaphrodites usually don't self-fertilize), sex requires the development of reproductive structures, and the act of copulation may bring increased vulnerability and therefore risk of being detected by a predator. During copulation, flight in fruit flies (genus *Drosophila*) is impaired. Male frogs chirp to attract mates, leaving them vulnerable to predation by bats foraging in the night. Although most fish and amphibians use external fertilization, internal fertilization brings male and female genitalia into intimate contact. Under these conditions, pathogens such as those found in sexually transmitted diseases (e.g., *Chlamydia psittaci*) have excellent opportunities to infect new hosts. Sex can eliminate successful genotypes. Sex is a gene-shuffler, for better or for worse. With many genetic loci contributing to fitness, recombination chops up good combinations with efficiency, leaving the adaptability of the new genotype uncertain. With recombination, each progeny is only 50 percent related to the parent, the maternal genotype is lost, and the population growth rate is slow. Sex is risky business!

Why, then, did sex evolve? And, are the conditions that favored the evolution of sex different from the conditions that now maintain sex? One of the dominant theories proposed for the evolution of sex, interestingly enough, has nothing to do with reproducing. It argues that sex/recombination evolved originally or primarily to purge, repair, or mask defective genes or DNA from the system.[8] For example, a single mutation in the gene that codes for human hemoglobin is deleterious. This deleterious allele (a) (an allele is an alternative form of a gene) in the homozygous recessive state (aa) results in an individual with sickle cell anemia. (This mutation, if you're interested, is caused by a single base substitution from thymine to adenine at nucleotide 2 in the hemoglobin gene. This mistake, in turn, codes for single amino acid change at position 6 in a protein chain of 146 amino acids long that is one of four chains comprising the hemoglobin molecule).

However, this same allele in the heterozygous state (Aa) results not only in an individual without the disease, but an individual resistant to malaria. The dominant allele (A) masks the effect of the deleterious one. This would be impossible through asexual reproduction. Margulis and Sagan argue that DNA repair is the original function of sex.[9] According to these researchers, high-intensity UV light unimpaired by the early Earth's atmosphere, imposed life-threatening danger of DNA damage. This situation required a repair mechanism. That mechanism was sex. Sex became an important source of new DNA. When the atmospheric oxygen built up as well as the ozone layer (result of proliferation of photosynthetic organisms), the UV threat was reduced. Repair by means of DNA recombination was less urgent. Sex remained as a carryover, or excess baggage, no longer needed for its optimal purpose.

Thus, the unintended consequence of the evolution of DNA repair mechanisms through recombination is genetic and phenotypic variation, and as a result, a new evolutionary pathway opened. This variation, in the words of Roughgarden, "constantly rebalances the genetic portfolio of a species and ensures its long-term survival."[10] Sexual reproduction is the dominant form of reproduction among higher organisms and has a selective advantage over asexual species, because it constantly provides new phenotypes, or evolutionary experiments, that lead to short-term gains in fitness as a buffer against extinction.

The evolution of sex remains an exciting topic. One plausible series of hypotheses sees sex as evolving as a proofreading and repair mechanism. Once it evolved, it had the unintended consequence of providing a means of sharing "opportune modifications." A beneficial mutation in one lineage could now be combined with a different beneficial mutation from another lineage. This may increase the speed of adaptive evolution and increase the likelihood that a population can successfully adapt to changing conditions. Also, sex had the unintended consequence of permitting additional methods of shuffling the genetic "deck" of two parents, coming up with many more combinations of phenotypes among their offspring. This may be advantageous for providing a form of evolutionary "bet-hedging" against environmental uncertainty.

Evolution of Genders

Meiosis is the process by which a diploid first duplicates its complement of genetic material and then divides twice to produce haploid cells. By diploid, we mean that the cell contains two sets of each gene. In the haploid condition, only one version of the gene is present in the cell. In this way, meiosis segregates the paired genes of the "parent" into "gametes." It is the fusion of parental gametes that combine to produce an "offspring." When two gametes come from the same parent, we call it "selfing," whereas gametes from different parents result in sexual reproduction. Even some single-celled protists exhibit cell division by meiosis and the production of gametes. However, these gametes are of similar size and composition, they have no "gender" identity, and each can fuse with any other to produce a new diploid cell. This is isogamy, when gametes are of equal size and can often function interchangeably. The road to genders and a concept of "maleness" versus "femaleness" requires anisogamy (the production of gametes of very different sizes).

The evolution of anisogamy had great impact, evolutionarily speaking, but it likely originally evolved for much more mundane reasons. Consider oak trees and the trade-off that can be associated with the movement of pollen, the production of ovules, and, eventually, the manufacturing of acorns: Pollen is wind-dispersed and permits individual oaks to breed with other oaks, sometimes many kilometers away. But the pollen (the "male" gamete) carries little in the way of reserves—just enough to grow a pollen tube and fuse its cell with an ovule ("female" gamete). Consider the acorn: it is rich in energy reserves that facilitate the early growth of the young oak; these reserves give the seedling a "leg up." A fair amount of growth and development can occur before the seedlings produce leaves and photosynthesis can take over. But the acorn (even with the assistance of squirrels, jays, and other seed dispersers) can expect to travel only a matter of meters to hundreds of meters from its mother.

Anisogamy may have evolved for the simple reason that there is a trade-off between the dispersible nature of a gamete (being smaller allows it to travel more easily or efficiently than if it were larger) and the inheritance of nutrients provided by the parent (larger gametes can provide more stored reserves than smaller ones). This may have selected for smaller versus larger gametes as opposed to gametes of an intermediate size. The smaller gametes, we know as sperm or pollen, and the larger, as eggs or ovules. But the original function of the small gamete may have been to aid dispersal, providing the opportunity to efficiently distribute genetic material, and the original function of the large gamete may have been to provide sufficient resources (nutrition) for the development and growth of the offspring.

Once evolved, anisogamy introduces an immediate (and perhaps cruel) asymmetry. The production of smaller gametes will generally be "cheaper," and larger gametes, more "expensive." This distinction becomes important, because in the Darwinian game of sex, each gamete that succeeds in fusing into new offspring (be it the larger or smaller) provides equal Darwinian fitness to the parent. Hence, the payoffs to maleness and femaleness are the same regardless of the asymmetries in costs of producing these gametes. So, the pollen that contributes to the acorn gives equal Darwinian rewards to the "male" parent as the "female" derives, having invested so much more in the ovule and subsequent acorn. The "maternal" side of the oak expended more energy in the effort of reproduction, while both maternal and paternal sides are equally represented, genetically speaking, by the offspring.

The asymmetry of costs introduces an evolutionary opportunity for an individual to forgo the greater effort of femaleness and flood the hermaphrodite scene with the cheaper, smaller gametes. By specializing on being "male," an individual may have been able to contribute to more than twice the number of offspring than if it stuck to the original orthodoxy of hermaphroditism. Certain species and systems of hermaphrodites may have been susceptible to invasion by males. Once males evolved and became introduced to the species, the hermaphroditic strategy may have seen a marked decline in the fitness rewards received from their production of small, male gametes. This may have selected for those hermaphrodites to have specialized in producing larger, more expensive gametes. Once males invaded the hermaphrodites, females may have been selected for in a species composed of males and hermaphrodites.

Once anisogamy evolved, the die was likely cast for many systems of hermaphrodites to give way to the evolution of males first and then the subsequent evolution of females. Quite simply, the evolution of male versus female may be a matter of the specialization of producing the smaller versus larger gamete, respectively. However, another unintended consequence cropped up—the cost of males. The small, cheap gamete selects for males to "flood the market," and, so, the large, expensive gametes become the limiting factor in the production of offspring. Perhaps hermaphrodites can produce twice as many eggs and allow for twice as many offspring as a population in which half the population simply produces the surplus gamete.

So, males may not be the optimal means of a species maximizing its output of offspring, but that is not what natural selection favors. It favors adaptations that maximize fitness, given the circumstances. Further, it appears that in the past, under many circumstances, hermaphrodites were highly susceptible to "invasion" by male phenotypes, and that once established as a system with distinct genders, hermaphrodites may no longer be the optimal strategy given these circumstances. Distinct genders become evolutionarily stable. However, the costs and benefits associated with different gender strategies likely varies considerably with the taxonomic group of the species and with environmental conditions. Small shifts in the costs and advantages associated with maleness, femaleness, and hermaphroditism might shift the gender habits of a species dramatically. The amount of variation found among plants and animals in gender strategies is phenomenal.

Among fish species, some species are monogamous while others exhibit polygamy and polyandry. It is common for fish to change sex. Anemone fish are sequential hermaphrodites alternating between male and female sexual behaviors. The timing of the sex change depends on a social trigger, such as the disappearance of a dominant male or female. The sea bass are simultaneous hermaphrodites. Some fish populations are unisexual. The Texas silverside (*Menidia clarkhubbsi*) is an all-female species. Females produce female offspring with no male involvement. As seen in the genus *Fundulus,* when population numbers become too high, some fish in the population stop reproducing altogether. Fish test the limits of species definitions. Fish often mate with fish of other species, produce fertile hybrids, backcross, and wipe out the mitochondrial DNA history of the parental species.

This diversity in sexual or reproductive strategies is not limited to fishes. Turtles exhibit temperature-dependent sex determination, while the whiptail lizard is parthenogenetic; the list goes on. Clearly, sexuality and alternative reproductive strategies are quite plastic among lower vertebrates. Variation in reproductive modes and sexuality is common among higher vertebrate and nonhuman primate populations as well. According to Bagemihl, over three hundred vertebrate species display same-sex courtship and genital contact.[11] Data suggest that in the spotted hyena, fetal hormones can actually direct adult sexuality. Sexual diversity among vertebrates is not new or surprising to biologists. If it is not a surprising phenomenon among vertebrates, why should sexual diversity and variation among human beings be surprising? In fact it is not.

HUMAN SEX AND GENDER DIVERSITY/ VARIATION/DIFFERENTIATION

Human sexual differentiation and diversity is a multifaceted and complex subject, and a comprehensive analysis of all its components is beyond the scope of this chapter. Yet, in the framework of variation, we shall consider the biological basis for sexual differentiation and its multiple permutations. Knowledge of biological variation allows us to conceptualize the less frequent middle spaces as natural, although statistically unusual.[12]

That being said, sexual reproduction usually involves differentiation into sexual forms. How this evolved is speculative. It has been hypothesized that dioecy (individuals that produce sperm or egg, but not both) evolved from a gain in genetic diversity from cross-fertilization, and that males and females are just products of simple chance mutations, and that is all.[13] Suffice it to say, in higher organisms, selection has resulted in one form producing a large gamete that provides nutrition to the developing embryo and the other producing small gametes, sperm—female and male, respectively. For many organisms, including human beings, sex determination is associated with chromosomal differences between the two sexes, the female (XX), and the male (XY), with the (Y) chromosome often being smaller and mostly inactive except for male-determining and male-fertility genes. Hence, the heterogametic (XY) can potentially produce two kinds of gametes, while (XX) can produce one.

Sex differentiation, however, is not as simple as X and Y, but the result of series of genetic and hormonal steps that influence the development of both the internal and external genitalia.[14] It is estimated that intersexed children are born at a rate of 1.7 percent each year.[15] This is most likely an underestimate, but the point is, many intersexed people exist. Genotypic variations are many. Common examples of karyotypic variation include individuals with 45 chromosomes (the standard complement is 46) with only one X (referred to as Truner's syndrome) or those with the sex chromosome arrangement of XXY (referred to as Klinefelter's syndrome). Truner's can result in females lacking secondary sex characteristics, while with Klinefelter's, men exhibit gonadal dysgenesis and breast enlargement.

Hormonal or biochemical mechanisms of human sex differentiation and their interplay with genetics are complicated, and often poorly understood. However, beginning with an undifferentiated gonad, a fetus with the XY genotype will express two genes: the SOX9 gene found in all male vertebrates, and the SRY gene found on the short arm of the Y chromosome in mammals. These genes are responsible for a series of biochemical reactions that result in the production of the testis. The developing testis in turn produces two hormones: Müllerian inhibiting substance (MIH) and testosterone. Müllerian inhibiting hormone inhibits the formation of the Müllerian duct that would eventually gives rise to the female internal genitalia (i.e., uterus, oviduct, cervix, and upper vagina). So, in the presence of MIH, the female reproductive system does not develop, but the male system does. Testosterone, as we well know, is responsible for male secondary sex characteristics and the production of DHT (dihydrotestosterone), which is involved in the morphogenesis of the penis and prostate. Two genes have been associated with the female cascade leading to the production of ovaries. These are DAX1 (antagonizes the function of SRY) and WNT4a; both genes are thought to reside on the X chromosome. So, these two genes, in the absence of SRY and SOX9, will initiate the biochemical pathway leading to the formation of the female internal genitalia and the production of estrogen.

Discordance in any one of the steps of the pathways described above may result in an intersexed individual. For example, an individual with an XY genotype could form a testis that produces testosterone, but only if MIH is inactive. This would result in an individual with male genitalia (vas deferens, epididymis) and also fallopian tubes, a uterus, and part of a vagina.[16] Another example is an individual with an XY genotype, but who is androgen-insensitive. Although testosterone is produced, there are no receptors on the cell membranes for testosterone to bond with, resulting in an individual with a feminine body type, yet no femalelike organs.

Another example of intersex results from a 5-ÿ-reductase inactivity. The enzyme 5-ÿ-reductase found on the genital skin, converts testosterone to dihydrotestosterone. In this case, male internal structures are formed, but without dihydrotestosterone, the external genitalia do not become developed, and the child is mistaken for a girl. At puberty, with an increase in the production of androgen, testosterone binds with dihydrotestosterone receptors now causing an enlargement of the penis and male characteristics. The girl finds out that she is, by some biological definition, a boy. Examples of pathway alterations are many. Randomly switching off a gene, the inactivation of an enzyme or hormone, the absence of binding sites on the surface of gonadal tissues, or alterations still unknown can result in a individual who no longer fits the stereotype but is considered intersexed. When intersexed persons are infertile (mostly but not always the case), it is likely that these conditions arose from or are maintained via natural selection. But, the large morphological and physiological shifts that can occur from just a few genes or developmental pathways illustrates how much variation in sexual morphology, physiology, and behaviors likely exists for natural selection, even in humans.

Darwin's Sexual Selection

Once genders evolved as maleness and femaleness, the evolution of more-or-less distinct gender roles could not have been far behind. Once females and males evolved, there evolved ways to best be a male or female, and these gender-conditional strategies evolved and influenced one another. Sexual selection likely began with the first species exhibiting maleness and femaleness. Sexual selection can be defined as an aspect of natural selection. Sexual selection involves adaptations with respect to courtship, morphological adornments, and other behavioral, morphological, and physiological strategies by which individuals improve the quantity or quality of matings.

Darwin's theory of sexual selection, besides tackling the question of mating strategies, resolves the paradox that many highly elaborate behaviors and morphologies seem utterly maladapted in light of natural selection aiming to improve the survivorship of a lineage. For example, the long tail feathers of male widow birds (*Euplectes progne*) make these birds easier to find and catch by predators, and growing such tail feathers takes considerable energy better spent elsewhere. In Costa Rica, male frogs calling loudly for mates may also be summoning a predatory bat rather than an eligible female. A "marsupial" mouse of the genus *Antechinus* gets so hormonally worked up during the breeding season that the males die after just one mating season.

Both early proponents and critics of natural selection felt that Darwinian evolution could not explain such traits. Enter sexual selection, stage left! Sexual selection can be seen as resulting from the differential reproductive successes due to variation among individuals in succeeding at procuring mates. Quite simply, sexual selection is an aspect of natural selection that relates mating behaviors and traits as adaptations of the organism. The object of sexual selection is to pass genes on to the next generation. In that light, sexual selection points to different selection pressures for females and males to be successful in this goal. Eggs or pregnancies are more "expensive" than ejaculations.

For example, in adult orangutans, males and females mate during brief encounters. If pregnancy occurs, the female of about 40 kilograms will carry the fetus for eight months, give birth to an $11^3/_4$ kilogram baby, nurse it for about three and a half years and protect her offspring for about seven to eight years. The 70 kilogram male on the other hand, invests a few grams of sperm that is replaced in a few hours. Apparent asymmetries in selection pressures between males and females have led to notions of behavioral consequences and limits on fitness. Male reproductive success in most species is limited by access to mates, and the reproductive success of females in most species is limited by the capacity to successfully produce and rear offspring. Male reproductive success is challenged by male-to-male competition (i.e., intrasexual selection), and female reproductive success is played out in female choice and competition for males. Succinctly, while Roughgarden and Fausto-Sterling take issue with this kind of descriptive language, many biologists see sexual selection most often manifesting in this way: males are aggressive, competitive, and promiscuous; females are choosy.

Moreover, in contrast with some of Roughgarden's claims found in this volume and elsewhere, we contend that the existence of sexual dimorphism is a common fact. But what do these differences amount to? The work of Wikelski and colleagues and Wikelski and Trillmich suggest that sexual dimorphism in marine iguanas (*Amblyrhynchus cristatus*) living in the Galápagos is the result of sexual selection.[17] In this species, males are larger than females. Large males eat more algae and, thus, gather more energy. However, they also expend considerably more energy on metabolism. Studies further showed that in two consecutive years, small iguanas ran a net energy surplus, but large iguanas ran a net energy deficit.

Interestingly, data from these studies show that the optimum body size for iguanas (balancing energetics) is that of a larger female. Why, then, are the males so much larger than the females? This seems nonadaptive. These researchers argue that this is consistent with sexual selection. The males stake out territories where the females bask freely. The larger males can hold on to territories better than smaller ones. Holding territories involves combat. Male iguanas get bigger because bigger males get more mates, and, therefore, pass on more of their "big-male" genes.

Sexual selection and male combat has also been reported in the form of infanticide in lions and chimpanzees. In lions, new male leaders of the pride will kill all cubs not yet weaned (these cubs do not have the new pride leader's genes). As a result, the females return to breeding condition about eight months earlier than they otherwise would have. According to Bertram, infanticide by males is the cause of about 25 percent of all cub deaths in the first year and over 10 percent of all lion mortality.[18]

Turning to females, in general, females exhibit some degree of mate choice, but not always (e.g., lion-tail macaque). Are females, and in some cases males, choosing mates because of their good genes? Probably not, and perhaps the more interesting questions to ask are: "Why do females mate?" and, "Is mating always directly related to reproduction?" Roughgarden cautions that preconceived notions of male-female relationships may lead researchers to miss what is really going on in nature.[19] Is there more going on in nature than passing genes to the next generation? The answer is yes.

We will not reiterate the entire argument that Roughgarden makes in this volume and elsewhere. We will, however, point to a few observations Roughgarden makes that offer expanded explanations for sexuality. Females choose mates for a variety of reasons. Females often mate with males with no sperm transferred (for reasons such as to guard against infanticide, keep males around longer, and distribute the probability of paternity to ensure offspring safety). As Roughgarden points out, sex facilitates cooperation and sharing. In bonobo populations, female same-sex relations are used for reconciliation, to help integrate new arrivals into the group, and to help form coalitions against males. As a consequence, the group now better controls resources. In addition, in nature, females often express phenotypic traits stereotypic of males, and in many fish species conventional sex roles are reversed (such as among pipefish and sea horses). In general, there is much going on in nature that does not fit the strict sexual selection model.

Does this mean that, according to Roughgarden, sexual selection is falsified? No, not in our view. Instead, we contend that we simply have another unintended consequence of adaptive evolution. As soon as courtship, sexuality, and gender roles (or lack thereof) evolve for the purposes of procreation, these behaviors, morphologies, and physiologies may now, in unintended ways, serve to promote other fitness-enhancing activities. Among these are reciprocal altruism, jockeying for position within a dominance hierarchy, signaling or advertising of other behavioral intents or aptitudes, bonding for social foraging, and presenting novel avenues for aggression or cooperation.

Thus, sexual selection likely, seamlessly but unintentionally, opens the door for Roughgarden's "social selection." Social selection does not replace sexual selection; it simply expands the fitness-enhancing roles that sexuality can play once courtship, gender roles, and mating strategies have evolved as adaptations for procreation. In fact, nothing precludes these other social values of sexuality from eventually appearing more conspicuous than the actual production of offspring. That elephant noses do so much more than just breathing does not negate the inclusion of elephants in a study on breathing. It just shows (beautifully) how a trait evolving for one purpose in a group of organisms can unintentionally and wonderfully become adapted for so much more than its original purpose.

This point is worthy of discussion, but the basic tenet of natural or sexual selection is survival and reproduction in order to successfully pass genes on to the next generation. Although many of the sexual strategies mentioned previously may not directly result in reproduction, they aid in the survival of either offspring (continuing the lineage) or adults, who, in turn, will survive to reproduce (i.e., the goal of sexual selection).

Sexuality and Human Beings

Like many other mammals, females lactate and males cannot. The unique production of milk, from highly modified sweat glands evolved uniquely within *Mammalia,* gives females a special role in child rearing that is not necessarily seen in other species. Human beings show elements of the stereotypic roles of males emphasizing quantity and females emphasizing quality, which are typical of mammals. No mystery there, just the history of life and the evolutionary constraints and opportunities dealt to mammals. Mammals have distinct sex chromosomes wherein the male chromosome is a rather degenerate and relatively nonoperative form of the X chromosome. We, like other mammals, exhibit sex-linked traits in which only the maternal gene is manifested in males—greatly increasing the likelihood of things like color blindness and hemophilia occurring in males versus females. During their lifetime, and unlike fish and many other species, human males cannot morph into females, or vice versa, as a conditional strategy. In many ways, maleness and femaleness appear to be much more deeply channelized in mammals than other organisms.

Like many mammals, human beings can exhibit monogamy, polygamy, and, to a lesser degree, polyandry and various degrees of serial polygamy or extrapair copulations. It has been argued that because of these behaviors, females can benefit from protection, food resources, and other necessities from a male mate, and often, "in exchange" for this, will provide a greater "certainty" of paternity. If the certainty of paternity is diminished, individual males are not inclined to participate in the care of offspring that may not be their own.

So, in what regard have human beings gone beyond their traditional mammalian blueprint? Human beings seem intelligent, but in what way? Human communication, sense of self, and empathy all seem to point to an adaptation for playing nonzero sum social games more than perhaps any other organism. By "game," we mean that an individual's ideal behavior depends upon the behaviors of others. One is not master of one's fate, but somewhat at the mercy of the behavior of others. One's own behavior still matters, of course. Yet, "social" refers to games and interactions occurring between humans rather than between humans and nonhumans. How human beings behave toward others, and vice versa, may have significance beyond that yet seen in other species. By "nonzero," we refer to the capacity to select behaviors that both influence the size of the collective whole and the portion of the whole that each individual in the social group gets.

In all, human beings have evolved a phenomenal capacity for recognizing the consequences of each person's actions for the group as well as for the individual. Human beings obsess, much more so than other organisms, over matters such as motive, social responsibility, social contracts, and inequity. It is probable that very early, with the last explosion of human beings out of Africa, social games became paramount to the normal factors influencing how most humans became adapted to acquire and use resources and avoid hazards. This self-referential social environment then became the most important factor determining fecundity and survivorship and ongoing human evolution.

UTILITY VERSUS FITNESS MAXIMIZATION

If the previous discussion is a plausible Darwinian scenario for human beings, the human sense of morality, ethics, guilt, shame, vengeance, and so forth becomes the behavioral modulators that make human beings good at playing this sort of Darwinian game. Human preoccupation with motives over facts, reputation, reciprocity, friendship, and other social tags may be adaptive conditioners for developing social contracts and making the best of one's situation within these constructs. Consequently, it is not so surprising that human beings manifest just about every form of sexuality found among mammals, and that this sexuality begins to resemble much more social selection. Copulation and courtship become behaviors associated with the larger social game between and within the sexes.

Then something unintended happened . . . human capacity for technology created a world that, in recent centuries, has seen an accelerated change in the environment. Human beings have engineered entirely novel circumstances, and an accelerating gap exists between factors that limit their population size. Currently, resources and food exceed that required for simple subsistence (relative to the ecosystems of other organisms). In the Darwinian struggle for existence, improvements in resource availability (or safety) results in higher populations that require resources, thereby limiting growth and keeping the population within a range. Human beings exist in a world for which they did not evolve, and in reaction to this world, normal motivators and emotions may no longer serve their original Darwinian purpose. In a sense, human beings are no longer fitness maximizers, but utility maximizers. The sense of well-being that might be interpreted as utility or satisfaction may simply be the unintended manifestation of human emotions and social behaviors operating far beyond the circumstances for which they evolved.

IS NATURAL SELECTION IN HUMAN BEINGS DEAD?

Let us finally turn to the topic of fitness. Fitness, in the Darwinian sense, is once again tied to reproductive success (i.e., essentially how many offspring an organism produces in its lifetime). An individual who has one offspring in his or her lifetime is less fit, in the Darwinian sense, than one who produces more. Broadening this to a global scale, how does fitness play out among human populations? Demographics show for example, that people living in the United States and most of Europe, where birth rates are down, have lower reproductive fitness in comparison to people living in developing countries, where birth rates are up (e.g., in Sweden, the birth rate is 10.2 births/1000 people; in Tanzania, the birth rate is 35.95 births/1000 people). If the birth rate demographics change, so will fitness.

Up until now, we have been talking about human beings who reproduce (i.e., heterosexual males and females). What about people who do not fit this definition of sexuality? Nonreproductive sexual behavior seems nonadaptive, counterintuitive to selection, and in time, should disappear. This, however, doesn't seem to be the case. So, what is going on? Are other modes of sexuality adaptive? Has evolutionary theory (i.e., selection) failed us in understanding human sexuality? Why does homosexuality persist in our population if it is not adaptive? Or, is it?[20]

One can only speculate. However, one question to be asked is: "Do homosexuals really have lower lifetime reproductive success?" This is inconclusive due to lack of solid data, but many self-described homosexuals do have children. Homosexuality can possibly be perceived as adaptive if one considers kin-selection. One would not have to produce offspring to ensure genetic survival assuming that one's close relatives actually reproduce. In many species (e.g., ants), not all individuals of the population reproduce. Those that do not reproduce help ensure that genetically related offspring survive. A social contract among population members was forged that resulted in apparent altruism.

Maybe sexuality is not entirely about reproduction. Social selection theory provides that sex is not just about exchanging gametes, but it is also about forming bonds and negotiating access to the resources necessary for survival. If this is true, negotiations will take place as much within sexes as between sexes. If sex becomes primarily about relationships, and only secondarily about gamete exchange, it would explain why more sex than reproduction occurs. Homosexuality functions in the same way as heterosexuality with respect to negotiating social bonds and access to resources. So then, what can biology tell us about human sexuality? Maybe that human sexual behavior does not differ from that of other vertebrates—that sexuality is very complex, involving a sophisticated interplay between biology and the environment in which human beings live (i.e., the social contracts made with society).

Can an understanding of evolution help predict the future of human sexuality? Probably some, but not completely. Environmental feedback becomes extremely important when dealing with natural selection in species displaying high degrees of sociality and cultural inheritance. Changes in one trait via natural selection can influence and be influenced by the population's social interactions and culture. The environmental factors may amplify, mitigate, or completely change the fitness value of a given trait. This makes predicting human evolution rather difficult. In other words, all bets are off.

Finally, what does such thinking mean for Christians and sexual ethics? In the spirit of interdisciplinary dialogue, which is what this book intends, we would like to offer up a provocative question: If the function(s) of sex/gender is constantly evolving and allows room—even if unintentionally—for nonprocreative expressions, can Christian traditions claim a timeless and ordained model of human sexual behavior? While we will not attempt an answer, we think such a complex question might point a way forward for ongoing reflection and discussion among various disciplines and communities.

Notes

Robin Colburn is a member of the Research and Collections Committee, Field Museum, and Science Committee, Chicago Botanical Garden.

1. Buss and Schmitt, "Sexual Strategies Theory."
2. Trevithick, "On a Human Preference for Monandry."
3. Borgerhoff Mulder, "Serial Monogamy as Polygyny or Polyandry?"
4. Buss, *The Evolution of Desire*.
5. Vincent and Brown, *Evolutionary Game Theory, Natural Selection, and Darwinian Dynamics*.
6. Liem, "Functional Design of the Air Ventilation Apparatus and Overland Excursions by Teleosts."
7. Shubin, *Your Inner Fish*.
8. Bernstein et al., "Genetic Damage, Mutation, and the Evolution of Sex."
9. Margulis and Sagan, *Origins of Sex*.
10. Roughgarden, "The Evolution of Sex."
11. Bagemihl, *Biological Exuberance*.

12. Fausto-Sterling, *Sexing the Body.*

13. Strickberger, *Evolution.*

14. Kemp, "The Role of Genes and Hormones in Sexual Differentiation."

15. Fausto-Sterling, *Sexing the Body.*

16. Kemp, "The Role of Genes and Hormones in Sexual Differentiation."

17. Wikelski et al., "Energy Limits to Body Size in a Grazing Reptile"; Wikelski and Trillmich, "Body Size and Sexual Size Dimorphism in Marine Iguanas Fluctuate."

18. Bertram, "Social Factors Influencing Reproduction in Wild Lions."

19. Roughgarden, *Evolution's Rainbow.*

20. Some researchers have hypothesized that sexuality has a genetic component, and quest for the "gay gene" goes on (Hamer and Copland, *The Science of Desire*). Data from a "twins study" is suggestive of a genetic component. For example, if one dizygotic male twin is homosexual, his brother has a one-in-four likelihood of also being gay. If one monozygotic male twin is homosexual, his identical brother has a 50% chance of also being gay. If such a gene (or genes) exists, it might remain in the population because it is adaptive. Could the gay gene be x-linked (i.e., found on the x-chromosome)? Could it increase the reproductive success of men who carry it? The presence of such a gene does not mean that every man carrying it is gay, or not exclusively so. Suppose the gene (assuming there is one), attributed to excessive "female" behavior in male homosexuality does not benefit the lineage of the male, but the presence of that gene in his sister increases the likelihood of her successful mating and subsequent reproduction. This would explain homosexuality as a reasonable "selection." Maybe the gene really does not have a selective advantage, but survives evolution because of a high rate of mutation? Could a gay gene have evolved in the first place? Are there genes for sexuality in general? There are genes for sex determination, so why not genes for sexuality?

8

Interpreting the Theology of Creation
Binary Gender in Catholic Thought

JOHN MCCARTHY

*It is necessary first of all to emphasize that the theology of
procreation is called to grow in its relation to its articulation in
the theology of creation. . . . Thus can be seen the importance of
the affirmations we made earlier when we indicated that every
theology of human procreation, must, in the last analysis, stem
from the theology of creation.* "Male and female, he created
them," Genesis states; it is immediately suggested that the
man and the woman are called to be a sign of the gift without
reserve of the Father to the Son and of the Son to the Father,
in a loving embrace that proceeds from the Father and from
the Son and has the Holy Spirit for its name. This Trinitarian
reality of the divine family, and with it the notion of the man
and woman as being created in the image of God and called by
him to collaborate in the transmission of the gift of life, must be
borne in mind in all theological reflection and in all preaching
on the family.

—Pontifical Counsel for the Family,
The Family in Human Procreation, no. 27.

Addressed to Pope Benedict XVI, this 2006 document from the Pontifical Counsel for the Family is presented as both a study of the role of procreation within the Roman Catholic teaching on the family and as a tribute to
the current pope's dedication to, and defense of, truth. Prominent is the importance of the theology of creation, as foundational not only for a theology of
procreation, but also for the understanding of man and woman as "the image
of God" and "collaborators in the transmission of life." The logic of this Roman
Catholic position on sexuality and family involves an interlocking coherence
of several positions, foregrounding the God-given gift of life, the worth of the
human person at all stages of life, the importance of marriage and family unity,

the right relationship of truth and freedom, and the divinely created order of humanity as male and female.

Because the Roman Catholic position on sexuality is so thoroughly integrated with the Church's central theological teachings on God as love, Trinity, and the source of life, it is not interpretively responsible to isolate any single topic from this matrix as if it were the key to the Roman Catholic position on right-ordered sexual activity. And yet not all the elements of the Roman Catholic position bear equal weight in supporting many of the Church's more normative positions. The Pontifical Council's document is helpful in identifying the role of the theology of creation as foundational for informing positions on sexuality, procreation, and family.

With this in mind, I want to consider the role of interpretation in a theology of creation for warranting the right understanding of human gender as either male or female (a gender binary). Assuming that "exclusive gender binarity" has been a fundamental aspect of Roman Catholic thought on human sexuality, and that this binarity is normatively important in the moral evaluation of certain acts and conditions, the question that I want to explore is this: how might interpretation within a theology of creation inform an authentic Roman Catholic position on gender binarity and thus on sexuality and gender? The position that I will take is roughly this: By looking at gender through an understanding of how a Christian theology of creation mediates the fundamental binary of God/not-God, an authentically Christian discussion might be opened within the Roman Catholic understanding of sexuality looking to a theology of creation as the place from which it is "to grow." In other words, the very theology of creation, presented so richly and diversely in the Catholic tradition itself, may very well provide ways in which this tradition can see beyond too literal a reading of the human as either, and exclusively, "male" or "female."

The Hermeneutics of Exclusive Gender Binarity in Recent Roman Catholic Documents

The phrase, "exclusive gender binarity," is not a phrase that is found in any contemporary ecclesial document, and so it must be recognized that I am using this term to summarily interpret the various ways in which these documents advance the understanding of the human person as exclusively and fundamentally—that is, ontologically and theologically—either male or female. Direct statements, like the one found in the *Letter to the Bishops of The Catholic Church on The Collaboration of Men and Women in The Church and The World,*—"Male and female are thus revealed as belonging ontologically to creation and destined to outlast the present time, evidently in a transfigured form"[1]—are not the norm. More frequently, exclusive gender binarity is embedded almost axiomatically in larger positions on the value of life, the importance of marriage, or the triune nature of God. But it is clear that this view of exclusive gender binarity is taught and assumed throughout contemporary church statements.

When orientation and actions associated with gender are addressed in Church statements, they are addressed with authoritative intent insofar as the Church sees a theological, moral, pastoral, or pedagogical dimension involved. This has an important bearing on how the documents consider both the role of the biological and social sciences in the discussion of gender, as well as the type of contribution that the Church understands itself to be required to make. The biological sciences are, by and large, understood to make a significant contribution to our knowledge of the genetic, biochemical, and evolutionary understanding of gender and sexuality. Sociology and anthropology contribute information regarding the frequency and social meaning of sexual behaviors. And psychology is informative for the understanding of the stages of human development and counseling practices that are involved with pastoral care and the informed pedagogy that is the responsibility of the Catholic family.[2] The authoritative contribution that the Church understands itself to make is in the area of clarifying "the meaning of existence and of human progress" in light of information gained from the sciences. It is clear, however, that theological, moral, pastoral, or pedagogical understanding does not take its principles or warranting structures from science or from the results of scientific investigation.[3]

If exclusive gender binarity is less argued than implied in Church statements, and if natural and social scientific research is not fundamentally determinative for responsible ecclesial positions on gender issues, how might the Catholic position on exclusive gender binarity be argued? The likely argument would be one that made clear the indispensable role of exclusive gender binarity for the integrated theological, moral, pastoral, and pedagogical position of the Church on life and human sexuality. And indeed this position is a highly integrated understanding involving the human person; the dignity and equality of the genders; the fundamental relationship of love to human sexuality; the importance of the family and marriage; the inseparability of the unitive and procreative functions of sexuality; the sacramental role of sexuality in the ongoing presence of the triune God in human life; the importance of chastity; and the increasing threat that many forms of modern science, popular culture, media, advertising, and education create for a true understanding of the meaning of human existence.

Again it may be helpful to turn to a specific statement in order to recognize the interlocked theological and moral reasoning as well as the relation of this authoritative reasoning to science:

This guide is meant to be neither a treatise of moral theology nor a compendium of psychology. But it does owe much to the gains of science, to the socio-cultural conditions of the family, and to the proclamation of gospel values which are always new and can be incarnated in a concrete way in every age.

3. In this field, the church is strengthened by some unquestionable certainties that have also guided the preparation of this document. Love is a gift of God, nourished by and expressed in the encounter of man and woman. Love is thus a positive force directed toward their growth in maturity as persons. In the plan of life which represents each person's vocation, love is also a precious source for the self giving which all men and women are called to make for their own self-realization and happiness. In fact, man [sic] is called to love as an incarnate spirit, that is soul and body in the unity of the person. Human love hence embraces the body, and the body also expresses spiritual love. Therefore, sexuality is not something purely biological; rather it concerns the intimate nucleus of the person. The use of sexuality as physical giving has its own truth and reaches its full meaning when it expresses the personal giving of man and woman even unto death. As with the whole of the person's life, love is exposed to the frailty brought about by original sin, a frailty experienced today in many socio-cultural contexts marked by strong negative influences, at times deviant and traumatic.[4]

Such an integral statement on the right understanding of sexuality and gender is quite typical of Catholic teaching. Reduced to its minimum, the Catholic position is this: starting from the understanding of the human being as an embodied person, created by, and oriented to, a loving God of life, gender, and sexual activity find their proper role when clearly located within this order. Human sexuality is a participation in, and an expression of, the relationship with this loving Triune God of life. As embodied in creation where the human person, man and woman, is in the image of God, sexual activity participates in the creative transmission of life, both unitively and procreatively. Sexuality is a form of human, loving activity that achieves a special kind of unity signaled by the desire of woman and man for each other and nurtured within the relationship of marriage.

While we may learn more about the history, sociology, psychology, or biology of all this, there are unchanging created values that must guide as well as protect the expression of sexual love between human beings. Expressions of human sexual activity that do not embody these unchanging values are theologically, ontologically, and morally incomplete; "disordered"; or wrong. And because they are so, they could endanger what a properly understood pastoral and pedagogical program should be as explained and exercised by the Catholic Church. Conversely, human sexuality understood properly within this theological and moral framework ought to guide correct pastoral and pedagogical practice.

Within this matrix of reasoned values is the argument for exclusive gender binarity. Maybe the most direct recent statement to this effect is the following from the 2004 document, *On the Collaboration of Man and Woman:*

> A second tendency emerges in the wake of the first. In order to avoid the domination of one sex or the other, their differences tend to be denied, viewed as mere effects of historical and cultural conditioning. In this perspective, physical difference, termed *sex,* is minimized, while the purely cultural element, termed *gender,* is emphasized to the maximum and held to be primary. The obscuring of the difference or duality of the sexes has enormous consequences on a variety of levels. This theory of the human person, intended to promote prospects for equality of women through liberation from biological determinism, has in reality inspired ideologies which, for example, call into question the family, in its natural two-parent structure of mother and father, and make sexuality and heterosexuality virtually equivalent, in a new model of polymorphous sexuality.
>
> While the immediate roots of this second tendency are found in the context of reflection on women's roles, its deeper motivation must be sought in the human attempt to be freed from one's biological conditioning. According to this perspective, human nature in itself does not possess characteristics in an absolute manner: all persons can and ought to constitute themselves as they like, since they are free from every predetermination linked to their essential constitution.
>
> This perspective has many consequences. Above all it strengthens the idea that the liberation of women entails criticism of Sacred Scripture, which would be seen as handing on a patriarchal conception of God nourished by an essentially male-dominated culture. Second, this tendency would consider as lacking in importance and relevance the fact that the Son of God assumed human nature in its male form.
>
> In the face of these currents of thought, the church, enlightened by faith in Jesus Christ, speaks instead of *active collaboration* between the sexes precisely in the recognition of the difference between man and woman.[5]

The Moral Hermeneutic of Creation and Natural Order

If the above is a relatively accurate statement of the integral Roman Catholic theological position on gender binarity, how more specifically related would this "called to grow in relation" be to its articulation in the theology of creation? One way to get at this question is to examine first the way in which the theological understanding of creation contributes to a style of moral reasoning. For the most part the theological understanding of human sexuality is related to a theology of creation through some form of interpretation of the first two chapters of Genesis.

Mulieris dignitatem is a good example. It asserts the importance of the Genesis language in this way:

Let us enter into the setting of the Biblical "beginning." In it the revealed truth concerning man as "the image and likeness" of God constitutes the immutable basis of all Christian anthropology. "God created man in his own image, in the image of God he created him; male and female he created them." (Gen 1:27) This concise passage contains the fundamental anthropological truths: man [sic] is the high point of the whole order of creation in the visible world; the human race, which takes its origin from the calling into existence of man and woman, crowns the whole work of creation; both man and woman are human beings to an equal degree, both created in God's image. This image and likeness of God which is essential for the human being, is passed on by the man and woman, as spouses and parents, to their descendants: "be fruitful and multiply, and fill the earth and subdue it." (Gen 1:28) The creator entrusts dominion over the earth to the human race, to all persons, to all men and women, who derive their dignity and vocation from the common "beginning."[6]

Emphasized in this document's subsequent discussion is the role of understanding Genesis as a moral warrant for maintaining the essential equality of men and women as persons as well as an essential, relational unity of male and female that draws "the man" from "his father and mother" in order to become "one flesh."

Indeed, this creation passage is identified as instituting marriage, as well as disclosing a natural order of sexual love in creation.

Thus in the same context as the creation of man and woman, the Biblical account speaks of God's institution of marriage as an indispensable condition for the transmission of life to new generations, the transmission of life to which marriage and conjugal love are by their nature ordered: "be fruitful and multiply, and fill the earth and subdue it." (Gen 1:28)[7]

Along with the "revealed moral order" spoken about in this understanding of the Genesis creation story—which, to be sure, is by no means idiosyncratic to *Muliaris dignitatem*—an allusion is made to the order of nature. It is this conjunction of a revealed moral order with a natural moral order known through the right understanding of the creation story that typifies a Roman Catholic style of moral reasoning in matters relating to gender.

To see the close connection between a revealed and natural moral order characteristic of this style of moral reasoning, it might be helpful to look at the *Letter to the Bishops of the Catholic Church on the Pastoral Care of Homosexual Persons*. Here we find some of the careful distinctions that are part of this form of moral approach:

However, the Catholic moral viewpoint is founded on human reason illumined by faith and is consciously motivated by the desire to do the will of God our Father. The church is thus in a position to learn from scientific discovery but also to transcend the horizons of science and to be confident that her more global vision does greater justice to the rich reality of the human person in his spiritual and physical dimensions, created by God and heir, by grace, to eternal life . . . [referring to the 1975 document, *On Certain Questions Concerning Sexual Ethics*]. At the same time the Congregation took note of the distinction commonly drawn between the homosexual condition or tendency and individual homosexual acts. These were described as deprived of their essential and indispensable finality, as being intrinsically disordered, and able in no case to be approved of . . . Although the particular inclination of the homosexual person is not a sin, it is a more or less strong tendency ordered toward an intrinsic moral evil; and thus the inclination itself must be seen as an objective disorder.[8]

Beginning with the final observation in this passage, namely a distinction between a condition or tendency and an act, the moral reasoning suggests at least four perspectives in the proper analysis of homosexual behavior. At one level, the behavior is a set of actions and at this level the actions may be described as disordered, that is, not in accord with the natural end of sexual acts. At a second level, homosexuality is a condition or tendency, and at this level, it is not capable of being described as sinful. At the same time, the inclination itself is objectively disordered, that is, the tendency to homosexual behavior is not in accord with the natural end of sexual behavior as a whole. At a third level the individual, whose condition is homosexual, is a human person with reason, and thus is capable of moral understanding consistent with the Catholic viewpoint precisely because of a created natural moral order. And fourth, the individual person's natural understanding is further situated in the revealed awareness that the end of all human life is eternal life with God, the gifted end of such created life.

Thus in this style of moral reasoning the theology of creation is understood to have a direct bearing on the understanding of human acts through the recognition of an order of nature based in the creative action of God. While scientific research may be able to inform or clarify this order, it is the responsibility of the Church to identify and proclaim this order as the truth of human life. This position, clearly detailed for instance in the encyclical, *Veritatis splendor,* links the human person "created by God," to the rationally understood moral order in which the final goal of all creation is union with God:

The morality of acts is defined by the relationship of man's [*sic*] freedom with the authentic good. This good is established as the eternal law by divine wisdom, which orders every being toward its end: this eternal law is known both by man's natural reason (hence it is "natural law"), and—in an integral and perfect way—by God's supernatural revelation (hence it is called "divine law"). Acting is morally good when the choices of freedom are in conformity with man's true good and thus express the voluntary ordering of the person toward his ultimate end: God himself, the supreme good in whom man finds his full and perfect happiness.[9]

The Moral Hermeneutic of Creation, Personhood, and Difference

While it is clear that this style of moral reasoning, which interprets the creation story through a hermeneutic of natural moral order, is characteristic of the way in which the theology of creation is related to moral positions on gender, it is also clear that in the same documents a theology of creation is not reduced to a hermeneutic of natural order. And this is important to recognize, for if the "theology of procreation is called to grow in its relation to its articulation in the theology of creation," we might look to other aspects of the theology of creation in these documents. This is not done without attention to the integrity of the Catholic position on life and love. It is done because of the theology of creation itself. So if we were to look to other hermeneutical options for a theology of creation, what might they look like? Let me suggest just two.

CREATION OF PERSONS

A prominent aspect of contemporary Roman Catholic teaching on the creation of human life in the image of God is the emphasis on the human being as a person created for love. In these discussions the contribution of a theology of creation seems less focused on the issue of natural order, and more focused on the essential God-related constitution of the human as a person. *Mulieris dignitatem* states it this way:

> With these words, the council text presents a summary of the whole truth about man and woman—the truth which is already outlined in the first chapters of the book of Genesis, and which is the structural basis of Biblical and Christian anthropology. Man—whether man or woman—is the only being among the creatures of this visible world that God the creator "has willed for its own sake"; that creature is thus a person. Being a person means striving towards self realization (the Council text speaks of self discovery), which can only be achieved "through a sincere gift of self." The model for this interpretation of the person is God himself as trinity, as the communion of persons. To say that man is created in the image and likeness of God means that man is called to exist "for" others, to become a gift.[10]

Roman Catholic teaching on sexuality often refers to the Trinitarian understanding of God in order to better explain the theological importance of love and to relate the generativity of human love to Trinitarian generativity.

At the same time, the Trinitarian understanding is not limited to this observation. The association of creation with the Trinitarian God also leads to a non-binary/unifying understanding of each person—"whether man or woman"—as creature "willed for [her/his] own sake"—as a person established as gift and called to be a gift for others. Rather than creation understood primarily as order, creation is *gift,* with the person placed within the "gifted order" rather than "natural order." This shift orients moral understanding toward both "personhood" and the responsibility of being the gift for another. Such a direction in the theology of creation tends then to lead the Roman Catholic discussion to the discussion of dignity and respect.[11] Even within the Congregation for the Doctrine of the Faith's (CDF) letter on the *Pastoral Care of Homosexual Persons,* this same vision of the role of creation can be seen:

> The human person, made in the image and likeness of God, can hardly be adequately described by a reductionistic reference to his or her sexual orientation. Everyone living on the face of the earth has personal problems and difficulties but challenges to growth, strengths, talents and gifts as well. To date, the church provides a badly needed context for the care of the human person when she refuses to consider the person as a "heterosexual" or a "homosexual" and insists that every person has a fundamental identity: the creature of God and by grace, his child and heir to eternal life.[12]

CREATION AND DIFFERENCE

Since the Genesis accounts of creation are used in modern ecclesial documents, the awareness of contemporary scriptural scholarship is to be expected. When related to other biblical passages, the Genesis creation accounts are placed within a much more textured theology of creation, particularly when read together with Christological passages speaking about the New Adam, or the new creation, or the Kingdom of God. In general, this eschatological aspect of the theology of creation tends to mute division and difference, especially as the result of sin. Recreation imagery speaks of restoration, unity, and the unity of all in the true image of God, Jesus:

> Herein lies the absolute originality of the gospel: many times in the Old Testament, in order to intervene in the history of his people, God addressed himself to women, as in the case of the mother of Samuel and Samson. However to make his covenant with humanity, he addressed himself only to men: Noah, Abraham, and Moses. At the beginning of the new covenant, which is to be eternal and irrevocable, there is a woman: the Virgin of Nazareth. It is a sign that points to the fact that "in Jesus Christ there is neither male nor female" (Gal. 3: 28). In Christ the mutual opposition between man and woman—which is the inheritance of original sin—is essentially overcome. "For you are all one in Jesus Christ," Saint Paul will write.[13]

But along with this more classical form of interpreting Biblical passages by reading them alongside other passages, there is a clear awareness that the passages speaking about the image and likeness of God must be read with something akin to a "creation hermeneutic."

And this "creation hermeneutic" discloses one of the central features of a theology of creation, namely that "creation" names a relationship of difference: all that is not God is created, and all that is created is not God. For *Mulieris dignitatem* this aspect of the theology of creation is given significant attention:

> At the same time, the language of the Bible is sufficiently precise to indicate the limits of "likeness," the limits of the "analogy." For Biblical revelation says that, while man's [*sic*] "likeness" to God is true, that "non likeness" which separates the whole of creation from creator is still more essentially true. Although man is created in God's likeness, God does not cease to be for him the one "who dwells in unapproachable light" (I Tim. 6:16): he is the "Different One," by essence the "totally Other." . . . This characteristic of Biblical language—it's [*sic*] anthropomorphic way of speaking about God—points indirectly to the mystery of the eternal "generating" which belongs to the inner life of God. Nevertheless, in itself this "generating" has neither "masculine" nor "feminine" qualities. It is by nature totally divine. It is spiritual in the most perfect way, since "God is spirit" (Jn. 4: 28) and possesses no property typical of the body, neither "feminine" nor "masculine."[14]

This form of a "creation hermeneutic," developed specifically for the discussion of the language of "image and likeness to God," must disturb any literal correlation of the human gender to the generative and creative powers of the Trinitarian God. While the document is clearly guarding against language that would attribute to God male or female characteristics, the "creation hermeneutic" emphasizes the difference between creator and creation as "more essentially true" than the likeness regarding the central correlation of generativity and gender. Such a "creation hermeneutic" must also affect the tendency of either a natural law or a Trinitarian creation hermeneutic to read the phrase, "in the image of God he created them, male and female he created them," as if this gender binarity is a privileged moment in which difference and otherness are momentarily suspended in favor of an almost literal disclosure of the "essence" or "will" of God.

The Breadth of Creation Theology

Thus far I have discussed several features in contemporary Roman Catholic thinking which are deeply informed by a theology of creation: the image of God, male and female, interpreted as a gender-exclusive binary; the role of science in informing the discussion of the image of God; the relation of creation to a natural order, rationally known; the style of moral reasoning this utilizes; and some of the places in contemporary ecclesial statements that display other approaches to a theology of creation than one that prioritizes the hermeneutic of natural moral order. What follows now is a constructive suggestion about how other hermeneutical avenues within a theology of creation might allow the "theology of procreation to grow in its relation to its articulation in the theology of creation," precisely by attending less exclusively to a hermeneutic of natural order and by engaging with these other authentically Christian aspects of a theology of creation.

But before going any further with this argument, I want to be clear about what is being claimed: This is not a constructive offering about what ought to be the place of various natural, life, or social sciences in the discussions of sexuality and gender within a Catholic context; it is not an argument about whether the more public and official statements of the Roman Catholic Church about sexuality and gender are right or wrong, too restrictive, outdated, or whatever; it is not an argument about the values instantiated by the normative discourse of these statements. I think that arguments can be made about all of these issues and more, many of which are engaged in other chapters of this collection.

My concern is one that seems logically and practically fundamental, namely: the warranting structures for the Catholic Church's position on sexuality and gender practices as based on an interpretation of the Genesis story. The Church's reading of the story is presented as an ultimately authoritative reading, one that presents, for theological reasons, why the story should be read in this way and what the normative results are. Other ways of reading and sources of commentary—even those contained in the Church's teachings—are systematically marginalized in the process, at least in so far as they might affect the normative discourse established by a reading of creation.

Thus, my concern is not about the exclusivity of gender, although there may be clear implications for these discussions. It is about the *authoritative reading of a creation narrative within the theology of creation,* specifically whether the normative reading is broadly informed enough by the Catholic position on creation. So here is where I hope to contribute to a discussion of a faithful Catholic account of sexuality and gender: Are the statements of the Roman Catholic Church on sexuality and gender informed deeply enough by a Catholic theological reflection on creation, especially when an understanding of "creation" is so foundational to the normative discourse? My constructive argument is that the normative reading of creation exemplified in the texts and positions above is an overly restrictive reading of the Catholic tradition on creation. Let me finally then offer an outline of how the Catholic position on sexuality and gender might "grow in its relation to its articulation in a theology of creation."

INTERPRETING CREATION AS BINARY DIFFERENCE

First, within the Catholic theological tradition(s) "big words" like "salvation, God, church, good," and, of course, "creation" have a fair amount of semantic flexibility. These words are part of several forms of discourse, all of which have taken place in the history of the Catholic tradition(s): liturgical, pastoral, doctrinal, spiritual, theological, polemical, apologetic, and more. In approaching any of these ideas, the first, hermeneutically responsible, theological approach to a long history of usage like this is to recognize that these words have "semantic tendencies" that are the result of various, sometimes complementary, sometimes conflicting, discourse situations. These "semantic tendencies" are not what we think of as precise definitions: a "precise concept" in theology is not one that is marked primarily by a univocal, or very restrictive range of meaning. A "precise term" in theology, is one where the range of questions and issues that the term has been used to deal with is clearly known and respected. Precision works differently in theology than it does in more empirically based discourses. A precise understanding of "creation" is not, theologically, achieved by limiting the semantic range to as narrow a field as possible. That may in fact be a loss of precision.

Second, in its most basic sense, theology is the ordered process of considering whatever we are talking about in relation to God (*theos*). This, of course, gets quickly complicated and controversial, but if we lose sight of this basic perspective in theology, forms of more authoritarian and sectarian discourse are not far behind. In this theological perspective there is no real "doctrine of creation" in Catholic thought. More properly, there is a doctrine (and basically this term simply means a tradition of discussions that sometimes come to more classic statements, sometimes not) of "God as Creator." This is the theological statement of "creation." This distinction is hermeneutically quite important. "Creation" is, theologically, first and foremost a "relationship" between what is God and what is not God. It is not first and foremost a moment, a beginning of everything, nature, matter, the nonhuman, or whatever else often comes to mind when we use the term "creation" in ordinary discourse. Theologically, God is "uncreated," and everything else is "created."

Third, the relation of God and not-God presents more than a few questions. There are lots of ways of raising these questions. The questions about the relation may be "why" questions, "how" questions, "when" questions, or even "come on now; you can't be serious" questions. But all of these questions probe the issue of "difference." The central theological issue of creation as relationship in the theological tradition is, I would argue, this "betweenness" that is the God, not-God relation. In the Catholic theological tradition there are several ways of dealing with this, since this tradition surely wants to maintain that there is a relationship, and that it is ongoing, and that it matters. So everything from "trinity," to "incarnation," to "grace," to "salvation," to "church," to "sacraments," to "spirituality," to "ethics," and more can be seen as playing some role in this "betweenness" that is structured by the idea of God as creator.

Fourth, from this point of view the real issue in a creation theology is "theo-diversity," that is, the many ways in which this relationship of difference negotiates, theologically and ontologically, the central incarnational conviction of Christianity. Creation as structured in the Catholic tradition involves one dominant binary pair: *uncreated/created*. At the same time, it maintains that this binary pair is *not* a radical difference but a relationship, even a very bodily relationship. Within the discussion of the doctrine of "the incarnation" in the Catholic tradition, the positions that get roundly trounced are ones that maintain that either the historical person of Jesus just "seemed" to have a body (and thus did not really bridge the "betweeness" of uncreated/created) or was not really God (and thus did not really bridge the "betweenness" of uncreated/created). And it is Christ who is seen to be the "true image" of God. The "theo-diversity" issue in the Catholic tradition is full of discussions where the foundational binary of creation—uncreated/created—is always overcome: icons, sacraments, salvation, and, most centrally, in the person of Jesus.

Fifth, the tradition of theological reflection on creation in the Catholic tradition is not one that puts a lot of attention on creation as the establishment of eternal, unchanging laws. The situation seems to be quite the contrary: the tradition speaks of the relationship between created and uncreated as certainly quite changeable. Creation involves re-creation, the New Adam, the resurrected body, the eschatological. Indeed, many of these notions are seen as foundational for interpreting Jesus as "announcing the coming of the kingdom," which is not portrayed as "keeping eternal and unchangeable laws in place." It is portrayed much more like Dorothy's realization: "Toto, I've got a feeling were not in Kansas anymore." What is permanent and unchangeable in the theology of creation is that there is a relationship, that the "betweenness" is not a "no-man's" or "no-God's" land, that it is ongoing, that it unites, and that it matters.

Sixth, the "betweeness" staked out in the theology of creation will always be negotiating the "icon-idol" issue, namely, when does the "created" become transparent to the "uncreated," the essence of the "icon" (and thus allow the "betweeness" to be in play). and when does the "created" substitute itself for the "uncreated," the essence of the "idol" (and thus stop the play of the "betweeness"). The book of Job may be important on this score. The official interlocutors of Job are sure that they represent the right interpretation of Job's plight. And they have every good reason for thinking so. They are looking at the situation through the lens of a covenant theology which was a prominent part of "a story" that, for their interpretive intentions, was "the story." In light of this, Job should have been able to select from his memory what got him into the unhappy position he was in, and he should have been able to determine what his future project was to be.

The problem for Job was that this story of covenant just did not fit his life. What intervenes in the situation is the well-known response of God to both Job and his interlocutors, a response that is a description of creation (Job 38–42). It can hardly be said that "God's" response portrays any sense that the tradition of the rational covenant order has got it right. In a rather angry and terrifying reminder that we don't know what we are talking about when we are talking about created orders, God announces his "wrath" against those who are spokespersons for the covenant position, and, in an echo of the Genesis command to be fruitful and multiply, gives Job twice as much as he had before his proverbial roof caved in. It is surely helpful to note in any theology of creation that Genesis 1 is not the only story in the Christian book.

Seventh, one final suggestion for a direction in a more poetically informed normativity in regard to a theology of creation: What happens in the Christian story when God does a little bit of "theo-bending" and "creation-bending" with the "incarnation"? It seems a lot of people in the narrative of the Gospel get really uncomfortable and upset. The fundamental binary interpretive categories that have to do with God and idols, worship and blasphemy, God and human have been violated. The response is the religious version of "Disgusting! Impossible! Disordered!" There may be several reasons for the final response—the crucifixion—to this bending of good order, but surely one of the important reasons is that norms, much beyond the ethical and determined by a larger religious narrative, were understood to be violated.

By playing in the "betweenness" the figure of Jesus becomes "strange"—indeed, a kind of stranger, one who "looks like us" but you can't quite trust is like "us." There are many ways to handle strangers: build higher and longer walls; invoke laws; avoid them; subjugate them; send them back to where they were, feed them, invite them in, look at them; redefine "us-ness." A normative response to "strangeness" is surely one way, but not the only way. Various forms of "re-creation" are also options suggested by a theology of creation. If creation is eternal and unchangeable order, "the strange" becomes eternally outside and potentially chaotic. But if creation is itself the relation of constantly transacted "betweeness," the ethical perspective might more authentically develop a poetics of hospitality and invitation to the neighbor rather than continue a certain hermeneutic of divine and natural law.

And, indeed, something of this theo-poetic combination of the eschatological reordering of a new creation combined with the emphasis upon agapic love is advocated in Benedict XVI's 2005 encyclical, *Deus caritas est*. The encyclical, fittingly, culminates by directly associating "creation in the image of God" not with difference, natural order, or binarity, but with love. "Love is possible, and we are able to practice it because we are created in the image of God. To experience love and in this way to cause the light of God to enter into the world—this is the invitation I would like to extend with the present Encyclical."[15]

This understanding and invitation for love is lavishly developed by Benedict XVI through the reflection on a variety of important theological topics: agapic love, the image of God/image of man in the light of this love, the meaning of incarnate love in Jesus and the Church, the practice of love in communion and charity, and the hope that this love can bring to the world.

What is important to notice is the interpretive, theo-poetic vision this brings to the characteristically highly integrated and normative theological reflections on matters like gender. To be sure, the underlying hermeneutical issue in the Catholic theology of creation is not whether a hermeneutic of order, natural law, new creation, image of God, trinity, or the like are part of the complexity of a more fully developed understanding. The more pressing hermeneutical issue is the interpretive hierarchy of value accorded to the symbols within a theology of creation. If, as Benedict XVI suggests, Christianity is such a love-suffused tradition, the odd, disordered, unexpected axiology of love of neighbor and invitation to the stranger must, theologically, have an interpretive impact on the theology of creation.

The stranger is indeed an "other" to me, but the "binary other," is also a person, and in the process of recognizing and loving this person I am not only tolerating the binary other but recognizing this "binariness" as the very structure of "the neighbor." Becoming a neighbor is, theologically, participation in the love of God that makes the human a person. Were a theology of creation that informs a Catholic position on sexuality to orient itself around this axiology of neighbor, hospitality, and invitation, it might do well to read the creation as deeply eschatological, recognizing the "odd order" of love.

When Benedict XVI does this, the image and implication of the parable of the Good Samaritan as the abolition of previous limits is highlighted. A theo-poetic axiology of binarity as love, hospitality, and invitation, rather than a determination of the limits of love by a "natural order" of exclusive gender binarity, might then be deeply informed by Benedict's words:

> The parable of the Good Samaritan (cf. Lk 10:25–37) offers two particularly important clarifications. Until that time, the concept of "neighbor" was understood as referring essentially to one's countrymen and to foreigners who had settled in the land of Israel; in other words, to the closely knit community of a single country or people. This limit is now abolished. Anyone who needs me, and whom

I can help, is my neighbor. The concept of "neighbor" is now universalized, yet it remains concrete. Despite being extended to all mankind, it is not reduced to a generic, abstract and undemanding expression of love, but calls for my own practical commitment here and now. The church has the duty to interpret ever anew this relationship between near and far with regard to the actual daily life of her members. Lastly, we should especially mention the great parable of the Last Judgment (cf. Matt. 25:31–46), in which love becomes the criterion for the definitive decision about a human life's worth or lack thereof. Jesus identifies himself with those in need, with the hungry, the thirsty, the stranger, the naked, the sick and those in prison. "As you did it to one of the least of these my brethren, you did it to me" (Matt. 25:40). Love of God and love of neighbor have become one: in the least of the brethren we find Jesus himself, and in Jesus we find God.[16]

Notes

1. Congregation for the Doctrine of the Faith [hereafter CDF], *Letter to the Bishops of The Catholic Church on the Collaboration of Men and Women in the Church and in the World,* 2004, no. 12.

2. The following statement is representative of the informative role given the sciences: "God created man in his own image and likeness: 'male and female he created them' (Gen. 1:27), entrusting to them the task of 'having dominion over the earth' (Gen. 1:28). Basic scientific research and applied research constitute a significant expression of this dominion of man over creation. Science and technology are valuable resources for man when placed at his service and when they prompt his integral development for the benefit of all; but they cannot of themselves show the meaning of existence and of human progress. Being ordered to man who initiates and develops them, they draw from the person and his moral values the indication of their purpose and the awareness of their limits." CDF, *Instruction on Respect for Human Life in Its Origin and on the Dignity of Procreation: Replies to Certain Questions of the Day,* 1987, no. 2.

3. Representative of the interaction between the sciences and the authoritative responsibility of the Church is the following statement from John Paul II's encyclical, *Veritatis splendor:* "Certainly moral theology and its teaching are meeting with particular difficulty today. Because the church's morality necessarily involves a normative dimension, moral theology cannot be reduced to a body of knowledge worked out purely in the context of the so-called behavioral sciences. The latter are concerned with the phenomenon of morality as a historical and social fact; moral theology however, while needing to make use of the behavioral and natural sciences, does not rely on the results of formal empirical observation or phenomenological understanding alone. Indeed the relevance of the behavioral sciences for moral theology must always be measured against the primordial question: What is good or evil? What must be done to have eternal life? . . . In fact, while the behavioral sciences, like all experimental sciences, develop an empirical and statistical concept of 'normality,' faith teaches that this normality itself bears the traces of a fall from an original situation—in other words, it is affected by sin. Only Christian faith points out to man the way to return to 'the

beginning' (c.f. Mt. 19:8), a way which is often quite different from that of empirical normality. Hence the behavioral sciences, despite the great value of the information which they provide, cannot be considered decisive indications of moral norms. It is the gospel which reveals the full truth about man and his moral journey, and thus enlightens and admonishes sinners; it proclaims to them God's mercy, which is constantly at work to preserve them from both despair and their inability fully to know and keep God's law and from the presumption that they can be saved without merit. God also reminds sinners of the joy of forgiveness, which alone grants the strength to see in the moral law of liberating truth, a grace filled source of hope, a path of life." John Paul II, *Veritatis splendor*, no. 111–12.

4. Pontifical Council for the Family, *The Truth And Meaning of Human Sexuality*, no. 2–3.

5. Pontifical Council for the Family, *The Family and Human Procreation*, no. 13–14.

6. John Paul II, *Mulieris dignitatem*, 1988, no. 6.

7. Ibid.

8. CDF, *Letter to the Bishops of the Catholic Church on the Pastoral Care of Homosexual Persons*, no. 2–3.

9. *Veritatis splendor*, no. 72.

10. *Mulieris dignitatem*, no. 7.

11. Benedict XVI's recent encyclical, *Deus caritas est*, gives a good example of this when it associates the "image of God" language with the form of action and respect characteristic of institutions like the Church governed by charity: "Here I would clearly affirm what my great predecessor John Paul II wrote in his Encyclical, *Sollicitudo Rei Socialis*, when he asserted the readiness of the Catholic church to cooperate with charitable agencies of these churches and communities, since all have the same fundamental motivation and look for the same goal: a true humanism, which acknowledges that man is made in the image of God and wants to help him live in a way consonant with that dignity. His Encyclical *Ut Unim Sint* emphasized that the building of a better world requires Christians to speak with the united voice in working to inculcate 'respect for the rights and needs of everyone, especially the poor, the lonely and the defenseless.'" Benedict XVI, *Deus caritas est*, no. 30. By uniting the Genesis language of "the image of God" with true humanity, the moral reasoning highlights respect for the dignity of all, precisely because they are created in the image of God. In a passage like this respect for dignity is not prescribed as a pastoral fall back position. Rather the recognition of created personhood eclipses other understandings.

12. *Letter to the Bishops of the Catholic Church on the Pastoral Care of Homosexual Persons*, no. 16.

13. *Mulieris dignitatem*, no. 11.

14. Ibid., no. 8.

15. *Deus caritas est*, no. 39.

16. Ibid., no. 15.

9

"Passing" and Identity

A Literary Perspective on Gender and Sexual Diversity

PAMELA L. CAUGHIE

> From the idea that the self is not given to us,
> I think that there is only one practical consequence:
> we have to create ourselves as a work of art.
>
> —Michel Foucault, "On the Genealogy of Ethics," 351

Sex, French historian Michel Foucault tells us, has a history. And gender, I would add, has a rhetoric. My goal in this chapter is to bring literature and gender theory into our discussions of sexual diversity and gender identity. The interdisciplinary nature of this anthology reminds us of the importance of defining our concepts; for we don't all mean the same thing by even the most commonsense terms, such as *truth* or *identity*.

For the literary scholar as for the gender theorist, truth is what makes sense in terms of a particular narrative. What is true is not simply that which corresponds to the real; rather, what is true is *what is accepted as being true* within a given discourse, institution, or discipline. Unlike biologists, literary scholars don't ask "Is it true?" but "How is it true?" This question requires interrogating the normative standards by which claims of truth, authenticity, and legitimacy are established. And that means learning to read people the way many of us have learned to read literature, taking into account the discursive structures, the narrative conventions, the character assignments, and the historical and social contexts within which narratives operate.

From a literary perspective, then, gender and sexual identity depend upon the narrative tropes we have available for representing our experiences. Tropes are figures of speech that, when repeated in cultural narratives and across disciplines, can easily become "naturalized" so that the figure becomes the "ground." Or, as Foucault puts it, what we assume to be the origin or "real thing" is an *effect* produced by discourse (specialized knowledge). Building on the work of Foucault, the contemporary gender theorists discussed below argue that gender is a rhetorical and linguistic construction, making this theory all the more compatible with literary studies.

Anne Fausto-Sterling, professor of biology and gender studies at Brown University, writes:

> European and American culture is deeply devoted to the idea that there are only two sexes. Even our language refuses other possibilities [. . .]. But if the state and legal system has an interest in maintaining only two sexes, our collective biological bodies do not. While male and female stand on the extreme ends of a biological continuum, there are many other bodies [. . .] that evidently mix together anatomical components conventionally attributed to both males and females. [. . .] If nature really offers us more than two sexes, then it follows that our current notions of masculinity and femininity are cultural *conceits*.[1]

Fausto-Sterling's assertion that gender is a conceit, an extended metaphor or cultural trope, echoes scholars in other fields. For example, in "The Egg and the Sperm," Emily Martin, an anthropologist of science, argues that culture shapes our understanding of nature. Analyzing accounts of fertilization in biology textbooks for their metaphoric language, Martin exposes the normative assumptions about gender that structure descriptions of natural processes. Eggs behave "femininely" (they are passive and dependent), sperms "masculinely" (they are active, even aggressive). When we think we are learning about natural processes, Martin says, we are actually learning about cultural beliefs "as if they were part of nature"[2] and so cultural assumptions about masculinity and femininity appear natural.[3] While the biologist (Fausto-Sterling) argues that cultural notions of gender are based upon an erroneous concept of sex, the anthropologist (Martin) argues that descriptions of sex are thoroughly imbued with cultural assumptions about gender. That is, the two notions of identity—as sex and as gender—can never be clearly distinguished, nor can we escape the implications of metaphoric language.

"It may seem only natural to those who equate gender with biology," writes Susan Bordo in *The Male Body*, "that the presence of a penis would confirm that the body who has it is male."[4] Bordo uses a scene from Neil Jordan's film *The Crying Game* to make us rethink the tendency to equate gender with biology. Dil, a male-to-female transsexual who has not had sexual reassignment surgery (SRS), goes home with Fergus, an unsuspecting IRA agent who has fallen for her. When Dil disrobes, Fergus vomits at the sight of the penis on the woman he desires. Dil's body creates what Marjorie Garber terms "category crisis";[5] for despite the penis, Dil is still a girl, Bordo writes, "according to the cultural grammar of gender" (23), that is, her dress, her body type, her walk, her speech—in short, her performance of femininity. Bordo's point is that "the body [is] not only a physical entity" but also "a cultural form that carries *meaning* with it" (26). "The way we experience our bodies is powerfully affected by the cultural metaphors that are available to us. [. . .] Whatever the input of biology, culture is always present, providing language and categories to help interpret that input" (38–39).

Bordo suggests that cultural conceits interpret a prior sexed reality. Judith Butler argues instead that gender precedes sex. Butler's *Gender Trouble* challenges the notion of sex as primary or prior, the idea that sexual identity exists before culture. "*Gender is a kind of imitation for which there is no original,*" Butler asserts, using "catachresis," a figure of speech for which there is no literal referent.[6] Following Foucault, Butler argues that to be sexed is to be subject to the law, that is, to discourses that categorize sex. There is no doer behind the deed, but rather, the deed creates the doer.[7] This is known as the "theory of performativity."[8]

The power, if not priority, of cultural conceits is exposed by other feminist philosophers. Marilyn Frye, for example, has argued that the demand for two distinct sexes requires that we insistently and continually announce our sex: "One must be female or male, actively," she says, asserting our sex again and again, through costume and performance. In doing so, we collude with the medical, legal, psychiatric, and philosophical discourses that create a world of sex dimorphism, "a world in which it seems to us that we *could* never mistake a woman for a man or a man for a woman,"[9] the kind of mistake that makes Fergus retch.

Sandra Lee Bartky makes a similar point in discussing "feminine bodily discipline." "Discipline," as Foucault defines it, is an imposed system of authority that produces a subject who is subjected to institutionalized forms of knowledge.[10] Dieting is one such disciplinary practice that "produce[s] a modality of embodiment that is peculiarly feminine" (27). It is not that dieting is always and only a "form of subjection," Bartky says, but that "it is not always easy in the case of women to distinguish what is done for the sake of physical fitness from what is done in obedience to the requirements of femininity" (29). The fact that we do not formally punish women who do not comply, writes Bartky, "does not mean that a woman who is unable or unwilling to submit herself to the appropriate body discipline will face no sanctions at all" (38). (One sanction, she notes, is "the refusal of male patronage," which can have severe consequences, such as the loss of intimacy and income potential.) Disciplinary practices become internalized, incorporated into the "structure of the self," thereby producing a form of psychic oppression or self-policing, but also—and importantly—providing the individual with a sense of identity, a "sense of oneself as a distinct and valuable individual" (38).

So what feminism is really calling for in resisting forms of oppression is women's relinquishment of a certain sense of identity. Not just our beliefs or our politics, but our very identity as women, and men, is at stake in feminist resistance to disciplinary regimes that produce femininity and masculinity. Insofar as one must have a sexed identity, that one must *be* male or female actively, as Frye says, any political project that seeks to dismantle the sex/gender system will be a threat to identity. No wonder feminism is so menacing to so many people.

The transgender movement, as Fausto-Sterling and others argue, can potentially provide a means of resisting disciplinary practices that insist on a dimorphic system of gender. To effect a sexual revolution, transgender theory, Bartky says, must reconceptualize sexual difference itself. "Femininity as a certain 'style of the flesh,'" she says, "will have to be surpassed in the direction of something quite different—not masculinity, which is in many ways only its mirror opposite, but a radical and as yet unimagined transformation of the [gendered] body."[11] That transformation is transgender.[12]

Yet some gender theorists, such as Bernice Hausman, argue that the transgendered person may reinforce normative assumptions about gender and sex that feminist and gender scholars want to challenge. The demand that we recognize more diversity in human sexuality and gender identity can serve to buttress the notion that gender is essential to society and to personal identity. Similarly, the argument that transsexuals should have access to medical procedures as a way of aligning one's body with one's felt identity has sparked debate. Some argue that a truly inclusive society would make such surgeries unnecessary, others that using an illness model for transsexuals (where they are seen to have an ailment that requires treatment) risks pathologizing the condition.[13] Where Jay Prosser says that treatments such as sexual reassignment surgery produce new narratives of the body that "allow the transsexual individual to emerge as a subject," Hausman responds that the illness model of transsexualism ends up changing the body to comply with the narratives, reinforcing rather than dismantling the sex/gender system.[14]

Feminists and gender theorists like Bordo, Hausman, and Bartky seek to challenge the gendered meanings attached to bodies and "embodied practices"; these theorists conceive gender as an analytic concept, not as some truth about the body. Gender, writes Hausman; "is always only a mode of perceiving and experiencing the world that is attributed and *narrativized.*"[15] While transgender theorists who argue for sexual reassignment surgery strive to make bodies more coherent within the current social organization, feminist gender theorists work to transform that organization in such as way as "to loosen its grip on our bodies."[16]

It is Michel Foucault who is, perhaps, the best-known theorist of sex and sexuality and whose work informs many of the theories presented above. In *The History of Sexuality*, Foucault argues that "sex" is a complex idea that is produced by a range of social and discursive practices. "The notion of 'sex,'" writes Foucault, "made it possible to group together, in an artificial unity, anatomical elements, biological functions, conducts, sensations, pleasures; and it enabled one to make use of this fictitious unity as a causal principle, an omnipresent meaning, a secret to be discovered everywhere."[17] Foucault doesn't deny biological sex and sexual organs; rather, he is saying that in the nineteenth century a range of very different things were grouped together under the category of "sex": biological distinctions, body parts, psychological reactions, social meanings.[18] More importantly, Foucault shows how sex came to be treated as fundamental to the *identity* of the individual ("homosexual" and "heterosexual" came to name identities rather than simply to distinguish practices). Then, after this artificial unity is in place, it becomes the *cause* for the very things that had been grouped together to create the concept in the first place. Something posited becomes the secret to uncover, the key to identity or behavior. Thus, far from being something natural that the Victorians repressed, Foucault says, "sex" was produced, talked about everywhere in various nineteenth-century discourses. (Surprisingly, perhaps, Joan Roughgarden offered a similar insight in a seminar gathering that preceded the writing of these chapters when she remarked, "The wild type may be a myth that we're burdened with.")

In 1980 Foucault published *Herculine Barbin*, the memoirs of a nineteenth-century French hermaphrodite whose life story became the subject of medical discourses dating from 1865. *Herculine Barbin* also contains several medical reports published in that decade, along with a scandalous fictional account published in Germany in 1893 by Oscar Panizza. It thus serves as an excellent text for illustrating the different ways sexual identity is "narrativized." Foucault opens this work with a provocative question: "Do we *truly* need a *true* sex?"[19] The reiteration of *true* already raises doubts.

As a historian, Foucault responds by tracing changes in how hermaphrodites (intersexuals in today's language) have been treated by law and in medicine. In the Middle Ages and the Renaissance, he says, the one who named the child (typically the godfather) chose the sex at the time of baptism, but upon reaching adulthood and before entering into marriage, the individual could decide which sex he/she preferred, the only stipulation being that the sex couldn't be changed again later. Yet in the eighteenth and nineteenth centuries, "biological theories of sexuality, juridical conceptions of the individual, forms of administrative control" (such as birth certificates), and moral theories aligned not just to determine but to *necessitate* a "true" sex.[20] Individual choice gave way to medical, legal, or moral expertise.

Challenges—legal, political, social—to sexual dimorphism in the late nineteenth and early twentieth centuries had a profound effect on concepts of sexual identity. "Homosexuals," only recently named (c. 1870), were showing up in ever-increasing numbers, notes Alice Dreger, and the rise of gynecology and more medical attention meant more hermaphrodites were being discovered as well. Around the same time, Freud was challenging the sacrosanct nineteenth-century belief in a natural, biologically rooted sexual dimorphism by posing a universal bisexuality in children. In the 1910s, anthropologists were writing about the Native American "Berdache," men living and dressing as women.[21] By the 1920s, transsexual surgery was being performed in Germany (Meyerowitz). On the social scene, women were advocating for equal rights and access to the professions and universities, and the "new woman," a cultural icon of this era, was cutting her hair, wearing pants, smoking in public, playing sports, and traveling alone, challenging notions of femininity. No wonder Virginia Woolf wrote in 1929, "No age can ever have been as stridently sex-conscious as our own."[22] In response, doctors, anxious over the increasing instability of sexual identities and worried that "physical sexual confusion" could "amplify social sexual confusion," offered various definitions of sex meant to maintain clearly demarcated lines between two sexes and thereby stem confusion.[23]

A highly publicized trial in Britain in 1929 captures the anxiety at this time over changing understandings of sexual and gender identity as well as an emerging sense of identity as something one *acquires* rather than something one *is*. Colonel Victor Barker, alias Valerie Arkell-Smith, was tried for perjury in 1929 for passing as a man. In this case, the identity of her "true" sex was not in dispute, nor was her sexuality the legal issue, even though she was married to a woman. The perjury trial centered instead on what we now call "gender identity," raising questions about how to classify this anomalous woman. Was she a sexual invert? A pervert? A "new woman"? The spectacle of Arkell-Smith, with closely cropped hair and forced to wear a dress throughout the trial, testifying that she had always felt herself to be a man before a male judge wearing a gown and a wig of curls must have struck witnesses even then as perverse. Add to this that the trial took place at a time when the androgynous fashions of the day (pants for women, the Sheik look for men) and the "new woman" were arousing anxiety over what were thought to be clear-cut sex differences and we can see that whatever the outcome of Arkell-Smith's trial for fraud, the trial itself exposed the fraudulence of the sex/gender system.[24]

In "Passing as Modernism," I argue that "passing" (the strategic adoption of a culturally empowered identity, as in passing as white or passing as a man) is the peculiar identification at the heart of turn-of-the-century modernism. The fluidity of identity boundaries that we have come to identify with our contemporary era has as much to do with the historical conditions of the early twentieth century as with recent (trans)gender theory. Insofar as all passing is marked by a discrepancy between what one professes to be and how one is actually positioned in a society, institution, or discourse, it mimes the *experi-*

ence of identity in a world in which, as evidenced above, boundaries of all kinds were being crossed. Passing, in my use, signifies the *dynamics* of identity and identification—the social, cultural, and psychological processes by which a subject comes to understand his or her identity in relation to others. Although passing is often understood as fraudulence or betrayal, as a sin against authenticity, authenticity is itself a historically specific concept, one whose meaning and value were being challenged in the modernist era. If authenticity and identity are cultural conceits, not truths, then we can rethink "passing." Whereas some might argue that a "passer" like Arkell-Smith lived a lie, I would say instead that she *refused* to live a conventional fiction.

While we might agree, says Foucault, that one could "adopt a sex that is not biologically his [or her] own," as transsexuals do, such a possibility does not dispel the belief in a true sex, nor does it undo the "essential relationships between sex and truth."[25] It is precisely this relationship between identity (sexual or racial) and truth that makes "passing" seem morally and politically reprehensible, and that leads people to condemn passing as deceit or fraud. We may no longer believe that a feminine man or a masculine woman or same-sex relations are crimes, Foucault says, but we retain "the suspicion that they are fictions, which, whether involuntary or self-indulgent, [. . .] it would be better to dispel" (x). A reading of *Herculine Barbin*, along with Virginia Woolf's 1928 novel, *Orlando*, supports the view that sexual identities are, indeed, fictions, or in Roughgarden's words, "myths that we are burdened with."

In brief, here is the story of Alexina, a nineteenth-century French hermaphrodite, whose life was the subject of much medical and legal discussion and of whom Foucault writes in *Herculine Barbin*. After her father dies when she is very young and her mother cannot afford to support her, Alexina spends her childhood and youth in various convents and Catholic schools. Initially Alexina feels her difference from the other girls because of her social class. It is not until her adolescence that she begins to be aware of her physical difference from the other girls: for example, a certain "hardness" of features, excessive body hair, a "ridiculously thin" build. Later she describes the terrible physical pain she suffers from time to time that eventually leads to the discovery of her anatomical difference. She is "instinctively ashamed of the enormous distance that separated me from them, physically speaking" (26), and when she is sent off to a Catholic normal school to become a teacher, she shudders upon entering the room filled with other young women in training, overcome by "sensations" that she says she blamed herself for "like a crime" (26, 33). Such shame and guilt are the moral consequences of disciplinary practices that "produce a modality of embodiment"[26] that must be either feminine or masculine.

At her first teaching position, Alexina meets Sara, another young teacher. The two women share an intense emotional and physical bond, what in the nineteenth-century was referred to as "romantic friendship" and later would be stigmatized as "lesbianism."[27] Their physical intimacy leads to Alexina's identity crisis, as we might call it today. She feels guilty about their intimacy but then defends herself by saying that the fault wasn't hers but was due to those physical sensations she couldn't resist. That is, the intimacy was "pure" because involuntary, not a matter of conscious choice. When we read the medical reports published at the end of the text, we learn that Alexina's physical features meant that penetration had likely occurred.[28] "What, in the natural order of things, ought to have separated us in the world had united us," Alexina writes (51). Here the nature of their relationship confounds the binary system of sexual and gender identity. Alexina admits to being Sara's "lover" (52), but was the "crime" that Alexina defends herself against that of same-sex sexual relations, or illegitimate heterosexual relations? Alexina feels guilty because she was, as she puts it, "usurping a place [. . .] that human and divine laws forbade" (52), making the crime less about sexual relations than about gender identity. As with the shifting adjectives and pronouns she uses to refer to herself in the original French version, the language of sexual relations eludes her as well, not just because the subject was taboo but because its nature was "impossible."[29]

Alexina ends up "confessing" her "false situation" three times, presenting different moral scenarios for responding to such sexual indeterminacy. She first confesses to the curé of the parish where her school is located, a man she detests for his power over the schoolteachers. He is horrified by her confession and responds with insults and scorn, grudgingly pardoning her (55). Her second confession is to an unknown priest in the town where she attends a retreat. He, too, is astonished by her confession but responds more indulgently. He recognizes that she is now "entitled" to call herself a man, but to make this claim publicly would create a "scandal," while continuing to pass as female in her current position is also impossible. Thus, he advises her to "withdraw from the world and become a nun" (62). While the first priest's "unspeakable moral code" (55) allows no compassion for what is outside the bounds of legitimate discourse, the second priest is no less culpable in Alexina's eyes for his "don't ask, don't tell" solution.

Eventually Alexina's physical sufferings grow so intense that she agrees to have Sara's mother, in whose home she lives, send for a doctor. The doctor, shocked to discover what we learn later was the presence of testes, advises the mother to send Alexina away, thereby freeing himself of any responsibility. Alexina is as disgusted by his failure of duty as she was by the curé's scorn. "His duty traced out another line of conduct for him," she writes. "In such a circumstance, indecision was not permitted; it was a grave fault, not only morally but in the eyes of the law" (70). The two-sex system has moral as well as legal consequences, or rather, as Fausto-Sterling puts it, moral and legal discourses demand two sexes so that clear lines of appropriate behavior may be drawn. One must choose "a true sex." When it comes to sexual identity, indecision is not permitted.

The doctor's moral failing leads Alexina to confess a third time. This time the priest consults with his doctor, "a man of science in the full sense of the word" (77), and together these "experts" plan a course of action to "rectify" Alexina's civil status (78). Alexina's legal, if not bodily, identity is changed from female to male. But whether in legal language (to rectify an error) or medical language (to correct a disability), changing the sexual identity complies with the sex/gender system rather than interrogating it.

On the one hand, Alexina feels it was her "duty" to reveal her physical condition to the authorities; on the other hand, she feels even this solution is wrong because her change in status "offend[s] all the laws of conventional behavior" (79): "Was it likely that society, which is so severe, so blind in its judgments, would give me credit for an impulse that might 'pass' for honesty? Wouldn't people try to falsify it instead and treat it as if it were a crime on my part?" (79). The ambiguity of "it" exposes the impossibility of this choice. Is the impulse that might pass for honesty the impulse to confess her difference or the impulse that led her to act sexually on that difference? Where's the crime: engaging in sexual relations of an ambiguous moral as well as physical nature, or defying conventional behavior by failing to have a "true" sex? Alexina's confessions expose the limitations of "imaginary conceptions," the lack of cultural conceits, that might allow for the possibility of a different truth. She refers to herself as "I, who am called a man" (107), unable or unwilling to embrace that identity but no longer able to deny it. "Dissembling," she says, was no longer possible. But dissembling what? Is she now "passing" as a man, or was she "passing" as a woman before?

As a man, Alexina (now called Abel) has trouble finding work.[30] As she quips at one point, in discussing her past work experience, "Abel" could hardly say he had been a schoolmistress and a lady's maid. Her experiences are that of a woman, her legal identity that of a man. As a result, Alexina suffers terrible poverty and isolation. The narrative ends with Alexina's decision to accept a job as a waiter's assistant on a ship bound for the United States, although it's unclear if she ever sailed. Alexina killed herself in Paris in February 1868.

Although in the fictional story based on Alexina's life, "A Scandal at the Convent," the "scandal" is the discovery of a male body in the convent, Alexina says that her very life is a scandal (99). What's scandalous is having no "true sex" in a culture that insists on such a distinction, and in a culture structured by binary gender. Her isolation is signified by new pronouns in the closing pages, where she refers to herself as "you" and "it." The pronoun "it" in particular brings out into strong relief the very insight of contemporary gender theory: namely, that one cannot be a "person" outside the discourses of gender. Alexina literally cannot name herself or convey her "true" experiences, not because they are *outside* the laws of conventional behavior, as she puts it, but precisely because they are structured *by* those laws, by a "cultural grammar of gender."

In this narrative the language of deception and fraudulence (the traditional notion of "passing") is tied to what is beyond belief, what hasn't been narrated. That is, the moral failing is not the fault of the individual but a failure of language, and thus of the cultural imagination. The notion of a "true" sex is the real scandal, as Foucault suggests when he asks, "Do we *truly* need a *true* sex?" Alexina's identity is not fraudulent, based on a misrepresentation or suppression of the truth; rather, in her case, the truth "goes beyond all imaginary conceptions" (87), and thus is "unreal," unbelievable. It's not, I would argue, that we need more identity categories so we might get the labels right; what we need are more imaginary conceptions, more life-sustaining fictions. Alexina has no "true" sex at the end; instead, as a man, she is living a conventional fiction, a role that kills her.

We may not be able to get rid of the category of sex altogether, as some feminist theorists argue, but we can investigate how the category of sex came to be discursively defined and how (not what) it *means*—socially, legally, rhetorically. This is where the concepts of *transgender* and *passing*, can prove helpful. For *trans*, like *passing*, is a dynamic; it signifies movement. And while these terms are often read as connoting movement from one identity category to another, whether legitimately or fraudulently, I suggest that they be read as defying the notion of fixed categories or bounded identities, as Woolf's novel can illustrate.

I first published on Virginia Woolf's *Orlando* (1928) twenty years ago in an essay that I realize now was about the rhetoric of transgender. Written for Woolf's bisexual friend and lover, Vita Sackville-West, *Orlando* is a mock biography of a character who lives for nearly four centuries, changing from a man to a woman at the turn of the eighteenth century. The novel isn't just a story about a transsexual (the eponymous protagonist); the novel also disrupts, rhetorically, sex dimorphism; the rhetoric of *Orlando* is as unstable as the sex of Orlando.[31]

The novel opens in the sixteenth century with Orlando as a young boy practicing his swordsmanship and ends in 1928 with Orlando as a young woman shopping at Selfridges. The opening words of the novel upset our certainty about anything in this text. We read, "He—for there could be no doubt of his sex," and immediately our doubt is aroused. The emphasis on what should be obvious makes it seem unnatural; the emphasis on an innocent pronoun makes it suspect. Long before any sex change is ever anticipated in the plot of the novel, that declarative sentence arouses uncertainty about what even fiction takes to be real: namely, sexual identity.

The sexual and textual indeterminacy of this narrative links language and identity. Orlando is associated with writing throughout. She writes the same poem for nearly four centuries; she is read like a book by the narrator, her fictional biographer (25); and she refers to herself as in the "process of fabrication" (175). That is, the novel is a text about writing, about constructing lives, histories, identities, and fictions. Thus, it encourages us to read Orlando's transsexualism not in terms of some notion of a "true" sex, but in terms of the relation between language and identity. One must assume a sexual identity in order to take one's place in language, yet we have no pronouns available for any indeterminate sex. Thus does grammar reinforce the two-sex system.[32] Woolf brings out the arbitrariness of that identity, and of language itself, not just through Orlando's sex change but through her own shifting rhetoric in this novel. Transsexualism in *Orlando* calls into question both conventional assumptions about sexual identity and conventional assumptions about language. The point of the vacillating rhetoric and the epicene protagonist of Woolf's novel is that language and identity are learned together. One famous passage from the novel, the famous clothes philosophy passage, most clearly makes this point.

Now a woman and living in the eighteenth century, Orlando in this chapter is becoming acutely aware of her new sex as she faces a legal challenge to her property rights, as she parries the sexual advances of the Archduke, and as she contends with "the coil of skirts about her legs" (153). Initially unchanged by the sex change, or so the narrator says, in the eighteenth century Orlando is assuming a more feminine identity. The narrator writes: "The change of clothes had, some philosophers will say, much to do with it. Vain trifles as they seem [. . .] they change our view of the world and the world's view of us" (187). According to this philosophy, our identity is as changeable as our apparel. Clothes make the man, or in this case, the woman.

The difference between the sexes would seem, then, to be conventional. However, the narrator continues: "That is the view of some philosophers [. . .] but on the whole, we incline to another. The difference between the sexes is, happily, one of great profundity. Clothes are but the symbol of something hid deep beneath. It was a change in Orlando herself that dictated her choice of a woman's dress and a woman's sex" (188). This is the view many contemporary memoirs by transsexuals take, that sexual difference is ontological, something "deep beneath" dictates the outward change.

But then, two sentences later, the narrator offers the statement often taken as Woolf's theory of androgyny: "For here again, we come to a dilemma. Different though the sexes are, they intermix. In every human being a vacillation from one sex to the other takes place, and often it is only the clothes that keep the male or female likeness, while underneath the sex is the very opposite of what is above" (189).[33] This statement contradicts the earlier assertion that Orlando was unaffected by the sex change as well as the philosophy that says we put on our identity with our clothing, but it also contradicts itself. For the narrator begins by saying that clothes are a symbol of something deep beneath, one's "true sex," and ends by saying that often what is deep beneath is the opposite of the outward appearance. That is, clothes are at once natural and fitting, and arbitrary and possibly deceiving. Similarly, rhetoric is seen as both a mere ornamentation of thought and as what makes a thought possible. Such contradictions are not surprising in this fantastic novel. What *is* surprising is that readers pass over the contradictions to focus on one statement as the author's position, accepting the narrator at his word, which is to take the rhetoric of the novel for granted. Reading through the rhetoric to the author's "true" point beneath is to privilege one understanding of rhetoric (as ornamentation) over the other offered in the novel.

Critics who accept the androgyny passage as a straightforward statement of Woolf's philosophy of identity focus on what the novel *says*, not what it *does*. Yet in this novel, language is not *expressive* but *performative*. Every time the narrator tries to clarify the ways Orlando has changed with the sex change, he ends up making stereotypical remarks; for he can make such sexual distinctions only by relying on conventional assumptions about sexual difference. Woolf knows that any language she can use to describe Orlando is already embroiled in certain conventional assumptions about gender and identity. There is no getting outside language in discussing sexual identity, and *this* is the insight we gain from this novel, not any one theory of sexual identity. One must attend to historical context and rhetorical language in any discussion of sexual identity. There is no way that the eighteenth-century philosopher and the twentieth-century gender theorist are talking about the "same" phenomenon when they write about human sexuality and sexual identity, because embodiment has a history as well as a style.

For me, the significance of the androgyny passage, then, is that it threatens meaning by breaking down those conventional oppositions that allow us to make meaningful distinctions. Far from doing away with sexual difference, as some readers conclude, *Orlando* enacts it, exploits it, makes a spectacle of it, thereby calling attention to its conventional and contextual "nature." Divesting Orlando of her property and patronym in this chapter, putting both her paternity and her propriety into question, Woolf does not liberate her identity but calls attention to the categories by which identity is determined and legalized. That is, it is not that the appropriate identity is androgynous, but that the metaphor of androgyny defies the notion of an appropriate identity or "true sex." Androgyny in *Orlando* is less a psychosexual category than a rhetorical strategy. Alexina asks, "Doesn't the truth sometimes go beyond all imaginary conceptions?" (87); Woolf might respond, imaginary conceptions are necessary to comprehend truth.

Sex as a fiction, a cultural conceit, a grammar, a metaphor—such conceptualizations enable us to *read* sexual identity as an historically specific narrative, making textual analysis an ethical imperative. A commonly held view of narrative ethics assumes that stories give us versions of real-life events so that we can exercise our moral judgment, hone our skills in making ethical decisions. This view holds that we learn to make ethical judgments by learning to sympathize with others' experiences as reflected in literature. We put ourselves in "their" place and thereby come to expand our notion of what it means to be human. Ethics lie in being able to bridge the gap between our position and theirs. In this sense, literary studies serves as a "handmaiden," so to speak, to philosophical, historical, or scientific studies.

In my writings on "passing," however, I have suggested that we rethink this common notion of narrative in order to rethink where ethics takes place in the study of literature. Woolf's *Orlando* and Alexina's memoir provide a different model for narrative ethics, *an ethics without identification*. What they teach us is not how to read characters as if they were people, but how to read people as if they were texts. To read through the rhetoric to the meaningful content beneath is like reading through the surface appearance to the "true sex" beneath. To read instead with attentiveness to the performative dimensions of language is to open up new imaginative possibilities that may lead to new forms of being. Literary scholar Biddy Martin writes that "our literary training [. . .] may hold out the greatest promise for new interdisciplinary discussions since it is at [the] level of language, of metaphor, and of rhetoric that new connections across fields can begin to be imagined" (371). No longer the handmaiden, serving other disciplines, literary studies, insofar as it produces knowledge, is now one of the boys!

Notes

1. Anne Fausto-Sterling, "Two Sexes Are Not Enough" (my italics).

2. Martin, "The Egg and the Sperm," 485.

3. Ibid., 486.

4. Bordo, *The Male Body*, 23.

5. "Category crisis" designates "a failure of definitional distinction, a borderline that becomes permeable, that permits of border crossings from one (apparently distinct) category to another" (Garber, 16).

6. Butler, "Imitation," 127.

7. Butler, *Gender Trouble*, 142.

8. An accessible example of this theory is the use of "we" in the Declaration of In-

dependence. "We the people" does not refer to citizens of the United States but brings that category of subjects into being. That is, the "we" isn't *referential*, pointing to a prior identity, but *performative*, producing that identity.

9. Frye, *The Politics of Reality*, 26.

10. Bartky, "Foucault, Femininity, and the Modernization of Patriarchal Power," 37.

11. Ibid, 40.

12. "Transgender" refers to the social phenomenon of people who live as a sex different from that to which they were assigned at birth, whether or not they have surgical or hormonal sex change to facilitate their lives as the "other sex."

13. For a critique of the medical management model, see Kessler, "The Medical Construction of Gender," 3–26.

14. Quoted in Hausman, "Recent Transgender Theory," 471.

15. Ibid, 476 (my italics).

16. Ibid, 485.

17. Foucault, *The History of Sexuality*, 154.

18. A related point is that certain biological sexual identities and sex organs predominately appear in some specific forms more than others. For example, biological male and female human beings, each with his/her respective and specific sex organs, are found more often in nature than transgendered males or females or individuals with ambiguous genitalia. Many natural scientists refer to these predominant types existing in nature as "wild types."

19. Foucault, *Herculine Barbin*, vii.

20. Ibid, xiii.

21. *La'mana*—called the Berdache by colonialists who saw them as homosexual transvestites or male prostitutes—undergo a ceremony that marks their passage into a new identity and a third gender. Elsie Clews Parsons, who published on the Zuni *la'mana* in 1916, writes: "This native theory of the institution of the man-woman is a curious commentary, is it not, on that thorough-going belief in the intrinsic difference between the sexes which is so tightly held to in our own culture" (qtd. in Babcock, *Pueblo Mothers and Children*, 9). For a fuller discussion of two-spirit people, see Roughgarden's *Evolution's Rainbow*, chapter 18. See also my "Passing as Modernism."

22. Woolf, *A Room of One's Own*, 99.

23. Dreger, *A History of Intersex*, 6, 10.

24. In October 2008, a transgendered politician in Georgia, Michelle Bruce, won a lawsuit brought by her opponents, who had accused her of fraud for running as a woman and claimed she had used a "fictitious" name.

25. Foucault, *Herculine Barbin*, x.

26. Bartky, "Foucault, Femininity, and the Modernization of Patriarchal Power," 27.

27. On the history of lesbianism, see Faderman's *Odd Girls and Twilight Lovers*. "Romantic friendship" referred to emotional and physical bonds between women that were culturally sanctioned, not "immoral."

28. The medical reports refer to this organ variously as "a penial body," "a monstrously developed clitoris" and "this little member as far removed from the clitoris as it is from the penis in its normal state" (Foucault, *Herculine Barbin*, 126–27).

29. French, of course, is a gendered language, dividing all subjects along the binary. Foucault notes that in the English translation, "it is difficult to render the play of the masculine and feminine adjectives which Alexina applies to herself," noting such difficulty "is an ironic reminder of *grammatical*, medical, and juridical categories that language must utilize but that the content of the narrative contradicts" (ibid., xiii–xiv; my italics).

30. I retain Alexina and the feminine pronoun, for that is the point of view from which the narrative is written.

31. Woolf uses the more philosophical concept "androgyny," rather than "transsexual," even though that word could have been available to her in 1928.

32. Fausto-Sterling refers to "the linguistic convenience" that gives us only two pronouns for the sexes. "Nor is the linguistic convenience an idle fancy. Whether one falls into the category of man or woman matters in concrete ways."

33. Androgyny is a "cultural conceit," to use Fausto-Sterling's phrase; intersex is the physical condition. Kari Weil distinguishes between the androgyne as an "aesthetic ideal" and the hermaphrodite as a "monstrous reality" in nineteenth-century literature. Whereas the androgyne designates an ideal of complementary wholeness, the hermaphrodite is a figure of warring bodies, an incompleteness "haunting the ideal of androgyny" (Weil, *Androgyny and the Denial of Difference*, 11).

10

Monogamy and Sexual Diversity in Primates

Can Evolutionary Biology Contribute to Christian Sexual Ethics?

JAMES CALCAGNO

The primary reason why anthropologists began studying nonhuman primates in the mid–twentieth century is straightforward and important to the discipline. As our closest living relatives in the animal kingdom, primates inform us both about our past evolution and our present human condition. However, using primatological insights to reflect upon (and even possible modify) Christianity and morality is quite new to me.[1] I am very grateful for my inclusion in such a dialogue, though I do have one caveat.

Most evolutionary biologists neither see nor seek connections between their work and religious teachings, whether the exchange is with more traditional views or newly revised ideas that take more recent scientific accounts into consideration. As this anthology demonstrates, science and theology operate in different ways, with different assumptions. On the plus side, despite those differences, "moral lessons" derived from each perspective can be quite similar, thus some consilience is possible. Yet, the implications of evolutionary theory can fundamentally challenge and be in direct disagreement with some religious beliefs. Although philosophers and theologians may comment that through greater reason one achieves greater faith, that may not always be the case. In the long run, faith and evolutionary reason may eventually work together in harmony, but they can also contradict one another in significant ways.

My initial task in this chapter is to address what evolutionary biology, biological anthropology, and specifically primatology may offer regarding human sexual pair-bonding and family structures. True to the anthropological tradition, this perspective is based on the premise that we can learn about ourselves through a comparison with our closest relatives, the primates. However, the possible relevance of this approach first needs significant qualification. Take, for example, the issue of monogamy.

Monogamy among Mammals and Primates: A Rare Breed

Monogamy is rare among mammals, and scientists commonly and ultimately attribute this to anisogamy, the basic difference between the sex cells of females and males. Mammalian females produce ova that are much larger and nutrient packed compared to the sperm of males, which are essentially tiny DNA packets with a small propeller. After an egg is fertilized, the difference between mammalian females and males continues to widen, given that females then carry this rapidly growing zygote inside for a lengthy time period. In stark contrast, the male's life, both physiologically and behaviorally, is relatively unchanged in the majority of mammals. Once the offspring is born, the bulk, if not all, of parental care is usually done by the female. The offspring receives its nutrition from the mother, and in most cases, rarely leaves the mother for months or years, while males are often not associated with either the mother or infant. In other words, for most mammalian mothers life will never be the same, whereas for fathers, well, life is basically the same.

Of course, there are many exceptions to any general rule relating to animal behavior, and this brief theoretical summary cannot do justice to the many complications of the scenario just presented. However, commonly scientists understand these exceptions to support the basic idea that the sex that possesses the "more limited reproductive resource" tends to have greater investment and more parental care in offspring. Usually, that limited resource is the eggs of females.

For males, life does change in some social structures more than others, especially in pair-bonded (commonly referred to as "monogamous") species. There tends to be greater paternal care, less sexual dimorphism in morphology, and greater similarity between the sexes behaviorally within monogamous species. However, among mammals, only about 3 percent have been reported to be monogamous.[2] Primates were thought to be the exception to the mammalian rule, as estimates of at least 10–15 percent of primate species being monogamous were accepted not long ago.[3] Yet upon closer examination and under more exact definitions of what constitutes monogamy, Fuentes contends that monogamy occurs among roughly 3 percent of all primates, the same as in mammals in general.[4]

Given our anthropocentric nature, the question of greatest concern to most humans, especially those wishing to promote or investigate Western traditions and values, is: "Are we part of that monogamous 3% ?" Seemingly implied by those hoping for a positive answer is: 1) if monogamy is innate to our species, it must be good; and 2) if we are among the rare 3 percent, then what the other 97 percent of mammals is doing is irrelevant to our ethical analysis. The latter view is not a good scientific response for at least two reasons. First, if the reverse were true (i.e., only 3 percent of mammals and primates were *not* monogamous), countless works would probably have been written regarding the divine basis of monogamy in animals. Clearly, however, we cannot discard data that do not fit our hopes, simply because they do not fit a desired agenda.

Second, and more importantly, "exceptions to the rule" often provide fascinating insight into a better understanding of the rules. Thus, a better question would be: "Why do 3% of mammals follow a mating pattern different from 97% of their mammalian kin?" What factors make monogamy a better strategy to increase reproductive success, and how do those factors compare with our modern human situation? Before addressing that issue, I will comment on the possible relevance of examining other primates.

Environment of Evolutionary Adaptedness

Evolutionary psychologists have coined the term "Environment of Evolutionary Adaptedness" (EEA) when discussing adaptations that evolved during our evolutionary past that help shape our current behavior. In other words, are we genetically predisposed to particular behaviors that were selected for in prehistoric environments, even if such environments have changed greatly or no longer exist today? Although an EEA can be a reasonable concept in general, biological anthropologists and archaeologists are often frustrated by its usage, because some evolutionary psychologists assume one particular human past to be true throughout time and geographic space. For many reasons, trying to construct a reasonable model of an EEA is an extremely difficult task. Nonetheless, anthropologists do share a desire to understand past human environments and the selective pressures they likely presented to members of our lineage, and although the difficulty of establishing an EEA is clearly daunting, it should not be frightening.

To understand human evolution and possible EEAs, at least three familiar approaches are generally used in anthropology. First, paleoanthropologists study the biological, fossil evidence of human evolution. Second, archaeologists examine the cultural remains of past hominins. Although it is difficult to use these two major routes to assess something like monogamy or pair-bonding, there are possible skeletal indicators of monogamy. For example, living primates who pair-bond exhibit little or no sexual dimorphism in body size. Early hominins are highly sexually dimorphic, and unlikely to have been monogamous, although nothing can be stated with certainty on the issue. Archaeologically, it is also difficult to derive specific information on mating patterns from material cultural remains of ancient populations. And the further back in time, the more meager is the cultural evidence. Primatology offers a third approach toward understanding ourselves, through the comparison of shared morphologies and behaviors of living primates as they relate to possible human ancestral conditions. One must be aware that we did not evolve from the living primates we see today, but instead from common ancestors who were different from any extant primates, since all species have evolved over time. All caveats aside, this approach might work with easy examples, but as one might guess, monogamy is far from simple.

THE CONCEPT OF HOMOLOGY:
AN "IF ONLY SO SIMPLE" EXAMPLE

Homology refers to shared traits among different species due to shared ancestry. An easy example in primates would be pentadactyly, or five digits at the end of each appendage. Humans, apes, monkeys, and prosimians all share this trait for one reason: The ancestor that gave rise to primates had this trait. Over the past 55 million years, primate species have changed in different ways, with some developing elongated digits, others having shortened some digits, and some species going both routes at once (e.g., elongated fingers with stumplike thumbs). Yet it is a safe assumption that the basic condition of pentadactyly is part of our evolutionary heritage, since suggesting that it independently evolved countless times among the primates would be neither parsimonious nor logical.

Pentadactyly is not solely related to morphology, but involves behavior as well. Although morphological traits are easier to trace evolutionarily, the same basic principle of homology can be employed with behavioral tendencies. For example, primates share more than just five digits, but also a very important ability to grasp objects with their hands and feet. Grasping behavior is of critical significance to the success of primates and an extremely important part of our human heritage. If that sounds surprising, imagine your life if you possessed hands like your pet dog or cat. Thus, it is most parsimonious and highly logical to assume that our EEA was comprised of people with grasping hands, regardless of whether there is a stitch of material culture present to indicate how those hands were used, nor a set of fossil hands to be found in any hominin species.

Again, this instance of homology is easy to establish. However, relevant data for ancestral mating patterns are far more difficult to grasp, due to the lack of clear patterns of homology. One need not examine all mammals or even all primates in this case, because the problem is readily apparent when looking at the apes alone. Our closest living relatives, the chimpanzees and bonobos, are found in what has been labeled "fission-fusion communities." Communities may consist of as many as fifty individuals, but one would never find fifty chimps traveling together simultaneously. On the contrary, females forage primarily as solitary individuals (unless accompanied by their infants). Related males often travel together, but also go off on their own at times. All of these individuals reside within a larger multimale, multifemale community, sometimes temporarily joining to form larger groups (fusion), which split again later (fission). Once larger groups are formed, they may divide into different smaller groups than existed prior to the fusion, although mothers will not split away from dependent offspring. In these communities, females generally mate with numerous males in the group, and there is little paternal care of offspring.

The grouping pattern of gorillas is much different from that of chimps and bonobos. Gorillas are found in more stable and cohesive units, commonly containing one adult "silverback" male that mates exclusively with three to four females. If there are two silverbacks, it is similar to having two polygynous units traveling together with their offspring. Although mothers predictably display great maternal care toward their offspring, silverbacks exhibit more paternal care than chimps, probably due to the fact that they likely fathered the offspring of their female companions. (Please note that this in no way implies that they need to be "aware of fatherhood," but instead that they simply act less agonistically toward offspring of those females that they have mated with in the past.) Among our two closest ape relatives discussed so far, we already have two very different types of mating patterns, and the situation only gets more diverse.

Orangutans are characterized as being solitary, while again noting this also assumes that mother and offspring remain together. Thus, females forage on their own, as do males. More recent research has shown that orangs may tend to be more gregarious when food sources permit grouping,[5] but this does not alter the fact that solitary adult males try to monopolize multiple solitary female home ranges. Males unable to maintain such territories may try less to defend such areas and instead sneak copulations whenever possible.

Finally, gibbons and siamangs have been characterized as being monogamous and found in nuclear families. Although this may seem promising to anyone hoping to find a biological basis for the endorsement of human monogamy, many cautions against doing so are warranted. First, gibbons and siamangs are the most distantly related apes to humans, and thus any similarity here in mating patterns is unlikely to be the result of homology. Second, it is inappropriate to single out one species as "evidence for primate monogamy" while ignoring the other 97 percent of species. Third, the monogamous lifestyles of gibbons involve some of the same attributes that humans lament about our own monogamy today, such as high rates of infidelity and the dissolution of pair-bonds.

In sum, if great homology existed among all primates regarding a monogamous mating pattern, the question addressed here may have been "why do humans have such a tough time adhering to what is so natural?" The fact that lifelong pair-bonds are hard to find among primates, and mammals in general, may explain why the presence or absence of human pair-bonds still provides plenty of grist for academic mills across multiple disciplines today. Regardless, animals are not similar by homology alone, which brings us to another important and necessary method of comparison.

THE CONCEPT OF ANALOGY

When primate behavior was first studied in the wild by anthropologists around 1960, the concept of homology was of key importance to help explain shared similarities among humans and our closest relatives. However, equally important was the concept of analogy, where similar traits in different species could be due to similar environmental pressures selecting for those traits. As one classic example, the wing of a bat is skeletally homologous to the human arm, but functionally it is analogous to an insect wing.

Closely related species can provide interesting examples of parallel evolution, where from the start they have much in common due to homology, but also develop similar traits under similar but independent circumstances. For example, New World and Old World monkeys evolved apart independently for millions of years, and independently developed similar traits (as well as numerous unique traits) to adapt to their forested environments. Regarding humans, an early focus on savanna baboons assisted in the understanding of our own past, under the assumption that early hominins may have faced similar challenges as they entered more open environments, unlike the heavily forested habitats of apes. Savanna baboons happen to live in larger, multifemale, multimale groups that are unlike any of the apes already noted, and the mating system is far from what anyone would call monogamy.

Clearly we cannot single out one primate species to justify or refute a human pattern, nor assume that what baboons specifically do today is how the first hominins lived long ago. Yet the concept of analogy itself remains highly relevant and relates to a key question in primatology and animal behavior: What social and environmental factors may relate to whether individuals in a species are solitary or monogamous, found in small or large groups, or shift between these categories we have constructed? In other words, how does an animal's socioecology affect its social organization and mating strategies?

Socioecology

Like biology itself, monogamy is not destiny. Yet some ecological factors may make some mating systems more likely to occur than others. In primates, numerous and sometimes overlapping suggestions have been offered as to why monogamy occurs, perhaps each of them with some merit under particular circumstances. The following are some of the best points or key elements:[6]

> 1. If females are solitary, and males cannot defend a territory that contains the home ranges of two or more females, nor can males have greater reproduc-

tive success (RS) by simply roving from one female range to another, a pair-bond is most successful.

2. If females who raise young alone have far less RS than those with male assistance, and males benefit from assuring greater female RS in their mates as opposed to mating with multiple females who are unlikely to then have viable offspring, pair-bonding works well. (Note: This may account for why pair-bonding is so prevalent among birds, where roughly 97 percent of species are monogamous. Females produce multiple and very large eggs relative to their own body size, and male assistance in foraging for the young is essential. However, given more recent abilities to conduct DNA analyses, the offspring in any given nest are fathered by another male at a rate much higher than once thought.)

3. If females require added defense for their offspring, either due to predation pressures or infanticidal males within one's own species, pair-bonding can benefit both sexes.

Regardless of which of these ideas has the most merit, it is clear that a mating pattern does not imply a lifelong commitment in any species. Monogamous males may shift toward polygyny if multiple female ranges become more simultaneously defensible. Increased food resources, or decreased predation or infanticide pressures, could lessen the need for monogamy, and females may benefit by having more diverse offspring fathered by different males. Animals that are primarily solitary can become more gregarious, and vice versa, with changing food supplies or predation concerns. Primates are not genetically programmed to be monogamous, but some situations are more likely to lead to monogamy than others.

Conflict between the Sexes: Observed and Expected

Given the previous discussion, it may seem that mammalian males and females have different agendas, but will pair-bond when it satisfies their own selfish interests. If so, then you're on the right track. Although Roughgarden would strongly oppose any suggestion of sexual selection at work in any species,[7] such a viewpoint is in stark contrast to views of virtually all evolutionary biologists and behavioral ecologists today.[8] As a result, strategies for reproductive success can differ greatly for females and males. In a comparison of extremes and given the high cost of maternal investment in their young, females will benefit from as much help as they can get to raise offspring, which often comes from close kin or unrelated males. Yet males are not wild about polyandry (an extremely rare mating pattern among animals, where multiple males share only one female reproductive partner), because they would be less likely to produce offspring of their own. Indeed, in rare instances where polyandry does occur, it is generally explained as males having no better options given the stresses on females to be able to successfully raise offspring. In contrast, males can have unusually high reproductive success if they can fertilize many females while not investing parental care, if it does not detract from the female's ability and success in raising her young.

Usually, however, neither sex can have its theoretically extreme ideal situation, and thus compromises must be reached to achieve greater reproductive success for both sexes. Monogamy, as well as any other mating pattern, could be viewed as a compromise reached by the sexes, for possible reasons discussed in the previous section. Out of this compromise, tremendous cooperation can, and needs to, arise.

Given the added costs of maternal care in primates to sustain a pregnancy, give birth, produce milk, and raise incredibly helpless offspring, food is of critical importance to females. Better fed and well-nourished females tend to reproduce earlier in life, have healthier offspring, have shorter interbirth intervals, and live longer to reproduce. As a result, females organize and distribute themselves in ways to gain the most from available food sources. Although males certainly need to eat, the key to their reproductive success is not access to food, but access to females. Thus, males generally must react in response to the cards dealt to them by females, since females may forage as solitary individuals or benefit from being in groups. Regardless, males often compete vigorously with each other for access to females. If there is any doubt about the consequences of that competition, note that despite the huge costs placed on primate females to raise young throughout their reproductive span, male mortality is almost always higher and their average lifespans almost always shorter.[9]

Human Monogamy

Many Americans assume that humans are a "monogamous species," while some "deviant" cultures are exceptions that can be found in issues of *National Geographic* or in Utah. Ironically, lifelong monogamy appears to be the more deviant, or at least the more unusual, system. Murdock's classic survey of nearly 900 cultural groups still surprises introductory anthropology students today when they learn that he could classify only 16 percent as having exclusively monogamous mating patterns.[10] Moreover, even in cultures where monogamy is highly valued, "serial monogamy" is commonly much more likely than a lifelong pair-bond. However, it should also be noted that in most "polygynous societies," most males cannot attract more than one wife, and monogamy may be more common than polygyny in so-called polygynous cultures. Fisher has suggested that if women are more economically independent, lifelong monogamy is less likely, because both males and females have more options to consider after they have passed through their "attraction" and "attachment" phases (the former lasting long enough to generally produce an offspring, and the latter getting that child through the toughest first two years of life).[11] Thus, her explanation is quite similar in principle to the second hypothesis suggested above for nonhuman primates.

As Fuentes suggests, part of the problem with our concept of monogamy is that given our largely Western and inescapably anthropomorphic perspective, we seem to be looking for monogamy in primates with the same ideals hoped for in humans (fidelity, unselfishness, everlasting love).[12] Yet animals don't get married and exchange vows, nor do they pair-bond for cultural reasons. Thus, what we might learn from animals about monogamy is muddled by confusing human ideals with animal mating patterns. In order to avoid this problem, Fuentes limits the term monogamy specifically to "a pattern wherein individual females and males mate exclusively with one partner over successive mating periods."[13] Defined as such, monogamy is not a "social system," nor a "social organization" (commonly used interchangeably in the literature), but simply a mating pattern. Other mating patterns in any one species would comprise its mating system, which would be only one part of the overall social organization. As a result, Fuentes not only classifies fewer primates as monogamous, as previously mentioned, but strongly cautions against the assumption that the term has the same meaning in humans and nonhumans.

Within primates alone, mating systems are extremely diverse. Although polyandry has already been noted to be very rare in the animal kingdom, it does occur in some primates. Similarly, although monogamy is very rare among mammals, it does occur in some primates. Some primates are solitary and breed for a very short time period only once a year, whereas others mate often and throughout the year. In some species, females leave their natal groups to find mates, whereas in other species they stay put while males exit, and in some species both sexes leave their natal groups. Primate sexuality is not only diverse and varied across species, but often within species as well.

Sexual Diversity: The Good News?

Anyone searching for evidence of sexual diversity in the animal kingdom will surely be pleasantly surprised, if not startled and amazed. Variation in sexual activities among different species is more than diverse; it's downright bizarre by even the most liberal human standards. Homosexuality, bisexuality, transsexuality, and sexuality in unimaginable ways is not only common throughout the animal kingdom, but the diversity makes our sexual interactions appear mundane by comparison. Consider, for example, hermaphroditic earthworms that pierce another earthworm's body wall with 40 or more needlelike setae during copulation.[14] The resulting transfer of hormones can both increase the chances of fertilizing eggs in the recipient and allow sperm to migrate to where the recipient's sperm is stored to be passed on later during copulation with another individual.

Heterosexuality can be equally amazing in some species. For example, some deep sea worms have great difficulty locating each other, and microscopic males have evolved. When a female is found, numerous (over 100 in some cases!) males crawl inside her reproductive tubes and stay there, making fatherhood more likely for each male while providing a reliable supply of sperm when needed for her. If not odd enough to our human perspective, the sex of the fertilized eggs is likely determined environmentally, depending upon whether the larvae settle on a female or on the whale bones that they eat.[15] But what do worms have to do with human sexuality? Probably nothing, other than to serve as a reminder that in comparison to the animal kingdom overall, and regardless of religious restrictions placed upon sexual activity, we are a relatively boring species sexually.

Perhaps the most fascinating example of sexual diversity within a primate species is provided by one of our two closest relatives. Bonobos not only have sex throughout the year, but they usually have it throughout the day, and they are extremely inclusive. Females rub genitals together with males as well as females, and males enjoy that variety as well. Young individuals have sex with elders and peers, and old individuals do not discriminate by age either. In other words, you name the possible combination of sex partners, and bonobos do it (outside of closely related kin, since after all, animals need only natural selection, not written laws, to avoid incest).

Even more interesting in this regard is that bonobo society is characterized by very low levels of violence, especially in comparison to their closest relatives, chimpanzees. Chimps can be extremely violent, attacking others within their own species with brutal and deadly consequences. Females must be wary, and often are weary, of males. In contrast, female bonobos can dominate males and enjoy much greater power within the community. When tension arises, rather than resorting to violence, bonobos commonly resort to genital-genital (g-g) rubbing. I imagine it is either too difficult to remain angry in these positions, or once in the process, perhaps bonobos simply forget what was so upsetting.

The fact that sexual diversity is rampant in the animal kingdom, from our most distant to our closest relatives, may be interpreted as "good news" by some and "immoral" by others. However, these are simply some facts of life, and one cannot jump from what behavioral ecologists describe in one species to moral judgments about what humans ought to do. The use of animals to inform us about human behavior must be done wisely and cautiously. Clearly, I do not expect worldwide acceptance of g-g rubbing as a viable way to reduce human conflict. However, perhaps we can learn from our primate kin to find better solutions to our problems that are more appropriate to our own species, if only in the form of an example reminding us that "biology is not destiny." Given our desire to boast about our massive brain-to-body size ratio, it seems reasonable to use our abundant grey matter to resolve conflicts in ways that differ significantly from male baboons flashing large canines.

Evolutionary Biology and Consilience: The Bad News?

The underlying focus of this anthology is to investigate how a reflection on evolutionary biology (along with other disciplines) might contribute to a faithful, Christian account of human sexual diversity. I hope this essay has shed some light on that issue. At the same time, it is necessary to note some concerns that faithful Christians might have about the perspective of evolutionary biology and the possible risks involved. Regardless, hopefully the benefits of this alliance of ideas will outweigh its risks.

In my opinion, this merging of ideas cannot occur at every level. Although insights from evolutionary biology may inform, enhance, and/or modify moral arguments, Christian teachings should not alter how scientific data are gathered or interpreted. Certainly some questions raised in theological and philosophical circles are investigated by science, especially those involving ideas about what constitutes "human nature." Like most evolutionary biologists, I view a scientific, evolutionary approach as a major strength to understand our world effectively, and to address the many problems confronting species on our planet, including our own. However, nothing written here, as in science itself, implies any supernatural causation, design, or purpose. Any commentary upon how God operates is not within the realm of science and thus better left to other disciplines.

I raise this issue partly because several chapters in this volume try to interpret the mind of God by examining the ideas of theologians and biblical scholars through time. For the evolutionary biologist, such an investigation is foreign at best and futile from a purely scientific perspective. To understand sexual diversity from a scientific perspective, few if any scientists care about the declarations of a fourth-century theologian on the subject. Ideally, the beauty of science is that phenomena can be interpreted regardless of whether someone is Christian, or female, or Democrat, or wealthy, or from India, with the hope that some ideas will gain global credence through empirical forms of verification, independent of one's cultural biases. Of course, such an unbiased ideal is never reached within any individual, let alone an entire community, but the goal should always be to try to recognize and minimize those biases, not to make them more prominent.

Notes

1. I am pleased and honored that the views of an evolutionary anthropologist are being consulted in the critical and constructive assessment of Christian teachings, or any religion. Having taught at Loyola University Chicago for many years, however, I am not surprised that such an invitation arose from a university devoted to the promotion of the "Jesuit tradition." After teaching "Human Origins" from an evolutionary perspective for over two decades, I am delighted by the fact that I have not had even the slightest conflict with the university regarding what is taught in my courses.

2. Kleiman, "Monogamy in Mammals."

3. Kinzey, "Monogamous Primates"; Rutberg, "The Evolution of Monogamy in Primates."

4. Fuentes, "Re-Evaluating Primate Monogamy" and "Patterns and Trends in Primate Pair Bonds."

5. van Shaik, "The Socioecology of Fission-Fusion Sociality in Orangutans."

6. See Fuentes, "Re-Evaluating Primate Monogamy," for a more comprehensive review of models.

7. Roughgarden, *Evolution and Christian Faith,* and chapter 6 in this volume.

8. See Kappeler and van Shaik, *Sexual Selection in Primates,* as one significant example.

9. Strier, *Primate Behavioral Ecology.*

10. Murdock, *Ethnographic Atlas.*

11. Fisher, *Anatomy of Love.*

12. Fuentes, "Re-Evaluating Primate Monogamy."

13. Ibid., 900.

14. Koene et al., "Piercing the Partner's Skin Influences Sperm Uptake."

15. Rouse et al., "*Osedax.*"

"In God's Image" and "Male and Female"

How a Little Punctuation Might Have Helped

ROBERT DI VITO

"When words used literally cause ambiguity in Scripture, we must first determine whether we have mispunctuated or misconstrued them."
—Augustine, *On Christian Doctrine,* 3.2)[1]

The interpretation of Genesis 1–3 found in several recent Vatican documents, among them John Paul II's encyclical *Mulieris dignitatem,* shows the continuing relevance of the Bible to today's discussion of sexual and gender diversity and provides the point of departure for this chapter. While Susan A. Ross is correct in noting that the interpretation found in these documents relies on the use of a kind of traditional typological method,[2] their actual application of this method has also resulted in what can amount to a novel recasting of the tradition. A case in point is what happens to the early Christian understanding of what baptism in Christ means for the distinction in sexuality in Gen. 1:27.

I begin with an analysis of the interpretation of Genesis 1–3 found in recent Vatican documents as it relates to the subject of sexual diversity. I then turn to a historical-critical reading of the same biblical texts, though limitations of space and time mean the focus is primarily on Gen. 1:26–28 and its understanding of humanity's creation in the divine image. In sharp contrast to the Vatican documents cited, this reading results in an interpretation that disassociates completely the clause "male and female He created them" in Gen. 1:27 from the preceding statement regarding creation in the divine image. In the third section I turn to Galatians 3:26–28, a Pauline text that alludes back to Gen. 1:27. It is this text's interpretation of Genesis 1–3 that is largely thwarted in the novel "traditional" Vatican reading and which today needs to be retrieved in its full vigor by the Church. Finally, in a very brief conclusion, I suggest two ways in which this study contributes to the discussion of sexual and gender diversity today.

Genesis 1–3 in Recent Ecclesiastical Writing

In *Mulieris dignitatem* (hereafter *MD*) John Paul II presents an interpretation of Genesis 1–3 in the course of a "meditation" on the anthropological and theological "bases" for understanding the dignity and vocation of being a woman and a man, but on this the occasion of the Marian Year (1988), especially of being a woman. The issue, as the Pontiff frames it, is a question of understanding "the reason for and the consequences of the Creator's decision that the human being should always and only exist as a woman or as a man" (*MD*, 1). As a "meditation," the approach, of course, particularly in dealing with Scripture, is a fairly traditional one, heavily dependent upon the use of allegory and typology, and one in which Mary as the model of both humanity and "the woman" becomes central to the entire reading.

RECASTING GEN. 1:27: CREATED MAN AND WOMAN TO IMAGE GOD

The meditation begins, "in the beginning," with Gen. 1:27, which is declared (*MD*, 6) quite simply the "immutable basis of all Christian anthropology." What makes this text so important is its assertion of "fundamental anthropological truths," not the least being that man and woman are "human beings to an equal degree, both created *in God's image*." As such, what this text expresses is nothing less than "the truth of the personal character of the human being," which is to say that "Man is a person, man and woman equally so, because both were created in the image and likeness of the personal God." Although for *MD* this human "likeness to God" initially gets specified as a rationality unique among all living creatures, this distinction is quickly displaced by intimations of another line of thinking reflected in the second account of human creation in Gen. 2:3–3:24, ascribed to the Yahwist source.

Clearly, John Paul II recognizes that there is a second account of human creation, one in which man and woman, to be known as Adam and Eve, are now created sequentially rather than simultaneously, and with Eve being taken by God from Adam's side while he is in a trancelike slumber. But John Paul II does not see in the differences a contradiction of the first account. Far from it! For *MD* this second account by the Yahwist merely clarifies what takes place in the first account from the Priestly school (hereafter P), simply using different language "to express the truth about the creation of man," *and especially of woman* [italics mine]. As such, it develops all the more deeply "the fundamental truth" that Gen. 1:26–28 contains about humankind "created as man and woman in the image and likeness of God" (*MD*, 6).

The subtle rephrasing here of the text of Gen. 1:27, with man and woman in the image and likeness of God now the *object* of God's creation, is not without consequence for the document's development of the implications of creation in God's image. It suggests that it is precisely the articulation as male and female that is decisive for understanding the image of God, that it is as male and female that humanity reflects the divine likeness. Such in fact is the explicit and unequivocal contention of the Congregation for the Doctrine of the Faith's (CDF) 2004 letter to bishops "On the Collaboration of Men and Women in the World." Of Genesis 1's description of humanity as "articulated in the male-female relationship," this letter asserts without hesitation: "This is the humanity, sexually differentiated, which is explicitly declared 'the image of God'" (5; comp. *MD*, 7). Put differently, what being created in the image of God (aka "personhood") amounts to is nothing less than being created for a (heterosexual) relationship either as a male or a female.[3]

WHAT GEN. 2:4–3:24 CLARIFIES:
CREATED TWO FOR A "UNITY OF THE TWO"

For *MD* this is the truth that is clarified, if not substantiated, in the second account of creation, where the woman is created out of the man's rib and placed with him as "a help corresponding to him." Essentially unlike the animals also created in Eden, because only she is man's equal as a person, woman is able to overcome man's "original solitude" as "another I." That is why this second account of creation for John Paul II must be read with the first, because the "original solitude" of man and the need for relationship it posits serves to ground the differentiation of gender within a common humanity. "From the beginning" the complementarity of the sexes is immutably and unequivocally inscribed in the very notion of gender as either male or female. Distinct though the sexes are, the second account of creation makes plain, as *MD* has it, that maleness and femaleness complete and explain each other only as a "unity of the two" made in the image and likeness of God (*MD*, 23). ". . . [M]an cannot exist 'alone' (cf. Gen. 2:18); he can exist only as a 'unity of the two,' and therefore *in relation to another human person*. It is a question here of a mutual relationship; man to woman and woman to man" (*MD*, 7).

MD is clear in its statement that in "the unity of the two" man and woman are called "to exist mutually 'one for the other'" (*MD*, 7) and in an equality corresponding to their individual dignity as persons (*MD*, 10). Yet here in *MD* as in other recent documents from the Vatican treating sex and sexuality, the kind of complementarity envisioned between man and woman finally makes more, as Jung has explained,[4] of the differences between the sexes than what biology might suggest. Indeed, for *MD* sexual complementarity cannot be reduced to biology because complementarity is fundamental to the human capacity for love and to give of oneself: "This capacity to love—a reflection of the image of God who is love—is disclosed in the spousal character of the body, in which the masculinity or femininity of the person is expressed" ("On the Collaboration of Men and Women," 8). Thus, what is most fundamental to human being, namely the capacity to love, is in this view actually gendered as male or female, as "spousal," in analogy to God's love for humanity, characterized as the love of a Bridegroom for His bride.

Nor is there room in this understanding for any blurring of the basic distinction between the two. What we are talking about here are differences that go to the very core of human being "in the unity of the two" that grounds "the dignity and vocation resulting from the specific diversity and personal originality of man and woman" (*MD*, 10). *MD* continues:

> Consequently, even the rightful opposition of women to what is expressed in the biblical words "He shall rule over you" (*Gen* 3:16) must not under any condition lead to the "masculinization" of women. In the name of liberation from male "domination," women must not appropriate to themselves male characteristics contrary to their own feminine "originality." There is a well-founded fear that if they take this path, women will not "reach fulfillment," but instead will *deform and lose what constitutes their essential richness.*

Maleness and femaleness comprise the original dimorphic state of humankind at creation and what is essential to the definition of each is simply taken for granted in many of these documents: receptivity and a mother's nurturing for the female, initiation and activity typically for the male.[5]

THE "UNITY OF THE TWO" AS IMAGE OF THE TRIUNE GOD

That Genesis 1–3 can be read together as a consistent account of human creation rather than as two separate, not entirely consistent, accounts from two different Pentateuchal sources (as posited by modern historical criticism), is certainly no innovation of recent ecclesiastical writing. But in contrast to the kind of unitary reading advanced in *MD* and the other Vatican documents referred to above, in ancient Jewish, Christian, and later Gnostic readings the creation of man and woman in Genesis 2 frequently was seen as a kind of "loss" of a more primordial unity suggested by the simultaneous creation of male and female in Genesis 1—or at least as the introduction of duality in place of an original unity. To be sure, the "sting" occasioned by this introduction of duality may have been intensified with Adam and Eve's disobedience and subsequent expulsion from Eden; and the two moments are not sharply separated. But for these ancient readings duality is there all the same in the account of the creation of woman in Genesis 2, even if for the biblical author it is the likeness to Adam that stands out.

Of course, for *MD* the creation of woman is less an introduction of duality than a further articulation of the "unity of the two" in a common humanity (Gen. 1:27). But it is also not just the articulation or differentiation of a common humanity. As *MD* makes clear, what is at stake is the human translation of the divine image in which humankind is created, the divine image that itself mirrors the communal life of God in the Trinity. Put succinctly:

> Being a person in the image and likeness of God thus also involves existing in a relationship, in relation to the other "I." This is a prelude to the definitive self-revelation of the Triune God: a living unity in the communion of the Father, Son, and Holy Spirit [*MD*, 7].

In other words, as Father, Son, and Spirit constitute three distinct Persons in the unity of the Godhead, so analogously man and woman—distinct persons—are one in the humanity they share (itself a reflection of the divine) and the "unity of the two" mirrors the "unity of the Three."

So, again, it is not the creation of woman after man in Gen 2: 22 that strikes a discordant note in the "unity of the two" revealed in Genesis 1. That comes on this reading—to be sure, with plenty of textual warrant—only in the "sin" of the "first parents" recounted in Genesis 3. Only there is the "unity of the two" actually threatened, because only there is the image of God "obscured" and "diminished" as a result of sin [*MD*, 9]. In the sin of Adam and Eve the original relationship between man and woman is ruptured: "Your desire shall be for your husband, and he shall rule over you" (Gen 3:16). Where before there had been simply "the unity of the two" now as a result of sin what emerges is "a break and constant threat precisely in regard to this 'unity of the two' which corresponds to the dignity of the image and likeness of God in both of them" [*MD*, 10]: "Sin brings about a break in the original unity which man enjoyed in the state of original justice: union with God as the source of the unity within his own 'I,' in the mutual relationship between man and woman ('*communio personarum*') as well as in regard to the external world, to nature" [*MD*, 9].

Genesis 1–3 in a Historical-Critical Reading

John Paul II is explicit in framing *Mulieris dignitatem* as "in the style and character of a meditation" (*MD*, 2), one that, as indicated above, relies heavily on a kind of traditional allegorical-typological reading of the Bible with no explicit acknowledgment of current critical scholarship. So at first blush engaging this document from a historical-critical perspective might well seem pointless. Suggesting otherwise, however, is not only the use of the same sort of "reflection" in other Vatican documents that are explicitly prescriptive but the fact that *MD* characterizes itself as a response to a recommendation from the October 1987 Synod of Bishops for "a further study of the theological and anthropological bases that are needed to solve the problems connected with the meaning and dignity of being a woman and being a man." That orientation to practical pastoral application alone warrants, at least in the Roman Catholic tradition, a broad engagement of theological disciplines and other sources of human knowledge and moral wisdom, including obviously the natural and social sciences. And the expectation is, particularly when it comes to articulating concrete moral norms, that in the end, at least, a real coherence and congruence of viewpoints emerges and not irreconcilable contradiction.[6]

WHAT IS BEHIND CREATION IN GOD'S IMAGE: DOMINION

That the introduction of the Christian triune God into the reading of Genesis flies in the face of historical-critical efforts to read these texts in the context of their composition in Second Temple, or First Temple, Judaism, scarcely needs to be said (even as such a reading is hardly innovative). What is remarkable, however, is that by means of this classical trinitarian understanding of the *imago dei*, *MD* tries to ground the distinction and stability of maleness and femaleness on the stable identity of the Persons of the triune God. ("The model for this interpretation of the person is God himself as Trinity, as a communion of Persons," *MD* 7.) Perhaps it would be going too far to suggest that in *MD* a gendered concept of the human person is *rooted* in the godhead; but, given the trend in current studies of human sexuality to emphasize sexual polymorphism and the fluidity of gender roles, the contrast in viewpoints is unmistakable. In any case, from a historical-critical point of view, what demands our attention in this discussion is the understanding of what it means for humankind (*hāʾādām*) to be created in the image of God. Is there any basis for ascribing to humankind either maleness or femaleness—or both?

There is no denying that in the Priestly statement "male and female God created them" an assumption of sexual dimorphism is most likely taken as normative in the human community. What becomes problematic, however, for the biblical scholar, is a statement such as that issued by the Vatican saying, with reference to this text and without qualification, "This is the humanity, sexually differentiated, which is explicitly declared 'the image of God.'"[7] In point of fact, humanity is never declared *to be* the image of God—in the manner of the Egyptian pharaoh or certain Assyrian or Neo-Babylonian kings.[8] Such an unqualified and immediate identification of God and humankind in P, which takes considerable pains, of all the Pentateuchal sources, to assert the fundamental distance between God and humankind (comp. here J in Gen. 2:4b–3:24) is hardly thinkable.[9]

But even more troublesome than the equation of humanity and the divine image is the implication that to be created in the image of God means to be created as either male or female or that it is precisely *as male and female* that humanity reflects the divine likeness (see *MD*, 6 above). Such an explication of the statement simply misunderstands the position and the function of the qualifying phrase "male and female He created them" both within vv 26–28 and in the overall Priestly account of creation in 1:1–2:4a. As a result, it ends up ignoring the fact that in the preceding parallel statement "in God's image He created it (humankind)" (v 27ab), God (*'ĕlōhîm*) is the defining term and as such gives no warrant for attributing any sort of sexual differentiation either to humankind (*'ādām*) or to the divine likeness. Indeed, that is precisely why the qualification is added, "male and female He created them" (v 27b).[10]

To understand then why the latter phrase has to be disassociated from the preceding statement about God's image it is necessary to examine the logic of vv 26–28 and their twofold theme: one relating to the order of creation and humanity's position in it; the other, to the theme of blessing and fertility. To the first theme of creation belongs the notion of humanity's creation in God's image and likeness in vv 26a and 27a. Here the correspondence is articulated grammatically by means of two adverbial prepositional phrases qualifying God's creative activity, "And God said, 'Let us make humankind (*'ādām*) in our image (*bĕṣalmēnû*), according to our likeness (*kidmûtēnû*) . . .'" (v 26a). The consensus among biblical scholars is that the two terms used here to describe indirectly *'ādām*'s (humankind's) correspondence to God, *ṣelem* and *dĕmût*, are almost, if not, synonymous. In their combination here, then, the basic meaning of *ṣelem* as "formal, plastic replica" (1 Sam. 6:5, 11)[11] is qualified by *dĕmût*, itself an abstract meaning basically "likeness" that helps to blur, if not actually to correct, the lines of the more concrete word in the pair.[12] Together these terms serve to designate humanity's overall resemblance to God but yet in such a way that neither indicates precisely *in what* that resemblance or similarity consists.

In fact, this shows that it is not the *nature* of the resemblance that is important for P but what that resemblance *means for humanity in the order of creation*. After all, God's intention in creating humankind in the divine likeness becomes clear only in the continuation of v 26b ("and let them rule over the fish of the sea . . ."), which grammatically cannot be separated from v 26a ("Let us make humankind in our image, according to our likeness"). This is what "and let them rule. . . ." does grammatically and logically: it draws out the implication of what being created in the divine image means. Just as God created the lights in the firmament to separate day from night (1:14), so God has made humankind: like the gods of the heavenly assembly ("in *our* image") and thereby *unlike* other creatures in Eden, precisely in order to exercise kingly rule over them. Creation in God's image sets humankind apart from other creatures, "by design," and makes humanity in some sense God's representative on earth.[13] By employing language at home in the royal court, where the king is the very image of the deity in the exercise of his rule and in the display of his power, here the language of image and likeness characterizes humankind as a whole in its relationship to other creatures of the earth as nothing short of godlike.[14]

A QUALIFICATION NECESSARY: DIFFERENCE FROM GOD AS THE GROUND FOR PROCREATION

Yet for all this, humankind is not divine; and within the context of vv 26–28, the parallel clauses of v 27 play a transitional role.

> 27ab in the image of God He created it (*'ādām*)
> 27b male and female He created them (*'ōtām*)

Like the animals over which it rules, if humankind is to endure in time, it must reproduce, which of course is the whole point of the "blessing" introduced in 1:28, as both command and empowerment: "Be fruitful and multiply and fill the earth." Not as God will they live on, but as creature—"male and female"—to whom God says in v 27: "Be fruitful!" (plural). In this way the bicolon of v 27 looks backward and forward: While the "image of God" asserts the resemblance of humanity to God and warrants humanity's special status in the created order, the addition of the "male and female He created them" looks forward to the command and blessing to "fill the earth," asserting humanity's placement among the creatures of the earth.

Phyllis Bird puts it well: "*Adam* is created *like* (i.e., resembling) God, but *as* creature, hence male and female. . . . The second statement adds to the first; it does not explicate it."[15] In fact, so *careful* is P to disassociate God from anything like reproduction in the manner of creatures that the break between the two statements about humanity is signaled in the text by a switch from singular pronouns referring to the collective "*'ādām*" designating the species ("in the image of God He created him/it"), to plural forms appropriate to the sexual dimorphism: "male and female He created *them*"). This is a case where—had the ancient author had modern punctuation and typeface—a little punctuation might have helped make clear the original intent.

The implications of this disassociation of sexual distinction from the divine image are of course considerable. The divine image, which here is referred to the species as a whole, belongs necessarily to the creation of every human being without regard to any sexual distinctions. Even more, it appears to exclude sexual distinction as a characteristic of *'ādām*, precisely and insofar as God is "the defining term" in humanity's correspondence to the divine.[16] And so, because the phrase "male and female" is concerned only with the blessing of fertility that follows, it, too, for its part, has no bearing on the "image" that qualifies the creation of the human species, nor on the God in whose image humanity is created, nor on the dominion given to the human species vis-a-vis other creatures and for which the divine image is the presupposition. What the phrase does do positively is to provide the presupposition for human fertility.

A further consequence of this disassociation of sexual distinction from the divine image involves the notion of gender equality in Gen. 1:27, particularly in view of the apparent simultaneity of the creation of man and woman (in contrast to their successive creation in Genesis 2). But even the language P uses here—viz., "male and female" (*zākār ûněqēbāh*) rather than "man" (*'îš*) and "woman" (*'iššāh*), terms that in Hebrew imply a distinctive social role and status, like "husband" and "wife"—points to the fact that nothing is being said in these verses about the roles of the sexes in society or about their relationship to one another or even about their equality or inequality.[17] The fact is, beyond Genesis 1:1–2:4a, P can scarcely be said to escape the androcentrism that marks the other biblical sources or to be indifferent to questions about the roles and the relative status of the sexes. When God speaks or acts, for P it is at the apex of a hierarchically conceived social order in which Israel's God exercises ultimate authority as *paterfamilias* over the "children" of Israel: "human and divine kingship are simply more inclusive forms of patrimonial domination."[18]

Yet even so, and despite its clear preference for the male in depictions of the human, P and its allied writings (e.g., Ezekiel) largely eschew the kind of anthropomorphisms typically in Yahwist depictions of the deity, even as P will take great pains to emphasize God's transcendence and distinctness from creation. That again is the point of the carefully wrought phrasing of Gen. 1:26–28, where the grammar alone precludes any "masculine identification to define the [divine] image."[19] In fact, given the clearly androcentric tenor of the totality of the Priestly writings, this restraint also makes the resulting limitation of the significance of the phrase "male and female" (to the status of a presupposition for procreation) perhaps all the more striking. It simply provides no support whatsoever for extending the distinction in sexuality it makes, or any distinction in sexuality for that matter, uncritically into what today is regarded as the domain of gender as opposed to biological sex. Sexual distinction marks the creation of humankind, not gender-related distinctions of status, roles, or responsibilities.

AN ENDORSEMENT OF SEXUAL DIMORPHISM?

Obviously, Gen. 1:27's phrasing "male and female" can be taken as a strong endorsement of sexual dimorphism, if not a normative heterosexuality; and certainly later Priestly legislation (Lev. 18:22; 20:13) will go in that direction (though without any appeal to Genesis 1). But even if the introduction of sexual distinction is related here to procreation as its necessary presupposition, this does not of itself mean that Gen. 1:26–28 thereby limits the ends of human sexuality (for social bonding, pleasure, etc.) solely to procreation. To be sure, one might argue that each of us as humans bears some, but certainly not the same or identical, responsibility for the tasks to which God assigns the species. Yet how any one of us at a particular age or station in life will "be fruitful and multiply," and contribute to "fill(ing) the earth," is no more specified in Genesis 1 than, for that matter, it is predetermined by this text how we are to "subdue it and rule (over it)."

It is clear that the Priestly school as part of an urban-dwelling elite for the most part simply *assumes* the sexual dimorphism it posits here in Genesis 1 for the human species, since it is neither argued nor explicitly debated. The matter-of-factness stems from the role and functional importance of procreation in the ancient Israelite family, which was itself an outgrowth of an agrarian subsistence economy. Here it is not an abstract human nature that determines "who does what" but practical necessity and the economic viability of the family unit in a harsh, unforgiving, physical environment.

In other words, the sexual dimorphism P assumes has its roots in the characteristic Israelite family, where the constant need imposed by the environment for a large supply of labor—coupled with high rates of infant mortality—accounts not only for the premium placed upon the reproductive capacity of women but also for the particular configuration of the family, which is designated in the Bible as "the house(hold) of the father" (*bêt 'āb*).[20] The terminology is revealing. Since the nature and the number of the tasks that had to be performed for a family to survive just at the subsistence level were simply beyond the capacity of the nuclear family, as both archaeology and the Bible attest to, the typical Israelite family, or "household of the father," was in reality a complex, multigenerational "extended family."

At any particular time, given the dynamic nature of all family life, it might well include not only a married couple with children, but grandchildren, the (male) children's spouses, the odd more or less distant relative, widows, indentured servants, concubines, and finally transients (sojourners). Obviously, this was not the "typical" twenty-first century American family! Indeed, the biblical witness to both polygamy and concubinage (e.g., in the case of the patriarchs Abraham, Isaac, and Jacob in Genesis) underlines again the "economics" of sexuality in the Bible, where pragmatic necessity rather than metaphysics determined gender roles. In this "economy," as Carol Meyers notes, production and reproduction, rather than representing competing categories of a woman's [or a man's?] existence,[21] are simply the kind of functional specialization demanded for the family to survive, whether that specialization comes from biology or not.

Hopefully, enough has been said to make it clear that the Bible's sexual dimorphism, as well as its gender assignments, must be understood within the context of its understanding of the family and of the ancient Near East. At the same time, this dimorphic view of sexuality also provided powerful support for the overall Priestly vision of reality, insofar as the latter's world view was constituted by an understanding of creation as the imposition of order upon primeval chaos—an order that emerges largely out of the introduction of separation and proper division into a preexistent chaos, as the light was separated from the dark (Gen. 1:4).

Indeed, in this way the entire world comes eventually to be organized, as clear boundaries define the Priestly ordering of time, space, and society. But boundaries are not enough, and so the boundaries are further reinforced in P by means of a comprehensive scheme of graded degrees of holiness that ensure the harmony of the various entities in the ordering of time, space, and society as well as of the hierarchical relationship in which each being stands to another. As the temple of Jerusalem is strictly demarcated from the city that surrounds it and sacred time defined over against ordinary time, so the priesthood is separated from the laity and man differentiated from woman. Everything has its place; everything has its time—even as the violation of the boundaries threatens incalculable disaster. The threat from chaos has only been checked, not eliminated. So what becomes critically important for P is the maintenance of this complex, interconnected system of boundaries. The stability of the entire created order depends upon it.[22]

Consequently, much is riding for the Priestly school on the separation of the sexes and the clear definition of their identity, since confusion at any level might spell disaster. But if this danger provides the proper context for understanding P's statement of sexual dimorphism, this same context also underlines the limitation of its understanding of sexuality and the emphasis on definition, separation, and division—which even in the OT are called into question and challenged (Jer. 7; Isa. 56; 65:1–16, esp. 1–7; 66: 1–6). And certainly that is no less true of the New Testament witness (Mark 7:1–23; Matt. 23:23–24; Luke 11:27–44; Acts 10: 9–16; 15; Rom. 14:20).

Galatians 3:28 and the Early Christian Subversion of Sexual Differentiation

Perhaps the most direct challenge to this priestly conception and the "either/or" of sexual dimorphism comes in Paul's citation in Gal. 3:28:

> For all of you who were baptized into Christ have clothed yourselves with Christ. There is neither Jew nor Greek, there is neither slave nor free person, there is not male and female; for you are all one in Christ Jesus. (*NAB*)

Here Paul employs, as part of his argument relativizing the Mosaic law's significance for the Christian believer, an even earlier Christian baptismal formula that makes a direct allusion to Gen. 1:27's "male and female." (Note how the conjunction "and" breaks the parallelism of the three pairs of opposites.) So this is not just some idiosyncratic statement by Paul about baptism but the recollection, and adaptation by Paul, of an antecedent pre-Pauline Christian baptismal tradition, one most likely at home in the Galatian community and elsewhere.[23] Indeed, Dennis MacDonald identifies as the source of the tradition behind Paul's allusion a dominical saying in early Christian literature now attested in slightly different forms in the fragmentary *Gospel of the Egyptians* (known from Clement of Alexandria), *2 Clement,* and the *Gospel of Thomas:* "When you tread upon the garment of shame, and when the two are one, and the male with the female neither male nor female."[24]

With roots in the Hellenistic Jewish exegesis of Genesis 1–3, this saying and the baptismal tradition it reflects takes as its point of departure the two Genesis creation accounts, not as two literary sources from distinct authors but simply two successive stages in a single "story" of the creation of "*Adam.*"[25] In the context of this exegetical tradition, while the first "*Adam*" (lit., "humankind") created in God's image and likeness (Gen. 1:26) was "heavenly," and thus incorruptible, the second "*Adam*" was earthly, having been molded from the clay of the ground (2:7), and thus mortal and corruptible. But the distinction in the two human beings does not end there, of course, for in this line of interpretation it was only with the second "*Adam,*" molded from the clay of the ground, that sexual differentiation came, manifest now with the creation of woman (Gen. 2:21–22), whose introduction also marks for man the real beginning of his "fall" from grace. Ipso facto, the "first" heavenly Adam, created in God's image, can know no sexual differentiation in this view, but must be instead a "unity of the two" in which there is no "male and female"—in effect a kind of androgyne, which is not uncommon for the progenitors of the human race in ancient philosophizing.[26] Aristophanes' tale in Plato's *Symposium* immediately comes to mind.[27] Even rabbinic sources know this line of interpretation, preserving a Greek (LXX) rendering of 1:27f, which reads: "male and female He created *him* ['*ôtô*]."[28]

But even if the world we know is one of duality, with its differentiation of "male and female," implicit in the baptismal tradition behind Gal. 3:26–29 is the conviction that the End will be as it was "in the Beginning." Incorporation into Christ through baptism will overcome the primordial division of the sexes and the opposition of social roles it leads to. Baptism in this view is nothing less than a restoration of the divine image as it was "in the beginning," before the separation of Eve from Adam and the Fall. What had been divided of old in a time of fulfillment will once again be reunited "in Christ," starting with the abolition of that sexual dimorphism of "male and female" at the heart of the Priestly order.[29] Like the angels, there will be neither marrying nor giving in marriage (Matt. 20:30). In the face of the Greco-Roman world's growing awareness of the anomalies created by its various social and sexual hierarchies, tied as these were to its continued insistence on an ethnic, a social, or a sexual identity, here Christians with equal awareness proclaimed an end to division and a "reunification" of all "in Christ." No more duality; no more dichotomy; "in Christ" no more sexual dimorphism, "male and female."[30]

Dennis MacDonald is probably correct in his assessment of Paul's attitude to this baptismal tradition when he stresses how Paul has modified its language so as to distance himself from any apparent rejection of the created order by the precedence it gives to the "spiritual" Adam over the "earthly" Adam (cf. 1 Cor. 15:45–49). The problem is that in this understanding of the Adamic paradigm, salvation as experienced in the sacrament of baptism comes to mean a liberation from the body, or in the language of Colossians, a "putting off the old human" (aka, "the robes of skin" in Gen. 3:21).[31] Clearly, for Paul, it could not be a question of leaving the body behind at baptism in some mystical transport, but rather of finally "being clothed with Christ" (Gal. 3:27; comp. 1 Cor. 15:54), in a process that is fully achieved only in the eschaton. And so instead of emphasizing the anthropologically oriented language of "two [sexes] becoming one" and returning to a state of spiritual androgyny, the focus for Paul falls on "all"—Jew or Greek, slave or free, male and female—becoming one in Christ by membership in a community where the old distinctions and oppositions are in the process of being overcome.[32]

In addition to this difference in anthropological and soteriological perspective from the traditions Paul encountered among the Galatian Christians, equally clear is how Paul has also in some sense "historicized" the eschatological thrust of the dominical saying behind this tradition, with his insistence to the Galatians that right now "there is no Jew or Greek. . . ."[33] At the same time, from an anthropological point of view, he has also managed to radicalize the unity Christians achieve through baptism: "for you are all one (εἷς) in Christ Jesus" (3:28). Note that Paul uses the masculine form of the word for "one" here, rather than the neuter of the presupposed dominical saying, because the unified creation Paul has in mind is nothing other than Jesus Christ himself. Thereby the unity envisioned is not merely a sociological reality, as some have it, but a "new creation" (2 Cor. 5:17) that is radically anthropological because it is constituted by membership in Christ's own body, to which all Christians belong by baptism (1 Cor. 12:12–13; Rom. 12:5; cf. 2 Cor. 5:1–5).

So rather than simply abandoning an earlier anthropological perspective for a sociological one, in fact Paul has dramatically deepened it. And from this perspective, too, "neither does circumcision mean anything, nor does uncircumcision, but only a new creation" (NAB) (Gal. 6:15), one where, we might add, the "male and female" of dimorphic sexuality has been subsumed in a new unity.

To be sure, it is a unity still in process and awaiting the perfection that comes only at the Parousia, when "we shall also bear the image of the heavenly one," (1 Cor. 15:49; cf. 2 Cor. 5:2–4). But it is also a present reality here and now.

It needs to be emphasized that in this new unity the issue is "sexual dimorphism" and not something like sexual equality. That is clear again from the gender of the Greek "one" above: it is masculine (for Jesus Christ), not neuter. In other words, in an ancient context, the abolition of sexual differentiation, if not always (cf. Aristophanes' tale), at least typically does not imply sexual equality—even when the reference is to androgyny. For as Dale Martin insists, the ancients operate with a radically different notion of the body and sexual dimorphism.[34] Where in the modern view of sexual dimorphism the body comes in one of two different, relatively equal sexual types, male and female, to the ancients the human body was of one basic type, exhibiting a kind of spectrum along which all humans, male and female, could be placed and with a clear hierarchy of what was valued.

So, in contrast to the modern view, all human beings had male and female aspects, and the only question was how much of one versus the other they had and where the balance put one in terms of the hierarchy, that is, *more* male or *more* female. For the androgyne who is "reunified" by baptism and restored to the divine image, typically this would mean then merely the subsumption of the "weaker" female aspects into the "stronger" male aspects rather than an addition of male parts to the female or vice versa. From this viewpoint, as Martin puts it, "Ancient androgyny . . . embodies the unequal hierarchy of male over female; it does not dispense with it or overcome it."[35] In the androgyne there is quite simply "no male *and* female." So although Paul insists that women may hold leadership roles in the Church, praying, prophesying, and speaking in the assembly, this does not necessarily mean he also rejected the prevailing gender hierarchy with its clear subordination of women. "Equality was not the issue; division was."[36]

Paul's vision here is certainly complex, even as it is beyond the scope of this chapter to sort out how it squares with all Paul's other statements on the relationship of "male and female," or the implications for today. That said, it is interesting that only slight attention is given to the Galatians text in *MD* (once in *MD*, 11) and when it is, as we have already indicated, the point to be made is that the "break" in the "unity of the two" comes not with the creation of woman but only *after* the sin of the first couple. This placement of the "break" then leaves *MD* free to say that Christ overcomes only the "tension" or "opposition" between the sexes due to sin and not sexual distinction as such or the corresponding roles. Indeed, in "On the Collaboration of Men and Women in the World" the Vatican goes so far as to say that the distinction between man and woman will remain even at the end of time.[37]

Certainly, from the perspective of Gal. 3:26–28, this represents a rather different view, one that in several respects can undermine what incorporation into Christ meant for the early Church. By reinscribing the distinction between the sexes dualistically in terms of an essentialism that marks certain roles only for men and others only for women (for example, in stark contrast to Paul's own insistence on the ecclesial roles of women) these documents surely undermine the vision implicit not only in the baptismal tradition Paul found in Galatia but also his own adaptation of it. Blunting the ethical implications for Christian living that the ancient symbolism suggests, these documents appear to ally themselves with the very world Paul saw was "passing away" (1 Cor. 7:31).

Implications

It is not the place of the historical-critic, qua interpreter, to affirm the theological primacy of Gal. 3:27–28 over against, for example, the Priestly insistence precisely on "male and female." All the same, the critic can show how one represents an accommodation to prevailing norms while the other embodies a visionary insight that paves the way to a more just and humane society. Surely this is the case with Gal. 3:26–28 and its interpretation of baptism. Indeed, even its pre-Pauline formulation, with its symbolism of the androgyne, continued to flourish in subsequent Christian, Jewish, and Gnostic readings (some would argue it *prevailed* over Paul's own adaptation, to judge by Col. 3:9–11).[38] In any case, the retrieval of these early Christian readings today is more than an academic exercise, because it underlines the real continuity that exists between early Christian sources and certain movements today that actively embrace people marginalized by the model of sexual dimorphism that larger society or its dominant institutions endorses. And this is no small contribution.

The fact is that the Bible on this issue, and more generally, serves only poorly as a stable foundation for our knowledge of propositions regarding the moral life that can never be questioned. Yet what the Bible does provide to Christians today is a commonly accepted protocol by which people can confirm their own identity as Christians, by "locating" themselves in various of the Bible's texts or central metaphors. In what is really a continual process of remaking and sustaining the tradition, there they—like so many before them—take up and repeat as their own the Bible's "truth." In fact, the process is not so different at all from what those responsible for writing much of the Bible had engaged in. For every generation of those called to witness to God's purposes in history has to take up and read the sacred texts given to it by tradition, but also read them in the light of *their* own place in history, *their* own questions, and *their* experience, in effect reauthoring the tradition in a way that makes it authoritative for *their* age. The process did not end simply with the closure of the biblical canon.

Instead what the fixing of the biblical canon really did was to give an enduring structure to this ongoing activity of reauthorizing the tradition, as the tradition at once confirms, and is in turn confirmed by, God's people.

To be sure, there are always problems in using Scripture in ethical argument. All the same, the almost exclusive focus in documents such as *MD* on Genesis 1–3, to the omission of other relevant texts (e.g., Isaiah 56), or while ignoring the overall representation of sex and gender in the Bible as that is informed by its original historical context, is self-serving and unhelpful. So taking a cue from the OT, where sexual dimorphism and its understanding of gender roles must be understood within the context of the ancient Israelite extended "family," perhaps one might argue today for a biblically inspired contribution to the current discussion of sexual and gender diversity that emphasizes a broad, communitarian ethical framework. In this scenario the Catholic moral concept of "integrity" or "wholeness" would figure prominently but in such a way that the "proper object of integrity," to answer Aline H. Kalbian's question,[39] is a contemporary reformulation of the Israelite multigenerational, extended family, or community. In such a communitarian vision, where the interdependence of all the community's members is heightened, it would be then the "integrity" of the overall communal "moral project," to use Fred Kniss's language, that is critical for ethical understanding and, accordingly, how "the moral project of the individual" in its own way contributes meaningfully and authentically to it. As Kniss notes in his chapter in this volume,[40] issues of sexual diversity and reproductive ethics simply take on a different cast when the focus shifts from the individual to the community and its moral life. It is not, we would say, the conformity of an individual project to a single standard that matters now, but how each contributes to the moral well-being of the whole.

Notes

1. Robertson, trans., *Saint Augustine: On Christian Doctrine.*
2. Ross, "The Bridegroom and the Bride," 42, 46–48.
3. Jung, "Christianity and Human Sexual Polymorphism," 301.
4. Ibid., 302.
5. Ross, "The Bridegroom and the Bride," 40.
6. For a finely worded statement of this basic principle, see Jung, "Christianity and Human Sexual Polymorphism," 305; Ross, "The Bridegroom and the Bride," 48, 55.
7. The statement is drawn from the 2004 letter issued by the Congregation for the Doctrine of the Faith (CDF), "On the Collaboration of Men and Women in the Church and in the World," 5.
8. Westermann, *Genesis 1–11,* 52–54.
9. Von Rad, *Genesis,* 60.

10. See the very helpful discussion by Bird, "'Male and Female He Created Them,'" 146–50.

11. Theological Dictionary of the Old Testament [hereafter TDOT] XII, 390–91. The word ṣelem, however, may also be used of pictures and dream images.

12. TDOT III, 257–60, esp. 259.

13. Bird, "'Male and Female He Created Them'" 137–38.

14. For the association of the phrase "image of God" with the ideology of kingship in the ancient Near East, see the summaries of the discussion provided by Westermann, Genesis 1–11, 152–53; and Bird, 140–44.

15. Bird, 149–50.

16. Ibid., 148.

17. Ibid., 155.

18. King and Stager, "Of Fathers, Kings, and the Deity," 45.

19. Bird, 159.

20. On the nature of the Israelite family as well as the connection here between its configuration and economic survival, see the contributions of Carol Meyers, especially in Perdue et al., Families in Ancient Israel, 16–21, esp. 18.

21. Ibid., 8.

22. Boccaccini, Roots of Rabbinic Judaism, 73–76.

23. Meeks, "The Image of the Androgyne," 179, 183–87, 207. Throughout this section my analysis is indebted to Meeks.

24. MacDonald, There Is No Male and Female, 14–15.

25. For an outline of this exegetical tradition, particularly as it is exemplified in the works of the Jewish philosopher Philo, see MacDonald, 26–30.

26. Meeks, "The Image of the Androgyne," 185.

27. Symposium 189c–193e.

28. Meeks, "The Image of the Androgyne," 185.

29. Ibid., 179, 183–87.

30. Martin, Sex and the Single Savior, 87–90.

31. MacDonald, There Is No Male and Female, 11, 119.

32. Ibid., 119–23.

33. Ibid., 125.

34. Martin, Sex and the Single Savior, 83–84.

35. Ibid., 84.

36. Ibid., 87.

37. Jung, "Christianity and Human Sexual Polymorphism," 303.

38. MacDonald, There Is No Male and Female, 128.

39. Kalbian, "Integrity in Catholic Sexual Ethics," 55–69.

40. See chapter 3 in this volume.

PART 3

Sexual Diversity and Christian Moral Theology

12

Social Selection
and Sexual Diversity
Implications for Christian Ethics

STEPHEN J. POPE

When reading the chapters by Roughgarden, Grande and colleagues, and Calcagno in this volume, it becomes apparent that notable differences and disagreements about the significance and interpretation of scientific truth related to sex and gender exist within the scientific community, quite apart from any dialogue or disagreements that might also exist between natural scientists and theologians. Joan Roughgarden's theory of social selection[1] offers a significant challenge to the dominant Darwinian theory of sexual selection. Specifically, this theory attempts to expand the focus of evolutionary theory from a narrow concern with mating to a broader account of the social as well as material context that promotes successful reproduction. Inclusive reproductive fitness depends on the interaction of partners, cooperative assistance, and parental care along with the provision of food and physical security. Reproductive success is made possible by networks of relationships that reflect social selection.

This chapter considers social-selection theory as neither established nor discredited, but rather as a speculative position that, if shown to be plausible by further scientific investigation, might have significant implications for our understanding of sexuality and sexual ethics, and for Christian ethics in particular. The case Roughgarden makes for social-selection theory stands on its own scientific ground. Yet she is also interested in both the social-ethical and religious implications of her own discoveries regarding the function of sexual behavior, including in human behavior. She writes as a committed Christian about the ethical implications of her own biological observations and theory, and so provides a helpful context for assessing Christian ethics as it treats matters pertaining to sexual diversity.

This chapter assumes familiarity with Roughgarden's project, and focuses on relating it first to the traditional sexual ethics of Pope John Paul II and then to the more progressive perspective of ethicist Margaret Farley. The chapter argues that Roughgarden's theory, if established, would tend to weaken some of the descriptive support for the pope's theology of the body (and the sexual ethic that it supports) and tend to support Farley's sexual ethic. It also maintains that, whatever the scientific reception of Roughgarden's biological theory, the church needs to embody and promote greater inclusivity.

Pope John Paul II

Pope John Paul II shared the longstanding Catholic affirmation that what is learned by reason, philosophy, and science is ultimately compatible with what is revealed in Scripture and passed on in the Christian tradition. The person is not simply a soul or spirit, but also a body. The body is a kind of "primordial sacrament" in the sense that it makes visible the reality of the person. The pope explained that, "The sacrament, as a visible sign, is constituted with man [sic] as a 'body' by means of his visible masculinity and femininity. The body, in fact, and it alone, is capable of making visible what is invisible: the spiritual and divine. It was created to transfer into the visible reality of the world the mystery hidden since time immemorial in God, and thus be a sign of it."[2]

Human beings are made in God's image precisely as men and women, the pope emphasized (Gen. 1:27). Genesis reveals that God created men and women with certain distinctive and mutually complementary traits so that they could play special roles within marriage, family, and society.[3] The human body has been designed by the Creator as either masculine or feminine so that it can allow for the manifestation of its "nuptial meaning" in the mutual self-giving of husband and wife.[4] The deepest significance of the human body is displayed in the interpersonal love embodied in sexual intercourse within heterosexual marriage. The otherness of sexual differentiation is transcended by sexual attraction that moves to self-giving love—the man engages in self-giving in the mode of active self-donation and the woman offers herself in the mode of reception. The duality of sexual love is also transcended by the fruitfulness of procreation. The human family shows that love is intended to become incarnate, overflowing in procreation to generate communion between persons. The theology of the body regards sex as capable of functioning as an image of the Trinity, in which the mutual self-giving love of the Father and the Son is the self-giving love of the Holy Spirit.

The pope's personalist reading of sexual and gender identity leads him to make generalizations about the meaning of the biological dimensions of human sexuality. Individuals whose personal experience or internal affections do not conform to their ontological identity as male or female are defective in this regard. These persons possess equal human dignity because they too are created in God's image, but the pope seems to have considered their condition to be in some ways analogous to that of a person suffering from mental illness. The Vatican thus described transsexuals as suffering from a "pathology" and therefore as ineligible for ordination or membership in religious orders.[5]

The theology of the body has been subjected to extensive criticism, especially as regards its use of Scripture to support a narrow and conventionally patriarchal reading of sex and gender.[6] It is also criticized for promoting a naively romanticized view of nature that has little relation to empirical nature as it is observed by scientists. The pope taught the compatibility of the fact of evolution with Christian belief, yet he also wrote, for example, as if Adam and Eve were historical figures.[7]

John Paul II thus affirmed the unity of theology and science in principle,[8] but he did not himself draw upon science and in fact often wrote as if it has little significance for Christian theology.[9] The pope expected scientific discoveries and information to confirm what we already know from Scripture and the natural law, as they are properly interpreted by the magisterium. He granted no independent normative significance to empirical studies and biological theories like those produced by Roughgarden. The fact that a given human trait has a genetic or biological origin, or is found in the animal world, does not confer moral legitimacy on it. The fact that three hundred species are engaged in same-sex activity has no relevance to this personalist ethic, other than to indicate the nature of sex when detached from authentic interpersonal love. The naturalistic observation of nonreproductive sexual acts in the wild (e.g., bonobo same-sex activity) has no normative significance. Science can provide an etiology of disorders, but it does not yield positive moral guidance. Behavioral sciences, the pope wrote, "have rightly drawn attention to the many kinds of psychological and social conditioning which influence the exercise of human freedom,"[10] but these conditions neither override human freedom nor undermine the binding power of the moral law.

While the pope regarded any person as due respect and compassion because made in God's image, he also insisted that no biological, psychological, or emotional conditions render acts that are intrinsically disordered to be ethically permissible. Studies like those published by Roughgarden offer no helpful ethical guidance to Christians (or anyone else). The diversity of human sexual behavior, the pope insists, is simply an indication of how things can go wrong when people are given over to sin.

Roughgarden would regard the pope's reflections on the meaning of sex as ignoring the actual material reality of concrete human bodies in their particularity and particularly in their diversity. What the pope regarded as aberration, Roughgarden counts as part of the created order. The pope's generalizations about the universally human eclipse the details that distinguish different individual persons. For Roughgarden, this attention to the universal renders John Paul II's ethic excessively abstract and narrow.

Advocates of the theology of the body would respond that the pope does attend to nature, but that the nature of the person is much more profoundly understood in ontological and theological rather than in material, biological, or genetic terms. Roughgarden can concede that ultimately theology and ontology subsume biology, but she would also insist that a properly integrating theological vision cannot proceed by ignoring or manipulating the biological realities that it seeks to subsume. The higher integration must account for the complexity of the lower realities it seeks to accommodate, not oversimplify them to the point of irrelevance. Instead of a true synthesis, Roughgarden would argue, the theology of the body represents an ontologically idealistic position that rides roughshod over the complexity of the empirical biology of the body, or, put better, the biologies of bodies.

Defenders of the theology of the body would in turn charge Roughgarden with effectively reducing the meaning of sex and gender to its biological or reproductive function. They hold that the physical intimacy of sex, the penetration of female by the male and the reception of the male by the female, is oriented to a deeper spiritual union of these two persons. The sexual difference between male and female is the condition for the union of complementarities, a union that calls forth the self-transcendence of one into the other precisely because it involves embracing the other as other. Same-sex relations implicitly deny this complementarity and so by their nature must stall at an immature level of affectivity and spirituality. Individuals who are, for whatever reason, confused about their sexual identity face emotional and psychological obstacles to attaining the kind of loving union to which God calls mature and healthy adult couples.

Roughgarden would regard such a position as reductionistic as well as morally offensive. The many ways in which sex can function to aid cooperation, friendship, and procreative ends is ignored by those who adopt this position because they do not fit into the normative framework that is said to be God's plan. As we glimpse in both her chapter and the chapter she coauthored with Jung in this volume, Roughgarden regards God as more capacious, affirming, and generous than the theology of the body acknowledges. Her own theology also affirms a divine plan for sexuality, but her framework is much broader than that of John Paul II. Rather than insisting that sexual identity conforms to a simple binary paradigm and that sexual acts conform to a clear set of moral rules regarding permissible and impermissible acts, her perspective affirms a much more general divine will that sexual activities act as expressions of the virtues of love, kindness, and caring for others. Rather than regarding heterosexuals as healthy and everyone else as defective, then, Roughgarden would like each person to be evaluated according to appropriate criteria. Heterosexism is a form of bigotry akin to other kinds of unjust prejudice.

It is important to note, however, that both interlocutors in this debate insist that every person be treated with respect. Respect includes treating another person as bearing intrinsic dignity equal to one's own dignity. This implies for Roughgarden that we honor the choices made by others, so that respect might involve honoring a person's choice, for example, to act as a cross-dresser as an expression of his or her identity. Disapproving cross-dressing indicates a lack of respect for the cross-dresser in Roughgarden's ethic. The pope, on the other hand, would maintain that honoring this choice would actually be to engage in formal cooperation with an activity that is morally demeaning because it violates the cross-dresser's dignity as a man or woman. We ought to affirm the choices of others when they are in keeping with their dignity, the pope would teach, and indiscriminate affirmation is disrespectful in that it ignores and even cooperates in undermining the person's true good.

This judgment might sound narrowly paternalistic to Roughgarden. But she would also seem bound to a similar position when asked, for example, if she would respect the choices of homophobes to discriminate against gay people. Presumably she would distinguish between respecting the person and judging his or her choices to be morally acceptable—this would be, in effect, a version of "loving the sinner, hating the sin." Roughgarden would agree that respect need not entail unconditional acceptance of every person's acts.

These authors are not, then, divided about the duty of respect for others, but about what God wills as the content of true and complete human flourishing. The pope is informed about the divine will from his reading of Scripture and the Christian tradition as interpreted by the magisterium of the Catholic Church. He begins his reflection on sex and gender within what he takes to be two millennia of divinely authorized teachings regarding the divine plan for men and women. Lives that do not conform to this message stand in need of conversion, amendment of life, and a renewed commitment to goodness and even sanctity. True human flourishing is found in a perfection that is reached fully only through the gift of divine grace in the eternal vision of God. This dual sense of ecclesial authority and grace-empowered supernatural destiny affirms the relative value of knowledge attained by human reason in philosophy, the sciences, and ordinary human experience, but it treats these primarily as sources of insight that can complement and extend truths that are already held and preached by the church. Reason can falter, mislead, and misunderstand, but revelation is completely reliable and not subject to error.

Roughgarden does not share the pope's confidence in the clarity and certainty of revelation and, of course, as an Episcopalian she does not accept the authority of the Roman Catholic magisterium. Her reflection takes place from the perspective of someone sensitive to the abuse of power legitimated by prejudice, rather than as someone exercising supreme authority within a large institution. Roughgarden puts her knowledge of biology at the service of the liberation of people she regards as oppressed. Yet she sees the church not only as a cause of a great deal of this oppression, but also as a potential agent of liberation. True love of neighbor allows people to flourish in the distinctive manner that is most appropriate to their own particular identities. Love is promoted by complementarity, but complementarity exists in many more ways than is captured in the sexual complementarity of a man and woman.[11]

Margaret Farley

Feminist Catholic theologian Margaret Farley stands within the Catholic Christian tradition but represents a significant modification of it. Her 2006 book, *Just Love: A Framework for Christian Sexual Ethics,* is intended not only for the church, but also for the kind of broad public audience that one finds in contemporary pluralistic societies. She explains that "I have attempted not only to incorporate major Christian beliefs and concerns, but also to render the framework intelligible and persuasive as part of a more general sexual ethics."[12]

Whereas John Paul II took his starting point from Scripture and natural law, Farley spends the first few chapters of her book interpreting the various challenges to sexual morality presented by recent developments in politics and technology, and by new forms of knowledge developed in philosophy, theology, the natural sciences, history, and cultural anthropology. She then presents her own constructive sexual ethics centered on the principles of autonomy and mutuality. She agrees with John Paul II's rejection of sexual hedonism, individualism, and the commercialization of sex, but she does not accept his understanding of human sexuality or many aspects of the moral code he employs in evaluating sexual activities. Farley takes the Bible to be a major source for discerning how to conduct our lives, but she believes that it is most valuable not as a source of specific revealed moral rules concerning sexual behavior, but rather as indicating general ethical principles like justice and love. Farley is here closer to Roughgarden than to John Paul II.

Like both Roughgarden and the pope, Farley's ethical norms flow from her description of human sexuality. Sexuality is an expression of our nature as social, affective, intelligent, and responsible beings. Our nature as relational and autonomous beings gives rise to the two key norms of love and justice. Ethical responsibility involves acting with justice in love. The norms of sexual ethics focus on the moral quality of the relationship between two partners: they include doing no unjustified harm, doing nothing without the consent of one's partner, building a relationship based on mutuality and equality, maintaining fidelity to commitment, and generating fruitfulness in the lives of others.[13] Advocates of the theology of the body would regard Farley's position as excessively lax, but in fact it does offer substantive norms, consistent conformity to which requires maturity, self-knowledge, and virtue.

Farley extends the meaning of "procreative" to "fruitfulness," and then urges readers to recognize that there are "multiple forms of fruitfulness in love for others, care for others, making the world a better place for others than 'just the two of us.'"[14] Procreation constitutes a good but not the supreme good of marriage. She argues that the Catholic Church's elevation of the unitive good of marriage at the Second Vatican Council and in later documents not only makes room for non-procreative sex within marriage (though not through the use of artificial contraception) but even opens the door to recognizing the value of non-procreative sexual relations outside of marriage.

The potential and weakness of contemporary society are assessed here along the lines suggested by Roughgarden rather than John Paul II. Developments in the last few decades have encouraged greater tolerance in how we think about sexuality, challenges the stereotype of male and female complementarity, and allows for a more positive assessment of same-sex relations. Farley is critical of both John Paul II's ahistorical use of Scripture and natural law, particularly as it leads to a narrow reading of gender and its implications.

Like Roughgarden, Farley regards sex and gender as much more complex than does John Paul II. "No one doubts that human persons are in some sense gendered," she writes, "but what this means and whether or why it is important are disputed questions."[15] She goes on to note a point of supreme importance to Roughgarden: "Equally contested are the assumptions that there are only two genders and the question of whether and why gender should control social roles within human communities."[16] Contemporary knowledge has definitively discredited the kind of gender categorization developed by the "theology of the body." The binary categorization is not only quaint but dangerous in that it historically "formed imaginations, actions, and roles which in turn determined that he who embodied the active principle was greater than she who simply waited—for sex, for gestation, for birthing which was not of her doing and not under her control."[17] The equality and mutuality thus have to replace the hierarchy of complementarity and the sacralization of oppression.

Farley endorses Roughgarden's objection to binary categories. She has no doubt that the "masculine/feminine dualism" by its very nature tends to "breed hierarchy."[18] St. Paul's "no longer male and female . . . for all are one in Christ Jesus" (Gal. 3:28) provides a vision from which "to eliminate the binary construction of gender as such."[19] Farley regards the pope's language of "complete self-giving" as exaggerated, excessively idealistic, and naively open to being misused to justify the exploitation of self-sacrificing women by more powerful men.

This ethic of love is constituted by "an affective way of being in union, and an affective affirmation of what is loved."[20] The minimal expression of this kind of affirmation involves respect for persons, treating people as ends in themselves, regarding them as possessing equal worth to the self, and honoring their autonomy and capacity for free choice and self-determination.[21] Farley here speaks to a deep concern of Roughgarden that people be allowed to decide how to live their own lives and be respected for their decisions as long as these decisions reflect respect for others.

Farley understandably offers a much more extensive account of "true and good love"[22] than does Roughgarden. Farley avoids subjectivism and promotes a kind of moral realism when she argues that the criterion for a true and good love is not determined by one's feelings but rather is "the concrete reality of the beloved—of whoever and whatever is loved."[23] Love that distorts or ignores the truth is, to that extent, false. Conversely, love is "right and good insofar as it aims to affirm truthfully the concrete reality of the beloved."[24] Both authors would concur that one need not be heterosexual to exercise the capacity to affirm truthfully the concrete reality of the beloved. Their commitment to the autonomy of the agent, and to the moral possibilities of nonheterosexuals to achieve genuine interpersonal mutuality,[25] places this ethic at quite a distance from that of John Paul II. "Today we also know that the possibilities of mutuality exist for many forms of relationship—whether heterosexual or gay, whether with genital sex or the multiple other ways of embodying our desires and our loves."[26] Mature and just love involves "active receptivity and receptive activity—each partner active, each one receptive."[27] Farley's more robust ethic can be complemented by Roughgarden's empirical work, and the latter's somewhat sketchy ethic receives substantive support from the former.

Affective affirmation of others leads to a commitment to justice for them. We might not be able to attain intense mutuality for all persons, but we can be committed to justice for them. This includes not leaving people in positions where they are vulnerable to discrimination, abuse, or violence. Domestic partnership laws offer a legal remedy to the attitudes underlying discrimination.[28] Respecting persons requires that we take their stories seriously. Whereas the "revealed" natural law approach identifies the "normatively" human as what is given in the Scriptures and tradition as interpreted by the magisterium, Farley relies on, in addition to these important sources, the lived experience of people who do not fit conventional norms.

Our understanding matures as it is informed by the truth disclosed in these stories of what it means to live in love and justice. Farley argues that we ought to take seriously the "clear and profound testimonies to the life-enhancing possibilities of same-sex relations and the integrating possibilities of sexual activity within these relations. We have the witness that homosexuality can be a way of embodying responsible human love and sustaining Christian friendship."[29] The last part of Roughgarden's *Evolution's Rainbow* in fact explores such narratives. Farley maintains that while scientific studies can be helpful, the most valuable basis for assessing the morality of sexual conduct comes not from science but rather from the particular stories of those who live integrated, virtuous, and flourishing lives as covenanted gays or lesbians and from the particular stories of the roles these individuals play within their communities as good neighbors and citizens.[30]

Attentiveness to experience underscores sexual diversity. Farley's experienced-based ethic would seem to echo Roughgarden's scientific findings in this regard. Some people come to understand that they are gay from the time they were children, some women have felt attracted to both men and women from early adolescence, and some women choose to be lesbian for political and moral reasons. Farley maintains that whether gender identity is "given" or "chosen," sexual relationships and activities of persons "can and should be respected whether or not they have a choice to be otherwise."[31] This is not to say that all sexual relationships and activities should be respected—as we have seen, Farley spells out in some detail the traits of normatively acceptable sex. Roughgarden's normative position could be significantly enhanced by an infusion of Farley's ethical theory, which provides moral standards for sorting out the morally good and bad features of relationships. People in anomalous or unconventional conditions, Farley insists, ought to be encouraged to pursue the human and moral good concretely available to them. This includes people whose gender identity is in some tension with their biological sex, but also, as she puts it, individuals for whom, and for various reasons, "gender simply does not matter."[32]

Listening to individual stories tells us more about human flourishing in the concrete than does philosophical analysis, scientific research, or theological speculation. Whereas Roughgarden understandably places much more emphasis on the scientific basis of dismantling conventional gender roles, she would agree with Farley's judgment that one does not need scientific support for the ethical judgment that, "No one ought here to pass judgment on any configurations of gender."[33]

Farley holds that our growing awareness of sexual and gender diversity makes gender more important in one sense, but less so in another. It is more important "for those who must struggle to discover their gender identity and come to be at home in it." She avoids reducing the person to his or her gender identity. Yet at the same time, she adds, gender can also be considered less significant "as a way to exclude some identities from the circle of our common humanity."[34] By this she means that we can no longer assume that the violation of conventional generalizations about male or female identity constitutes a legitimate basis for denying someone's rights or excluding him or her from the circle of respect.

Nature for Farley is not normative. She regards God neither as Creator of a hierarchically structured moral order nor as the divine Teacher of a detailed Scriptural moral code that is meant to be applied to all times and places. The highest moral priority in her ethic is to promote loving and just relationships. Individuals ought to be free to live according to their own gender identities as long as they strive to shape their consciences to live up to the ethical standards of love and justice. If the church wants to imitate Jesus's concern for "the least" of our brothers and sisters, Catholics ought to focus their moral disapproval on those who discriminate rather than on the victims of injustice.

* * *

The opening of this chapter noted that the provisional nature of the scientific status of Roughgarden's social-selection theory makes any conclusions drawn from it somewhat tentative. Yet the theological and moral case for the values ascribed by both Farley and Roughgarden need not wait upon scientific valida-tion. This chapter has indicated that Roughgarden's work calls into question the binary ontology developed in John Paul II's theology of the body and the moral exclusion that it generates. Farley's critique of the theology of the body reinforces these doubts, and her work can be enriched by Roughgarden's research. At the same time, Farley's just love stands independently of scientific argumentation since it is essentially an experience-informed theological ethic. Farley provides an extensively developed ethical position that provides needed distinctions, nu-ances, and elaborations of what both she and Roughgarden identify as centrally important norms of love, justice, equality, and mutuality.

On the other side of the equation, John Paul II can remind us of three impor-tant aspects of Catholic faith that tend to be overlooked. First, Christian faith faces the reality of sin and regards human life as a grace-inspired journey to God marked by ongoing conversion; a renunciation of personal sin, selfishness, intemperance, and lust; and an embracing of a new way of life. This message challenges the popular centrality given to autonomy, personal preferences, and individual liberty. Second, Christian faith is communal and involves personal commitment to participation in the life of the church. This life depends upon an ordered and reasonable loyalty to the church and a commitment, as Paul put it, to "maintain the traditions even as I have delivered them to you" (I Cor. 11:2). Third, Christian faith is Eucharistic, a sharing in the bread given to the community and in the cup "poured out for the many" (Mark 14:25). The mys-tery of the Eucharist sustains the Christian community and its message that Christ is the savior of every human being. "With this in mind," wrote the pope, "how can we exclude anyone from our care? Rather, we must recognize Christ in the poorest and the most marginalized, those whom the Eucharist—which is communion in the body and blood of Christ given up for us—commits us to serve."[35] Farley and Roughgarden would add specification to who counts as the "marginalized."

This chapter closes with four sets of observations made on the basis of the work of Roughgarden, Farley and John Paul II. First, ethics and science need to be both distinguished and kept in contact with one another. Ethical positions rely in part on descriptions of human nature. These descriptions are usually philosophical and theological, but it is incumbent on ethicists to take into account relevant empirical data and theories made available by contemporary science. John Paul II's theology of the body is insulated from potentially correcting sources of insight coming from the sciences. Advocates of Catholic natural law tradition increase the plausibility of their positions to the extent that they show some empirical basis for them. Conversely, the danger of scientifically based discussions of ethical issues lies in a failure to note that empirical descriptions of nature do not, in and of themselves, justify moral claims about human conduct. Roughgarden as biologist makes a scientific case for her theory, but she has to make a theological and ethical case for the further normative argument she wishes to advance.

Second, all three authors identify the greatest human moral ideal as love, the affective affirmation of, and movement toward, what is recognized to be good.[36] John Paul II and Farley use their own words to communicate that an important challenge confronting human sexuality today is "humanization"—the need to direct this complex and multifunctional capacity to the service of love and commitment. The fact that we have the capacity to hold all three of these goods together—sex, love and commitment—radically separates us from other primates.[37] Human sexuality is much more than biology. Whereas animals go into heat, mate, and rear young according to patterns set by evolution, human beings undertake interpersonal and social commitments, forge strong affective bonds, engage in frequent sex, and deliberately take up a way of life that promotes the ongoing growth of the human purposes of sexuality.

Third, Farley and Roughgarden rightly note that social ethics needs to reflect more clearly on how social institutions in our pluralistic society can support love and commitment for couples existing outside the heterosexual context of the majority. John Paul II believed that the nature of genuine self-giving love entails the same heterosexual, monogamous, indissoluble, and procreative normative standards for every human being. One can argue, partly on the basis of Farley's and Roughgarden's work, respectively, that knowledge of evolution supports a greater sensitivity to concrete particularities in sex and gender because it does not draw such a strong normative connection between the natural reproductive end of sex and morally legitimate sexual activity. Evolutionary attentiveness to the diversity within populations underscores the difference between goods that in general contribute to human flourishing of most people and the specific and practical needs of concrete individuals who are striving to live well in the particular contexts of their own lives.

Finally, this realization bears a number of implications for the church's activity. First, it underscores the importance of promoting the dignity and worth of all members of the Body of Christ. Christ calls all Christians, John Paul II wrote, to be "heralds of human dignity." The church is supposed to be the "sacrament of the unity of humanity in Christ." It can meet this responsibility only by refusing to form "an identity based on exclusion"[38] and by undertaking a commitment to working for what Timothy Radcliffe, O.P., calls "the universal communion of the Kingdom."[39] This goal must be pursued on a number of levels.

Full incorporation of everyone into the Body of Christ is premised on the church's commitment to affirming, in thought, word, and deed, that every person possesses intrinsic dignity as a child of God, regardless of sexual identity. This affirmation can be advanced by serious pastoral engagement with marginalized members of the community in ways that involve effective listening, learning, and understanding. The central mystery of the life, death and resurrection of Jesus Christ is a sign of the universal reconciliation of all people in Christ. Radcliffe observes, "we can prepare ourselves for [this] gift by beginning to speak in ways that embody the capaciousness of God's Word."[40] The church needs to learn to speak with gays and lesbians, transsexuals and bisexuals, in ways that communicate a desire for understanding and friendship rather than contempt and rejection.

Respect, hospitality, and dialogue prepare the path for solidarity through community building and allow the church to be a sign of the unity of humanity in Christ. When this happens, as Radcliffe puts it beautifully, "people will be able to catch some hint of the mystery of God whose centre is nowhere and who[se] circumference is everywhere, and for whom no one is on the edge."[41] This goal of full inclusion requires the church first to eliminate injustice from its own institutional structures and practices. It should also lead the church to employ its moral authority in public discussions over sexual diversity and to condemn institutional injustice in the wider society and the irrational prejudice that often lies behind it. This prophetic voice should be complemented by public policy advocacy for equal access to human goods and equal respect for human and civil rights. These much needed modes of activity for full inclusion will probably not be exercised fully in the immediate future, but pursuit of the human good has always been a long-term project requiring patience, courage, and hope.

Notes

1. See Roughgarden, *Evolution's Rainbow* and "Challenging Darwin's Theory of Sexual Selection," 23–36.

2. John Paul II, *The Theology of the Body*, 76.

3. See the Apostolic Exhortation *Mulieris dignitatem*. See also John Paul II, *Man and Woman He Created Them*. Critical treatment is found in Johnson, "A Disembodied 'Theology of the Body,'" 111–27.

4. For a fine analysis, see Ross, "The Bridegroom and the Bride," 39–59.

5. Catholic News, "Vatican Bans Transsexuals from Religious Orders," February 3, 2003.

6. The pope was criticized for giving excessive attention to law at the expense of many other kinds of biblical symbols and literary genres and for not acknowledging significant issues of exegesis and hermeneutics raised by current biblical scholarship. See Jung, "The Promise of Postmodern Hermeneutics," 77–107 and Di Vito, "Questions about the Construction of (Homo)sexuality," 108–32. On the standard New Testament texts, see the somewhat dated but still instructive discussion by Scroggs, *The New Testament and Homosexuality*. The best concise discussion of the use of Scripture in ethics is Spohn, *What Are They Saying about Scripture in Ethics?*

7. For more detailed analysis, see Modras, "Pope John Paul II's Theology of the Body," 153–54.

8. See John Paul II, "Address to the Pontifical Academy of Sciences," 5; John Paul II, on the Galileo case, "Faith Can Never Conflict with Reason"; John Paul II, "Letter to the Reverend George V. Coyne," 377.

9. See Pope, *Human Evolution and Christian Ethics*, 32–55.

10. John Paul II, *Veritatis splendor*, no. 33, 54.

11. See Traina, "Papal Ideals, Marital Realities," 284.

12. Farley, *Just Love*, xii.

13. Ibid., 289. See also her more extended reflections in *Personal Commitments*.

14. Farley, *Just Love*, 290.

15. Ibid., 134.

16. Ibid.

17. Ibid., 221.

18. Ibid., 134.

19. Ibid., 140.

20. Ibid., 212.

21. Ibid.

22. Ibid., 200.

23. Ibid.

24. Ibid.

25. Ibid., 221.

26. Ibid.

27. Ibid.

28. See Williams, "Religion, Politics, and Gay/Lesbian Civil Rights."

29. Farley, "An Ethic for Same-Sex Relations," 338.

30. See Pope, "Scientific and Natural Law Analyses of Homosexuality;" and "The Magisterium's Arguments against 'Same Sex Marriage.'"

31. Farley, *Just Love*, 295.

32. Ibid., 153.

33. Ibid.

34. Ibid., 155–56.

35. John Paul II, "Respect for Human Rights."

36. See Farley, *Just Love*, 201 ff.

37. See Cahill, *Sex, Gender, and Christian Ethics*, 93–97.

38. Radcliffe, *What Is the Point of Being Christian?* 144.

39. Ibid., 143–44.

40. Ibid., 162.

41. Ibid., 163.

13

The Triumph of Diversity

Hopkins's "Pied Beauty"

FRANK FENNELL

I begin with the poem, written by Gerard Hopkins (the "Manley" came later) in the summer of 1877 while he was finishing his studies at the Jesuit novitiate of St. Bueno's in northern Wales:

Glory be to God for dappled things—
For skies of couple-colour as a brinded cow;
For rose-moles all in stipple upon trout that swim;
Fresh-firecoal chestnut-falls; finches' wings;
Landscape plotted and pieced—fold, fallow, and plough;
And all trades, their gear and tackle and trim.
All things counter, original, spare, strange;
Whatever is fickle, freckled (who knows how?)
With swift, slow; sweet, sour; adazzle, dim;
He fathers-forth whose beauty is past change:
             Praise him.[1]

Now I would suggest that we start by keeping in mind Helen Vendler's dictum that one can analyze a poem with the trained eye of a scholar, but that first one should read it as a human being. The scholar's analysis would enable us to recognize, for example, that this is an experiment in writing what Hopkins called a curtal sonnet, one that is a $^3/_4$ size replica of a full Petrarchan sonnet; to explain the application to this poem of Hopkins's idiosyncratic theories about poetry, including such concepts as *inscape* and *instress* and such methods as *sprung paeonic rhythm;* to discover the roots—in Greek poetry (Hopkins had won a rare double first in classics when graduating from Balliol College, Oxford, and he had taught Greek for two years in London); in Anglo-Saxon poetry (he was teaching himself Anglo-Saxon); and in Welsh *cynghanedd* (he had taken Welsh lessons from a local native speaker)—of his unusual poetic language. While I will return to *inscape* shortly, for the most part we can put such scholarly questions aside. They are important, but for another time and place.

Instead, let us take Vendler's recommendation seriously and ask of this poem some simple questions about what it means to us as thinking, feeling human beings. Any reader of this poem—better yet, any *hearer* or *reciter* (for Hopkins was convinced that all poetry was meant to be heard, not read)—will come away from the experience of "Pied Beauty" with several strong impressions:

* That the poet has been deeply moved, not by ordinary manifestations of beauty, but rather by unusual and diverse kinds of beauty: beauty that is "pied," that is to say spotted or mottled, like a piebald horse, beauty that is irregular, unusual, asymmetrical, untamed, natural.
* That nature, whether "animal, vegetable, or mineral," offers endless and finely detailed expressions of this offbeat kind of beauty, from cloud formations to trout to chestnuts to birds' wings.
* That human life affords countless examples as well, from plotted landscapes in rural areas to the "gear and tackle" of the manual laborer.
* That this wondrous variety—the poet does not just notice the diversity, he celebrates it—has an author, a source, to whom the poet gives a family name ("father") and urges us to offer praise.

For a full appreciation of the poem and its relationship to the theme of this book, I suggest that we begin by unpacking (dare I even say reveling in?) the evocative imagery of the poem. Notice that what the poet does first is simply give us a list, a list of "dappled things" for which he wants to give praise to God. Here is the list:

* *skies of couple-colour as a brinded cow.* The poet begins his list by directing our attention to the ways the clouds in the sky are constantly changing shape and color, constantly moving and reforming, just as in a herd of cattle no two animals have the same pattern of coloration (*brinded* or *brindled* means having irregular streaks or spots—think of Holstein cows like the ones on milk cartons).
* *rose-moles all in stipple on trout that swim.* Stippling is a painter's technique, much favored by the French Impressionists, of using the brush for dots or short touches rather than lines and then letting the dots form a pattern. The kind of trout that Hopkins knew have these little rose-colored dots on their sides, dots that also look like moles and that the poet imagines as having been put there by God-as-Impressionist-painter. And Hopkins is very accurate scientifically when he specifies that these are trout "that swim," because the rose-colored dots disappear the moment the fish is removed from water.
* *Fresh-firecoal chestnut-falls.* When chestnuts fall to the ground, their outer

covering often breaks away, revealing the wonderful red colors of the inner shell which gleam like fiery coals.

* *finches' wings.* Ever seen them? Beautiful wings, with variegated, light-colored bands running across them.

* *Landscape plotted and pieced—fold, fallow, and plough;* Here the poet, long in advance of airplanes, imagines what it must be like to see a landscape from high above, with fences or hedgerows marking off the irregular parcels of land, some of which have been plowed, some of which lie fallow, some of which are riven by streams or ditches. Unlike the earlier items in this catalog, nature now has been marked by human manipulation—we are the ones who put up fences, plow fields, dig ditches. But nature is still beautiful.

* *And all trades, their gear and tackle and trim.* Perhaps the most unusual entry in this catalog of pied beauty. The poet means the beauty of such simple, manmade artifacts as a carpenter's tools or a farmer's equipment for his horse—not at all the sorts of things we are accustomed to call beautiful, but all, looked at in the right way, looked at in the way the poet teaches, beautiful nonetheless.

What follows this catalog is the short series of generalizations we noticed before. First the poet wants to praise what he has just exemplified, namely "All things counter, original, spare, strange." *Counter* means things that go against, run counter to, the usual grain, the usual way, the usual form—we speak, for example, of counterarguments, of counterattacks. *Original* and *strange* we know. The beauty of *spare* we understand today, after being exposed to modern painting and modern architecture ("less is more"), but it was a rare notion in Hopkins's day.

The poet continues with his summing up: He praises the beauty of what is *fickle* (inconstant, changeful, capricious), of what is *freckled* (there again is that notion of delight in things spotted or pied—and any child who hated his or her freckles will cheer this indirect praise of their beauty). He praises also the beauty of opposites, creatures or things that are *swift* or *slow,* foods that are *sour* just as much as those that are *sweet,* items that are dull and dim just as much as those that dazzle our senses.

Finally, the poet points to the divine author of such beauty, the eternal one, the only one in the universe "whose beauty is past change" and in whose loving, parental care we all rest. Hopkins closes with a simple but forceful adjuration, "Praise him," in which he puns on the personal pronoun ("him") and the song of praise (hymn).

Hopkins's catalog of diverse beauties startles us, awakens us to diverse kinds of beauty we have perhaps missed. How much is there in life that we have dismissed, overlooked, thought was not beautiful because our culture has taught us it was not? Look again, says the poet. Forget what your culture has told you about how to look. Look at *everything, every thing,* because every created thing has its own special kind of beauty.

We could continue in this vein and gain a still fuller appreciation of the aesthetic aspects of the poem. But I want instead to ask two simple questions: Where did these ideas about "pied beauty" come from, and what if anything might they say about our joint endeavor to reflect on sexual diversity?

*   *   *

To answer the "where did these ideas come from" question, I will work backward in time, beginning with the poet himself and then tracing his intellectual forbears. As we move back in time we will also find ourselves touching on aspects of what might be called Hopkins's Christian heritage.

The "Pied Beauty" poem clearly begins in the poet's experiences. We know from his letters and journals that from an early age Hopkins was attracted to manifestations of natural beauty, especially beauty of an unusual kind. Consider this journal entry from March 1871, before Hopkins had resumed writing poetry:

> Bright morning; pied skies, hail. In the afternoon the wind was from the N., very cold; long bows of soft grey cloud straining the whole heaven but spanning the sky with a slow entasis which left a strip of cold porcelain blue. The long ribs or girders were as rollers/ across the wind, not in it, but across them there lay fine grass-ends, sided off down the perspective, as if locks of vapour blown free from the main ribs of the wind. (204)

That's a poet's journal entry even if he wasn't writing his mature poems yet. Note the minute observation, the fascination with "pied" cloud displays, the attempts to find metaphorical equivalents for what is being so carefully observed.

Perhaps even more to the point, consider this journal entry from a month later:

> This is the time to study inscape in the spraying of trees, for the swelling buds carry them to a pitch which the eye could not else gather—for out of much much more, out of little not much, out of nothing nothing: in these sprays at all events there is a new world of inscape. The male ashes are very boldly jotted with the heads of the bloom which tuft the outer ends of the branches. . . . (205)

The poet then goes on for another four long sentences on just what can be observed in the male ash tree. More key for our purposes is that word *inscape,* which I alluded to before and which appears twice in this entry. Inscape is a word of Hopkins's own coinage. It refers, not just to the minute observations themselves, but rather to the pattern, ever-shifting but instantaneously grasped, which nature affords to the careful and sensitive observer.

At each moment, depending on one's focus, there is a unique pattern evident in nature, a highly particularized and individualized perception. That pattern is fleeting, evanescent. But it can be "fixed" through a work of art, whether painting or poem or even journal entry. In fact, for Hopkins inscapes and inscaping (the word can function as both noun and verb) define poetry: "[D]esign, pattern, or what I am in the habit of calling 'inscape' is what I above all aim at in poetry," he tells his friend Robert Bridges (235). So important did this concept become, not only for Hopkins but for others, that inscape is now an entry in the *Oxford English Dictionary (OED)*, where it is defined as "the individual or essential quality of a thing; the uniqueness of an observed object, scene, event, etc."[2] So if it is the uniqueness, the individual quality, of a scene that we should treasure, and if the poem itself (and the poet's style) must be just as unique, just as individualized, we come a little closer to understanding "Pied Beauty" and the kind of beauty it praises.

But as original and unique as Hopkins may have been, he was not composing in an intellectual vacuum. He has intellectual forbears. Some were elder Victorian contemporaries, such as the art critics John Ruskin and Walter Pater (Pater had been Hopkins's "don," or tutor, at Oxford). But by the time Hopkins wrote "Pied Beauty" he was also a member of the Jesuit order, and as a Jesuit he had been formed, and was continuing to be formed, by religious mentors too.

First, of course, for a Jesuit was the *Spiritual Exercises* formulated by St. Ignatius. Those *Exercises* have many dimensions and requirements, but the most relevant for our purposes is the requirement that the exercitant compose meditations very specific in their time, place, and circumstance. In other words, the meditator first evokes a mental image of a particular place and circumstance—for example, a scene from the life of Christ. All of the senses should be engaged; mentally one must "be there" as fully as one can. Then, when one has supplied every sensory detail that one can, so that the scene is as completely present as it can possibly be, one should meditate on the spiritual significance of what has been "seen/touched/smelled." This meditation evolves into a colloquy, a colloquy for example with God in Christ, and thus the meditation ends with what amounts to a prayer.

Hopkins's poems, as David Downes[3] and others have shown, often follow this pattern he learned from the founder of his order. "Pied Beauty" begins with detailed observations, a series of them, inscapes of the world the poet knows and apprehends with his senses. Then comes the explanation of their significance ("He fathers forth whose beauty is past change"), followed by a brief prayer ("Praise him"). Indirectly the poem becomes an adjuration to us: we too can have access to these and similar inscapes, just as much as the poet can, and we too can utter a "praise hymn" in which we "praise him." This poem becomes an example of what Paul Mariani calls a poem "of double vision, of the spiritual inhering in the physical."[4]

Beyond this, the *Spiritual Exercises* offers a reason for requiring such careful compositions of place. "[A]ll good things and gifts descend from above, . . . just as the rays descend from the sun and the waters from the spring," the poet quotes approvingly from Ignatius.[5] All that we see and do and perceive, both the saint and his disciple believe, comes as gift, a gift for which the proper posture is one of thanks. While contemporaries like Annie Dillard[6] and others have articulated a similar idea, that posture does not have the same operative power in today's world that it once had. Nor did it have that power in Hopkins's own Victorian world. Nevertheless we cannot understand what Hopkins is trying to do with his poems without understanding this vital part of the Catholic intellectual heritage, which he received during his training as a Jesuit and which through annual retreats he maintained throughout his (relatively short) life.

But Hopkins encountered an even more formative influence during his years of training for the priesthood. In August of 1872 he came upon a two-volume edition, printed (in Latin) in Venice in 1514, of the works of the medieval philosopher Duns Scotus. Johannes Duns Scotus (1265–1308) was a Franciscan who taught first at Hopkins's beloved Oxford and then at the University of Paris. Known as the Subtle Doctor because of the complexity of his thinking, Scotus developed many ideas that Hopkins found attractive and stimulating. Among them four related concepts seem key:

* God's attributes are prototypes of the attributes of all created things.
* These attributes can be differentiated one from another, in created things just as much as in God.
* Such differentiation might more properly be called individuation—Scotus's term for it was *haecceitas*—and it is of fundamental importance to the world as we know it.
* Source and analog for this principle of individuation was the Incarnation of Christ, not (argued Scotus) a postlapsarian divine intervention but rather a foundational principle of creation from the very beginning.

In each of these instances Scotus was articulating a position that differed from that of other scholastic philosophers. Historically he proved to be arguing on behalf of a losing cause, because Thomas Aquinas and others carried the day and became the "official" theologians for the next seven centuries. But the influence of Scotus on Hopkins was profound and lasting—Hopkins even wrote a poem for him ("Duns Scotus' Oxford").

The effect of Scotus on Hopkins's poetry in general and on "Pied Beauty" in particular is clear. If "Pied Beauty" is anything, it is a poem about exactly those bulleted items above, in other words it is about individuation, about differentiation, and about the divine source for this differentiation and diversity. While the diversity and individuality of all created things may be found and celebrated in Hopkins's work before 1872—in his learnings from Ruskin and Pater, in his Jesuit tutelage, in his own concept of inscape—what Scotus and *haecceitas* gave him was a philosophical and theological justification for looking at the world in the way that he did.

Especially key was Scotus's idea that the wonderful diversity that we find in the world was something that was there from the very beginning, something that was always part and parcel of creation as we know it. Diversity was/is *prelapsarian;* in other words it predates the Fall as described in the Book of Genesis. (Even to say "predates" of course implies a chronology foreign to a God who transcends time, but language entraps us.) Diversity is not something we choose, not something imposed on our world because of our sins, not something meant to bewilder or distract us. Instead diversity is *who we are,* it is what nature is. Diversity reflects God's plan from the very start of the universe.

To frame the argument about diversity in this way, as Scotus and therefore Hopkins do, has important consequences. If diversity is part of creation from the very beginning, our customary ideas—in other words, the ideas "given" to us by our culture—may be askew. What we think is beautiful, that is, what our culture has taught us to think is beautiful, may be too limited. Perhaps we have been too blind to the diverse, "pied" kinds of beauty around us. If so, Scotus through Hopkins opens our eyes to new, infinitely variegated kinds of beauty and thus stretches our mind and our imagination. So, too, what our culture has told us to judge as "unnatural" or as "immoral" may be too limited. How can something, some human act or habit or characteristic or orientation, be "unnatural" or "immoral" just because it is different, diverse? If it is part of the created world, it is by definition, Scotus and Hopkins teach us, beautiful. There may be unnatural or immoral acts, but that is because of what humans choose to do to others, not because of what or who they are.

The importance of Scotus to Hopkins is underlined by the price Hopkins paid for adhering to the ideas of the Subtle Doctor. When, in 1877, Hopkins came up to the set of examinations that would determine whether he would stay at St. Bueno's for a fourth year and thus be eligible for administrative advancement in the Jesuit order, he "failed" them. He failed them, it now seems clear, not because of the inadequacy of his written and oral responses (this was a man with a double first at Oxford), but rather because of his stubborn adherence in his answers to the philosophy of Duns Scotus at a time when his examiners believed that Thomism, and Thomism alone, offered the definitive answers. Hopkins was sent off to be a parish curate, taking with him a hard-won allegiance to this part of his Catholic heritage.

We should move on now to the important question of the *consequences* of these ideas—not for Hopkins, but for us.

* * *

What might these ideas contribute to our reflections on diversity in general, and sexual and gender diversity in particular?

To clear the ground, let me first indicate that "Pied Beauty" does not *prove* anything. Poetry never does. As MacLeish puts it in "Ars Poetica":

> A poem should not mean,
> But be.

The action of a poem upon us will not be one of logic, of reason. We will not have been led by a chain of inductive or deductive reasoning to arrive at a conclusion, much less a series of such conclusions such as would be required for a philosophy or a theology.

So if poetry is not a logical demonstration, what is it? Good poetry is a *dramatization,* a putting into words of something seen, felt, experienced. It is a celebration of a moment, of a vision, of what Hopkins, following his beloved Scotus, called an inscape.

But no dramatization—of diversity or anything else—will be of any use to you as a reader unless you have fully encountered it, fully recognized what the poem is dramatizing, fully taken in what the poem is saying to you. To explain this important point better, we need to make a short detour into modern thinking on this topic. In his essay "A Way to Language," the German philosopher Martin Heidegger makes the distinction between speaking and what he calls "Saying." "Saying" is the way language—in this case, poetry—evidences its designs on us. Saying presumes listeners:

> We . . . listen to language in this way, that we let it say its saying to us. No matter in what way we may listen besides, whenever we listen to something we are *letting something be said to us.* . . . In our speaking, . . . we [then] say again the Saying we have heard.[7]

In other words, we are not the same people after the Saying of the poem as we were before. We are not the same people after we have read and heard "Pied Beauty" as we were before we read and heard it. If we have read and listened carefully, Hopkins's world and his way of looking at it will at least in some small way have been superimposed on our world and our way of looking, even if just for a moment.

So a poem or any text that fully *is,* that has worked its Saying on us, will have its deepest effect when we absorb it, take it in, own it, make it part of the furniture of our mind. Heidegger again: "This owning . . . we call Appropriation. . . .

Appropriation, seen as it is shown by saying, cannot be represented either as an occurrence or a happening—it can only be experienced as the abiding gift yielded by Saying."[8] Appropriation applies to any text, but it is indeed a gift; in other words it needs an active recipient or it will not happen. Moreover, that active recipient must go out to "meet" the text, to make it his or her own. If we as readers or hearers are distracted, have our minds elsewhere, appropriation will not happen; to paraphrase Thoreau, only that text dawns on us to which we are awake. Also if the text lacks a powerful language, if it does not really "Say," appropriation will not happen either. But when the gift is given, and when the gift is a beautiful one, and when the gift is gratefully accepted, the effect is powerful.

While appropriation can happen with any text, poetry, Heidegger goes on to claim, is often the most profound expression of this power of language to enact a Saying:

> If we listen to the poem . . . we then let the poet tell us, and let ourselves be told together with him, what is worthy of the thinking of a poetic being.
> To let ourselves be told what is worthy of thinking means—to think.[9]

This reciprocal relationship between poetry and thinking "aims to call forth the *nature* of language."[10] So complete is the claim that poetry has on us that it transcends historical circumstance, becoming a singing of poet's soul to listener's/ reader's soul so that both can sing, in perfect harmony, of mankind's destiny— "that is to say, [it] saves mankind."[11] Poetry as the singer of man's destiny, as the savior of mankind—no Romantic theorist, not a Fichte or a Lavater, makes a higher claim for poetry than this. And with reference to "Pied Beauty," it does not matter whether Hopkins was a Victorian British Jesuit priest (*his* "historical circumstance"), the only question will be whether his language truly "Says" something to us.

Reading and hearing a poem—really reading and hearing it—is therefore to appropriate it, so the reader of a poem engages in the most profound kind of thinking. But it is not the kind of thinking that builds a theological or philosophical structure. The attentive reader of "Pied Beauty" will, I contend, encounter a vivid, beautiful celebration of diverse kinds of beauty. If he or she appropriates the poem, really takes it in and rejoices with the poet over every imaginable kind of diversity, that is enough, and all the poet could hope for.

So if poetry is a dramatization rather than a chain of reasoning, do I mean to imply that "Pied Beauty" has nothing to do with the focus of this book, nothing to say to us today as we inquire into this subject of diversity, especially sexual and gender diversity? Again I would answer no. "Pied Beauty" can indeed be very relevant, precisely because you, if you are or have been a receptive hearer of the poem, may well have appropriated its Saying, may well have tucked this celebration of diversity away in the corner of your mind. The day may come, now, or soon, or many years from now, when your thoughts will turn to the topic of diversity—diversity in nature, diversity in human beings, diversity in human ideas and values and orientations. When that happens, if you have appropriated "Pied Beauty" in the way Heidegger describes, it may well be that it suddenly becomes the perfect vehicle for expressing what you are thinking and feeling and imagining. You will not just be reading the poem, you will *be* the poem, you will join the poet in reveling at what wonderfully diverse kinds of beauty God has given us.

Certainly there is no better poetic embodiment of the triumph of diversity in all of its forms than this poem. Not only does it praise diverse kinds of beauty, it teaches us how to *see* that beauty in the first place. We learn to look closely, minutely, to *find* the beauty that is there every minute, in a thousand fleeting forms, just as Hopkins did in his journal entries. We learn to *imagine* that beauty, as Hopkins did in his use of the *Spiritual Exercises.* And we learn to *accept* too, as Hopkins did through Duns Scotus. If diverse beauty, and diversity itself, is there from the very beginning, part of God's plan for the world and for us, then we too can accept and embrace it as part of that plan. It should come as no surprise to us, for example, that this diversity is just as much a part of our sexual world, our sexual nature, as it is of any other aspect of that world and nature. Arguments about what is "wrong" or "unnatural" become irrelevant, because sexual and gender diversity—just like every other kind of diversity—has been present from the very beginning.

A poetic grasp of diversity, which is what Hopkins gives us, does not *require* anything. But it makes for a wonderful celebration!

Notes

1. All Hopkins citations are from Phillips, ed., *The Oxford Authors: Gerard Manley Hopkins.* The poem is on pages 132–33. Works in copyright are quoted by permission of Oxford University Press on behalf of The British Province of the Society of Jesus.

2. *Oxford English Dictionary,* 2nd edition (1989), accessed online.

3. Downes, *Gerard Manley Hopkins.*

4. Mariani, *A Commentary on the Complete Poems of Gerard Manley Hopkins,* xxiv.

5. Hopkins, *The Sermons and Devotional Writings of Gerard Manley Hopkins,* 124.

6. Dillard, *Living by Fiction,* 144.

7. Heidegger, *On the Way to Language,* 124.

8. Ibid., 127.

9. Ibid., 155.

10. Ibid., 161.

11. Ibid., 196.

14

Christ as Bride

Toward a Christology of Diversity

SUSAN A. ROSS

The "Bridegroom-Bride" metaphor in Roman Catholic theology has become a prominent theme in recent decades, particularly in the works of John Paul II. In brief, this metaphor and its accompanying images have been used to develop a theological understanding of male-female complementarity, where God, Christ, the clergy, and men stand for the Bridegroom, and creation, humanity, lay people, and women stand for the Bride. John Paul II builds on the theology of Hans Urs von Balthasar (1905–1988), a Swiss theologian whose theology has, in recent years, received far more attention than it did during his lifetime, particularly by theologians unhappy with liberal tendencies in theology.[1] I developed and critiqued some of these ideas in an earlier article that focused on theological anthropology; this essay extends some of these reflections to Christology, that is, theological work on the meaning of Jesus Christ.[2]

The Bridegroom-Bride metaphor is an ancient one, going back well into the prebiblical traditions on which biblical writers relied. It was taken up by Paul in the New Testament and further developed by medieval mystical writers. In more recent years, however, it has become much more focused and deliberate.[3] Rather than being one of a number of metaphors for intimacy with God, the "nuptial metaphor" is now being used as the basis for gender essentialism, where the Bridegroom is the active partner, initiating and leading, and the Bride is the "receptive" partner (most church use of this language no longer uses "passive"), following and cooperating with the Bridegroom.

Christ as Bridegroom is a metaphor that was first developed by Paul in his epistles; this will not be my focus as I am not a Pauline scholar. I will focus rather on some of the recent ways that the metaphor has been used in relation to questions relating to women, and by extension to other "others," including sexual and gender minorities. I want to raise the question of the adequacy of this language, particularly if the Catholic (or any Christian) tradition aims to take reason and science seriously. In addition, I will raise the further theological question of the relationship of the historical Jesus to the "saving work" of Christ, and whether maleness is essential to this "saving work."

Christ as Bridegroom in Recent Magisterial Theology

In 1977, the Vatican issued its statement on the "Question of the Admission of Women to the Ordained Priesthood."[4] In this document, the Vatican argued against the ordination of women on the basis of two related lines of reasoning. The first was historical precedent. Jesus "did not call any women to be one of the twelve," including his mother, and this was affirmed in apostolic tradition. Since Jesus had countered his own Jewish tradition in a number of ways, the fact that he did not call women to be apostles was understood by the Vatican to be a deliberate decision on his part, and not simply due to historical circumstances. And in the Church's subsequent history, women had not been ordained to the priesthood. Thus there did not seem to be good reasons for changing this long-standing policy.

Some critics took issue with this argument, claiming that there was evidence for women's presbyteral leadership in the early church.[5] Advocates for women's ordination have pointed to the existence of iconographic evidence for women's leadership.[6] But even the Vatican itself acknowledged that history alone is not a sufficient reason for maintaining this rule. In fact its Biblical Commission argued that there was no compelling scriptural basis for either side of the argument.[7]

The Vatican declaration argued further against the ordination of women on the basis of the "sacramental mystery of the priesthood." This most controversial part of the Vatican's argument was the statement that there would not be a "natural resemblance to Christ" if women were ordained. The statement is worth quoting in full:

> The Christian priesthood is therefore of a sacramental nature: the priest is a sign, the supernatural effectiveness of which comes from the ordination received, but a *sign that must be perceptible and which the faithful must be able to recognize with ease*. The whole sacramental economy is in fact based upon natural signs, on symbols imprinted upon the human psychology: "Sacramental signs," says Saint Thomas, "represent what they signify by *natural resemblance*." The same natural resemblance is required for persons as for things: when *Christ's role in the Eucharist is to be expressed sacramentally, there would not be this "natural resemblance" which must exist between Christ and his minister if the role of Christ were not taken by a man: in such a case it would be difficult to see in the minister the image of Christ. For Christ himself was and remains a man* (*Inter Insigniores* 5; emphases mine).

This statement received an enormous amount of criticism, ranging from questions about the appropriateness of white western celibate males lacking a "natural resemblance" to Palestinian married men and whether racial differences counted for "natural resemblance."[8] (The Vatican's answer was that racial differences are not "essential" differences.) In subsequent discussions of women's ordination, the language of "natural resemblance" disappeared, and was more or less replaced by the language of Christ as Bridegroom. Official church statements argued that differences of sex constituted something that went much deeper than racial or ethnic difference. Yet the language of "natural resemblance" is significant. Aquinas observes that " . . . it follows that the sacramental signs consist in sensible things: just as in the Divine Scriptures spiritual things are set before us under the guise of things sensible," indicating, as Frank Catania notes in this volume, that "science," broadly speaking, is not an insignificant source for Aquinas's theology.[9]

In the writings of John Paul II, particularly his 1988 encyclical *Mulieris dignitatem* (hereafter MD), the spousal metaphor is developed further, particularly in relation to Mary, the mother of Jesus. Mary's "yes" to God becomes the model for humanity's response to God. Humanity in relation to God is "feminine," in that human beings take the role of responding to God, along the model of Mary. The "feminine" nature of the soul is also a very old idea; sources for this are especially abundant in medieval spirituality.[10] Interestingly, men are both "male and female": male in terms of their bodiliness and in relation to women, but female in relation to God as responsive to God's invitation.[11]

In his writings on the "theology of the body," John Paul II develops the complementarity of the sexes further.[12] Men and women are "ordered to each other," in a profoundly relational understanding of the self. Maleness and femaleness are seen as "essential" dimensions of the person that are not exchangeable. To be a woman is to be fundamentally "receptive" and open to the other. Thus, John Paul II is very critical of forms of feminism that seek to make women "like men." There is a "special genius" to womanhood that is oriented toward relationship and nurturing, so that every woman, whether she is a biological mother or not, has a "maternal" spirituality. Because of these "essential" differences, women cannot be ordained priests, and ought to be content with the "special" vocation unique to women. In his encyclical of 2005, *Deus caritas est*, Pope Benedict XVI concluded his reflections on love with a reference to the receptive Mary, which continues the same theme; it must be said, however, that he has not evidenced the same affinity for the "spousal" metaphor in the way that his predecessor did.[13]

In all of these papal statements, the maleness not only of the human Jesus but the divine Christ is emphasized; John Paul II in particular makes the point that Christ represents the bridegroom: "Since it is God's love, its spousal character is properly divine, even though it is expressed by the analogy of a man's love for a woman. The woman-bride is Israel, God's Chosen People, and this choice originates exclusively in God's gratuitous love." (MD, 23) For John Paul II, God really *is* male, not just by linguistic convention, but by nature—although this view is never put in quite these stark terms. Yet to be male is to be the origin, the source, the first, the initiator. To be female is to be derivative of the male and always profoundly dependent upon the male—indeed, to derive one's entire identity by relation and response to the male: "A woman's dignity is closely connected with the love which she receives by the very reason of her femininity; it is likewise connected *with the love which she gives in return.*" (MD, 30; emphasis in original). Moreover, there is no distinction between "sex" and "gender" in Vatican and papal writings: The two are identical since biology is, ultimately, human destiny. Consequently, this is one of the fundamental reasons for seeing "homosexuality" as a "disorder": clearly, something is wrong when a man desires another man, since he is *by nature* oriented towards women.

Feminist Theological Considerations of Christology

Contemporary feminist theologians have taken on the challenge of a biologically male-centered Christology by asking the question "Can a Male Savior Save Women?" In this chapter of *Sexism and God-Talk,* Rosemary Radford Ruether notes: "Behind this argument of the necessary maleness of Christ lies the theological assumption of the maleness of God"[14] And in her review of "alternative Christologies," Ruether observes that what many of them do is simply offer women an identification with the "feminine side" of Jesus, or a "splitting of the past revelation of Christ as the historical Jesus from the ongoing Spirit" (135). She goes on to argue that a new starting point for contemporary Christology involves "a reencounter with the Jesus of the Synoptic Gospels" where what is revealed is a "criticism of religious and social hierarchy . . . remarkably parallel to feminist criticism" (135). After reviewing the highlights of Jesus's "iconoclastic reversal" (136) of traditional values, Ruether concludes that "[t]heologically speaking, then, we might say that the maleness of Jesus has no ultimate significance. It has socially symbolic significance in the framework of societies of patriarchal privilege" (137). She distinguishes between the historical human being Jesus of Nazareth and Christ as the "redemptive person and Word of God" and concludes that "Christ is not necessarily male, nor is the redeemed community only women, but a new humanity, female and male" (138). She also argues that "those who have been liberated can, in turn, become paradigmatic, liberating persons for others" (138).

Elizabeth Johnson takes up the question of the "distortion" of the Christ in *She Who Is.* Johnson observes that " . . . of all the doctrines of the church Christology is the one most used to suppress and exclude women."[15] She agrees with Ruether in distinguishing between the historical person Jesus and the saving Christ: ". . . when Jesus' maleness, which belongs to his historical identity, is interpreted to be essential to his redeeming christic function and identity, then the Christ serves as a religious tool for marginalizing and excluding women." (151). She develops the consequences of this conflation by describing how "the maleness of Jesus is used to reinforce a patriarchal image of God" (152)—in effect, literalizing a metaphor. Moreover, Johnson notes how "men alone among human beings are able to represent Christ fully" (153), with the result being that men are not only more like Christ but more like God. Mary Daly's often-quoted quip "If God is male, then the male is God" expresses this point well.[16]

Like Ruether, Johnson shows how the Jesus of the bible is inclusive of those on the margins of society and treats women as fully human. She notes that in biblical accounts, after Jesus's death and resurrection, the "total Christ" is described by Paul and John in metaphors such as "the body of Christ" and "the vine and the branches" and thus "the reality of Christ [is] expand[ed] to include potentially all of redeemed humanity" (162). She further argues that ". . . the biblical symbol Christ, the one anointed in the Spirit, cannot be restricted to the historical person Jesus nor to certain select members of the community but signifies all those who by drinking of the Spirit participate in the community of disciples" (162). What is most significant is that *human bodiliness,* and *not male sexuality,* becomes the place where God enters into solidarity with human beings. "Jesus the Christ is the Wisdom of God *in a concrete, historical gestalt*" (167, my emphasis), which symbolizes God's full identification with humanity. The fact that male humanity has been seen as more appropriate for this identity is ultimately heresy, in that it suggests that women are less the image of God than are men.

In *Jesus: Miriam's Child, Sophia's Prophet: Critical Issues in Feminist Christology*, Elisabeth Schüssler Fiorenza rehearses these now-familiar arguments and observes that ". . . ecclesiastical arguments against women's access to all levels of church leadership through ordination have endowed the biological sex of the historical Jesus with theological significance."[17] But Schüssler Fiorenza takes Ruether to task for her assumption of the idea of "full humanity" as the lasting significance of Jesus without challenging "the Western sex/gender system and its androcentric language" (47). She includes womanist theologians in her critique as she argues "I do not think we can derive the criterion and norm of a feminist Christian theology from the option of Jesus for the poor and outcast. Rather, we must ground feminist theology in wo/men's struggles for the transformation of kyriarchy" (48).[18] Here, Schüssler Fiorenza argues against an "interpersonal" interpretive framework for understanding Christ in favor of a sociopolitical one. Countering both Ruether and Johnson, Schüssler Fiorenza says, ". . . a feminist liberationist exploration of Christian Scriptures does not begin its work with the biblical text but with a critical articulation and analysis of the experiences of wo/men" (61).

None of these writers questions the maleness of the human being Jesus of Nazareth, but each argues that maleness is not determinative of his theological significance. They all make a distinction between the human Jesus and the salvific work of Christ. While Schüssler Fiorenza argues against the "interpersonal" models of sex and gender, her point remains that the maleness of Jesus is without ultimate theological significance. "Christ" is a symbol of God's identification with the poor and marginalized and a way of the divine entering fully into human experience. The fact that this incarnation was in a particular person who was male is simply indicative of historical particularity, not of lasting significance.

Feminist critiques of androcentric Christologies have arisen in response to arguments for the exclusion of women from ordained ministry. These arguments are based on the normative significance of Jesus's maleness and assumptions that equate the maleness of Jesus with the maleness of God. If Christ is the *Logos* (the Word of God), then, the magisterial argument goes, the speaker of this Word (God) must be male as well.

Because of the weight of the sex-gender system (as Schüssler Fiorenza puts it) and because gay or transgender men can "hide" their sexuality by "acting" like "normal" (i.e., heterosexual) men—at least in public—there has not been as much theological discussion of the significance of the maleness of Jesus Christ by gay and transgender groups as there has been by feminists.[19] Yet, there have been a number of portrayals of Jesus Christ as gay. Terrence McNally's play "Corpus Christi" generated a great deal of controversy when it was produced in New York in 1998. A brief search by Googling "gay Christ" results in more than 10 million hits ("gay Jesus" resulted in 380,000). The same search method using the term "transgendered Christ" resulted in 173,000 hits ("transgendered Jesus" again yielded 380,000 hits). Because of space limitations, I will not pursue this particular line of questioning further, but will simply note that the issue of Jesus's sexual orientation raises similar issues as Jesus's biological sex.

Christa

In the spring of 2006, a group of graduate students in Loyola's Theology Department arranged to have Edwina Sandys's sculpture "Christa" brought to campus for a month-long residency. The sculpture portrays a naked woman on the cross (see Figure 14.1). The sculpture had originally been made for the celebration of International Women's Year in 1975 and had first been exhibited at the United Nations. In 1984, Christa had been exhibited at the Episcopalian Cathedral of

Fig. 14.1. Christa. Bronze Figure on Lucite Cross, Edition of 3. Copyright Edwina Sandys, 1975. Photographer, Adam Reich, 2009.

St. John the Divine in New York City during Holy Week. It generated much controversy among some church leaders (of various denominations) regarding the appropriateness of seeing a female form on the cross.

I was teaching a course, "Theology and the Arts," during the spring semester of 2006 and decided to use the Christa image, along with some other images of crucified women—some of them more violent and striking than the Sandys sculpture—as the basis for one of the classes. I photocopied images of Sandys's Christa and of images found in Julie Clague's article "The Christa: Symbolizing My Humanity and My Pain."[20]

That class was one of the most powerful sessions that I can remember in nearly 26 years of teaching. The students sat there, stunned, as they looked at photographs of Sandys's sculpture, and of much more brutal and sexually explicit sculptures. I shared with them some of the artists' own intentions and some of the reactions to these sculptures described in Clague's article, which ranged from condemnation to praise.

Then the students began to share their own reactions. Most were initially shocked, and one thoughtful young man argued strenuously that it celebrated something blasphemous and very evil—the brutalization of women. But then the women in the class began to speak. Interestingly, it was the women students who defended these images, and most of the male students who found them most offensive. The fact that the traditional portrayal of the crucifixion is *not* seen as scandalous is worth observing; as Sallie McFague has argued, the use of female images often serves to highlight the metaphorical process.[21] One student, who had been assaulted in her apartment only a few weeks before, talked about how she felt that her suffering was given a face and a voice. Later, in a paper, she wrote:

> The images of "Christa" that we looked at in class are shocking, but so are the acts of violence that are committed against women around the world at an alarming rate. I would hope that to learn about sex trafficking of women and girls, female genital mutilation, domestic abuse, or rape, would be an experience that inspires outrage; however, one is forced to ask, "where is the outrage?" because violence against women remains largely invisible around the world. Images of "Christa" can serve to shock people into actually seeing the violence that is committed against women, and into recognizing that violence as unjust, just as the torture of Jesus was unjust.[22]

Another student wrote of the *comfort* she experienced in seeing these images: as a survivor of childhood abuse herself, she felt that the suffering of women was not only named but honored. Both of these students volunteered to speak at a forum on the sculpture and a few weeks after the class shared their thoughts with a small group of students and faculty.

The responses of these students brought home to me again the negative and positive power of symbols, and also suggest that conceptions of the gender of Christ have only begun to be explored fully. Christology is one place where all sorts of significant issues converge: Christ is the symbol of the Christian tradition and so the placing of crucifixes in classrooms can become a symbol for a university's commitment to its Catholic Christian heritage, and possibly exclusion of those who are not Christian.[23] Portrayals of the Christ as female will often generate calls of blasphemy, although portrayals of Christ as African, Asian, Latino, and so forth, may not. When the *National Catholic Reporter* held a contest for an image for "Jesus 2000," the winning image was criticized because of its "feminization" of the image of Jesus.[24] In the 1990s, men's groups like the Promise Keepers emphasized the importance of the masculinity of Christ:

> Promise Keepers' mission is to help promote spiritual revival in the homes, churches and communities of this nation. This will be accomplished by modeling, praying for and instructing all men to grow in Christ-like masculinity, enabling them to become "promise keepers" to the Lord who loves them, to their wives who trust them, to their children who need them, and to the world which must be influenced by them.[25]

Christ: Sexuality, Catholic Tradition, and Biology

It seems clear that maintaining the theological significance of the maleness of Christ is central to magisterial Catholic (and to other Christian) ideas of gender, church order, and tradition. But is this conviction reasonable? Is this in line with the Catholic tradition's understanding of the relationship between reason and faith? In relation to the question of ordination, Cardinal Francis George once commented to me that it was clear to him that women were equally capable of *doing* what men did as priests, if one only considered the priest's functions. But priesthood, he said, was not just a function but rather a divine call and *persona*. This was one issue that one simply had to "take on faith," since he believed that Jesus Christ had "willed" that the priesthood be reserved to men alone. (I interpret this as actually a mixture of both historical precedent and magisterial interpretive privilege.) And while theologians will generally agree that at a certain point, the theologian will ultimately leave reason behind—consider the comment attributed to Thomas Aquinas at the end of his life that everything he did was "straw" or "chaff"—too often the directive to "take it on faith" has been invoked prematurely so as to close off further discussion. Hence, I argue that it is imperative to continue this discussion, particularly with reference to science and other forms of "reason."

The history of reflection on Christ's sexuality is, as one would guess, an interesting one. One provocative example of such work is Leo Steinberg's book

The Sexuality of Christ in Renaissance Art and in Modern Oblivion. An art historian, Steinberg undertook a study of portraits of the infant Christ in the arms of his mother and the adult Christ on the cross. What he found was that in portraits of the Mother and Child, Mary was portrayed as drawing the viewer's attention to Jesus's penis. This was done for a deliberate purpose: to "remind[ ] us that the humanisation of God entails, along with mortality, his assumption of sexuality."[26] In addition, Jesus's sexuality, in particular, "matters in abeyance"—that is, it "consecrates the Christian idea of chastity." And finally, Steinberg writes, "the freedom of Christ's sexual member bespeaks that aboriginal innocence which in Adam was lost." In depictions of the cross and especially the resurrection, Steinberg observes that Jesus's penis is sometimes depicted as erect. Steinberg attributes this theme as a revival of an "ancient topos"—that is, the erect penis as a symbol of power—and with reference to one painting, comments that this expresses "the unknowable mystery of a god's unmanned body in its resurgence" (91). It is worth noting here that normative humanity is seen as male and would confirm medieval arguments about the higher status of the male sex.[27]

Medieval women religious writers, as Carolyn Walker Bynum and Barbara Newman have reminded us, were well aware of their "inferiority" as women.[28] Bynum has written of the women who found their "lowly" humanity symbolized in the human Jesus rather than in the divine Christ, which would have been the preserve of men. Yet there was much "gender-bending" in the medieval period, with devotions to "Jesus as Mother," Julian of Norwich's references to the motherhood of Jesus, and Guerric of Igny's devotion to the "twin breasts of the church"—Peter and Paul. It has been my own speculation that at a time when gender roles are very stable, "gender-bending" is not only possible but frequently done. But at times when gender roles are more unstable, threatening the stability of religious and social institutions, "gender-bending" becomes much more dangerous for those institutions with the most to lose from gender instability.

Clearly, the present time fits into the latter category; religious, and especially papal, writings on the "spousal metaphor," which has long been used as a way to express intimacy, have been sharpened to express gender roles—that is, the metaphors have been literalized—and there are plenty of church writings that underscore the significance of these "metaphors." In the Dogmatic Constitution on the Church (*Lumen Gentium*) of Vatican II, a host of metaphors are drawn upon to describe the Church, one of them being the spousal metaphor. But the frequency of the use of this spousal language to determine gender roles has expanded, especially under John Paul II.

Yet Catholic (and more generally most of Christian) theology, as this volume argues, does not see itself in conflict with reason. Indeed, it is quite the opposite, for most of Christianity's history. This affirmation of reason has sometimes required a bit of fancy footwork as "reason" has come to conclusions that undermine traditional church teachings, for example, in the case of Galileo. Medieval arguments about women's unfitness for ordination relied on medieval biology: that is, when the male seed was understood to contain the "homunculus," which was nurtured in the fertile female womb, the "natural" outcome would be a male. A female was the result if something "went wrong"—that is, "an indisposition on the part of one of the partners or a moist south wind"[29]—thus the idea of the female as the "misbegotten male."

Scientific work on genetics and sexual development, at least from this writer's unscientific expertise, shows that there is no "ontological" priority of the male, and that the origin of life is complex. If anything, it seems that human development shows a sort of "ontological priority" of the female, in that the embryo is first female, and if and when the Y chromosome activates, the embryo then becomes male. Thus, theologically (and speculatively) speaking, there does not seem to be any "scientific" justification for considering the origin of life as necessarily male. It is certainly clear that patriarchy and the idea of a transcendent male god go together,[30] and although I am skeptical of "romantic" feminist ideas of a "primal matriarchy" as preceding the "hostile takeover" of patriarchy, there is plenty of evidence of goddess worship in the ancient world.[31]

Thus, if science is to shed any light on the idea of "Christ as Bride," it would seem to be in relation to the role of sex in the beginnings of life. But I have my doubts that this would solve any theological problems. Rather, it seems to me, this is fundamentally a question of the point at which one has to "take it on faith"—or, to put it differently, where revelation trumps reason—and is thus more a question of theological method, scriptural interpretation, and the ways that theology can or will draw upon "reason" or scientific knowledge.

In relation to the necessary maleness of Christ, it is as if we are in a "he said, she said" argument. The magisterium ("he said") says that God's Word is "most appropriately" or even necessarily expressed in the body of a man for reasons beyond human knowing. In the past, of course, the reason for God and God's Word being male were that men were of course superior to women. Feminist theologians and others sympathetic with the contrary train of thought ("she said") say that the maleness of Jesus is a contingent historical reality; the Word of God—or the Sophia of God, to use Elisabeth Schüssler Fiorenza's term—is beyond the limited categories of human sexuality. If "she" is right, there seems to be no reason why a gay or transgender Christ is not also a theological, if not a historical, possibility.

The issue of Christ's maleness is the point at which evolutionary biology has the potential to challenge theological claims for the ontological priority of the male sex, and of the inevitability of the maleness of God and of God's Word. But my suspicion—and the discussions in the symposia that preceded this book only confirm this—is that much more is at stake here than whether maleness is the most apt category for referring to God and/or Christ. Evolutionary biology raises questions not only of the relation of male and female, but also of heteronormativity in human sexual expression.

* * *

Can Christ be a Bride? While this essay has not taken up the many dimensions of Christ's saving work, it has pointed to the implications of the gender of Christ. The experiences of my students, new developments in Christology such as Muriel Orevillo-Montenegro's *The Jesus of Asian Women,*[32] and portraits of a sexually ambiguous or feminized Jesus—all testify to the power of the symbol of Christ to provide meaning and comfort to generations far removed from first-century Palestine. The Vatican's insistence on a male Christ as the Word of an implicitly male God will continue to generate questions among not only feminists, but also to theologians sympathetic to the emerging views of evolutionary biology. The question of the significance of Christ's gender is therefore a question that calls not only for further theological reflection, but also more dialogue between theology and the sciences.

Notes

1. See Dickens, *Hans Urs von Balthasar's Theological Aesthetics;* Steck, *The Ethical Thought of Hans Urs von Balthasar;* Nichols, *The Word Has Been Abroad.*

2. Ross, "The Bridegroom and the Bride," 39–59.

3. For a helpful review of this literature, see Stuhlmueller, "Bridegroom: A Biblical Symbol of Union, Not Separation," 278–83. See also Weems, *Battered Love.*

4. See Swidler and Swidler, *Women Priests,* 37–49. The Vatican statement, *Inter Insigniores,* the Pontifical Biblical Commission report, and a number of commentaries are all included in this helpful volume.

5. Macy, *A History of Women and Ordination.*

6. See the Web site of the Women's Ordination Conference, online: http://www.womensordination.org/why/html.

7. See the Pontifical Biblical Commission's report, "Can Women be Priests?" on the evidence for women's ordination in the scriptures contained in Appendix II of Swidler and Swidler, *Women Priests,* esp. 344–45.

8. See chapters 34–37 (by Cooke et al.) in Swidler and Swidler, *Women Priests,* 249–59, for examples of these critiques.

9. Aquinas, *Summa Theologiae,* III, q.60, a.4; see Frank Catania earlier in this volume.

10. Bynum, *Holy Feast and Holy Fast;* Newman, *God and the Goddesses.*

11. See Beattie, *New Catholic Feminism.*

12. See John Paul II's own work, especially *The Theology of the Body;* West, *Theology of the Body Explained;* West et al., eds., *John Paul II on the Body.*

13. *Deus caritas est,* esp. sections on Mary, 41–42.

14. Ruether, *Sexism and God-Talk,* 126. Further page references in the text above.

15. Johnson, *She Who Is,* 151. Further page references in text.

16. Daly, *Beyond God the Father,* 19.

17. Fiorenza, *Jesus: Miriam's Child, Sophia's Prophet,* 44. Further page references in text.

18. It is worth noting that Schüssler Fiorenza raises significant questions of methodology.

19. Biblical scholars also note that the idea of inferiority in one of two same-sex partners raises important questions. See, among many treatments of these texts, Martin, *Sex and the Single Savior.*

20. Clague, "The Christa: Symbolizing My Humanity and My Pain," 83–108.

21. See McFague, *Models of God,* 98. I am grateful to William George for his observation that the students, male and female, did not question the portrayal of the crucifixion itself.

22. Student paper; used with permission.

23. During the tenure of the previous president of Loyola University, a directive was issued to place crucifixes in all the classrooms.

24. The *National Catholic Reporter* held a contest for new images of Jesus for the twenty-first century. See http://www.natcath.com/NCR_Online/archives/051200/051200i.htm. The winning piece was "Jesus of the People" by artist Janet McKenzie.

25. "Promise Keepers—Ecumenical Macho-Men for Christ?" http://www.rapidnet.com/~jbeard/bdm/Psychology/pk/pk.htm (accessed 1/23/08).

26. Steinberg, *The Sexuality of Christ in Renaissance Art and in Modern Oblivion.* All quotations are from page 23.

27. For example, Aquinas's response to the question whether women were "misbegotten males." See *Summae Theologiae* I, 92, ad.

28. Bynum, *Jesus as Mother* and Newman, *Sister of Wisdom.*

29. Aquinas, *Summa Theologiae* I, q.92.

30. See Lerner, *The Creation of Patriarchy.*

31. For feminist works that argue for the historicity of such a "hostile takeover," see Eisler, *The Chalice and the Blade;* Stone, *When God Was a Woman;* Gould, *The First Sex.*

32. Orevillo-Montenegro, *The Jesus of Asian Women.*

15

Gender in Heaven

The Story of the Ethiopian Eunuch in Light of Evolutionary Biology

PATRICIA BEATTIE JUNG

AND JOAN ROUGHGARDEN

When one considers the weight of scientific evidence, it becomes evident that neither sexuality nor gender among human beings is as clear-cut as many assume. This chapter is the outgrowth of many conversations over a couple of years between two Christians: one an Episcopalian evolutionary biologist, the other a Roman Catholic moral theologian. Here we share some of our conversation with you. In what follows, we first summarize two important, but conflicting stories about human gender and sexuality. Then, we move to the heart of the essay, which explores whether there is any grounding within Christianity for understanding sexual and gender diversity as a part of, rather than as a defect within, nature/creation.

Two Conflicting Stories about Gender and Sexuality

According to the first story, namely the one that has come to dominate Christian thinking about gender and sexuality, persons should be either (unequivocally and exclusively) male or (unequivocally and exclusively) female. This way of being not only characterizes everyone but is central to human personhood. Furthermore, this dimorphic (meaning that human beings are essentially either completely male or completely female) design is God's graceful way of drawing people into communion with one another. For example, the Roman Catholic Church teaches that sexual "difference is oriented toward communion."[1] Quoting from Pope John Paul II's apostolic letter "On the Dignity of Women" (*Mulieris dignatatum*), the then prefect of the Congregation for the Doctrine of the Faith, Joseph Cardinal Ratzinger (now Pope Benedict XVI), argued in a letter to the bishops of the Catholic Church that "man and woman are called from the beginning not only to exist 'side by side' or 'together' but they are also called to exist mutually 'one for the other.'"[2]

Thus, this story of human sexuality grounds the body's significance in its potential for heterosexual spousal and reproductive relationships. "This capacity to love—a reflection and image of God who is love—is disclosed in the spousal character of the body, in which the masculinity or femininity of the person is expressed."[3] In short, in the cooperation of two distinct sexual identities and corresponding, complementary gender roles, heterosexual, married embodied persons are able to reflect and image God's love.

Within this dualistic framework, Pope John Paul II did make a notable change to 1900 years of Church teaching when he affirmed the essential equality of men and women in both public and private spheres. (See Jung's chapter in this volume.) Yet, history and a wealth of human experience testify to the fact that "the war" between the sexes will likely ultimately end only in heaven. For now, it is important to note, in this account of human sexuality and gender, that "male and female are thus revealed as belonging ontologically to creation and destined therefore to outlast the present time, evidently in a transfigured form."[4] In short, the Catholic Church teaches a person's gender identity as either male or female will abide—obviously in some transfigured way—in the new creation. Simply put, the present failures and harms of our intimate and sexual relations will pass away in the new world, but the reality of these two (and *only these two*) genders will not. Gender is eternal.

This is not a peculiarly Catholic point of view. This narrative about heterosexuality and its corresponding two genders dominates the story told about human sexuality in all Christian denominations. On this point, theological luminaries of the last century as disparate as Karl Barth and Hans Urs von Balthasar even agree. Indeed, while most Christian feminists dispute patriarchal versions of this account because they disadvantage women (and not incidentally harm men and children as well), even they have not mounted a serious challenge to the binary construction of gender. Instead, most are content to argue that human sexuality is simply not only heterosexual orientation. Until the modern era, this dimorphic paradigm seemed to account for most data related to human sexuality and gender. Indeed, in its original form, the theory was remarkably elegant.

And yet there is another story about human sexuality and gender. The scientific facts about the variation in human sexuality and gender dispute any simple binary account. In traits not directly related to sex, there is substantial overlap between men and women, for example, with respect to the difference in height between populations of men and women in various parts of the world. There are now a significant number of biomedical and evolutionary scientists who recognize that the difference between height statistics from Japan when contrasted with those from Scandinavia might equal or exceed the differences between men and women within a geographic section. Similarly, the differences in mental aptitudes for language and spatial relations between men and women are statistically significant if the sample sizes used are large enough, but they still amount only to a couple of percentage points, depending on the trait. Simply put, according to this second—more comprehensive but often neglected—story, it becomes a matter of convention as to what traits are taken to represent a "typical" man or woman.[5]

The huge overlap between males and females in non-sex-related traits motivates the search for some essential sex-related defining feature of a man or woman, say in anatomy. But then it turns out that one doesn't know which feature of anatomy to select as the defining trait. Is it the shape of the external genitals (how big, how small, how symmetrical, where placed, etc.) that matters? Well, about one in a thousand babies cannot be readily classified as male or female based on external anatomy, which amounts to 6.6 million people worldwide, given a global population of 6.6 billion in 2007. This is twice the population of Kansas, which has about three million people.[6]

Another possible strategy for finding the sex-related and defining feature of essential maleness or femaleness would be to ask whether people can identify their own gender. Again, about one in one thousand persons are transgendered, that is, they have an external genital anatomy sufficiently close to some conventional template that they were assigned at birth to a male or female category, only to grow up identifying with and living in a gender other than that to which they were originally assigned. Perhaps we can determine who is male and female by the direction of sexual attraction? Well, depending upon how homosexuality is defined, between one in ten to one in one hundred are gay or lesbian, indicating that a sizable minority of persons are not accurately described when it is assumed that erotic attraction coincides with heterosexual complementarity.

Not even examining internal gonads can be used as evidence sufficient to specify essential gender traits because many people—about one in ten thousand—are born without functioning gonads and/or with gonads possessing both testicular and ovarian tissue. To complicate matters further, all these various characteristics mentioned above (e.g., nonsex traits often associated with one gender or another, the presence and size of sex organs, self identification, sexual orientation, internal gonads) may not line up with one another, making a "biological" definition of man and woman problematic for a large minority of the human population. Evidence confirming the extent of this sexual and gender variation is substantial and growing.[7]

Consequences of the Predominant Story

Human communities, of course, have known for thousands of years that not all persons fit the dimorphic model well. Cultural anthropologists tell us that in other times and places, significant space—often sacred space—was created for those who were gender variant, that is, perhaps cross-dressers or hermaphrodites.[8] But historically, the first story has won the day thus far in terms of shaping common assumptions about gender identity. And such assumptions have led to problematic consequences for many people. It is important to realize that the dominance of this one story of gender identity has had serious, and very often hurtful, effects on the lives of real, embodied human beings. For example, in Eurocentric cultures, very little safe space was allocated to those whom today we might describe as transgendered. Though changing, it is still quite dangerous to be queer or gender variant in the United States.[9]

At its worst, some elements in Christianity sanction either explicitly or implicitly such hate crimes against those who are gender variant. Sally Gross reported that some fundamentalist Christians deny baptism to sexually ambiguous persons on the grounds that intersexed persons—because they are not determinately male or determinately female—do not satisfy what they interpret to be a biblical established criterion for being created human.[10] Pastorally, however, most Christian denominations condemn such responses and initiate both transgendered adults and infants into their communities through baptism.

However, in most Christian denominations, transgendered people are viewed as unfit for ministry and other leadership positions in the church. Consider the Roman Catholic position on this matter. According to canon law, only baptized males can be validly ordained (Canon 1024). Thus, the local bishop or religious superior must decide—all things considered—whether the candidate for ordination has been endowed with the physical qualities sufficient to meet the sexual requirements of this order (Canon 1029). All of this, of course, begs the question as to just what characteristics make a male.[11]

At their best, the majority of Christian denominations treat gender variation as a disorder or defect.[12] Such "gender deviation" (and not Christian cultural or theological anthropologies) is seen as in need of repair. The goal or end of "normal" human sexual development is presumed to be only either male or female.[13] Often in this dimorphic framework, if the developmental "problem" cannot be "fixed," it is simply viewed as a "cross to bear" or "trial" one suffers. For some transsexual people, cross-dressing, hormone treatments, and even surgery may be permitted in order to reduce the distress caused by the "mental disorder," but this is understood to be palliative care and not genuinely remedial. According to the logic of this view, ideally such gender instability should be "closeted." True and full healing—that is, identification with the decisively male or female gender one received at the Creator's Hand—must await resurrected life in Christ.

To reiterate, at best, Christian denominations see those who are transgendered as suffering from a defect or disorder. However, evolutionary biologists and other scientists have raised some important questions about this diagnosis. What is relatively new is the recognition that such sexual variation is common across species and that the rate of its incidence is incompatible with biological and evolutionary conceptions of disorder or defect (see chapters Roughgarden and by Grande and colleagues in this volume for more on this point).

The medical profession does not have a set definition of how to determine what a disease is. A typical definition of what constitutes a disorder is that is it diagnosable, causes pain and suffering, and interferes with normal function.[14] Most variation in gender expression and sexuality fails this definition because the traits are not painful, and the only suffering that arises from them results from social stigmatization. Nor do they interfere with normal function, because the "normal function" of gender expression and sexuality is not known, and anthropological and historical studies have revealed many sexual practices and standards of gender expression throughout the world and through history.[15]

A geneticist might define a genetic defect as a gene that is deleterious in all circumstances and is therefore opposed by natural selection. As such, its frequency is set by the balance between the rate at which natural selection eliminates it each generation and the rate at which it is replaced through recurrent mutation. The rate at which natural selection eliminates a deleterious gene depends on how harmful it is. Only genes that are very deleterious are speedily removed by natural selection, and genetic diseases like Hodgkins Disease are found in a frequency of around one in four thousand. The frequency of traits like homosexuality, transgender expression, and most forms of intersex are thousands of times too common to be consistent with the degree of rarity required by a hypothesis of genetic defect.[16] There are simply no biological grounds for treating the vast majority of variations in gender expression and sexuality as defects.

Furthermore, the rest of the animal kingdom reveals a degree of variability in gender expression and sexuality that could not have been imagined at the time Darwin wrote during the late 1800s. The most common body plan, when one includes both plants and animals, is for an organism to make both eggs and sperm during its life and thus to be both male and female. And in animals specifically, excluding the insects, about half of all species are both male and female at the same or different times during their lives. To illustrate: If you go snorkeling on a coral reef, about one-fourth of the fish you see swimming about come from species in which individuals change sex during their lives. And homosexual matings are now documented in peer-reviewed professional journals in over three hundred species of vertebrates, including our closest primate relatives, the bonobos.[17]

The surprising extent of natural variation in gender and sexuality throughout the animal kingdom in itself is evidence that some natural adaptive function is served by these phenomena. But what might be the adaptive value of natural variation in gender and sexuality? This question perplexes many evolutionary biologists today. Their attempts to answer it must be thought of as still speculative theories that await testing in future years. In the meantime, the camera doesn't lie, so to speak (even since the advent of Photoshop!), so the reality of a diversity of gender expression and sexuality throughout nature, including human beings, is a fact and we must now engage its theological significance.

Considering a New Story: Diversity and Christianity

Clearly, we take the second story seriously. The findings of evolutionary biology push us to reassess our premises about human gender and sexuality and the biblical and theological arguments they undergird. We contend that the erosion of the scientific basis for the dimorphic paradigm significantly challenges prevailing interpretations of biblical and traditional views of gender within Christianity. The overall purpose of this chapter is to begin the process of retrieving other models of gender within the Christian scriptures and tradition that are more congruent with what the Vatican has labeled the "theory of polymorphous sexuality" (delineated above). Put another way, the purpose of what follows is to explore whether there is any basis in Christianity for discarding (or at least de-centering) the binary construction of gender now being questioned within the scientific community or for seeing sexual and gender polymorphism as congruent with Christianity.[18]

We take the following four premises to be axiomatic. First, we are called as Christians to live in ways that bear witness to the already present and still coming reign of God. This is what we believe it means to pray: "thy kingdom come, thy will be done, on earth as it is in heaven." Both what we teach about gender now and how we treat those who are gender variant are very important to the Christian witness about our life to come. Our vision of what gender in heaven will be like is morally significant.

Second, we recognize that much of what exists now may be radically transformed, healed or simply left behind in the new creation. Clearly, judgments about how human communities *ought* to construct gender and about how individuals *ought* to embody it cannot simply be derived from what *is*. That would not only be fallacious, but it would deny the inherent character of sin. And yet, we think it is equally problematic—also for deeply theological reasons—to think that what ought to be can be completely discontinuous with what is. As

Christians, we believe there will be some continuity between what is now our experience (however broken) of God's original blessing and the life of the world to come in the new creation. The trick, of course, is to discern what will abide in our glorified risen bodily selves.

Third, we believe that change in common Christian convictions about sex—not only on earth, but in heaven—can occur. Developments in church teaching about such matters are possible. We know that some deeply embedded Christian traditions about risen life have radically changed over the centuries. For example, the Catholic Church no longer teaches that paternalism will become more fully benevolent and female submission more fully gracious in the life to come. Instead, despite centuries of biblical interpretation and Church teaching to the contrary, the Church now teaches that in heaven people of faith will join a communion of saints marked by the mutuality and reciprocity of friendship in Christ, not well-ordered patriarchal chains of command.

Fourth, while the heaven for which we long may not be a patriarchal company, it is hard for us to imagine that all human experience of sexuality and gender will be erased in heaven. Even if we take Jesus's cryptic remarks about the nature of our relationships with each other in heaven (Matthew 22:23–30) as literally descriptive (which their context suggests might not be advisable), one can reasonably conclude only that there will be no marriage (at least as a patriarchal institution) in heaven. This does not necessarily mean there will be no sex or gender in heaven. Even in the scriptures, angels are not always portrayed as asexual (Genesis 6:1–2).

One could, of course, conclude that there will be no sex or gender in heaven, but that does not fit well with other convictions we hold about resurrected life and about our future as a communion of saints before God. Many of us have known gender to invite not only (unjustified) discrimination but also intimacy and communion. In his chapter in this volume, John McCarthy aptly describes human sexuality as a form of hospitality, its performance an invitation into relationship. This truth has found expression in the traditional notion of the spousal character of the body. However, nothing about the experience of gender as inviting relationship requires its delimitation as a rigidly heterosexual binary.

And so, finally, it is clear why we are interested in thinking afresh about gender in heaven. Such arguments are clearly speculative but, as John Thiel has argued so well, there are many warrants in the tradition for the exercise of the eschatological imagination.[19] Such arguments are certainly no more (or less) speculative than arguments about gender in creation, that is, about gender in a pre-Lapsarian state of innocence about which we have no experience either. So deeply ingrained are dimorphic interpretations of gender that most Christians have simply lost sight of the fact that this model is itself a speculative construction based on reinforcing interpretations of the "facts" about human sexuality, the Bible and tradition.

But the scientific "facts" about gender are no longer settled. When confronted with the deepening erosion of the scientific bulwark for this model, we could not help but wonder whether only this heterosexual binary model could claim to have biblical and traditional foundations.

RETRIEVING AND REINTERPRETING ACTS 8:26–40

While it is difficult to know precisely what a baptismal formula like the one quoted in Galatians 3:28 might have meant, we would not be alone in suggesting that it seems to challenge dimorphic models of gender. In *Sex and the Single Savior*, Dale Martin points out that the Greek text is best translated as follows: there is "no male and female" in Christ. For Martin, this suggests several possibilities. In Christ, females could become males, males could become females, or gender could be interpreted as multiplex rather than duplex. Martin notes that as long ago as 1974 Wayne Meeks argued in a seminal article, "The Image of the Androgyne," that this Galatians text is not about equality in heaven, but rather about the recovery of an androgynous way of being in the life to come. Meeks argued that some early Christian communities believed gender dimorphism would be abolished in the life to come. What this most likely meant for the Pauline community was that females would undergo a process of "masculinization" and become asexual males.[20]

Many scholars—admittedly not without good intertextual and literary reason—wrestle with this passage from Galatians, and the questions it poses about gender in heaven, by interpreting it in light of their readings of Genesis 1–3 (See Robert Di Vito's chapter in this volume for very interesting and important biblical interpretative work on Genesis 1–3). However, in this chapter we hope to draw attention to another passage about baptism in the New Testament. We believe it might better illumine the eschatological hopes held by at least some early Christians: the story of the baptism of the Ethiopian eunuch found in the Acts of the Apostles 8:26–40.

This is the story of a Spirit-led encounter on the Gaza Road between the evangelist Philip and a pious, dark-skinned "god-fearer" who was reading aloud in typical fashion from a scroll from the prophet Isaiah. This traveler was headed home in his carriage toward a capital city in what we would now call northern Sudan. In the ancient Mediterranean world this destination, Meroe, would have been recognized by those who heard the story as the capital city of the southernmost ends of the earth, on the fringe of the Greek-speaking (that is, the "civilized") world. As told by the author of Luke-Acts, Philip clearly recognized this Ethiopian to be both the equivalent of the chief financial officer of the Candace (a line of Ethiopian queens) and a eunuch. Nevertheless, Philip baptized this unnamed eunuch because as the text itself puts it "nothing prevented it."

In the ancient Mediterranean world, the term "eunuch" served as an umbrella term for a wide variety of gender-variant realities (somewhat like our term "transgendered" today). Those classified as eunuchs by nature would have been born with undeveloped or underdeveloped male sex organs, and/or during puberty, their organs and typically male secondary gender characteristics would not have developed. They would have had long limbs, a curved spine, and the high voices and fat deposits usually considered more characteristic of females. Those classified as eunuchs by nature might have included some of those whom we today call intersexed. In ancient times, these "boys" might well have volunteered to be castrated and sold into slavery.

The appearance of those who were made eunuchs as a consequence of conquest or being sold into slavery also varied, depending upon when in their development castration occurred and how they were made eunuchs. Obviously, whether or not one's testicle(s) were crushed, scrotum tied off, or penis and/or the entire genitalia amputated affected one's genital appearance differently. It is possible for a eunuch to be quite "manly" in overall appearance, unless of course he was made a eunuch before puberty. Postpubescent castrati are sterile, but they may have significant degrees of some secondary male characteristics. Many still experience significant levels of sexual desire as well as the ability to penetrate others sexually. Of course, all eunuchs could satisfy the sexual desires of others—of any gender—through oral, manual and/or anal activities. Our point is that it is quite likely that the Ethiopian eunuch discussed in Acts was visibly gender variant. And it is certainly plausible that this label "eunuch" might today encompass many transgendered and transsexual (male to female) people.

The first thing we noticed about this text is that it has been much neglected and continues to this day to evoke little commentary. It was rarely represented in Christian iconography.[21] In addition to the Eurocentric prejudices that may have fostered that neglect, we believe it receives scant attention because the gender variance embodied by eunuchs still today threatens deeply rooted conceptions of gender. Certainly the outcome of the heated debates within the early church about gender-bending practices and self-castration resulted in the marginalization of this text and we believe still influence greatly modern interpretations of it.

For example, in her entry on the "Ethiopian Eunuch" for *The Anchor Bible Dictionary*, Beverly Roberts Gaventa notes that interpreters have puzzled over why the author of Luke-Acts identifies this particular Ethiopian as a eunuch.[22] And yet, Gaventa does not ask: *What is so puzzling?* If, on the one hand, this story recounts an actual event, its author would have made mention of this because many eunuchs are in fact recognizably (that is, morphologically) gender variant. Even though eunuchs reminded men and women alike of the tentative nature of the differences on which male privileges were predicated, still, the gender ambiguity of most eunuchs would not have been easy to ignore.[23]

Of course, we know very little about the actual treatment of eunuchs within Judaism early in the Common Era (CE), but we do know something about how they are considered in texts. Generally speaking, eunuchs (in Hebrew *sārîs*), whether born or made, had some of the same ritual and legal responsibilities of other males, including blowing the *shofar* and saying grace after meals, and so forth.[24] Nevertheless, they were clearly listed separately from other men in the literature of the period. They did not have all the privileges and obligations of other men; they were prohibited from participation in Levirate marriages, explicitly excluded from the holy priesthood (Leviticus 21:17–23), and not allowed to judge capital cases, and so forth (NB: They were permitted to judge civil cases). It is not certain whether this is because of their sterility (and the character deficits associated with childlessness) or rather, because they were seen as not quite "men."[25] Most commentators suspect that our Ethiopian pilgrim remained a "god-fearer" on the fringe of Judaism (rather than a proselyte) because he was unable to comply with the law of circumcision. (But this must remain speculative since he may only have been lacking testicles.)

If, on the other hand, this story expresses the poetic license of our historian author, the identification of this unnamed person as a eunuch must have served some theological purpose. And yet Gaventa does not ask: *What could that purpose have been?* In antiquity, eunuchs were socially permitted free association and travel with both women as well as men. They were not considered a true member of either group and so were excluded from neither. Their guardianship of women enabled an increase in women's relative independence. This provoked anxiety in the male heads of households because this increase in the mobility of women corresponded with a decrease of their control over women. Their appearance constantly disclosed the male/female binary with its accompanying power divisions to be arbitrary and socially constructed.

In his book *The Manly Eunuch: Masculinity, Gender Ambiguity and Christian Ideology in Late Antiquity* Matthew Kuefler notes that the gender instability that threatened all men in the ancient Mediterranean world was dramatically embodied by eunuchs. Even if "merely" symbolic, the full inclusion of the eunuch in early Christian communities—precisely without much comment—may reveal something about early Christians' (or at least the author of Acts) conception of life in Christ. Perhaps gender in heaven would not be simply male or female.

Instead of asking these questions, Gaventa concludes her (admittedly brief) entry by arguing that since the author of Luke-Acts does not comment on the restrictions within Judaism against full membership for eunuchs, he may have been less interested in that feature of the story. In reading this commentary, we could not help but ask: What more comment need the author have made than to have portrayed this "god-fearer" as reading aloud from the promises articulated by the prophet Isaiah about the covenant community to come? Most

Jewish hearers would have known that among these was the promise of the full inclusion of eunuchs (Isaiah 56: 3–8).[26]

We found another example of the marginalization of this text in *Eunuchs and Castrati: A Cultural History.* Here, Piotro Scholz notes that this story of a conversion to Christianity of a eunuch has been dismissed by many exegetes as a legend, and for the most part, he seems to join in that assessment. Furthermore, Scholz himself argues that this Ethiopian was probably not truly a eunuch (in the sexual sense), but only a high-ranking court official. Scholz argues:

> There was no compelling reason to emasculate court officials. We may therefore safely assume that in the Hellenistic period, the term *eunuchos* was used other than as a synonym for castrati. . . . In yet another respect Luke's account speaks against the notion that the Meroite official was emasculated. . . . Christianization took place in a time and world that knew not only pagan cults and mysteries with emasculation rites, but also widespread celibacy motivated by religion.[27]

We find this reasoning problematic for several reasons. First, while this may be true in some cases, this particular Ethiopian official was a student of Judaism. Though not altogether unheard of, celibacy was definitely uncommon among its adherents. Second, in late antiquity there were large numbers of eunuchs everywhere. Castration was not associated only with "Galli" priests, devotees of Cybele (Magna Mater) and the Scythian goddess. People were born or became eunuchs for a variety of reasons. Sometimes, if an infant was sexually ambiguous, he would be raised male but then sold into slavery as a eunuch. In the Roman empire of the Common Era, castration had long been the mark of slavery, especially of slaves brought in from outside the empire. Unlike the "Galli" priests who wore female clothing, heavy makeup, and long loose hair and lived in wandering missionary communities, slaves who were eunuchs worked in a variety of capacities at many levels of social and political life.

Third, the market for eunuchs was extensive. Sometimes adolescents were castrated to preserve their youthful beauty for pederastic purposes.[28] Most often, however, eunuchs were sought because women and children were thought to need guardians and tutors who could be completely trusted to preserve their chastity. Frequently, eunuchs served as military officers in charge of supply lines and war booty, or as court accountants in charge of important treasuries. Their inability to sire a dynasty of their own in the eyes of many suggested that they would be less likely to steal or become mutinous.

We found Benjamin Witherington's analysis of the text far more compelling. In his *The Acts of the Apostles: A Socio-Rhetorical Commentary,* he argues that the Ethiopian eunuch was certainly a eunuch in the sexual sense—indeed, most probably castrated and dismembered. This would have resulted in his inconsistent treatment within Judaism. On the one hand, his monotheism and high status in the court warranted considerable respect. On the other hand, as an effeminate and most probably impotent eunuch, he would have been classed among the most despised and scorned. Though a student of Judaism, conversion required circumcision of its male proselytes and this would presumably have been impossible for the Ethiopian eunuch. No longer really a gentile, this "god-fearer" was literally in no man's land, on the fringe of Judaism.

And yet, such an ambivalent response "would not be true among the followers of Jesus, who not only valued singleness (Acts of the Apostles 21:9; 1 Corinthians 7) but in fact spoke of it in terms of being a eunuch for the sake of God's dominion (Matthew 19:10–12)."[29] Witherington suggests that the vignette in this passage is structured as a chiasm, with the quotation of the passage from Isaiah serving as its hinge. Its climax follows Philip's explanation of the scriptures and proclamation of the good news; it comes when seeing the water, the eunuch asks rhetorically: "What is to prevent me from being baptized?" Nothing! The author of Luke-Acts sees the eunuch as a symbol of the fulfillment of Spirit's promise of radical inclusivity!

REINTERPRETING PATRISTIC TRADITIONS

It is fascinating to reconsider the debate in the early church about gender in heaven (and consequently about appropriate gender roles on earth) in light of what we now know to be scientific facts about human sexual diversity. In the early centuries of the Common Era, there was apparently considerable division among Christian communities about gender-bending practices.

Some groups of early Christians sought to obliterate social boundaries of all kinds, including those demarcated by gender. For some, eunuchs were signs of this new virtuous alterity. It has been well documented that male and female disciples traveled together as unmarried missionary pairs, as well as studied and cohabitated together in communities not bounded by gender. Remnants of these gender-bending practices survived into the third and fourth century and found expression in the spiritual and scholarly friendships that existed between women and ascetic men at that time.

Doubts about the ability of Christian disciples to sustain their mutual commitment to chastity were expressed by pagan and Christian critics alike. In his *Apology* Justin Martyr (138–161 CE) both documents and gives tacit approval to the impulse toward and approval of self-castration among some Christians. Though he sought to conceal it, Origin of Alexandria (185–254 CE), a theologian and teacher of both men and women, is thought by many to have addressed such doubts about his chastity by castrating himself, probably around 209 CE. By the middle of the fourth century, the practice continued to persist among Christians (despite the repeated condemnations detailed below).

Responses to this self-castration, as probably to many other gender-bending activities, were decidedly mixed. On the one hand, many worried about and eventually condemned them. Tertullian (155–230 CE) associated self-castration with dualistic doctrines and heretical (more precisely Marcionite) conceptions of the Creator. The Council of Nicaea (325 CE) banned castrated men from the clergy and excommunicated (for three years) laity who engaged in the practice. Self-castration became a mark of heresy; it was eventually seen as a practice scornful of God's created order. In 345 CE, a Council at Gangera condemned Christian women for assuming men's clothes and shaving their heads "under the pretext of piety." Both Basil of Ancyra (c. 364 CE) and then Cyril of Alexandria (378–444 CE) dismissed the notion that castration could guarantee chastity.

On the other hand, at least some others including Eusebius, Bishop of Caesarea (265–340 CE) viewed castration as an act of faith and self-control. Such approval is clearly exceptional in extant sources. It was Augustine's rigid, dimorphic view of gender, both in heaven and on earth, that came to dominate Christian views in the West. Nevertheless, we believe there was considerable division within Christianity over questions about gender in heaven for centuries before the onset of the Middle Ages.

Our point here is neither to endorse self-castration as a Christian virtue nor to condemn it as always and everywhere problematic. Rather, what we believe is important to understand is that castration—and the other gender-bending activities with which it was associated—was not a rare act of the lunatic fringe. In some quarters of the early church, these practices—for example, castration, female-to-male cross-dressing, coeducation, and cohabitation, and so forth—enjoyed a significant measure of acceptance. Binary gender roles may have been seen by these groups as altogether insignificant to discipleship, or at least they may have seen gender as a category as quite fluid.

Mary Rose D'Angelo identifies in late-first- and early-second-century texts, three strategies for both accommodating to, and resisting, the reassertion of the patriarchal and procreative "family values" of the Roman Empire of that era.[30] On the one hand, in the Pastoral Epistles gender roles are quite rigidly patriarchal and for women procreative. On the other hand, in Hermas the Shepherd both prophecy and household leadership are open to men and women (implicitly leaving women eligible for leadership in other arenas as well). D'Angelo sees the Luke-Acts corpus as falling somewhere between these two. Depictions of bad women were avoided and women were portrayed as truly called to discipleship (perhaps even teaching, if in the company of a male partner). And yet, male rule was confirmed as well.

We think it reasonable to presume that gender-bending strategies of several types were quite common among early Christians who understood themselves to be called to enact an eschatological future in which gender was transfigured. In a thought-provoking essay, Sarah Coakley compares Judith Butler's contemporary call to "perform gender" against the cultural grain to Gregory of Nyssa's (335–390 CE) ascetic call to the transformation of gender.[31] Though he gradually distanced himself from what became known as the heresy of Origenism (that is, from castration), Gregory certainly saw celibacy (and may have eventually even seen marriage) as countercultural school(s) of nonattachment to and non-enmeshment in systems whereby power and wealth were/are exchanged and transmitted. According to Coakley, what asceticism enabled for Gregory was gender fluidity, and even gender reversals. Ascetic practices enabled people to break the hold of gender systems over their lives. This is why, in contrast to Augustine, Gregory argues that the resurrected body would constantly be in flux, moving from glory to glory.[32]

*　*　*

Given the parameters of this chapter, we can do little more than sketch an argument we hope is suggestive and which we hope will foster sustained and extended study of the questions we raise here. Instead of interpreting Galatians 3:28 in light of the standard dimorphic interpretations of gender that accompany traditional accounts of Genesis 1–3, we suggest that baptism into Christ might incorporate the faithful into a future marked by gender fluidity. It is time to interpret Galatians 3:28 in light of the reinterpretations of certain biblical texts such as the story of Philip's baptism of the Ethiopian eunuch in Acts and in light of the recovery of certain visions of gender in heaven (like Gregory's) and the gender-bending practices as evidence (if only by their condemnation) among our earliest ancestors in the faith.

Minimally, these historical analyses establish that there was an openness in some Christian communities to not viewing gender binary as a requirement for acceptance into Christian communal life. More importantly, these historical analyses establish further that in some early communities the denial or transformation of social—even physiological—markers of gender binary may have been accepted, perhaps even encouraged, as expressive of fuller entrance into the Christian life. If such practices only embodied for their adherents steps toward a gender-free and sexless future, it is hard to imagine why they warranted such rebuttal from the West given its happy emphasis on virginity and celibacy. We think it makes most sense of the historical data (limited as it is) to see in such texts and practices a witness to a heavenly life to come in which both gender—and the status and power that accompany it—were envisioned as fluid.

Such a strand in the tradition would have been in tension with what is frequently labeled as the "traditional" Christian viewpoint on gender today. Indeed, we seek to establish that early Christian communities held a variety of views in this regard. Additionally, we hope to underscore the fact this particular perspective on gender appears on the face of it to be more congruent with emerging evolutionary accounts of the human potential for sexual fluidity and diversity.

A similar argument can be mounted with regard to what are truly biblical views of gender. Of course this pericope in the Acts of the Apostles on which we focus is not about gender dimorphism, but rather reveals that all of Isaiah's prophecies are fulfilled in Christ. Nevertheless, Philip's Spirit-led decision to baptize the Ethiopian eunuch could be interpreted as a scriptural challenge to rigidly dimorphic models of gender, whether on earth or in heaven, because such full inclusion was indeed among Isaiah's prophecies.

If what glorifies God is creation come fully alive—and if the promise of such life abundant comes with our incorporation into Christ through baptism—and if in baptism there is "no male and female"—Christians might well expect there to be some experiences of diversity and fluidity within human sexuality here and now. One often finds such rumors of angels. But in any case, all human lives are shaped at least in part by their expectations for the future. Christians are called to live in anticipation of the new creation established in Christ.

Notes

1. Congregation for the Doctrine of the Faith [hereafter CDF], "On the Collaboration of Men and Women in the Church and in the World," 6.

2. Ibid.

3. Ibid., 8.

4. Ibid., 13.

5. Roughgarden, *Evolution's Rainbow,* 26–28.

6. Ibid., 284–87.

7. Ibid., 207–61.

8. For example, in the southern state of Oaxaca, Mexico, the native Zapotec people recognize today, indeed socially sanction, a "third" gender. Called "muxes," these individuals are "males" who from "boyhood" have felt drawn toward living as "women." This can be traced back to cross-dressing Aztec priests and "intersex" Mayan gods. See Lacey, "A Lifestyle Distinct," 4. For additional contemporary examples see Roughgarden, *Evolution's Rainbow,* 377–86.

9. A recent report by Amnesty International (AI) tells stories of how members of the LGBT community in the United States are frequently abused by police. In these stories, transgender individuals are often targeted, and in the process their chosen gender is ignored. AI points out that when transgender individuals are arrested, they are often vulnerable to sexual violence because they are placed in holding cells with individuals of their biological, not chosen, gender. Through personal stories and reports, AI shows how transgender individuals are often forced to submit to inappropriate bodily searches and tells the story of one transgender woman who was searched vaginally. When responding to a hate crime against a transgender woman, several Los Angeles Police Officers asked paramedics to confirm the woman's male identity, but they refused. The AI

report points to studies that show that there are significant numbers of individuals who are homeless, unemployed, and underemployed within the transgender community and are discriminated against when they try to seek social services. And when transgender individuals encounter police, the police often assume they are sex workers and make arrests without valid cause. See Amnesty International, *Stonewalled—Still Demanding Respect.*

10. Gross, "Intersexuality and Scripture," 65–74.

11. In 2003, The Catholic News Service reported on a Vatican document drafted by the Italian canon lawyer, Urbano Navarrete, S.J. In the document, the Vatican is said to teach that whether one is male or female is determined at birth, and that baptismal records should under no circumstances be changed. Defined as having a psychic disorder, transsexual persons may undergo surgery, but priests in such circumstances can continue their ministry only if it does not produce scandal. Norton, "Vatican Says 'Sex-change Operation Does Not Change a Person's Gender.'"

12. This is reinforced by the *Diagnostic and Statistical Manual of Mental Disorders* (DSM), which still describes gender variance as a pathology. Most doctors refer to intersex as a "disorder in sexual development," (DSD). This, of course, connotes a need for repair. For a detailed discussion, see Reis, "Divergence or Disorder?" 535–43.

13. We argue that it is more accurate to think of gender-variant people as embodying divergent, rather than disordered, patterns in sexual development, even if they are statistically unusual within this spectrum. Such terminology does not invite medical intervention, and in fact, shifts the burden of proof should intervention be considered.

14. See definitions in online medical dictionaries: http://www.nlm.nih.gov/medlineplus/dictionaries.html.

15. Rougharden discusses several of these, see *Evolution's Rainbow,* 352–76.

16. Ibid., 281–82.

17. Roughgarden discusses the "animal rainbow" at length. Ibid., 13–184.

18. Not surprisingly, from Rome's point of view, this theory not only distorts important truths about the normative nature of sexuality "by the obscuring of the difference or duality of the sexes," but has many harmful implications for the family. CDF, 2.

19. Thiel, "For What May We Hope?" 517–41.

20. Martin, *Sex and the Single Savior.* For Martin's full discussion of the Galatians text, see chapter 6, "The Queer History of Galatians 3:28," 77–90.

21. This was true until it became a popular subject in seventeenth-century Netherlands. There have been various theories about its role in confessional squabbles but one need only look at some of these paintings to see how they might have served to sacralize the colonization of Africa.

22. Gaventa, "Ethiopian Eunuch," 667.

23. Kuefler, *The Manly Eunuch.*

24. They were distinguished from those of indeterminate or androgynous sex by rabbis.

25. Sarra Lev, from Reconstructionist Rabbinical College, has argued compelling for the former rationale in her essay, "They Treat Him as a Man and See Him as a Woman: The Tannaitic Understanding of the Congenital Eunuch." Unpublished Essay.

26. This promise is given as well in Wisdom 3:14–15.

27. Scholz, *Eunuchs and Castrati.*

28. Pederasty commonly refers to sexual relations between an adult male and a boy.

29. Witherington, *The Acts of the Apostles,* 295–96.

30. D'Angelo, "'Knowing How to Preside over His Own Household,'" 265–96.

31. Coakley, *Powers and Submissions,* 153–67.

32. Augustine asserts that in heaven we will recognize each other as men and women. See *City of God* XXII, Ch.17.

Conclusion

Descriptive and Normative Ways
of Understanding Human Nature

AANA MARIE VIGEN

O Lord, you examine me and know me . . .
You created my inmost self,
knit me together in my mother's womb.
For so many marvels, I thank you: a wonder am I,
and all your works are wonders.

—Psalm 139: 1, 13[1]

"Who am I?" This deceptively complicated question has dogged humanity for all recorded history. And in one way or other, it nips at the heels of all of the essays in this volume. Who are human beings—at root—in terms of our gender and sexual identities? How do we come to understand and know what is ultimately true about these identities? What can the sciences (both "hard" and "soft") tell us? What do the humanities contribute? These scholars from varied and distinct disciplines, and in their own unique voices and methods of inquiry, attempt partial answers to this question as they explore the social, literary, philosophical, theological, and scientific bases and/or constructions of categories related to human gender and sexuality.

At the crux of these chapters is a central question of ethics: How, if at all, do we move from descriptive accounts of *what exists* in creation to prescribing *what ought to be?* How do we move from description to pre(or pro)scription? Ethics, and specifically, Christian social ethics, is never content merely with asking "Who am I?" It always addresses the question of: "Who *ought* I be?" Moreover, pondering this question is never ultimately a solitary endeavor (though it can feel that way at times). Instead, the most integral shape of this quest is community oriented: "Who *are we* and who *ought we* become?" And of course, the next question quickly presents itself: "What should I/what should we *do?*"

Who are we . . . who should we strive to be . . . what should we do . . . ? Questions of "being, becoming, and doing" seem inextricably bound up with one another. In this concluding essay, I want to step back from directly probing the complexities of sexuality and gender to reflect on matters of method in ethics. In particular, I want to explain why human experience (broadly construed) ought to be given more weight in reaching normative claims about human sexuality and gender than it often receives in Christian ethics. But before I make that case, a few words are needed about how I define ethics and understand the sources for Christian ethics.

Ethics Defined

Instead of simply employing the term, "ethics," a brief description of what I mean by it may be helpful. Let's start with a nutshell definition: "Ethics is the critical reflection on morality."[2] Here, *morality* refers to the values, virtues, norms (aka ground rules) that structure/govern a given individual and/or society, and *ethics* is the discipline that critically examines these ground rules.[3] The task of ethics is to ask whether the values/virtues/norms/ground rules are adequate. Do they need revision? Ethics also explores what sources and moral theories are used in creating and defending particular normative claims. In other words, ethics, as a discipline, does *not* simply relate to what one thinks about particular moral questions. Rather, it involves *how* one thinks about them. Ethics considers and reveals what sources or moral wisdom, methods of evaluation, and even blind spots are evident in how one approaches moral questions.

The process of ethical reflection necessarily involves four discrete tasks:

1. Critically reflect upon common assumptions. Open yourself to learning new information.
2. Seek out all the information (from a rich combination of varied sources and disciplines) needed to craft a "thick description"—accurate, multifaceted—of the ethical situation, conflict, issue, or question at hand.
3. Develop a theoretical framework using various moral theories and sources of information. Here a focus on duties, obligations, consequences, principles, and norms play a central role. Philosophical and theological sources figure prominently, but the sciences can also be an integral resource at this juncture.
4. Create constructive moral imagination. The work of ethics is never done at the point of critique! What vision do you offer? How could/should things change? What do you propose as the ethical way forward?

Enumerating these four steps may be deceiving because the process of moral deliberation is not so much a linear process (you finish one step and move to the next) as a spiral. Each step feeds back into the others. And the process is never really done as long as we are living and conscious creatures. Of course, we must arrive at conclusions that are final for specific moments (and these may be rather prolonged). Yet, a dynamic openness to new information—to reconsidering issues as new information becomes available—keeps our ethical decisions vibrant and relevant to the particular moments and questions in which we find ourselves.

Beyond this definition, I want to mention two other qualities integral to the work of ethics. First, the discipline of ethics wrestles with the tension between what "is" and what "ought" to be. If there are no disagreements—over values, principles, or social, economic, political needs, there is no need for ethics. So, rather than be disturbed by arguments, we should expect them! The work of ethics is intertwined with conflicts and is usually, and one could argue, *should be* rather "messy." Most times, the answers to central moral questions of the day are not clear cut or easy to determine. Making any compelling argument is complicated and laborious work—it involves a lot of nuance and wrestling with complexity. Moreover, resolutions are not arrived at without self-critical reflection and a perpetual openness to new evidence or arguments that may cause one to reevaluate one's position. In other words, the work of ethics is never done as long as we have working brains, beating hearts, and critical awareness.

Second, ethics is the property of all—alive in daily decisions in how we craft our lives little by little and in big decisions—as individuals and as communities/society. It is a common vocation of all human beings; no one is exempt. Thus, you can't simply fall back on laws, sacred scriptures, or what others have told you to do the work of ethics for you. You have to risk making arguments about what is morally good and ethically defensible for yourself—informed by others of course, but you can't take a pass on this fundamental responsibility and gift that comes with being human.

Sources in Christian Ethics

What are the central sources or tools needed for the doing of this work? Christian ethics commonly identifies four sources for the doing and theorizing of ethics: the Christian scriptures, Church tradition, human Reason (often denoting philosophy), and experience.[4] However, beyond this basic identification, there is much disagreement about sources in ethics. Various theologians and ethicists weigh these four rather differently. For example, they don't only disagree about *what* constitutes moral relations and actions with respect to human sexuality and gender; they fundamentally disagree over *which sources* should be given the most authority for making such determinations. Some, perhaps most, Christian theologians and ethicists give the lion's share of importance to sacred scriptures. They see scripture as the normative standard and guide by which to judge human decisions and relationships, and by which to evaluate the insights from other sources. Others weigh scriptures and the teachings, traditions, and doctrines of their ecclesial body equally. Still others try to strike a dynamic balance among the four sources.

SCRIPTURE'S ROLE AND PLACE

With respect to sexuality and gender, and especially homosexuality, many Christians prioritize scripture as the authoritative source. Di Vito's chapter helps us see how vital it is that we recognize that the scriptures must be interpreted and that our biblical interpretations must be nuanced. Simply quoting Romans, Leviticus, or Genesis to settle the matter is not sufficient. Furthermore, a tenuous, but essential fact to acknowledge is that Christians, (along with people of other religious traditions), operate with a "canon within the Canon." Not all scriptures are treated as equally authoritative for contemporary communities of faith, as evidenced by the fact that Christians no longer use scripture to sanction slavery, to mandate the separation of women when they are menstruating, or to prohibit other "abominations" (wearing mixed fabrics, mixing wine with milk products) mentioned in the Holiness Code.[5]

In a related vein, if we are honest, Christians will acknowledge how little scripture says overall with respect to human gender and sexuality. The paltry number of biblical verses focusing on sexual practice or gender roles contrasts starkly with the lengthy, pointed, numerous, and often challenging, passages throughout both Testaments that address economic obligations and justice for various marginalized groups. Note the strong exhortations against the accumulation of excessive wealth, for example.[6]

Yet, beyond the careful use and interpretation of scripture, when seeking to discover who we are—in terms of gender, biology, and sexual identity—scripture alone does not provide all the information we need. For example, the kind of same-sex activity rejected by biblical writers may likely have little in common with contemporary practices and relationships. The biblical authors do not envision just, loving, committed relationships as being possible between two men or two women. Rather, they have things in mind such as rape, coerced sexual relations, incest, and sex between and adult and a child. Many GLBT people, including Christians, have been vocal in their rejection of these same practices. However, their experience tells them that same-sex relationships are vital ways in which they experience grace, love, compassion, mutuality, respect, caring, and deep bonding. They also argue that same-sex relations are not characterized by such problematic traits any more than heterosexual ones are.

Another reason that the Bible alone is not a sufficient source is because some of the biological understanding undergirding it is flawed. As we make clear in the Introduction, (and Jung discusses elsewhere), the scriptures appear to presume women contributed to the gestation but not to the conception of a child. If not barren, women's bodies only provided the fertile ground for the already complete seed provided by the man. The scriptures utilize a mistaken biology.

For reasons such as these, many Christians hold scripture in dynamic tension with lived experience and with what we continue to learn from psychology, sociology, and biology about sexual orientation. However, institutional religious bodies have some catching up to do. A real problem is that many ecclesial dialogues (most notably in Protestant denominations) considering institutional policy changes around the blessing of same-sex relationships and the ordination of GLBT persons in relationships are either 1) consciously or unconsciously informed by inaccurate psychology, sociology, biology; and/or 2) they do not fully consider these scientific sources because scripture is assumed by church authorities and numerous lay members to be more normative than these others. The collective content of this book asks whether such an approach can be justified any longer. Indeed, this book aims to surface and critically examine the way insights from these other sources of wisdom may inform our biblical interpretations.

As a Lutheran, I grew up in a *sola scriptura* religious tradition, and scripture is still a fundamentally significant source for articulating Christian lifestyles, practices, and moral norms. The scriptures, along with church teachings and tradition are vitally important to my sense of the moral life, of who I am and of who I ought to be, because they powerfully speak about the responsibilities human beings owe one another and creation (to care for, to love, to embody justice in our individual and social relationships, etc.). These sources profoundly speak of the intrinsic goodness and beauty of humanity, while also casting sharp illumination on our inherent limits and imperfectability. In short, the scriptures and church teachings reveal much of what I believe God wants for us, who God is for us, and who we are called to be for one another.

I also deeply believe that there is a greater unity and integration among all the various sources of wisdom. There is but one truth. Ultimately, what I learn about the truth from biology, psychology, and all the rest will enrich my faith and not undermine it. Conversely, my faith will strengthen my appreciation of the wonders discovered by these scientific sources.

REEVALUATING THE RANGE OF SOURCES
NEEDED IN CHRISTIAN ETHICS

This chapter will certainly not resolve religious debates about the interpretation and authority of scripture; in fact, it seeks to make a very different point. My central concern regarding the sources in ethics does not revolve around how comparatively authoritative scripture is. Rather, it makes three rather different methodological claims about the sources for Christian ethics: 1) The list of four sources of moral wisdom (scripture, tradition, reason, and experience) is incomplete in the sense that not enough kinds of valuable information are highlighted by these categories. 2) How we understand the categories themselves needs fuller development so that we see how each one is already interdisciplinary (uses multiple and different kinds of information). 3) How we understand the category of experience merits more respect and development than it is often given in Christian ethics. I address this last concern in the section that follows.

With respect to my first concern, while the list of four primary sources is a good start, if it is seen as a complete catalogue, it is simply too short. Indeed, a glaring hole in the "list of four" is that "science" isn't explicitly mentioned! Historically, moral thinkers (e.g., Aristotle, Aquinas) assumed that what we now call science was included within the domain of philosophy. Thus, some Christian ethicists see the sciences as being an implicit part of the category "Reason." Given the complex moral quandaries associated with twenty-first-century science (stem cells, genetics, ecological crises, nanotechnology, etc.) and that the information from the sciences is so rich and varied (represented by collections of distinct disciplines and subdisciplines), contemporary theologians and ethicists must pay attention to the sciences and name the sciences explicitly as a source needed in the doing of ethics.

In short, I would like to expand the list of sources in Christian ethics beyond the four. Consider this working list: (*and keep in mind that all of these sources need interpretation/critical reflection and social analysis*):

* Reason (intellectual, critical thinking on all of the following sources)
* Sacred Scriptures
* Christian Traditions/Doctrines
* Deeply held Cultural Traditions
* Laws and Legal Traditions (historical and contemporary)
* Experience (individual and communal; historical and contemporary)
* Community (We all participate in and need communities of moral formation and deliberation.)
* Professional Disciplines (clinical, legal, psychological, pastoral, and so forth)
* Academic Disciplines, such as (but not limited to):
    * Theology, Ethics, and Biblical Studies
    * Natural Sciences
    * Social Sciences
    * Literature, Narrative, Biography, Documentary, Ethnography, and so forth

Even as it is a long list, it is by no means exhaustive. Rather, it is illustrative. Indeed, the fact that the sources for ethics are so many and so varied is one of the main reasons why interdisciplinary conversation is crucial to the development of sound moral arguments.

More substantive, however, is my second methodological claim. Fully appreciating the sources relevant for Christian ethics goes beyond completing any given "laundry list" of items to include or prioritize. Instead, nuanced understanding of each category is needed.

For example, the teachings, doctrines, and traditions of a community of believers and institutional religious body are certainly essential for patterning common ways of being and communal identity as they relate both to spiritual and moral ways of life. In other words, religious tradition and doctrine help define the common commitments and characteristics that distinguish a particular people from another. It gives them a common sense of who they are and of who they ought to be in the world as members of a faith community. However, no church or religion exists in a vacuum. Instead, churches and other religious institutions are shaped by particular contexts and histories—social, economic, political, linguistic, cultural, and so forth. In his chapter, Kniss, a sociologist, illustrates this fact by mapping the distinct evolutions of differing religious bodies in the United States.

Furthermore, the category "Tradition" needs to include not only explicitly Church traditions, but also deeply held cultural ones that grow out of the particular soils in which the church or religious community is planted—historically, linguistically, culturally. We see evidence of this reality in the dynamic conversations, pieties, and amalgamations characteristic of Christianity in the Global South (Africa, Asia, Latin America) where indigenous cultures and languages shape, as they too are shaped by, this faith tradition.[7]

The category "Reason" also needs more elaboration. "Reason" does not simply equal "Philosophy." It is a more comprehensive term, which refers to the human ability to reflect critically. Human beings are able to use our unique intellectual capacities to work with and study knowledge that comes from various disciplines: for example, philosophy, sociology, literature, theology, and the natural and social sciences. In other words, reason is not so much a discrete source associated with one scholarly discipline but rather refers to the way in which we learn from, reflect upon, and analyze various sources of information.

Given this definition of reason, perhaps the sources for ethics—however many we list—do not exist as separately and as independently as some might imagine. In other words, perhaps the categories do not represent wholly separate domains of knowledge, but rather overlap. I do not mean that scripture is the same as reason. We definitely need some distinctions. Rather, the point is simply that there is some level of inherent interrelationship among the different sources. The general categories of "Experience" and "Reason" are both examples of this kind of interaction among multiple sources of knowledge.

Experience (Re)Defined

I want to reflect substantively on the role of human experience in the doing of ethics. This category has historically been viewed with the most suspicion by Christian ethicists—fearing that it is too subjective, too individualistic, too sentimental, too biased—to be authoritative in ethics. One prevalent concern raised is that taking it seriously leads to moral relativism—a kind of "anything goes" ethic; a hands-off "you have your ethical views, I have mine and there is no greater sense of what is just, good, moral" kind of thinking. Simply put, a claim to have experienced something true and valuable for moral discernment is dismissed as "soft"—willy-nilly. How would we distinguish between a "real insight of value" and a rationalization/justification of whatever a person or community wants to do/be? In contrast, tradition, scripture, and rationality are praised as "harder"—more trustworthy, more "objective"—guides for moral knowledge.

With respect to discussions of human sexuality and gender, some religious leaders specifically want to sideline the experience of GLBT folk, claiming the centrality and authority of scripture over against what such persons might claim because, the leaders claim, their moral vision is muddied by specific political agendas (same-sex marriage legislation, the establishment of civil or religious unions). They also raise the concern that their moral arguments are biased and "disordered" by the very experiences they contend are illuminative (unnatural acts, unhealthy experiences, orientations, and identities). In particular, some suggest that GLBT experience seeks to subvert the preemptive authority of the other sources (most notably scripture and ecclesial tradition). In short, GLBT experience—lives, histories, and witness—is not a trustworthy source of moral wisdom because it is not objective. Instead, some view it as riddled with subjective, hidden goals, and by doing so they imply that heterosexual experience is somehow free of such subjectivity.

But is subjective viewpoint all there is to the category of experience? A more robust definition of the category is profoundly needed. And here I wish to make a couple of distinctions. First, I will define what I mean by experience—and the two main ways human beings access it. Second, I want to describe two distinct functions of experience for moral deliberation. And third, and most provocatively, I will argue that the category of experience is not simply one among many on the list of potential sources for ethics, but rather *is a primary means* for utilizing and interpreting *all* of the sources.

To begin, what do I mean by "experience"? The term should not be reduced to a superficial or individualistic level, "my personal experience matters most." Instead, "experience" refers to a thick and multidimensional body of information about lived reality. Susan L. Secker succinctly distinguishes between two basic types of information about experience: "(1) knowledge . . . that is provided by the human, natural, and social sciences, and (2) personal reports of individuals concerning the situation in which they find themselves and about which they can provide firsthand reflection. . . ."[8] Thus, experience is accessed through a variety of mutually corrective sources, including sociological, psychological, biological, anthropological data; narratives constructed in literature or heard and recorded in documentaries and ethnographies; and firsthand accounts of particular lived experience, often found in personal storytelling.

Moreover, not only are there multiple sources of information about human experience, but the category serves two distinct purposes, which relate specifically to the divisions between description and prescription mentioned above. First, Secker explains, appeals to human experience serve as "empirically-based descriptions of the way things are."[9] This is the most familiar ethical use of experience. It aids in the crafting of the full, accurate, and complex reporting of what exists—in nature and culture as constitutive of human identity. Such descriptions are integral building blocks for subsequent normative claims. Descriptive accuracy is absolutely essential for the creation of ethical judgments. Such a move does not give undue authority to selfish whims or subjective desires. Rather, it simply takes seriously "particular experiential reports which are representative of a generalized reality."[10] Before making a case for what ought to be, one must—as fully as possible—understand and describe what is.

Here is an example that illustrates how important such accuracy is in shaping what people think is normative. If all, or the vast majority of, the scientific evidence indicates that it is not possible to "reorient" one's experience of sexual desire, recommending that GLBT people attempt such change makes no logical sense. This is why many Christian denominations commend lifelong sexual abstinence to homosexual persons instead of trying to change the person's orientation. In other words, such Christians accept the scientific evidence that it is not realistic to expect homosexual people to "change" their sexual orientations and so they prescribe a different course of action, namely celibacy. Of course, for these Christians, the "ought" of this norm implies that they assume homosexual persons "can" embody such abstinence.

Numerous Christian ethicists have long signaled the centrality of human experience as a source for discerning moral norms and actions. And, interestingly, they are not alone. As point of fact, entire fields within various scholarly disciplines are dedicated to reporting accurately the depth and complexity of experience. (And they are not limited to the disciplines of psychiatry, psychology, or pastoral care.) Large domains within ecology, biology, chemistry, and physics also focus on such exploration. In all, numerous scholars in varied disciplines (such as those represented in this book) dedicate their lives to the fundamental and complex task of describing faithfully what is. And to do this, exploring the history and a full range of human experience is absolutely essential.

Secker also notes that there is a second, more complex and extensive, function of the category in which "appeals to human experience are introduced to provide normative criteria according to which judgments can be made about situations once they are accurately and fully understood."[11] When using experience in this way: "The ethicist seeks to identify features of the human which are so fundamental that normative ethical arguments cannot ignore them. Experience in this sense *functions as an ethical authority;* that is, as a type of truth claim."[12] Thus, experience does not merely tell us relevant facts about lived human reality when doing ethical reflection; *in itself it contains moral knowledge,* authority, and truth. Secker adds: "[T]he point of this usage is to correct the criteria and rules that guide moral judgment and define moral agency by refining them in light of an adequate conception of normative human reality."[13] To illustrate: If scientific studies of the many species that reproduce sexually (such as those reported by Roughgarden) indicate that in many of them, same-sex activity serves to enhance a group's survival rate by strengthening the group's ability to rear young; and if cross-cultural studies indicate that same-sex activity has surfaced steadily in human societies, and at a rate that exceeds what a genome tolerates for abnormalities,[14] this factual information would appear to challenge ethical norms that contend that heterosexual relations and practices are inherently morally superior to homosexual ones. One cannot "jump" from fact to value, and yet, values cannot be widely disconnected from truth about our lives. I elaborate this point further below.

For now, what is important to understand is that some Christian ethicists recognize what Secker identifies as the first function as valid, but they take issue with the second, more extensive use. The reason why the second function can be controversial is because it means that experience as a source may be used to reform or correct the other sources. For those ethicists who recognize this more expansive use, "empirical examination of contemporary human experience . . . can be expected to qualify the ethical role of biblical and theological texts which were themselves products of socio-cultural presuppositions."[15] In other words, experience may play a part in adjudicating what information from the other sources is relevant (and even authoritative) with respect to a particular ethical question. Experience can function in this way because the existence of the other sources is also intertwined with human experience—human history, socioeconomics, cultural systems, and so forth, have all shaped our collective interpretations and uses of scripture, tradition, and reason. I return to this point below.

Margaret Farley strongly emphasizes the importance of both the above functions. In particular, Farley gives women's experience a strong role in checking the validity of other sources in the doing of sexual ethics. Secker succinctly summarizes Farley's view: "Ethical appeals based on a notion of personhood which violates women's intrinsic self-understanding . . . cannot be legitimately claimed to have authority, even if such appeals can be grounded in Scripture or theological tradition."[16] For example, ethical claims that posit women as intrinsically inferior to men or that prescribe strict gender roles for men and women—whether or not it is possible to support them with quotations from scripture or from appeals to a religious doctrine or tradition—are nonetheless morally indefensible given all we now know about women and men (biologically, culturally, philosophically, etc.); about the socioeconomic and political contexts that play a part in constructing gender roles and inequalities; and given all the ideals of justice, right relationship, mutuality, and individual rights that represent the philosophical foundation of democratic societies.

The third and last point regarding experience I wish to make, already signaled above, is the most controversial. What the preceding analysis pushes us to consider is that experience is not simply a category among other discrete categories for Christian ethics. Rather, it is the way human beings access the wisdom of *any* source for ethics. It is the interpretative vehicle. We mediate all moral knowledge through our very bodies, minds, hearts, and conscience. Lutheran ethicist, Christian Scharen, pointedly contends:

> While many disagreements over the proper balance of these four sources exist in the scholarly literature, I wish to point out that experience is never simply just one among the four sources. Rather, it infuses all the others, as a sort of founding source or means of knowing. So, for example, Holy Scripture records people's experience and reception of God and God's revelation in Jesus Christ; the church's traditions represent the collective experiences of God's pilgrim people over time; and it is now common to assume scholarly work to be influenced by the experiences of the scholar her- or himself. In addition, our experiences deeply influence how we interpret the data drawn from sources: how and what we draw from Scripture, tradition, and the secular disciplines.[17]

Trying to figure out how to weigh and balance the sources for ethics is not sufficient for scholars such as Scharen and Farley. They call for recognition that experience is not simply a separate source of knowledge among other sources; instead, it serves as an interpretative lens and test of the adequacy of truth claims from other sources (e.g., appeals to tradition or scripture). Human beings necessarily utilize our rational capacities in order to make sense of data from history, biology, tradition, scripture, and individual and collective lives. Experience is inextricably woven into all of the sources of human knowledge—how we tap into them, interpret them, preserve them, and revise our understandings and truth claims as more knowledge become available. There is no direct link to truth that is unmediated. All knowledge—whether it comes from biology, philosophy, scripture, and so forth—must also pass through reflective human minds, hearts, fingers, eyes, ears, and noses.

For some Christians, such a view threatens a sense of the transcendent divine presence in creation (that is uniquely contained/revealed in scripture and tradition). And yet, others argue that such an understanding is instead a way to take God's incarnation in the world seriously. If God is truly transcendent, we mortals cannot place spatial or time limits on how God reveals God's self to us. The Christian scriptures testify throughout to a God intimately and profoundly present within all creation. In this light, the possibility that God speaks to humanity through biological data should not be so shocking or unnerving.

*   *   *

It would be premature to offer conclusions regarding the descriptive or normative nature of human gender and sexuality. Together, the chapters and authors of this book reach no formal consensus. Instead, taken collectively, the essays embody a sustained, sincere, thoughtful interdisciplinary dialogue and make the point that such dialogue is essential to a nuanced understanding of human sex and gender. This collection models open and serious exchange in the hope that it will inspire others to attempt the same.

And yet what are we to conclude? What are we to make of all that we have read and reflected upon? Upon reading various chapters, perhaps some readers are thinking: "Just because seahorses, certain species of fish, and birds embody multiple, or even changing, genders, certainly that does not mean that human beings ought to attempt the same?! And just because bonobos exhibit certain sexual behaviors or relations outside of monogamy and/or heterosexual mating, surely that does not mean that human beings ought to cast heterosexual monogamy aside!" Certainly we cannot flatly deduce what ought to be from what exists in nature. And yet the diversity and complexity within nature is not normatively insignificant information either.

What relationship exactly is there between what exists in creation and what we as human and responsible, moral beings find as morally permissible/desirable for human identities and relations? This concluding chapter does not offer definitive answers to this query; yet amid all the complexity, of this I am certain: Questions of "being, becoming, and doing" along with those of "what is and what ought to be" are inextricably bound up with one another. And these varied and complex chapters offer readers helpful resources for pondering and responding to this very question in their own lives.

Some readers may want a more definitive statement explaining the relationship between description and prescription, between "is" and "ought." Yet, I think the very nature of the question defies complete resolution. Rather, it seems more adequate to say that while we cannot simply deduct what ought to be from what is, clearly this book's collected analysis shows how we dare not ignore what is in terms of social and natural scientific understandings of human sex and gender in any ethical claim of what ought to be or change in human relations. So rather than doing the difficult work of moral discernment on such matters for readers, I have hoped, in this chapter, to point out things that will assist readers in their own ethical reflection and deliberation. Thus, I sought to signal central, thorny questions and issues that merit engaged reflection and to complexify our collective appreciation of the process of moral reflection and the sources integral to it.

By way of a conclusion, I want to offer two final provocations for our collective consideration. They represent my own questions at this juncture—not conclusions—and I hope they inspire fruitful reflection. My questions revolve around questioning first the separation of "facts" from "values" and then the relationship between experience, truth, and values.

On the surface, some disciplines (the natural and social sciences) primarily attempt explore "being, becoming, and doing" in descriptive terms. Scientists dedicate themselves to observing *what is* and reporting what they see and understand. Other disciplines and scholars (theology, ethics, philosophy) more boldly speak in "ought" language—what *should be* and offer a moral vision related to "being, becoming, and doing." When they do so, they are said to be speaking in normative terms, not simply descriptive ones.

Ethicists and some theologians spend much of our lives offering normative accounts; however, we may not all or always spend enough time making sure we utilize the best and most accurate descriptions before making a normative argument. And while many natural and social scientists do not see anything but accurate description and fact reporting as part of their vocational task, many recognize—as, for example, Joan Roughgarden makes plain in this volume and elsewhere—that they, too, have their own subjective assumptions that influence what they see, how they report it, and, yes, their basic descriptions of "what is."

So, perhaps scientists are not wholly objective or free from a desire to shape societal understanding of what should be. And why should they be? Think for a moment about global climate change. How can any scientist documenting the runaway melting of the polar ice cap and the drastic effects on thousands of living species not want to alter the course of this human-fashioned trajectory if at all possible? What good is describing what is, if it does not somehow meaningfully inform human action, choices, relations, and responsibilities?

For their part, theologians and ethicists are not shy about their claims to describe adequately and accurately human nature—in light of the revelation available in sacred scriptures, Church traditions, human reason, and human experience. Perhaps they could benefit from greater humility and from more rigorous exploration of the depth and breadth of experience. Christians pay attention to experience when reflecting on the justification (or lack thereof) for war; we read census data on poverty and lack of insurance to determine what kind of moral response is required; we look to the testimonies of immigrants and citizens along the border to reflect on immigration policy, we listen to scientists when assessing the dangers and possible solutions to global climate change. So why not with respect to gender and sexuality?

In all, perhaps a tidy division between description and prescription, or between the articulation of facts and values, as Stephen Pope suggests in his chapter, is not really possible. Perhaps both the scientists and the theologians do more of both than they fully acknowledge or realize. The truth of "how life is" is neither strictly fact nor value. Biological discoveries may indeed communicate values—for example, about biodiversity, ecological interdependence—that convey in and of themselves vital ethical information for a planet in peril. So, even as the scientists themselves may or may not be people of any particular faith, what they discover may reveal something about God's handiwork, at least for those who see the world through such a lens.

Even if bonobos are not a role model for the ideal human relations, they are part of God's good creation. For their part, secular moral theorists will connect the biological explanations with categories and imaginative frames from secular philosophy and the humanities, both to understand the world and to make arguments about how we should live and respond in ethical ways. Either way, the biological scientists do more than report facts, and the theologians and philosophers do not own the copyrights to "values" language.[18]

In short, we may not be able to separate neatly facts from values and designate the former as the realm of scientists and the latter as the domain of theologians and secular moral philosophers. If both generally construed domains are concerned with truth, and if, for people of faith, truth is not separate from God, perhaps we need to consider the possibility that there is theological truth—about who we are, our nature—that can be discovered through careful and probing scientific inquiry. While I am not a proponent of "intelligent design" schools of thought, I do think that learning as much as we can about creation, even about the gender identities and sexual practices of bonobos, seahorses, and the rest does tell us something about God—about God's infinite imagination and delight in diversity, if nothing else. In this sense, then, perhaps describing what exists in nature—as fully, as carefully, and as accurately as possible—is a kind of theological work, a vocation in a sense. For in understanding more of God's creation, we come to understand more of God.

The second area of questions that hound my consciousness comes back to the authority of experience. In my view, there cannot ultimately be a significant disconnect between human experience and what is objectively, essentially true about sex and gender. In other words, when there is a disconnect between what a significant number of people report as true to their experience related to sex and gender and what predominant scientific understanding reports as "true" about sex and gender, then something has to be amiss—either the scientific data is off or the reporting and interpreting of the human experience is skewed. Either way, the disconnect does not make sense.

If something is profoundly rooted in our nature related to our sexuality or gender, when values conflict with what is rooted in our nature, we—as individuals and as communities—ultimately reject or revise the values. For example, up until 1973, the American Psychiatric Association classified homosexuality as a mental illness. It changed its official position in response to years of GLBT people and others insistently and publicly reporting and documenting their experience that homosexual orientations do not equate illness.

Other moments in history testifies to this fact. By in large, most of U.S. society has rejected previous religious admonitions against masturbation. Similarly, many Christians reject both scientific claims and religious ones alike that do not defend the essential equality of women and men. Western scientific communities no longer use eugenics to contend that one race or ethnicity is superior to others as Nazis (*and also* white American researchers and physicians) did up to the notorious Nuremburg Trial of 1947 and even beyond it (e.g., Tuskegee Syphilis Study 1932–1972).[19] Christians all over the world reject slavery, despite biblical passages that took it for granted as part of society.

So rather than see claims to knowledge based in experience as oppositional to objective facts and transcendent values, perhaps we should entertain the notion that an individual's and a society's values will shift over time so that they resonate more fully, or conflict less, with the deepest truths known via individual and communal experience. It could be argued that such a view is consistent with what Jesus meant when he promised the Spirit would lead the Church deeper into the truth (e.g., John 14:25–26; 16:12–14). The question for Christians may be this: "Do we trust the Holy Spirit to guide us deeper into the truth?"

The scientific evidence and bulk of theological elaboration over the centuries are both seemingly irrefutable and in basic agreement on at least this one aspect of human identity: Human beings, as a species, are a discrete and distinctive part of a much larger, complex, diverse and interdependent creation. Whether we, as individuals and as societies, acknowledge it or not, our future is bound up with that of other living organisms and larger ecosystems. Our future is woven together with others (plants, animals, organic material) in a common existence on a fragile planet. Whether we take this fact seriously or not, our ethical thinking and concrete actions will determine whether we have a future of relations and identities (sexual, social, gender, etc.) to contemplate.

Apart from this above claim and after reading and reflecting on the array of analyses offered in this volume, I am not sure how much can be said definitively of an "essential human nature," whether in biological, theological, philosophical, or ethical terms. For example, Caughie's chapter powerfully shows how human gender is, to a very significant degree, a socially constructed reality. Jung, Rough-garden, and Grande et al. give additional, provocative, scientific, theological, and ethical reasons why a dimorphic understanding of human gender and sexuality is inadequate.

Yet, even as human discourse, institutions, practices, and customs create, or at least fundamentally shape, what we understand to be "natural" to human be-ings, one feature seems fairly integral to human nature: We are inquisitive and self-aware creatures. We tend to be restless in our search to know and under-stand ourselves and our world. Indeed, together, these essays testify to a restless, searching quality alive within human beings. This volume, we hope, is a begin-ning. May we begin or continue the conversation and the search . . . and may the divine smile at our discoveries.

Notes

1. Translation from *The New Jerusalem Bible*.

2. See Birch and Rasmussen, *The Bible and Ethics in the Christian Life*, 38–39.

3. I use the adjectives, "moral" and "ethical" interchangeably.

4. For more on the history of the elaboration of these four sources, see the work of Albert Outler, a Methodist historian, and that of James Gustafson. In particular see Gustafson, *Ethics from a Theocentric Perspective*. See also Farley, *Just Love*, 182. Farley cites Gunter, *Wesley and the Quadrilateral*. And see Cahill, *Between the Sexes*, 5.

5. Leviticus 17–26 is referred to as the Holiness Code by biblical scholars.

6. For a treatment of these themes in Christian ethics, see McFague, *Life Abundant;* Moe-Lobeda, *Healing a Broken World;* Wheeler, *Wealth as Peril and Obligation;* and Brubaker et al., *Justice in a Global Economy*.

7. If such dynamic "cross-fertilization" seems troubling or problematic, remember that that is *exactly* what was going on in sixteenth-century Germany as Martin Luther translated and interpreted the sacred scriptures and tradition in light of the particular German peoples in the midst of massive economic and political shifts. And it happened again in the fertile soil and founding documents of what would become the United States. In both these examples, economic and political shifts bled (literally and metaphorically) into ecclesial ones, just as the religious reformation provoked economic and political change.

8. Secker, "Human Experience and Women's Experience," 579.

9. Ibid.

10. Ibid., 585.

11. Secker, 580.

12. Ibid. (emphasis mine).

13. Ibid., 581.

14. Roughgarden shows that the rate of same-sex sexual reproduction and/or activity in both nonhuman and human species significantly exceeds that which scientists associate with defect and/or harmful genomes, or disease, abnormality. In other words, such activity and relations occur at a higher rate than genomes tolerate if they are defective and/or hurtful to the species. See Roughgarden, *Evolution's Rainbow.*

15. Secker, "Human Experience and Women's Experience," 587.

16. Ibid., 587–88. Secker explains further: "Farley suggests a twofold hermeneutical function for women's experience. Negatively, borrowing from Rosemary Radford Ruether, she claims that 'whatever diminishes or denies the full humanity of women must be presumed not to reflect the divine or an authentic relation to the divine or to reflect the nature of things, or to be the message or work of an authentic redeemer or a community of redemption.' Positively, she calls for an objective construal of the normatively human which is inclusive of women's understanding of women's personhood as component part of human personhood." Ibid., 588.

17. Scharen, "Experiencing the Body," 101.

18. I want to acknowledge a helpful, clarifying conversation with Christian Scharen in December 2008 that deepened my sense of this point.

19. For information on the tragic history of eugenics in the United States, see Washington, *Medical Apartheid* and Kuhl, *The Nazi Connection.*

Bibliography

Adkins-Regan, E. "The Love That Dare Not Bark Its Name." *BioScience* 49 (1999): 926–27.

Akçay, E., and J. Roughgarden. "Extra-Pair Reproductive Activity in Birds: Review of the Genetic Benefits." *Evolutionary Ecology Research* 9 (2007): 855–68.

Altman, Dennis. *Global Sex.* Chicago: University of Chicago Press, 2001.

Amnesty International. *Stonewalled—Still Demanding Respect: Police Abuses against Lesbian, Gay, Bisexual, and Transgender People in the USA.* Oxford, U.K.: Alden Press, 2006.

Aquinas, Thomas. *Commentary on the Nicomachean Ethics.* Translated by C. I. Litainger, O.P. Library of Living Catholic Thought, vol. 1. Chicago: Henry Regnery and Co., 1964.

———. *Summa Contra Gentiles.* Vol. 3. Cura et Studio Sac. Petri Caramello. Taurino et Romae: Marietti, 1950.

———. *Summa Theologiae.* Vol. 1, Prima Pars et Prima Pars Secundae Partae; et Vol. 2, Tertia Pars. Cura et Studio Sac. Petri Caramello. Taurino et Romae: Marietti, 1950.

Associated Press, "Caster Semenya Withdraws from Competition amid Speculation" September 12, 2009, http://www.nytimes.com/2009/09/12/sports/12runner.html?_r=1&scp=3&sq=semenya&st=cse.

Augustine. *City of God (De Civitate Dei).* Cambridge: Aris and Phillips/Oxbow, 2007: xi–251.

———. *Saint Augustine: On Christian Doctrine* (Library of Liberal Arts). Translated by D. W. Robertson, Jr. New York: Macmillan Publishing, 1958.

———. *St. Augustine on Marriage and Sexuality.* Edited by Elizabeth A. Clark. Washington, D.C.: Catholic University of America Press, 1996.

Aulette, Judy, Judith Wittner, and Kristen Blakely. *Gendered Worlds.* New York: Oxford University Press, 2009.

Babcock, Barbara, ed. *Pueblo Mothers and Children: Essays by Elsie Crew Parsons, 1915–1924.* Sante Fe, N.Mex.: Ancient City Press, 1991.

Bagemihl, Bruce. *Biological Exuberance: Animal Homosexuality and Natural Diversity.* New York: St. Martin's Press, 1999.

Barnes, Barry, and David Edge. *Science in Context: Readings in the Sociology of Science.* Cambridge: MIT Press, 1982.

Bartky, Sandra Lee. "Foucault, Femininity, and the Modernization of Patriarchal Power." In *The Politics of Women's Bodies,* edited by Rose Weitz, 25–45. Oxford: Oxford University Press, 2003.

Beattie, Tina. *New Catholic Feminism: Theology and Theory.* New York: Routledge, 2006.

Bernstein, H., H. C. Byerly, F. A. Hopf, and R. E. Michod. "Genetic Damage, Mutation, and the Evolution of Sex." *Science* 229 (1985): 1277–81.

Bertram, C. R. "Social Factors Influencing Reproduction in Wild Lions." *Journal of Zoology* 177 (1975): 463–82.

Biblical Discernment Ministries. "Promise Keepers—Ecumenical Macho-Men for Christ?" http://www.rapidnet.com/~jbeard/bdm/Psychology/pk/pk.htm (accessed January 23, 2009).

Birch, Bruce C., and Larry L. Rasmussen. *The Bible and Ethics in the Christian Life.* Revised Edition. Minneapolis, Minn.: Augsburg Fortress Press, 1989.

Bird, P. A. "'Male and Female He Created Them': Gen 1:27b in the Context of the Priestly Account of Creation." *Harvard Theological Review* 74 (April 1981): 129–59.

Bleiweiss, R. "Asymmetrical Expression of Transsexual Phenotypes in Hummingbirds." *Proceedings of the Royal Society of London B* 268 (2001): 639–46.

———. "Widespread Polychromatism in Female Sunangel Hummingbirds (*Heliangelus:* Trochilidae)." *Biological Journal of the Linnean Society* 45 (1992): 291–314.

Boccaccini, G. *Roots of Rabbinic Judaism: An Intellectual History, from Ezekiel to Daniel.* Grand Rapids, Mich.: William B. Eerdmans Publishing, 2002.

Boethius, A. M. S. "A Treatise against Euthyches and Nestorius." In *The Theological Tractates,* English translation by H. F. Stewart, E. K. Rand, and S.J. Tester. Loeb Classical Library. Cambridge: Harvard University Press, 1978.

Bordo, Susan. *The Male Body: A New Look at Men in Public and Private.* New York: Farrar, Straus, and Giroux, 1999.

Borgerhoff Mulder, M. "Serial Monogamy as Polygyny or Polyandry? Marriage in the Tanzanian Pimbwe." *Human Nature* 20 (2009):130–40.

Botterweck, G. Johannes, ed. . *Theological Dictionary of the Old Testament.* Grand Rapids, Mich.: Eerdmans, Northam, Roundhouse, 2004.

Bowler, Peter. *Reconciling Science and Religion.* Chicago: University of Chicago Press, 2001.

Brooke, John. *Science and Religion: Some Historical Perspectives.* Cambridge, U.K.: Cambridge University Press, 1991.

Brown, Peter. *The Body and Society: Men, Women and Sexual Renunciation in Early Christianity.* New York: Columbia University Press, 1988.

Brubaker, Pamela, Rebecca Todd Peters, and Laura A. Stivers, eds. *Justice in a Global Economy: Strategies for Home, Community, and World.* Louisville: Westminster John Knox Press, 2006.

Burns, Gene. *The Frontiers of Catholicism: The Politics of Ideology in a Liberal World.* Berkeley: University of California Press, 1992.

———. "The Politics of Ideology: The Papal Struggle with Liberalism." *American Journal of Sociology* 95 (1990): 1123–52.

Buss, D. M. *The Evolution of Desire: Strategies of Human Mating.* New York: Basic Books, 1994.

Buss, D. M., and Schmitt, D. P. "Sexual Strategies Theory: An Evolutionary Perspective on Human Mating." *Psychological Review* 100 (1993): 204–32.

Butler, Cuthbert. *The Vatican Council 1869–1870,* edited by Christopher Butler. Westminster, Md.: Newman, 1962 (orig. ed. 1930).

Butler, Judith. *Gender Trouble: Feminism and the Subversion of Identity.* New York: Routledge, 1990.

———. "Imitation and Gender Insubordination." In *The Judith Butler Reader,* edited by Sara Salih with Judith Butler, 119–37. Oxford, U.K.: Blackwell Publishing, 2004.

Bynum, Caroline Walker. *Holy Feast and Holy Fast: The Religious Significance of Food to Medieval Women.* Berkeley: University of California Press, 1988.

———. *Jesus as Mother.* Berkeley: University of California Press, 1982.

Cahill, Lisa Sowle. *Between the Sexes: Foundations for a Christian Ethics of Sexuality.* Minneapolis, Minn.: Augsburg Fortress, 1985.

———. *Sex, Gender, and Christian Ethics.* New York: Cambridge University Press, 1996.

Catania, Frank [Francis J.]. "Science." In *Medieval France: An Encyclopedia,* edited by William W. Kibler and Grover A. Zinn, 864–65. New York: Garland Publishing, 1995.

Catholic News. "Vatican Bans Transsexuals from Religious Orders." (February 3, 2003; accessed October 5, 2007), http://www.cathnews.com/news/302/4.php.

Caughie, Pamela L. "Passing as Modernism." *Modernism/modernity* 12, no. 3 (September 2005): 385–406.

Chao, Lin. "Fitness of RNA Virus Decreased by Muller's Ratchet." *Nature* 348 (1990): 454–55.

Christiansen, F. B., S. P. Otto, A. Bergmann, and M. W. Feldman. "Waiting with and without Recombination: The Time to Production of a Double Mutant." *Theoretical Population Biology* 53 (1998): 199–215.

Clague, Julie. "The Christa: Symbolizing My Humanity and My Pain." *Feminist Theology* 14, no.1 (2005): 83–108.

Coakley, Sarah. *Powers and Submissions: Spirituality, Philosophy and Gender.* Oxford, U.K.: Blackwell Publishing, 2002.

Code, Lorraine. *What Can She Know? Feminist Theory and the Construction of Knowledge.* Ithaca, N.Y.: Cornell University Press, 1991.

Collins, Francis. *The Language of God: A Scientist Presents Evidence for Belief.* New York: The Free Press, 2006.

Curry, Oliver. "Who's Afraid of the Naturalistic Fallacy?" *Evolutionary Psychology* 4 (2006): 234–47.

Daly, Anthony C. "Aquinas on Disordered Pleasures and Conditions," *The Thomist* 56 (October 1992): 583–612.

Daly, Mary. *Beyond God the Father: Toward a Philosophy of Women's Liberation.* Boston: Beacon Press, 1983.

D'Angelo, Mary Rose. "'Knowing How to Preside over His Own Household': Imperial

Masculinity and Christian Asceticism in the Pastorals, Hermas and Luke-Acts." In *New Testament Masculinities,* edited by Stephen D. Moore and Janice Capel Anderson, 265–96. Atlanta, Ga.: Society of Biblical Literature, 2003.

Darwin, Charles. *The Descent of Man, and Selection in Relation to Sex.* Facsimile Edition. Princeton, N.J.: Princeton University Press, 1871.

Daum, Meghan. "The Case of Caster Semenya," *Chicago Tribune,* September 23, 2009; online: http://www.chicagotribune.com/news/opinion/chi-oped0923daumsep23,0,481879 .column

Davies, N. B., I. R. Hartley, B. J. Hatchwell, and N. E. Langmore. "Female Control of Copulations to Maximize Male Help: A Comparison of Polygynandrous Alpine Aaccentors, *Prunella collaris,* and Dunnocks, *P. modularis.*" *Animal Behaviour* 51, no. 1 (January 1996): 27–47.

Dawkins, Richard. *The God Delusion.* New York: Houghton Mifflin, 2006.

———. "Is Science a Religion?" *The Humanist* 57, no. 1 (January/February 1997): 26–29.

Dean, Cornelia. "Faith, Reason, God and Other Imponderables," *New York Times,* July 25 2006.

de Tocqueville, Alexis. *Democracy in America.* Translated by George Lawrence and edited by J. P. Mayer. Garden City, N.Y.: Anchor Books, 1850/1969.

Dickens, W. T. *Hans Urs von Balthasar's Theological Aesthetics: A Model for Post-Critical Biblical Interpretation.* Notre Dame, Ind.: University of Notre Dame Press, 2003.

Dillard, Annie. *Living by Fiction.* New York: Harper and Row, 1982.

Dillon, Michele. *Catholic Identity: Balancing Reason, Faith, and Power.* New York: Cambridge University Press, 1999.

Di Vito, Robert A. "Questions about the Construction of (Homo)sexuality: Same Sex Relations in the Bible." In *Sexual Diversity and Catholicism,* edited by See Patricia Beattie Jung, 108–32. Collegeville, Minn.: Liturgical Press, 2001.

Downes, David. *Gerard Manley Hopkins: A Study of His Ignatian Spirit.* New York: Bookman, 1960.

Dreger, Alice Domurat. "A History of Intersex: From the Age of Gonads to the Age of Consent." In *Intersex in the Age of Ethics,* edited by Alice Domurat Dreger, 5–21. Hagerstown, Md.: University Publishing Group, 1999.

Durkheim, Emile. *The Elementary Forms of Religious Life.* London: Allen and Unwin, 1912/1979.

Ecklund, Elaine Howard. "Initial Findings from the Study of Religion among Academic Sciences." *Chronicle of Higher Education,* October 31 2006.

Ecklund, Elaine, Jerry Park, and Phil Veliz. "Secularization and Religious Change among Elite Scientists." *Social Forces* 86, no. 4 (2008): 1805–39.

Eisler, Riane. *The Chalice and the Blade.* Cambridge, Mass.: Harper and Row, 1987.

ELCA News Service, "2009 ELCA Churchwide Assembly Addresses Variety of Topics." August 28, 2009; online: http://www.elca.org/Who-We-Are/Our-Three-Expressions/ Churchwide-Organization/Communication-Services/News/Releases.aspx?a=4278

Faderman, Lillian. *Odd Girls and Twilight Lovers: A History of Lesbian Life in Twentieth-Century America.* New York: Columbia University Press, 1991.

Farley, Margaret A. "An Ethic for Same-Sex Relations." In *Readings in Moral Theology No. 8: Dialogue about Catholic Sexual Teaching,* edited by Chares E. Curran and Richard A. McCormick, S.J., 340–48. Mahwah, N.J.: Paulist, 1993.

———. *Just Love: A Framework for Christian Sexual Ethics.* New York: Continuum, 2006.

———. "New Patterns of Relationship: Beginnings of a Moral Revolution." In *Introduction to Christian Ethics: A Reader,* edited by Ronald R. Hamel and Kenneth R. Himes, 63–79. N.Y.: Paulist Press, 1989.

———. *Personal Commitments: Making, Keeping, and Changing.* San Francisco: Harper and Row, 1986.

Fausto-Sterling, Anne. *Sexing the Body: Gender Politics and the Construction of Sexuality.* New York: Basic Books, 2000.

———. "Two Sexes Are Not Enough." Excerpt from *Sexing the Body,* http://www.pbs.org/wgbh/nova/gender/fs.html.

Ferder, Fran, and John Heagle. *Tender Fires: The Spiritual Promise of Sexuality.* New York: Crossroads Publishing, 2002.

Ferngren, Gary, ed. *Science & Religion: A Historical Introduction.* Baltimore: Johns Hopkins University Press, 2002.

Ferrell, Michael J. "How Jesus 2000 Grew Wings, Keeps on Flying." *National Catholic Reporter.* http://www.natcath.com/NCR_Online/archives/051200/051200i.htm (accessed January 23, 2009).

Figert, Anne. *Women and the Ownership of PMS: The Structuring of a Psychiatric Disorder.* Hawthorne, N.Y.: Aldine de Gruyter, 1996.

Fiorenza, Elisabeth Schüssler. *Jesus: Miriam's Child, Sophia's Prophet: Critical Issues in Feminist Christology.* New York: Continuum, 1994.

———. *In Memory of Her.* New York: Crossroads Publishing, 1983.

Fisher, Helen. *Anatomy of Love: The Natural History of Monogamy, Adultery, and Divorce.* New York: Simon and Schuster, 1992.

Fisher, Ronald. *The Genetical Theory of Natural Selection.* New York: Oxford University Press, 1930/2000.

Foucault, Michel. *Herculine Barbin: Being the Recently Discovered memoirs of a Nineteenth-Century Hermaphrodite.* Translated by Richard McDougall. New York: Pantheon, 1980.

———. *The History of Sexuality: An Introduction, vol. 1.* Translated by Robert Hurley. New York: Random House, 1978.

———. "On the Genealogy of Ethics: An Overview of Work in Progress." In *The Foucault Reader,* edited by Paul Rabinow, 340–72. New York: Pantheon Books, 1984.

French, Roger, and Andrew Cunningham. *Before Science, the Invention of the Friars Natural Philosophy.* Brookfield, Vt.: Scholar Press, 1996.

Frickel, Scott, and Kelly Moore. *The New Political Sociology of Science: Institutions, Networks and Power.* Madison: University of Wisconsin Press, 2005.

Frye, Marilyn. *The Politics of Reality: Essays in Feminist Theory.* Freedom, Calif.: The Crossing Press, 1983.

Fuentes, Agustin. "Patterns and Trends in Primate Pair Bonds." *International Journal of Primatology* 23, no. 5 (2002): 953–78.

———. "Re-Evaluating Primate Monogamy." *American Anthropologist* 100, no. 4 (1999): 890–907.

Fujimura, Joan. "The Molecular Biological Bandwagon in Cancer Research: Where Social Worlds Meet." *Social Problems* 35, no. 3 (June 1988): 261–83.

Gaillardetz, Richard R. *By What Authority?: A Primer on Scripture, the Magisterium, and the Sense of the Faithful.* Collegeville, Minn.: Liturgical Press, 2003.

Garber, Marjorie. *Vested Interests: Cross-Dressing and Cultural Anxiety.* New York: Routledge, 1992.

Gaventa, Beverly Roberts. "Ethiopian Eunuch." In *The Anchor Bible Dictionary. Volume 2,* edited by David Noel Freedman. New York: Doubleday, 1992.

Gavrilets, S., and W. R. Rice. "Genetic Models of Homosexuality: Generating Testable Predictions." *Proceedings of the Royal Society of London B* 273 (2006): 3031–38.

Gerth, Hans Heinrich, and C. Wright Mills. *From Max Weber: Essays in Sociology.* New York: Oxford University Press, 1958.

Gieryn, Thomas F. "Boundaries of Science." In *Handbook of Science, Technology and Society,* edited by S. Jasanoff, G. Markle, J. Petersen, and T. Pinch, 393–443. Beverly Hills: Sage, 1994.

———. "Boundary-Work and the Demarcation of Science from Non-Science: Strains and Interests in Professional Ideologies of Scientists." *American Sociological Review* 48, no. 6 (December 1983): 781–95.

———. *Cultural Boundaries of Science: Credibility on the Line.* Chicago: University of Chicago Press, 1999.

———. "Cultural Boundaries: Settled and Unsettled." In *Clashes of Knowledge,* edited by Peter Meusberger, Michael Welker, and Edgar Wunder, 91–99. Dordrecht, Holland: Springer, 2008.

Gieryn, Thomas, and Anne Figert. "Ingredients for a Theory of Science in Society: O-Rings, Ice Water, C-Clamp, Richard Feynman and the Press." In *Theories of Science in Society,* edited by Susan Cozzens and Thomas Gieryn, 67–97. Bloomington: Indiana University Press, 1990.

———. "Scientists Protect Their Cognitive Authority: The Status Degradation Ceremony of Sir Cyril Burt." In *The Sociology of the Sciences Yearbook, Volume X,* edited by G. Bohme and N. Stehr, 67–86. Dordecht, Holland: D. Reidel, 1986.

Gieryn, Thomas F., George Bevins, and Stephen Zehr. "Professionalization of American Scientists: Public Science in the Creation/Evolution Trials." *American Sociological Review* 50, no. 3 (June 1985): 392–409.

Gilbert, G. Nigel, and Michael Mulkay. *Opening Pandora's Box: A Sociological Analysis of Scientists' Discourse.* Cambridge, U.K.: Cambridge University Press, 1984.

Goodstein, Laurie. "Episcopal Split as Conservatives Form New Group, *The New York Times,* December 3, 2008. http://www.nytimes.com/2008/12/04/us/04episcopal.html (accessed May 20, 2009).

Gould, Elisabeth David. *The First Sex.* New York: Penguin Books, 1971.

Gould, Stephen Jay. *The Mismeasure of Man.* New York: W. W. Norton and Co, 1996.

———. *Rocks of Ages: Science and Religion in the Fullness of Life.* New York: Ballantine, 1999.

Granfield, Patrick. *The Limits of the Papacy.* New York: Crossroads Publishing, 1987.

Gross, Sally. "Intersexuality and Scripture." *Theology and Sexuality* 11 (September 1999): 65–74.

Gudorf, Christine E. *Body, Sex and Pleasure: Reconstructing Christian Sexual Ethics.* Cleveland: Pilgrim Press, 1994.

Gula, Richard M. *Reason Informed by Faith: Foundations of Catholic Morality.* Mahwah, N.J.: Paulist Press, 1989.

Gunter, W. Stephens, et al. *Wesley and the Quadrilateral: Renewing the Conversation.* Nashville: Abingdon Press, 1997.

Gustafson, James M. *Ethics from a Theocentric Perspective: Ethics and Theology.* Volumes 1 and 2. Chicago: University of Chicago Press, 1983, 1992.

———. "Genetic Engineering and a Normative View of the Human," in *Ethical Issues in Biology and Medicine, edited by* Preston N. Williams, 46–58. Cambridge, Mass.: Schenkman Pub. Co., (distributed by General Learning Press), 1972.

———. "The Relationship of Empirical Science to Moral Thought." In *Introduction to Christian Ethics: A Reader,* edited by Ronald R. Hamel and Kenneth R. Himes, 428–38. New York: Paulist Press, 1989.

Haigh, John. "The Accumulation of Deleterious Genes in a Population—Muller's Ratchet." *Theoretical Population Biology* 14 (1978): 251–67.

Hamel, Ronald R., and Kenneth R. Himes, eds. *Introduction to Christian Ethics: A Reader.* Mahwah, N.J.: Paulist Press, 1989.

Hamer, D., and P. Copland. *The Science of Desire: The Search for the Gay Gene and the Biology of Behavior.* New York: Simon and Schuster, 1994.

Harris, Steven. "Roman Catholicism since Trent." In *Science & Religion: A Historical Introduction,* edited by Gary Ferngren, 247–60. Baltimore: Johns Hopkins University Press, 2002.

Hart, Stephen. *What Does the Lord Require?* New York: Oxford University Press, 1992.

Harvey, P. "A Bestiary of Chaos and Biodiversity." *Nature* 397 (1999): 402–03.

Hausman, Bernice. "Recent Transgender Theory." *Feminist Studies* 27, no. 2 (Summer 2001): 465–90.

Heidegger, Martin. *On the Way to Language.* Translated by Peter Hertz. New York: Harper and Row, 1996.

Himmelstein, Jerome L. "The New Right." In *The New Christian Right,* edited by Robert C. Liebman and Robert Wuthnow, 133–48. New York: Aldine, 1983.

Hopkins, Gerard Manley. *The Oxford Authors: Gerard Manley Hopkins,* edited by Catherine Phillips. Oxford: Oxford University Press, 1986.

———. *The Sermons and Devotional Writings of Gerard Manley Hopkins,* edited by Christopher Devlin, S. J. Oxford: Oxford University Press, 1959.

Hunter, James Davison. *Culture Wars: The Struggle to Define America.* New York: Basic Books, 1991.

Hutchison, William R. *The Modernist Impulse in American Protestantism.* Oxford: Oxford University Press, 1982.

Iannaccone, Laurence, Rodney Stark, and Roger Finke. "Rationality and the 'Religious Mind.'" *Economic Inquiry* 36, no. 3 (July 1998): 373–89.

Intersex Society of North America. "What Is Intersex?" http://www.isna.org/faq/what_is_intersex (accessed January 23, 2009).

Iyer, P., and J. Roughgarden. "Origin of Male and Female: Evolution of Anisogamy Reanalyzed." In review.

Johnson, Elizabeth A. *She Who Is: The Mystery of God in Feminist Theological Discourse.* New York: Crossroads Publishing, 1999.

Johnson, George. "Agreeing Only to Disagree on God's Place in Science." *New York Times,* September 27, 2005, http://www.nytimes.com/2005/09/27/science/27essa.html (accessed on May 20, 2009).

———. "A Free-for-All on Science and Religion." *New York Times,* November 21, 2006.

Johnson, Luke Timothy. "A Disembodied 'Theology of the Body': John Paul II on Love, Sex, and Pleasure." In *Human Sexuality in the Catholic Tradition,* edited by Kieran Scott and Harold Daly Horell, 111–27. Lanham, Md.: Rowman and Littlefield, 2007.

Jordan, Mark D. *The Ethics of Sex.* Oxford, U.K.: Blackwell Publishing, 2002.

Jung, Patricia Beattie. "Christianity and Human Sexual Polymorphism: Are They Compatible?" In *Ethics and Intersex,* edited by S. Sytsma, 293–309. Netherlands: Springer, 2006.

———. "Constructing a Consistent Ethic of Life." In *The Consistent Ethic of Life: Assessing Its Reception and Relevance,* edited by Thomas A. Nairn, 61–80. Maryknoll, N.Y.: Orbis Books, 2008.

———. "The Promise of Postmodern Hermeneutics." In *Sexual Diversity and Catholicism,* edited by Patricia Beattie Jung, 77–107. Collegeville, Minn.: Liturgical Press, 2001.

Kalbian, L. H. "Integrity in Catholic Sexual Ethics." *Journal of the Society of Christian Ethics* 24, no. 2 (2004): 55–69.

Kappeler, P. M., and C. P. van Shaik. *Sexual Selection in Primates: New and Comparative Perspectives.* Cambridge, U.K.: Cambridge University Press, 2004.

Karlin, S. "Sex and Infinity: A Mathematical Analysis of the Advantages and Disadvantages of Genetic Recombination." In *The Mathematical Theory of the Dynamics of Biological Populations,* edited by M. S. B. and R. W. Hiorns, 155–94. New York: Academic Press, 1973.

Keller, Catherine. *From a Broken Web: Separation, Sexism, and Self.* Boston: Beacon Press, 1988.

Kemp, S. "The Role of Genes and Hormones in Sexual Differentiation." In *Ethics and Intersex,* edited by S. E. Sytsma. New York: Springer, 2006.

Kerr, Fergus. *After Aquinas: Versions of Thomism.* Oxford, U.K.: Blackwell Publishing, 2002.

Kessler, Suzanne. "The Medical Construction of Gender: Case Management of Intersexed Infants," *Signs* 16 (1990): 3–26.

King, P. J., and Lawrence E. Stager. "Of Fathers, Kings, and the Deity: The Nested Households of Ancient Israel," *Biblical Archaeology Review* 28, no. 2 (March/April 2002): 43–45, 62.

Kinzey, W. G. "Monogamous Primates: A Primate Model for Human Mating Systems." In *The Evolution of Human Behavior: Primate Models*, edited by W. G. Kinzey, 87–104. Albany: State University of New York Press, 1987.

Kitcher, Philip. "The Many-Sided Conflict between Science and Religion." In *Philosophy of Religion*, edited by William E. Mann, 266–82. Oxford, U.K.: Blackwell Publishing, 2005.

Kleiman, D. "Monogamy in Mammals." *Quarterly Review of Biology* 52 (1977): 39–69.

Kniss, Fred. *Disquiet in the Land: Cultural Conflict in American Mennonite Communities*. New Brunswick, N.J.: Rutgers University Press, 1997.

———. "Mapping the Moral Order: Depicting the Terrain of Religious Conflict and Change." In *Handbook of the Sociology of Religion*, edited by Michele Dillon, 331–47. New York: Cambridge University Press, 2003.

Kniss, Fred, and Paul Numrich. *Sacred Assemblies and Civic Engagement: How Religion Matters for America's Newest Immigrants*. New Brunswick, N.J.: Rutgers University Press, 2007.

Knorr-Cetina, Karin. *Epistemic Cultures: How the Sciences Make Knowledge*. Cambridge: Harvard University Press, 1999.

Koene, J. M., T. Pfortner, and N. K. Michiels. "Piercing the Partner's Skin Influences Sperm Uptake in the Earthworm *Lumbricus terrestris*." *Behavioral Ecology and Sociobiology* 59 (2005): 243–49.

Komonchak, Joseph A. "Interpreting the Council. Catholic Attitudes towards Vatican II." In *Being Right: Conservative Catholics in America*, edited by Mary Jo Weaver and R. Scott Appleby, 17–36. Bloomington: Indiana University Press, 1995.

Kuefler, Matthew. *The Manly Eunuch: Masculinity, Gender Ambiguity and Christian Ideology in Late Antiquity*. Chicago: University of Chicago Press, 2001.

Kuhl, Stefan. *The Nazi Connection: Eugenics, American Racism, and German National Socialism*. New York: Oxford University Press, 1994.

Kurtz, Lester R. *The Politics of Heresy: The Modernist Crisis in Roman Catholicism*. Berkeley: University of California Press, 1986.

Lacey, Marc. "A Lifestyle Distinct: The Muxe of Mexico," *New York Times*, December 7, 2008, http://www.nytimes.com/2008/12/07/weekinreview/07lacey.html (accessed on May 20, 2009).

Latour, Bruno. *Science in Action: How to Follow Scientists and Engineers through Society*. Cambridge: Harvard University Press, 1988.

Lerner, Gerda. *The Creation of Patriarchy*. New York: Oxford University Press, 1987.

Lev, Sarra L. "They Treat Him as a Man and See Him as a Woman: The Tannaitic Understanding of the Congenital Eunuch." Unpublished essay.

Liem, K. F. "Functional Design of the Air Ventilation Apparatus and Overland Excursions by Teleosts." *Fieldiana: Zoology* 1379 (1987): 1–29.

Lindberg, David C. "Medieval Science and Its Religious Context." *Osiris*, 2nd Series 10 (1995): 60–79.

Lipset, Seymour Martin, and Earl Raab. *The Politics of Unreason: Right-wing Extremism in America, 1790-1977*. Chicago: University of Chicago Press, 1978.

Lonergan, Bernard. *Method in Theology*. New York: Herder and Herder, 1972.

MacDonald, D. R. *There Is No Male and Female* (Harvard Dissertations in Religion). Philadelphia: Fortress Press, 1987.

MacIntyre, Alasdair C. *After Virtue : A Study in Moral Theory.* 2nd ed. Notre Dame, Ind.: University of Notre Dame Press, 1984.

——. *Dependent Rational Animals: Why Human Beings Need the Virtues.* Peru, Ill.: Open Court, 1999.

——. *Three Rival Versions of Moral Enquiry: Encyclopaedia, Genealogy, and Tradition.* Notre Dame, Ind.: University of Notre Dame Press, 1990.

Macy, Gary. *A History of Women and Ordination.* Lanham, Md.: Scarecrow Press, 2003.

Margulis, L., and D. Sagan. *Origins of Sex: Three Billion Years of Genetic Recombination.* New Haven: Yale University Press, 1986.

Mariani, Paul. *A Commentary on the Complete Poems of Gerard Manley Hopkins.* Ithaca, N.Y.: Cornell University Press, 1970.

Marsden, George M. *Fundamentalism and American Culture: The Shaping of Twentieth-century Evangelicalism, 1870–1925.* Oxford: Oxford University Press, 1980.

Martin, Biddy. "Success and Its Failures." In *Feminist Consequences: Theory for the New Century,* edited by Elisabeth Bronfen and Misha Kavka. New York: Columbia University Press, 2001: 353–80.

Martin, Dale. *Sex and the Single Savior: Gender and Sexuality in Biblical Interpretation.* Louisville: Westminster John Knox Press, 2006.

Martin, Emily. "The Egg and the Sperm." *Signs* 16.3 (1991): 485–501.

Maynard Smith, J. *Evolution and the Theory of Games.* Cambridge, U.K.: Cambridge University Press, 1982.

McFague, Sallie. *Life Abundant: Rethinking Theology and Economy for a Planet in Peril.* Minneapolis: Fortress Press, 2001.

——. *Models of God: Theology for an Ecological, Nuclear Age.* Philadelphia: Fortress, 1987.

Meeks, Wayne. "The Image of the Androgyne: Some Uses of a Symbol in Earliest Christianity." *History of Religions* 13, no. 3 (February 1974): 165–208.

Merton, Robert. *Science, Technology and Society in Seventeenth-Century England.* New York: Harper and Row, 1938/1970.

——. *The Sociology of Science: Theoretical and Empirical Investigations.* Chicago: University of Chicago Press, 1973.

Meyerowitz, Joanne. *How Sex Changed: A History of Transsexuality in the United States.* Cambridge: Harvard University Press, 2002.

Miller, C. W., and A. J. Moore. "A Potential Resolution to the Lek Paradox through Indirect Genetic Effects." *Proceedings of the Royal Society of London B* 274, no. 1615 (22 May 2007): 1279–1286.

Modras, Ronald. "Pope John Paul II's Theology of the Body." In *John Paul II and Moral Theology,* edited by Charles E. Curran and Richard A. McCormick, S.J., 149–156. Mahwah, N.J.: Paulist Press, 1998.

Moe-Lobeda, Cynthia D. *Healing a Broken World: Globalization and God.* Minneapolis, Minn.: Fortress Press, 2002.

Moon, Dawn. *God, Sex, and Politics.* Chicago: University of Chicago Press, 2004.

Murdock, G. P. *Ethnographic Atlas.* Pittsburgh: University of Pittsburgh Press, 1967.

Namaste, Viviane. *Invisible Lives: The Erasure of Transsexual and Transgendered.* Chicago: University of Chicago Press, 2000.

Nash, George H. *The Conservative Intellectual Movement in America, since 1945.* New York: Basic, 1976.

Nelkin, Dorothy. *The Creation Controversy: Science or Scripture in the Schools?* New York: Norton, 1982.

———. "Science Controversies: The Dynamics of Science Disputes in the United States." In *Handbook of Science, Technology and Society,* edited by S. Jasanoff, G. Markle, J. Petersen, and T. Pinch, 444–56. Beverly Hills: Sage, 1995.

Nelkin, Dorothy, ed. *Controversy: Politics of Technical Decisions.* 3rd ed. Beverly Hills: Sage Publications, 1992.

Newman, Barbara. *God and the Goddesses: Vision, Poetry, and Belief in the Middle Ages.* Philadelphia: University of Pennsylvania Press, 2003.

———. *Sister of Wisdom: St. Hildegard's Theology of the Feminine.* Berkeley: University of California Press, 1987.

Nichols, Aidan. *The Word Has Been Abroad: A Guide through Balthasar's Aesthetics.* Washington, D.C.: Catholic University of America Press, 1998.

Norton, John. "Vatican Says 'Sex-change Operation Does Not Change a Person's Gender.'" Catholic News Service/U.S. Conference of Catholic Bishops, January 14, 2003, http://ai.eecs.umich.edu/people/conway/TS/CatholicTSDecision.html (accessed May 12, 2009).

Numbers, Ronald. *The Creationists: The Evolution of Scientific Creationism.* New York: Knopf, 1992.

Obituary: John Templeton (1912–2008). *Nature* 454, no. 7202 (July 17, 2008): 290.

Olson, Richard. *Science and Religion, 1450–1900: From Copernicus to Darwin.* Westport, Conn.: Greenwood Press, 2004.

Orevillo-Montenegro, Muriel. *The Jesus of Asian Women.* Maryknoll, N.Y.: Orbis Books, 2006.

Parker, G., R. Baker, and V. Smith. "The Origin and Evolution of Gamete Dimorphism and the Male-Female Phenomenon." *Journal of Theoretical Biology* 36 (1972): 529–53.

Parker, G. A. "Behavioural Ecology: The Science of Natural History." In *Essays on Animal Behaviour: Celebrating 50 Years of Animal Behaviour,* edited by J. R. Lucas and L. W. Simmons, 23–56. Amsterdam: Elsevier, 2006.

———. "Sexual Conflict over Mating and Fertilization: An Overview." *Philosophical Transactions of the Royal Society* B. 361 (2006): 235–59.

Perdue, L. G., J. Blenkinsopp, J. J. Collins, and C. Meyers. *Families in Ancient Israel.* Louisville: Westminster John Knox Press, 1997.

Pickering, Andrew. *Constructing Quarks: A Sociological History of Particle Physics.* Chicago: University of Chicago Press, 1984.

Platt, Gerald M., and Rhys H. Williams. "Religion, Ideology and Electoral Politics." *Society* 25 (1988): 38-45.

Pope John Paul II. "Address to the Pontifical Academy of Sciences." *L'Osservatore Romano,* English ed., November 29, 2000.

———. "Faith Can Never Conflict with Reason." *L'Osservatore Romano,* English ed., November 2, 1992.

———. "Letter to the Reverend George V. Coyne, S.J., Director of the Vatican Observatory." *Origins* 18.23 (November 17, 1988).

———. *Man and Woman He Created Them: A Theology of the Body.* Boston: Pauline Books, 2006.

———. *The Theology of the Body: Human Love in the Divine Plan.* Boston: Pauline Books and Media, 1997.

Pope, Stephen J. "Descriptive and Normative Uses of Evolutionary Theory." In *Christian Ethics: Problems and Prospects,* edited by Lisa Sowle Cahill and James F. Childress, 166–82. Cleveland: Pilgrim Press, 1996.

———. *Human Evolution and Christian Ethics.* New York: Cambridge University Press, 2007.

———. "The Magisterium's Arguments against 'Same Sex Marriage': An Ethical Analysis and Critique." *Theological Studies* 65, no. 3 (September 2004): 530–65.

———. "Scientific and Natural Law Analyses of Homosexuality." *Journal of Religious Ethics* 25, no. 1 (Spring 1997): 89–126.

Preves, Sharon. *Intersex and Identity: The Contested Self.* Piscataway, N.J.: Rutgers University Press, 2003.

Proctor, R. "The Destruction of 'Lives Not Worth Living.'" In *Deviant Bodies,* edited by J. Terry and J. Urla, 170–96. Bloomington: Indiana University Press, 1995.

Qvarnström, Anna, J. E. Brommer, and L. Gustafsson. "Testing the Genetics Underlying the Coevolution of Mate Choice and Ornament in the Wild." *Nature* 441 (4 May 2006): 84–86.

Radcliffe, Timothy, O.P. *What Is the Point of Being Christian?* New York: Burns and Oates, 2005.

Rahner, Karl. "Experiences of a Catholic Theologian," *Theological Studies* 61, 1 (March 2000): 3–15.

Ramirez, Margaret. "Lutherans Ask Bishops to Keep Gay Clergy in Ministry: Vote Urges Bishops to Avoid Discipline." *Chicago Tribune,* 12 August 2007.

Reis, Elizabeth. "Divergence or Disorder? The Politics of Naming Intersex." *Perspectives in Biology and Medicine* 50, no. 4 (Autumn 2007): 535–43.

Reuther, Rosemary Radford. *Religion and Sexism.* New York: Simon and Schuster, 1974.

———. *Sexism and God-talk: Toward a Feminist Theology.* Boston: Beacon Press, 1993.

Rogers, Eugene F., Jr. *Sexuality and the Christian Body.* Oxford, U.K.: Blackwell Publishing, 1999.

Rosenberg, Alexander. *Philosophy of Social Science.* 2nd ed. Boulder, Colo.: Westview Press, 1995.

Ross, Susan A. "The Bridegroom and the Bride: The Theological Anthropology of John Paul II and Its Relation to the Bible and Homosexuality." In *Sexual Diversity and Catholicism: Toward the Development of Moral Theology,* edited by Patricia B. Jung and J. A. Coray, 39–59. Collegeville, Minn.: Liturgical Press, 2001.

———. *Extravagant Affections: A Feminist Sacramental Theology.* New York: Continuum, 1998.

Roughgarden, Joan. "Challenging Darwin's Theory of Sexual Selection." *Daedalus* 136, no. 2 (Spring 2007): 23–36.

———. *Evolution and Christian Faith: Reflections of an Evolutionary Biologist.* Washington, D.C.: Island Press, 2006.

———. "The Evolution of Sex." *The American Naturalist,* 138 (1991): 934–53.

———. *Evolution's Rainbow: Diversity, Gender, and Sexuality in Nature and People.* Berkeley: University of California Press, 2004.

———. *The Genial Gene: Deconstructing Darwinian Selfishness.* Berkeley: University of California Press, 2009.

———. "The Myth of Sexual Selection." *California Wild* 53, no. 3 (2005): 18–23.

———. "Social Selection vs. Sexual Selection: Comparison of Hypotheses." In *Controversies in Science and Technology Volume II: From Climate to Chromosomes,* edited by D. Kleinman, K. Cloud-Hansen, C. Matta, and J. Handelsman, 421–63. New Rochelle, N.Y.: Mary Ann Liebert, Inc., 2008.

Roughgarden, Joan, M. Oishi, and E. Akcay. "Reproductive Social Behavior: Cooperative Games to Replace Sexual Selection." *Science* 311 (2006): 965–69.

Rouse, G. W., S. K. Gofffredi, and V. C. Vrijenhoek. "*Osedax:* Bone-Eating Marine Worms with Dwarf Males." *Science* 305 (2004): 668–71.

Rutberg, A.T. "The Evolution of Monogamy in Primates." *Journal of Theoretical Biology* 104 (1983): 93–112.

Rynne, Xavier. "The First Session." In *Vatican Council II,* 3–134. New York: Noonday Press, 1968.

Savolainen, V., and L. Lehmann. "Genetics and Bisexuality." *Nature* 445 (2007): 158–59.

Scharen, Christian. "Experiencing the Body: Sexuality and Conflict in American Lutheranism." *Union Seminary Quarterly Review* 57, no. 1–2 (2003): 94–109.

Schatz, Klaus. *Papal Primacy: From Its Origins to the Present.* Collegeville, Minn.: Liturgical Press, 1996.

Scholz, Piotro. *Eunuchs and Castrati: A Cultural History.* Translated by John A. Broadwin and Shelley L. Frisch. Princeton, N.J.: Markus Wiener Publishers, 2001.

Scroggs, Robin. *The New Testament and Homosexuality.* Philadelphia: Fortress, 1983.

Secker, Susan L. "Human Experience and Women's Experience." In *Dialogue about Catholic Sexual Teaching: Readings in Moral Theology vol. 8,* edited by Charles E. Curran and Richard A. McCormick, 577–99. Mahwah, N.J.: Paulist Press, 1993.

Shapin, Steven. *A Social History of Truth: Civility and Science in Seventeenth-Century England.* Chicago: University of Chicago Press, 1994.

Shapin, Steven, and Simon Schaffer. *Leviathan and the Air Pump: Hobbes, Boyle and the Experimental Life.* Princeton, N.J.: Princeton University Press, 1985.

Shubin, N. *Your Inner Fish: A Journey into the 3.5-Billion-Year-History of the Human Body.* New York: Pantheon Books, 2008.

Smith, John Maynard. *Evolution and the Theory of Games.* Cambridge, U.K.: Cambridge University Press, 1982.

Spohn, William C. *What Are They Saying about Scripture in Ethics?* Mahwah, N.J.: Paulist Press, Revised Ed., 1995.

Starr, Paul. *The Social Transformation of American Medicine: The Rise of a Sovereign Profession and the Making of Vast Industry.* New York: Basic Books, 1982.

Steck, Christopher. *The Ethical Thought of Hans Urs von Balthasar.* New York: Crossroad Publishing, 2001.

Steinberg. Leo. *The Sexuality of Christ in Renaissance Art and in Modern Oblivion.* Chicago: University of Chicago Press, 1997.

Stenmark, Mikael. "Science and the Limits of Knowledge." In *Clashes of Knowledge: Orthodoxies and Heterodoxies in Science and Religion,* edited by Peter Meusberger, Michael Welker, and Edgar Wunder, 111–20. Dordrecht: Springer, 2008.

Stone, Merline. *When God Was a Woman.* New York: Dial Press, 1976.

Strickberger, M. W. *Evolution.* 3rd Edition. Sudbury, Mass.: Jones and Bartlett Publishers, 2000.

Strier, K.B. *Primate Behavioral Ecology.* 3rd Edition. Boston: Allyn and Bacon, 2007.

Stuhlmueller, Carroll. "Bridegroom: A Biblical Symbol of Union, Not Separation." In *Women Priests: A Catholic Commentary on the Vatican Declaration,* edited by Leonard Swidler and Arlene Swidler, 278–83. NewYork: Paulist Press, 1977.

Sullivan, Francis A. *Creative Fidelity: Weighing and Interpreting Documents of the Magisterium.* Mahwah, N.J.: Paulist Press, 1996.

———. *Magisterium: Teaching Authority in the Catholic Church.* Mahwah, N.J.: Paulist Press, 1983.

Swidler, Leonard, and Arlene Swidler, eds. *Women Priests: A Catholic Commentary on the Vatican Declaration.* Mahwah, N.J.: Paulist Press, 1977.

Taylor, F. Sherwood. *St. Albert, Patron of Scientists: A Paper Read to the London Aquinas Society.* Oxford: Blackfriars, 1950.

Thiel, John E. "For What May We Hope? Thoughts on the Eschatological Imagination." *Theological Studies* 67 (2006): 517–54.

Torrell, J. P. *Saint Thomas Aquinas,* vol. 1. Washington, D.C.: The Catholic University of America Press, 1996.

Traina, Cristina H. L. "Papal Ideals, Marital Realities: One View from the Ground." In *Sexual Diversity and Catholicism,* edited by Patricia Beattie Jung, 269–88. Collegeville, Minn.: Liturgical Press, 2001.

———. "Under Pressure: Sexual Disciple in the Real World," in *Sexuality and the U.S. Catholic Church: Crisis and Renewal,* edited by Lisa Sowle Cahill, John Garvey, and T. Frank Kennedy, S.J., 68–93. New York: Crossroads Publishing, 2006.

Trevithick, A. "On a Human Preference for Monandry: Is Polyandry an Exception? *Journal of Comparative Family Studies* 28 (1997): 154.

Valentine, David. *Imaging Transgender: An Ethnography of a Category.* Durham, N.C.: Duke University Press, 2007.

van Shaik, C. P. "The Socioecology of Fission-Fusion Sociality in Orangutans." *Primates* 40 (1999): 69–86.

Van Valen, L. "A New Evolutionary Law." *Evolutionary Theory* 1 (1973): 1–30.

Vincent, T. L., and J. S. Brown. *Evolutionary Game Theory, Natural Selection, and Darwinian Dynamics.* New York: Cambridge University Press, 2005.

von Balthazar, Hans Urs. On the Tasks of Catholic Philosophy in Our Time." Translated by Brian McNeil. *Communio* 20 (Spring 1993): 147–87.

Von Rad, G. *Genesis: A Commentary.* Revised by J. H. Marks. Philadelphia: The Westminster Press, 1973.

Wallace, William A. *Prelude to Galileo: Essays on Medieval and Sixteenth-Century Sources of Galileo's Thought.* Boston: D. Reidel Publishing, 1981.

Washington, Harriet. *Medical Apartheid.* New York: Harlem Moon Broadway Books, 2006.

Weber, Max. *The Protestant Ethic and the "Spirit" of Capitalism and Other Writings by Max Weber,* edited by Peter R. Baehr, and Gordon C. Wells. New York: Penguin Classics, 1930/2002.

Weems, Renita. *Battered Love: Marriage, Sex, and Violence in the Hebrew Prophets.* Minneapolis, Minn.: Augsburg Fortress Press, 1995.

Weil, Kari. *Androgyny and the Denial of Difference.* Charlottesville: University of Virginia Press, 1992.

West, Christopher. *Theology of the Body Explained: A Commentary on John Paul II's "Gospel of the Body."* Boston: Pauline Books and Media, 2003.

West, Christopher, John M. McDermott, S.J., and John Gavin, S.J., eds. *John Paul II on The Body: Human, Eucharistic, Ecclesial.* Philadelphia: St. Joseph's University Press, 2007.

Westermann, C. *Genesis 1–11: A Commentary.* Translated by J. J. Scullion, S.J. Minneapolis, Minn.: Augsburg Publishing House, 1984.

Westfall, Richard. *Science and Religion in Seventeenth-Century England.* Ann Arbor: University of Michigan Press, 1958/1973.

Wheeler, Sondra E. *Wealth as Peril and Obligation: The New Testament on Possessions.* Grand Rapids, Mich.: W. B. Eerdmans, 1995.

Whitehead, A. N. *Science and the Modern World.* New York: Simon and Schuster, 1925/1997.

Wikelski, M., V. Carrillo, and F. Trillmich. "Energy Limits to Body Size in a Grazing Reptile, the Galápagos Marine Iguana." *Ecology* 78, no. 7 (October 1997): 2204–17.

Wikelski. M., and F. Trillmich. "Body Size and Sexual Size Dimorphism in Marine Iguanas Fluctuate as a Result of Opposing Natural and Sexual Selection: An Island Comparison." *Evolution* 51 (1997): 922–36.

Williams, Bruce. "Religion, Politics, and Gay/Lesbian Civil Rights." FSC Catholic Center, Fitchburg, Mass., http://falcon.fsc.edu/~bnogueira/gaylesbian.htm.

Wilson, David. "The Historiography of Science and Religion." In *Science & Religion: A Historical Introduction,* edited by Gary Ferngren, 13–29. Baltimore: Johns Hopkins University Press, 2002.

Witherington, Benjamin III. *The Acts of the Apostles: A Socio-Rhetorical Commentary.* Grand Rapids, Mich.: William B. Eerdmans, 1998.

The Women's Ordination Conference. http://www.womensordination.org/ (accessed January 23, 2009).

Woolf, Virginia. *Orlando: A Biography.* San Diego: Harcourt, Inc., 1956.

———. *A Room of One's Own.* New York: Harcourt, Brace, Jovanovich, 1981.

Zambelli, Paola. *The Speculum Astronomiae and Its Enigma: Astrology, Theology, and Science in Albertus Magnus and His Contemporaries.* Boston: Kluwer Academic, 1992.

Zoll, Rachel. "Episcopal Leaders Promise Restraint on Electing Gay Bishops in Face of Anglican Demands." *Associated Press,* September 26, 2007.

Ecclesial Documents Congregation for the Doctrine of the Faith. *Instruction on Respect for Human Life in Its Origin and on the Dignity of Procreation: Replies to Certain Questions of the Day.* 1987. http://www.vatican.va/roman_curia/congregations/cfaith/documents/rc_con_cfaith_doc_19870222_respect-for-human-life_en.html (accessed on May 15, 2009).

——. *Inter Insigniores: Declaration on the Question of Admission of Women to the Ministerial Priesthood.* 1976. http://www.papalencyclicals.net/Paul06/p6interi.htm (accessed on May 15, 2009).

——. *On the Collaboration of Men and Women in the Church and the World.* 2004. http://www.wf-f.org/CDF-LetteronCollaboration.html (accessed on May 15, 2009).

——. *On the Pastoral Care of Homosexual Persons.* 1986. http://www.vatican.va/roman_curia/congregations/cfaith/documents/rc_con_cfaith_doc_19861001_homosexual-persons_en.html(accessed on May 15, 2009).

Pope Benedict XVI. *Deus caritas est.* 2005. http://www.vatican.va/holy_father/benedict_xvi/encyclicals/documents/hf_ben-xvi_enc_20051225_deus-caritas-est_en.html (accessed on May 15, 2009).

Pope John Paul II. Apostolic Constitution "*Fidei Depositum,*" October 11, 1992, on the publication of *The Catechism of the Catholic Church.* http://www.vatican.va/holy_father/john_paul_ii/apost_constitutions/documents/hf_jp-ii_apc_19921011_fidei-depositum_en.html (accessed on May 15, 2009).

——. *Apostolos Suos.* 1998. http://www.vatican.va/holy_father/john_paul_ii/motu_proprio/documents/hf_jp- ii_motu-proprio_22071998_apostolos-suos_en.html

——. *Familiaris consortio.* 1981. http://www.vatican.va/holy_father/john_paul_ii/apost_exhortations/documents/hf_jp-ii_exh_19811122_familiaris-consortio_en.html (accessed on May 15, 2009).

——. *Mulieris dignitatem.* 1988. http://www.vatican.va/holy_father/john_paul_ii/apost_letters/documents/hf_jp-ii_apl_15081988_muli-eris-dignitatem_en.html (accessed on May 15, 2009).

——. "Respect for Human Rights: The Secret of True Peace." Message for the World Day of Peace, January 1, 1999, no. 13. http://www.vatican.va/holy_father/john_paul_ii/messages/peace/documents/hf_jp-ii_mes_14121998_xxxii-world-day-for-peace_en.html (accessed January 2, 2008).

——. *Veritatis splendor.* 1993. http://www.ewtn.com/library/encyc/jp2ver.htm (accessed on May 15, 2009).

Pope Paul VI. *Motu Proprio.* "Apostolica Sollicitudo," September 15, 1965. In *The Documents of Vatican II,* edited by Abbot and Gallagher, 720–724. New York: America Press, 1966. http://www.vatican.va/holy_father/paul_vi/motu_proprio/documents/hf_p-vi_motu-proprio_19650915_apostolica-sollicitudo_en.html (accessed May 14, 2009).

——. *Humanae vitae.* 1968. http://www.vatican.va/holy_father/paul_vi/encyclicals/documents/hf_p-vi_enc_25071968_humanae-vitae_en.html (accessed on May 15, 2009).

Pontifical Council for the Family. *The Family in Human Procreation*. 2006. http://www
.wf-f.org/FamilyandHumanProcreation.html (accessed on May 15, 2009).

———. *The Truth and Meaning of Human Sexuality: Guidelines for Education within
the Family*. 1995. http://www.vatican.va/roman_curia/pontifical_councils/family/
documents/rc_pc_family_doc_08121995_human-sexuality_en.html (accessed on
May 20, 2009).

United States Conference of Catholic Bishops. *Economic Justice for All*. 1986. http://www
.osjspm.org/economic_justice_for_all.aspx (accessed May 14, 2009).

Vatican Council II. *Christus dominus*. 1965. http://www.vatican.va/archive/hist_councils/
ii_vatican_council/documents/vat-ii_decree_19651028_christus-dominus_en.html
(accessed on May 20, 2009).

———. *Gaudium et spes*. 1965. http://www.vatican.va/archive/hist_councils/ii_
vatican_council/documents/vat-ii_cons_19651207_gaudium-et-spes_en.html (accessed May 15, 2009).

———. *Lumen gentium*. 1964. http://www.vatican.va/archive/hist_councils/ii_vatican_
council/documents/vat-ii_const_19641121_lumen-gentium_en.html (accessed on
May 20, 2009).

Contributors

JOEL BROWN is a professor of biology at the University of Illinois, Chicago. He is an evolutionary ecologist interested in game theory and its application to animal feeding behavior, ecological communities, and wildlife management. He is coauthor of *Evolutionary Game Theory, Natural Selection, and Darwinian Dynamics* and coeditor of *Foraging: Behavior and Ecology.*

JAMES CALCAGNO is a professor of anthropology at Loyola University, Chicago. His research interests include primatology, paleoanthropology, biocultural anthropology, and evolutionary theory. He is the author of *Mechanisms of Human Dental Reduction,* has published articles in numerous professional journals, and was the guest editor of an issue of *American Anthropologist,* which focused on the past, present, and future connections of biological anthropology within the discipline of anthropology.

FRANCIS J. CATANIA is emeritus professor of philosophy at Loyola University, Chicago, where he also served as a former chair of the philosophy department and former dean of the Graduate School. His research interests are in medieval philosophy, particularly the philosophy of Albert the Great and Thomas Aquinas.

PAMELA L. CAUGHIE is a professor of literature at Loyola University, Chicago. Her research interests are in postmodernism, feminist theory, and modernist literature. She is the author of *Virginia Woolf and Postmodernism: Literature in Quest and Question of Itself* and *Passing and Pedagogy: The Dynamics of Responsibility* and the editor of *Virginia Woolf in the Age of Mechanical Reproduction* and *Disciplining Modernism.* She has written articles for numerous scholarly journals, including *Differences* and *Feminist Studies,* and contributed chapters to anthologies such as *Gender in Modernism* and *The Blackwell Companion to Modernist Literature and Culture.*

ROBERT DI VITO is a professor of Old Testament at Loyola University, Chicago. He is the author of a book on personal religion in ancient Mesopotamia and editor-in-chief and translator for the *Revised New American Bible.* In addition to entries on theological anthropology for *The New Interpreter's Dictionary of the Bible, The Encyclopedia of the Bible and Its Reception,* and *Catholic Biblical Quarterly,* he has contributed chapters to various anthologies, such as *Sexual Diversity and Catholicism* and *The Whole and Undivided Self: The Bible and Theological Anthropology.*

FRANK FENNELL is a professor of literature and dean of the College of Arts and Sciences at Loyola University, Chicago. He specializes in the poetry of Gerard Manley Hopkins and is the author or editor of several books, including *Rereading Hopkins: Selected New Essays.* He has also published in professional journals, such as *Renascence* and the *Hopkins Quarterly* and is currently working on another book on Hopkins's poetry.

ANNE E. FIGERT is an associate professor of sociology at Loyola University, Chicago. Her research interests include health, sociology of science, and gender studies. She is the author of *Women and the Ownership of PMS: The Structuring of a Psychiatric Disorder* and coeditor of two books in sociology. Her scholarly articles include research on medicalization, psychiatric diagnoses, and HIV/AIDS services.

TERRY GRANDE is a professor of biology at Loyola University, Chicago. Her research interests are in evolutionary relationships and historical biogeography of fishes, focusing specifically on the development and evolution of morphological structures shared by related fish groups. She has published many articles in professional journals and contributed chapters to several edited volumes, including *Mesozoic Fishes: Systematics and Biodiversity.*

PATRICIA BEATTIE JUNG is a professor of Christian ethics and the Oubri A. Poppele Professor of Health and Welfare Ministries at Saint Paul School of Theology. She is currently coeditor of the *Journal of the Society of Christian Ethics* and has contributed multiple articles to journals such as *Word and World* and the *Journal of Religious Ethics.* She is coeditor of *Sexual Diversity and Catholicism: Toward the Development of Moral Theology* and *Good Sex:*

Feminist Wisdom from the World's Religions. She coauthored *Heterosexism: An Ethical Challenge.*

FRED KNISS is a professor of sociology and provost at Eastern Mennonite University and an affiliate research professor of sociology at Loyola University, Chicago. He is the author of *Disquiet in the Land: Cultural Conflict in American Mennonite Communities* and coauthor of *Sacred Assemblies and Civic Engagement: How Religion Matters for America's Newest Immigrants.*

JOHN McCARTHY is an associate professor of constructive theology at Loyola University, Chicago. He is the author of *The Whole and Divided Self: The Bible and Theological Anthropology* and contributed a chapter to *Broken and Whole: Essays on Religion and the Body.* He also contributed several entries to the *New Handbook of Christian Theology.*

JON NILSON is a professor of theology at Loyola University, Chicago. His research interests include ecclesiology and African American religious thought. He is the author of *Hearing Past the Pain: Why White Catholic Theologians Need Black Theology* and *Nothing Beyond the Necessary: Roman Catholicism and the Ecumenical Future.* He has also served as president of the Catholic Theological Society of America (2002–3).

STEPHEN J. POPE is a professor of Christian ethics at Boston College, and his research interests include Christian ethics and evolutionary theory. He is the author of *Human Evolution and Christian Ethics* and *The Evolution of Altruism and the Ordering of Love;* editor of *The Ethics of Aquinas;* and author of an entry on "Reason and Natural Law" in *The Oxford Handbook of Theological Ethics.*

SUSAN A. ROSS is a professor of theology and ethics at Loyola University, Chicago, and chairperson of the theology department. She is the author of *For the Beauty of the Earth: Women, Sacramentality, and Justice* and *Extravagant Affections: A Feminist Sacramental Theology;* coeditor of *Broken and Whole: Essays on Religion and the Body;* and author of a chapter in *Freeing Theology: The Essentials of Theology in a Feminist Perspective.* She has published articles in the *Journal of Religion* and the *Journal of the Society of Christian Ethics.*

JOAN ROUGHGARDEN is a professor of biological sciences and geophysics at Stanford University. She is the author of *Evolution's Rainbow: Diversity, Gender, and Sexuality in Nature and People; Evolution and Christian Faith: Reflections of an Evolutionary Biologist;* and *The Genial Gene: Deconstructing Darwinian*

Selfishness. She was awarded the 2005 Stonewall Prize for Nonfiction from the American Library Association for *Evolution's Rainbow.*

AANA MARIE VIGEN is an assistant professor of ethics at Loyola University, Chicago. She is the author of *Women, Ethics, and Inequality in U.S. Healthcare: "To Count Among The Living"* and has contributed chapters to several books including *Disrupting White Supremacy from Within* and *To Do Justice: Engaging Progressive Christians in Social Action.*

Scripture Index

Subject and Author Index

References to sex and gender are separated into these categories: gender (cultural expression); sex (anatomy); and sexuality (attraction, courtship, behavior). Often terms have double entries with tags distinguishing "human" and "nonhuman."

The University of Illinois Press
is a founding member of the
Association of American University Presses.

Composed in 10.5/13 Adobe Minion Pro
with Meta display
by Celia Shapland
at the University of Illinois Press
Manufactured by Edwards Brothers, Inc.

University of Illinois Press
1325 South Oak Street
Champaign, IL 61820-6903
www.press.uillinois.edu